FIGURE IT OUT ↑LIFE

A Thin Book on ⟨Figure⟩ Drawing

Umakanth Thumrugoti

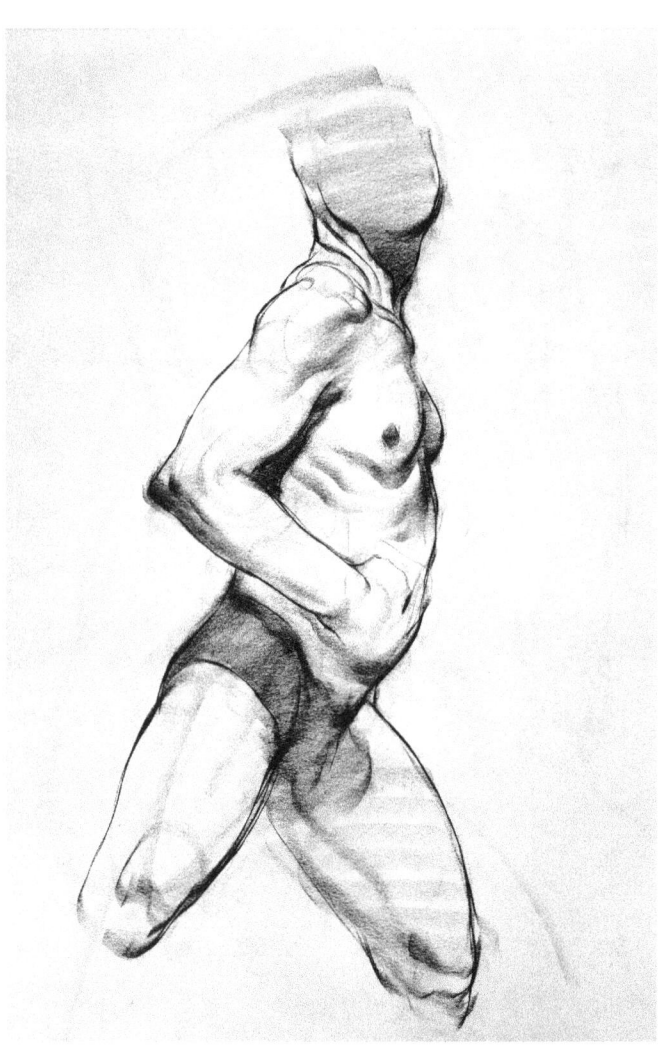

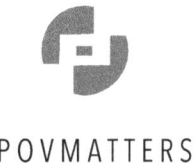

POVMATTERS

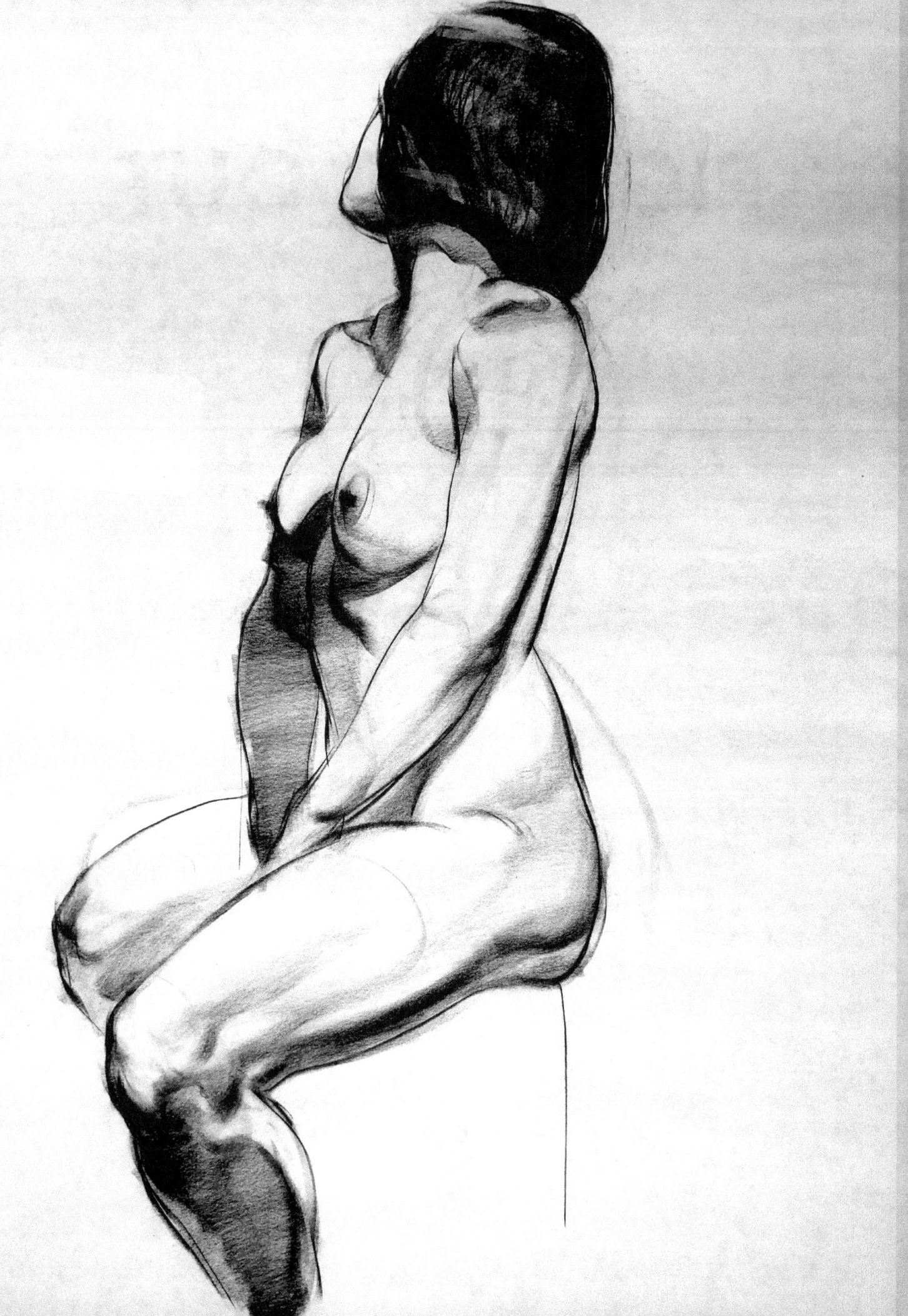

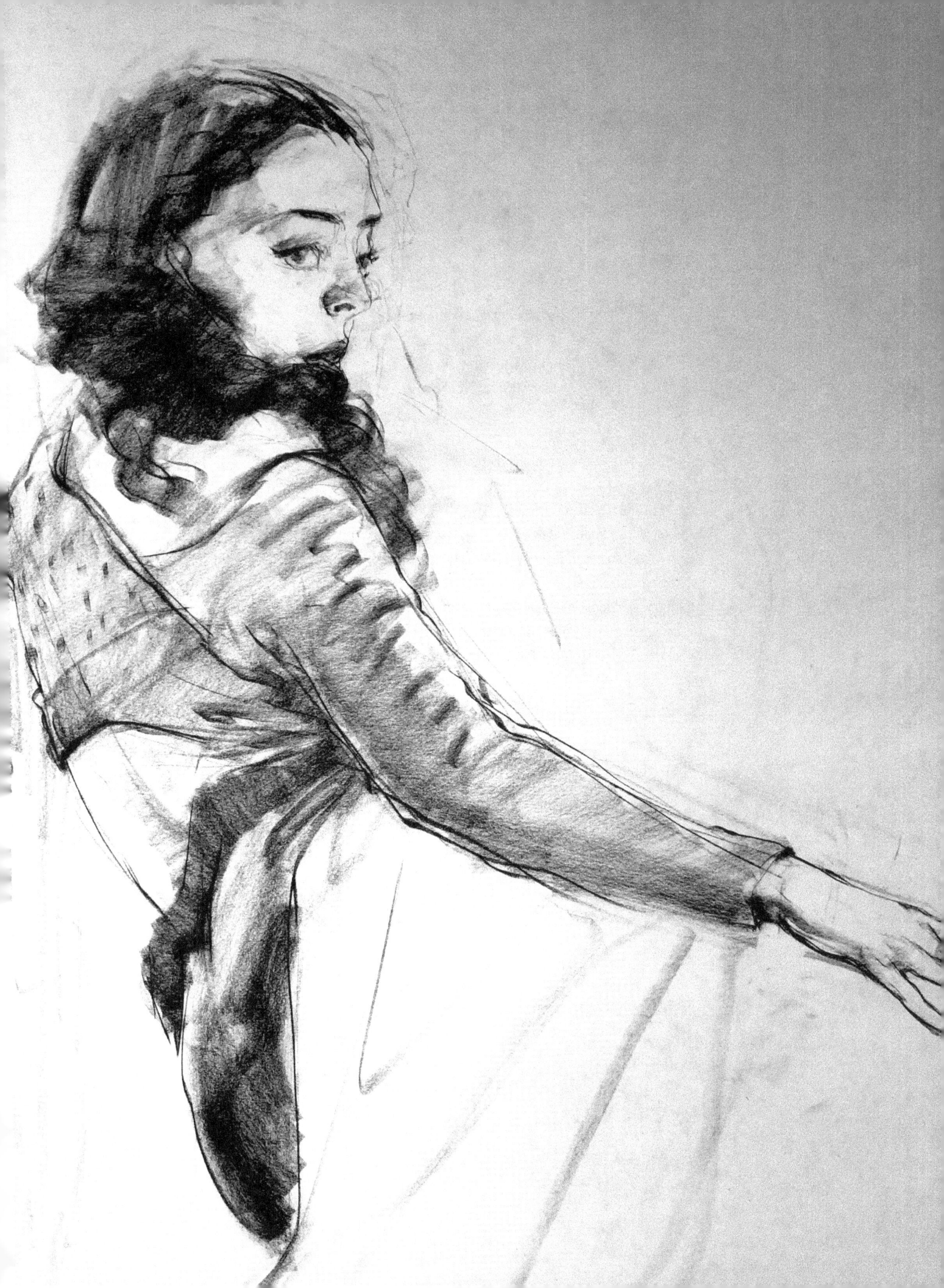

FIGURE IT OUT
A Thin Book on Life Drawing

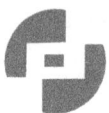

© 2020 by Umakanth Thumrugoti

Published by
POVMATTERS

Contact
info@povmatters.com

FIGURE IT OUT : A THIN BOOK ON LIFE DRAWING is copyright protected. All rights reserved. Copyright under international and Pan-American copyright conventions. No part of this book may be reproduced, stored in a retrieval system or transmitted in any other form, electronic, mechanical, photocopying, recording, computer networking or any other means without prior permission in writing by the copyright holder.

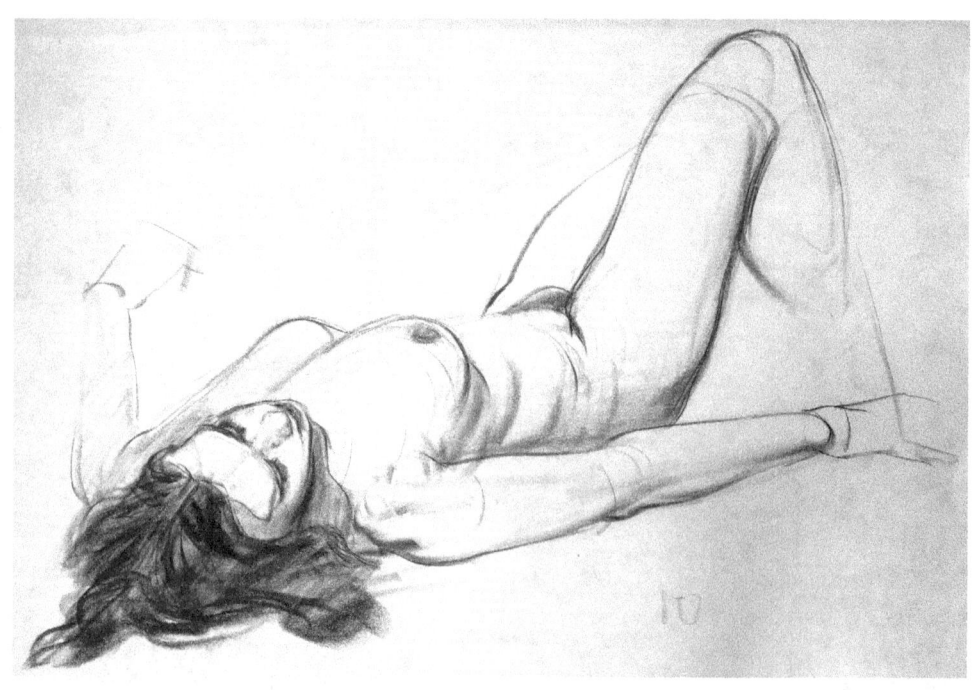

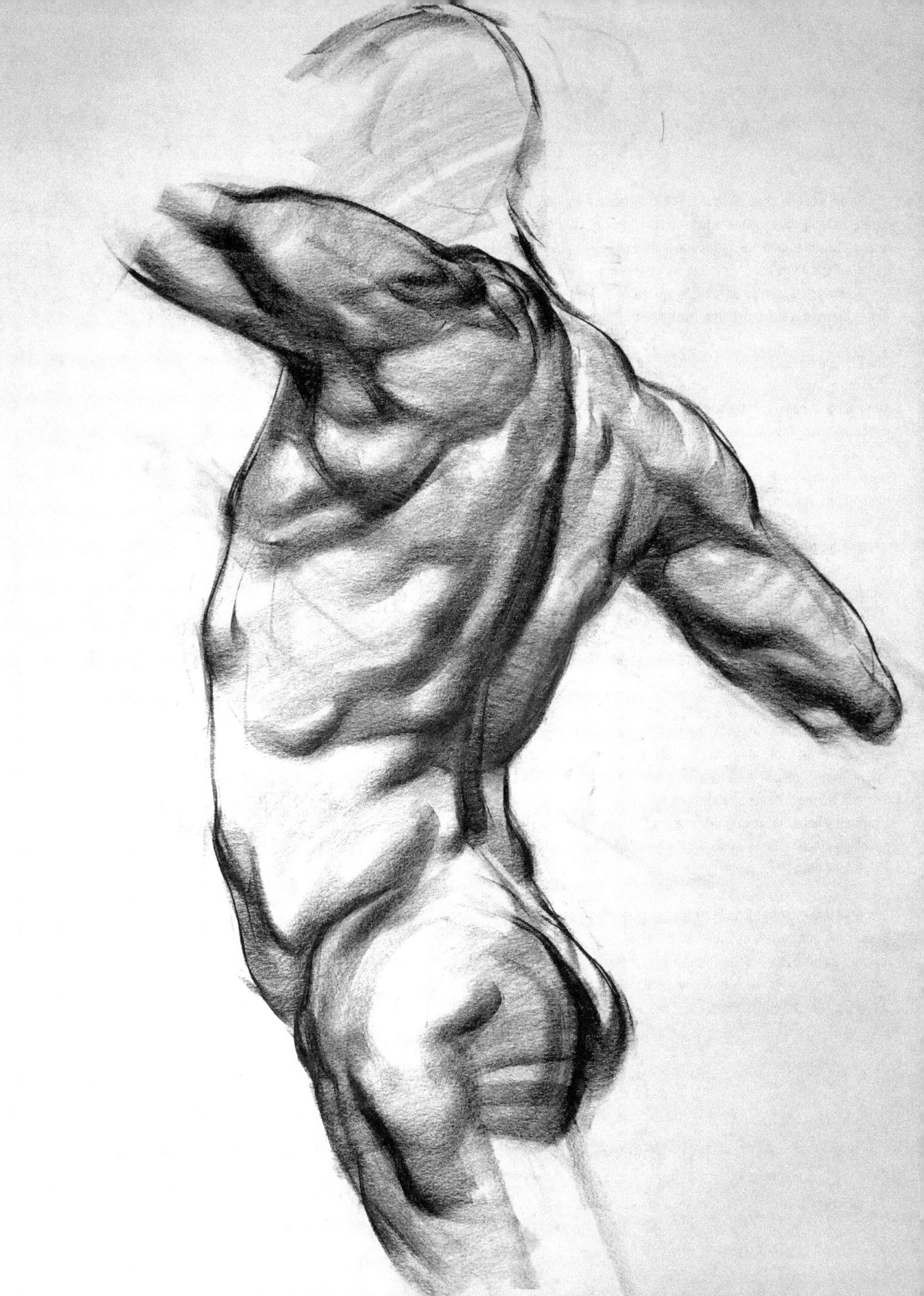

Why yet another book on life drawing?

"There are a billion already," you say. Well, while there may be a few about figure drawing, there are not as many on life drawing. Life drawing especially with short poses, forces one to develop tools and techniques to put down the figure quickly, capture the essence of the pose and omit unnecessary details. It's a different 'language' of drawing in contrast to figure drawing, which is not time constrained.

The first edition of this book was created for a workshop I taught on life-drawing at the Society of Illustrators. I expanded on the ideas and observations shared over the course of many workshops and classes in the following years. My education in engineering and a background in animation influences my thinking process quite a bit. I tend to be analytical when drawing - never copy the model, learn to 'see', and understand proportions, anatomy and lighting.

Most of the drawings presented in this book were short poses - 20 minutes or less, done at life-drawing sessions. A good, *unfinished* life drawing is a window into an artist's mind: the struggle of figuring out the model's gesture, proportions, anatomy and lighting, compressed into a short interval of time. That view is worth a thousand words. One has to labor through a few thousand bad drawings, each brimming with instructive missteps, to produce that final, successful one.

I have kept the text in this book to a minimum. Very rarely do I read instructional art books from cover to cover - but I do study the drawings/paintings presented in them for many hours. This particular point of view encouraged me to create a handy book with simple instructions but many drawings. I hope the life-drawings presented in this book help reveal my 'thinking process' : the rough lay in, the gestural lines, and finally the committed lines.

A special thanks to my friend Frank Nissen, an ex-Disney colleague, who helped me with the text, critiqued the drawings and provided a strong support for the book. A sincere and heartfelt thanks to all artists who publish art books, storybooks, comic books, illustration books etc., You have no idea how inspirational you are to me.

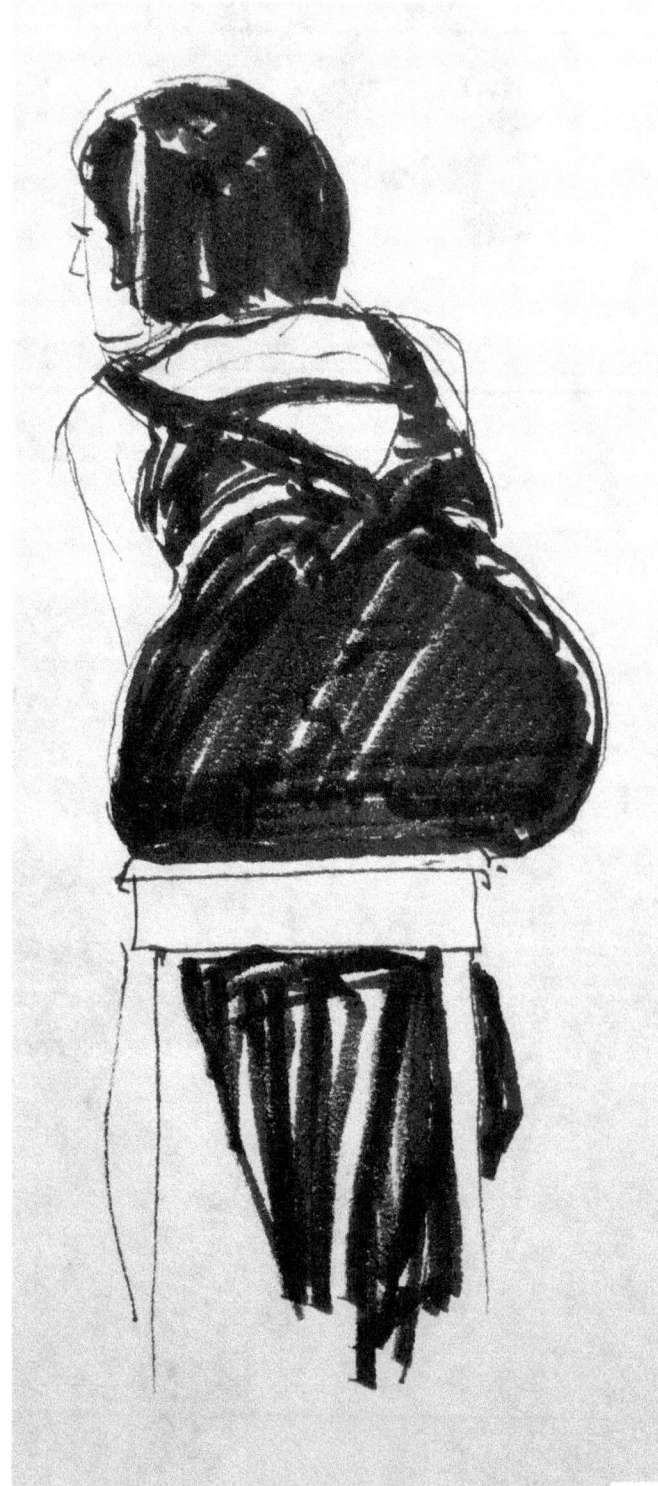

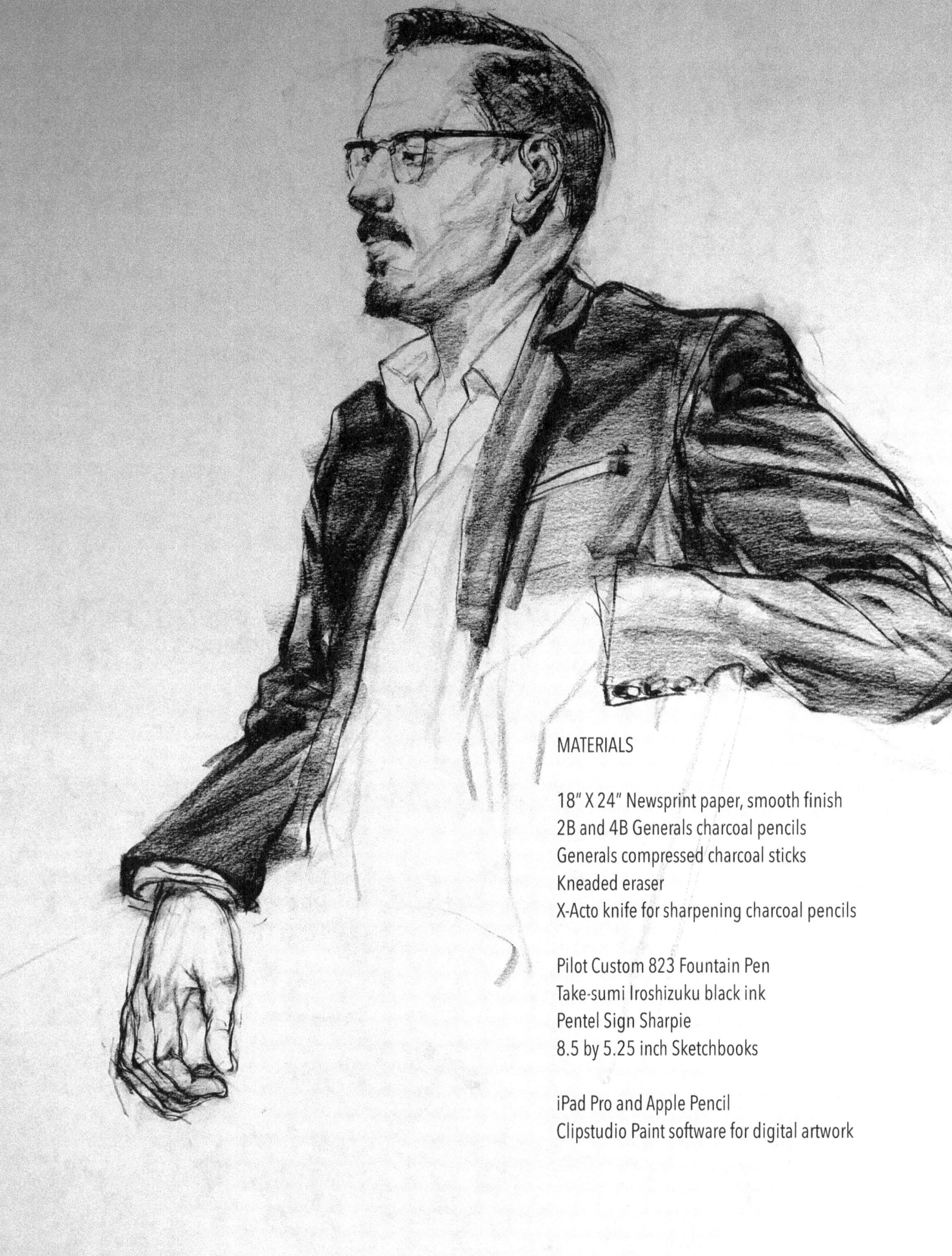

MATERIALS

18" X 24" Newsprint paper, smooth finish
2B and 4B Generals charcoal pencils
Generals compressed charcoal sticks
Kneaded eraser
X-Acto knife for sharpening charcoal pencils

Pilot Custom 823 Fountain Pen
Take-sumi Iroshizuku black ink
Pentel Sign Sharpie
8.5 by 5.25 inch Sketchbooks

iPad Pro and Apple Pencil
Clipstudio Paint software for digital artwork

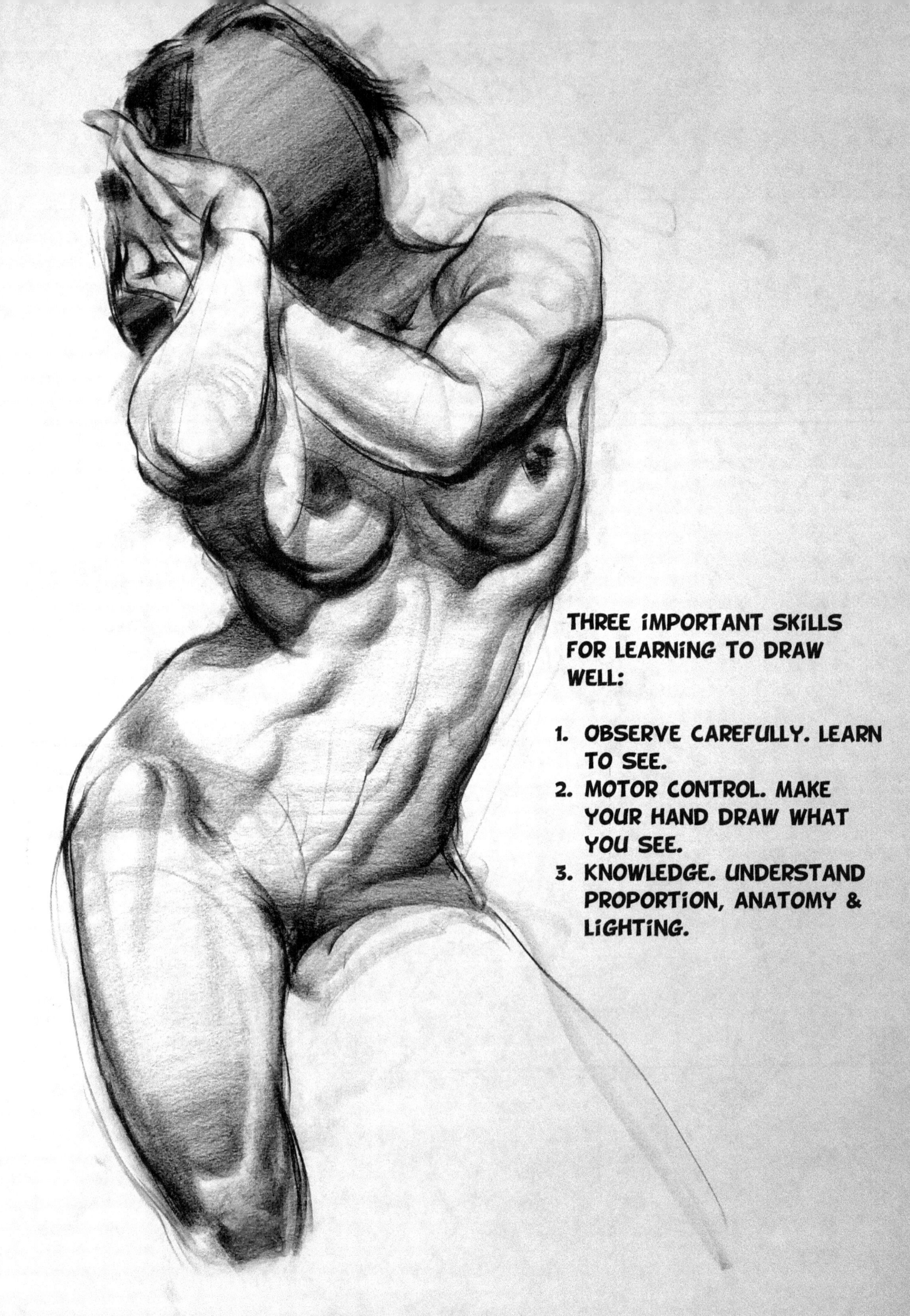

THREE IMPORTANT SKILLS FOR LEARNING TO DRAW WELL:

1. OBSERVE CAREFULLY. LEARN TO SEE.
2. MOTOR CONTROL. MAKE YOUR HAND DRAW WHAT YOU SEE.
3. KNOWLEDGE. UNDERSTAND PROPORTION, ANATOMY & LIGHTING.

When you are starting out in life-drawing, keep your materials consistent. Choose one set of materials, such as smooth newsprint, charcoal pencils, kneaded eraser etc., and stick with them for some time - a couple of years at least (assuming you will be drawing six hours a week). It takes practice to learn to put down a uniform tone (value), control the thickness of the line, choose which details to leave out. Keeping the same materials lets you concentrate on observation and motor control.

After you develop a certain expertise, you can chose whatever medium you want, and you'll be surprised at how quickly you can adapt to the new materials.

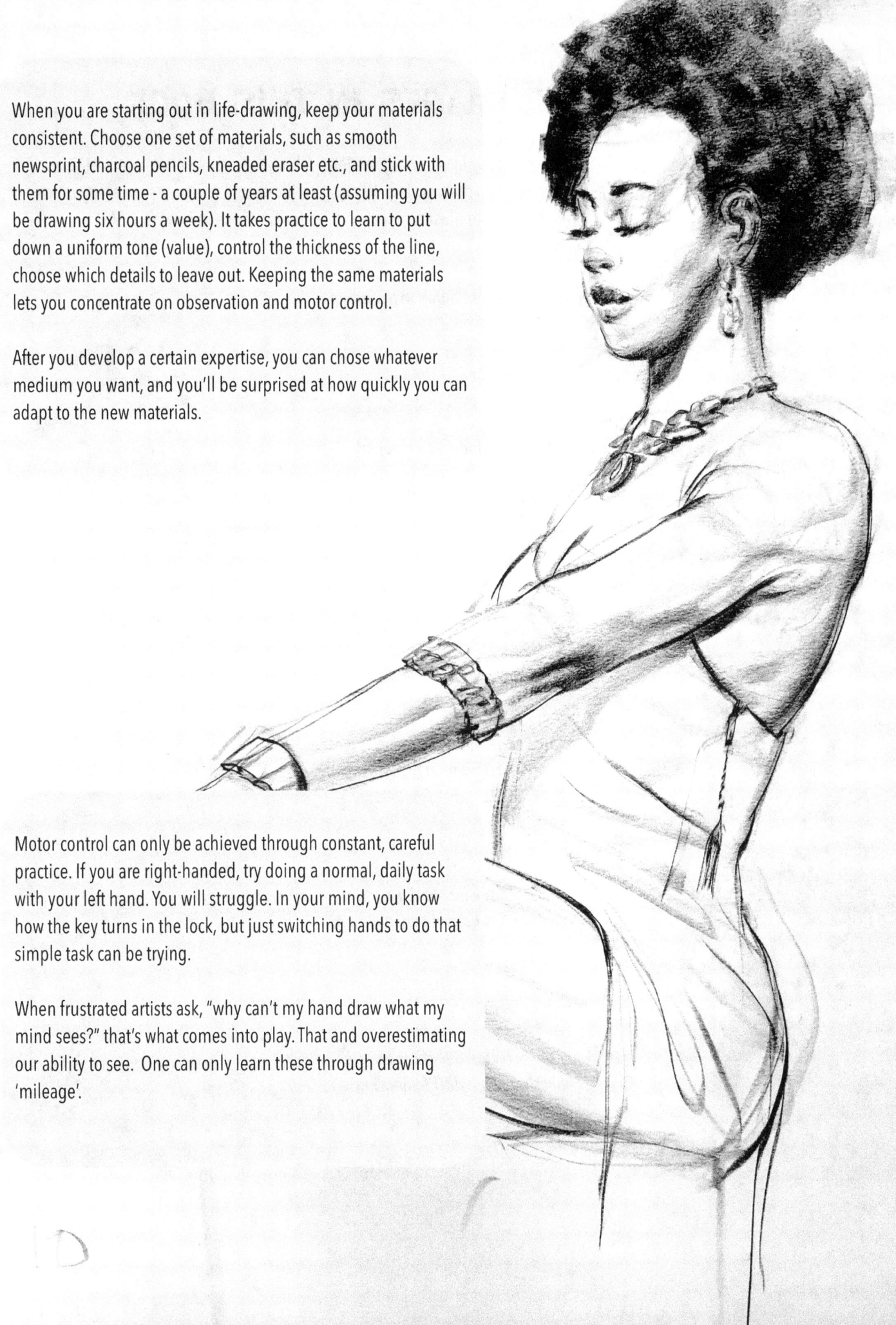

Motor control can only be achieved through constant, careful practice. If you are right-handed, try doing a normal, daily task with your left hand. You will struggle. In your mind, you know how the key turns in the lock, but just switching hands to do that simple task can be trying.

When frustrated artists ask, "why can't my hand draw what my mind sees?" that's what comes into play. That and overestimating our ability to see. One can only learn these through drawing 'mileage'.

A NOTE ON THE IMAGES IN THIS BOOK

Most charcoal and pen & ink drawings in this book were done at life-drawing sessions. All poses were twenty minutes or less. Whenever possible, I noted the pose duration in a small box on the drawing. What you will see in these pages are pretty much the raw life drawings done at crowded sketch nights at Society of Illustrators and Art Students League in New York City.

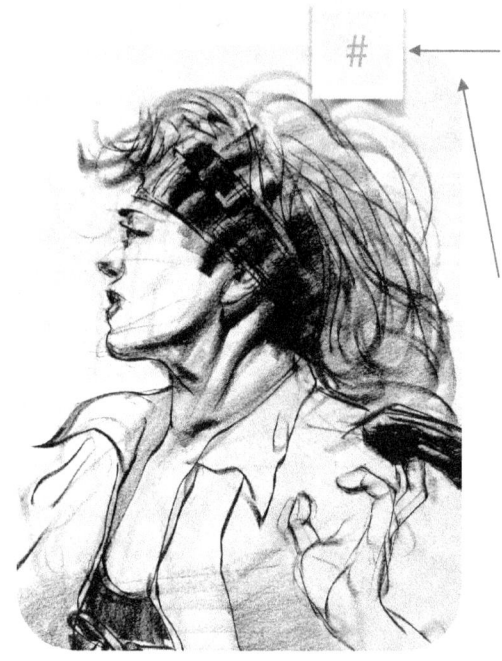

← Represents the pose duration in minutes.

← Rounded corners indicate a cropped image.

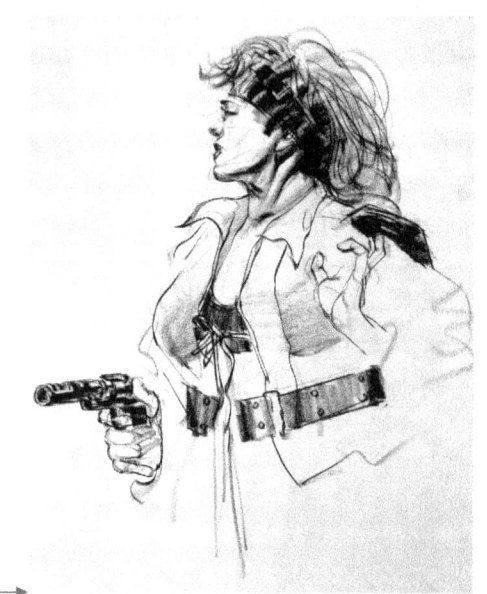

Square corners indicate the complete image →

← A framed edge with the shadow indicates a timed pose from my imagination.

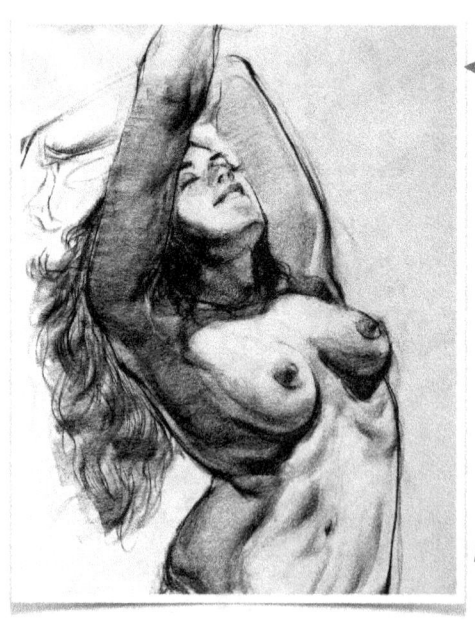

Black lines over white background are digital drawings from my imagination. →

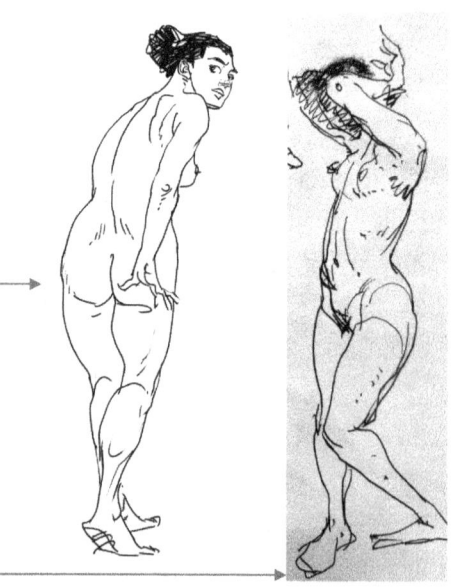

Black lines over textured background are physical pen & ink life-drawings.

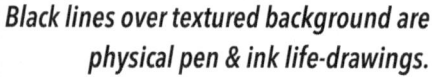

I left out pose duration stamps on full page spreads for aesthetic reasons.

Umakanth Thumrugoti

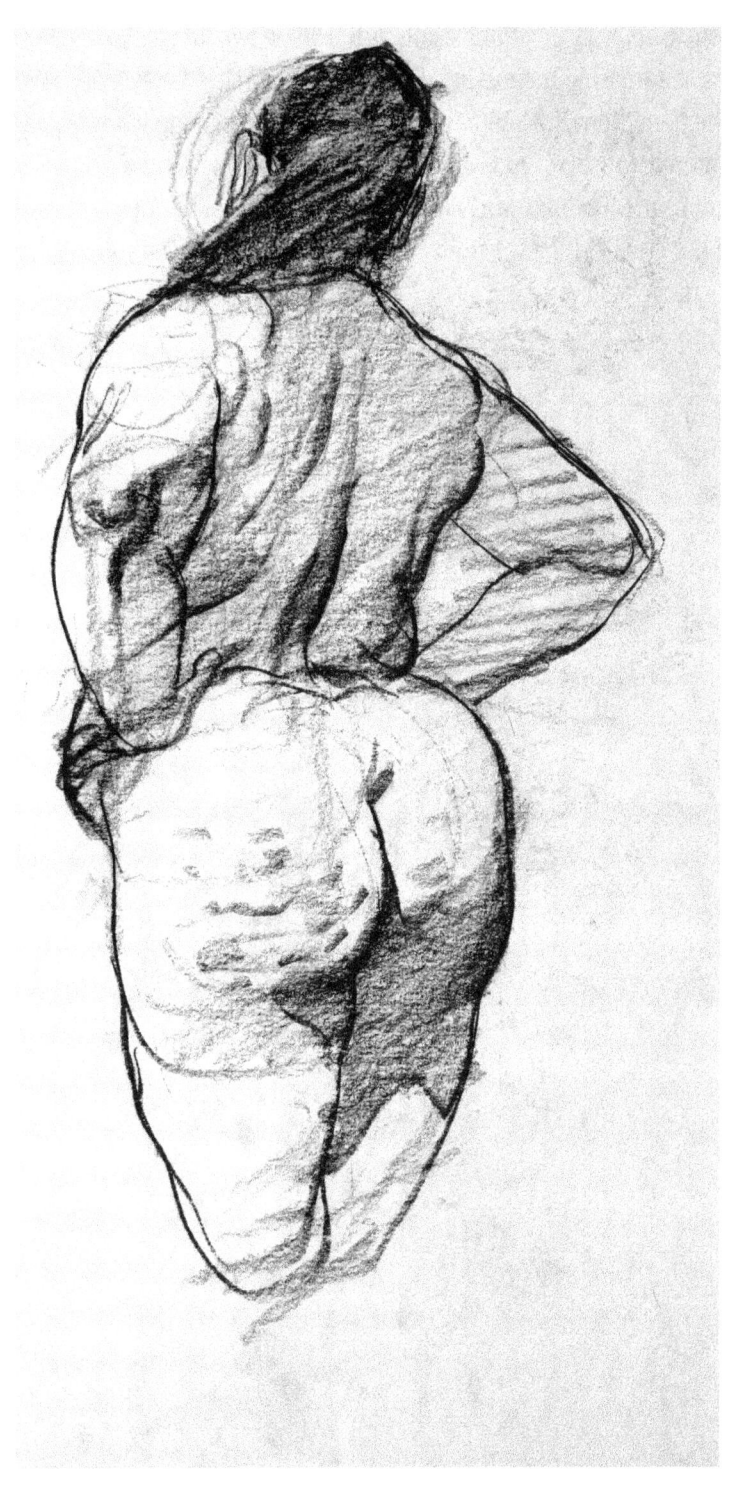

A FEW BASICS

Two goals - observation & motor skills

Improve your observational skills. Is the spine twisting? Is the knee crossing the median line of the body? How far away is the hand from the lateral side of the other leg? Along with learning to observe, you will also need to train your hand to produce the line/tone you want. The latter part is easy. You can get good at it by sheer practice. Remember the first time you got on a bicycle?

Do not copy - observe and reproduce

Do not copy the model - an example of this practice is using the 'grid method' (google this if you are interested). Instead, observe the model, interpret your observations with your knowledge of *proportions*, *anatomy*, and *lighting* and reproduce them. Do this long enough and you may not need a model.

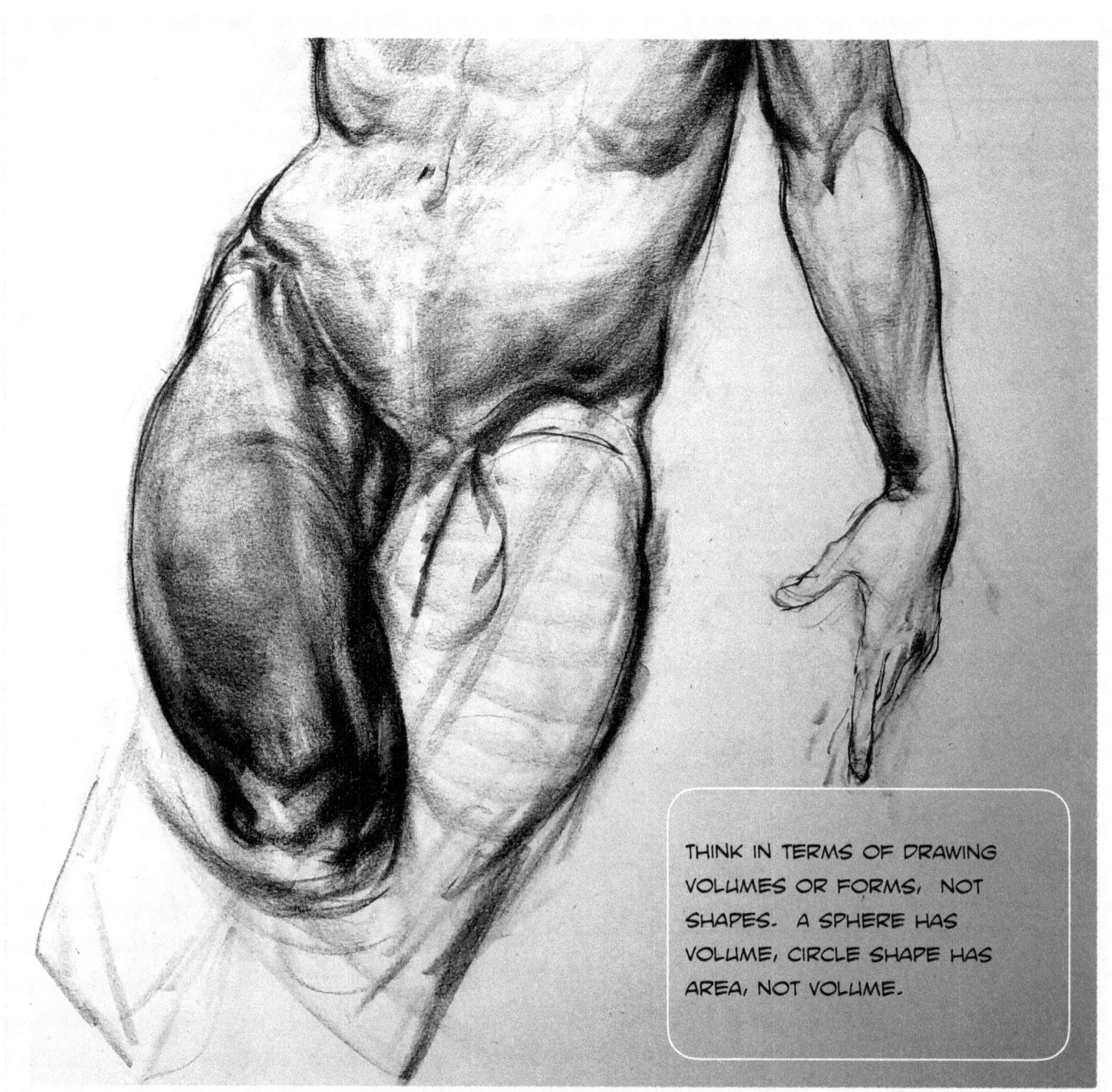

THINK IN TERMS OF DRAWING VOLUMES OR FORMS, NOT SHAPES. A SPHERE HAS VOLUME, CIRCLE SHAPE HAS AREA, NOT VOLUME.

Lines versus Tones

Do a rough lay in by drawing with *tonal-lines*. Once you are happy with your lay in, you can 'commit' by drawing the *axial-line*. See the image below right for a definition of axial & tonal lines.

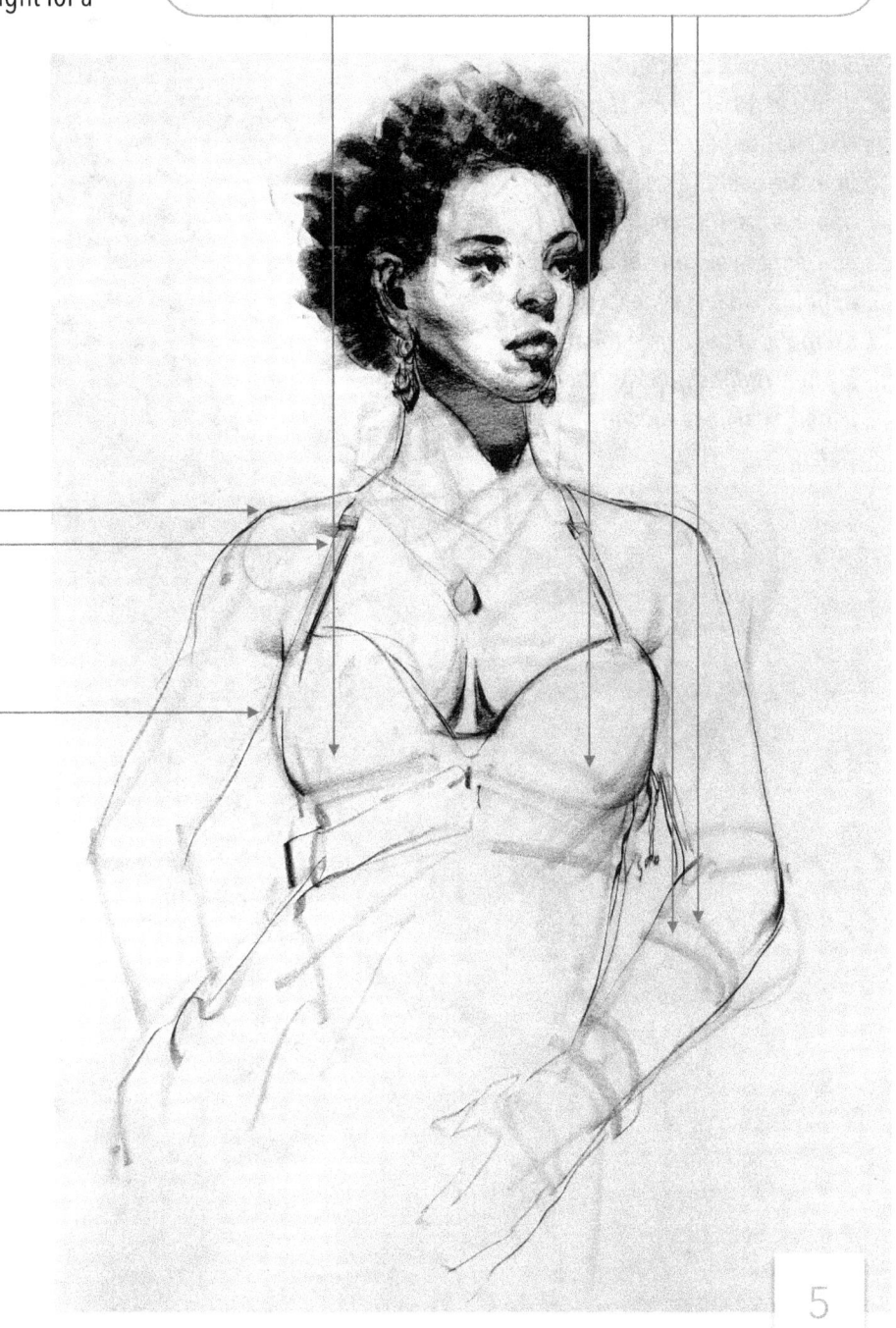

Tonal-line is simply a line drawn very lightly, using the side of the charcoal tip. They are erasable. I use tonal-lines for the rough lay in.

Axial-lines are those that are drawn along the axis of the charcoal pencil. They tend to be dark and sharp, difficult to erase. With a slight variation in the tilt of the charcoal tip, you can get thick and thin lines.

Focus on accuracy - style follows

If you draw a chair a thousand times, your one thousandth drawing of the chair might be a single line, but that line will capture your understanding and interpretation of the chair completely. That's how one develops one's own style. Draw a bazillion!

Drawing analytically

Drawing is an analytical process. Use your observations of the model, and your knowledge of human proportions, anatomy, and lighting to analyze the marks you have made for accuracy. More on this in the following pages.

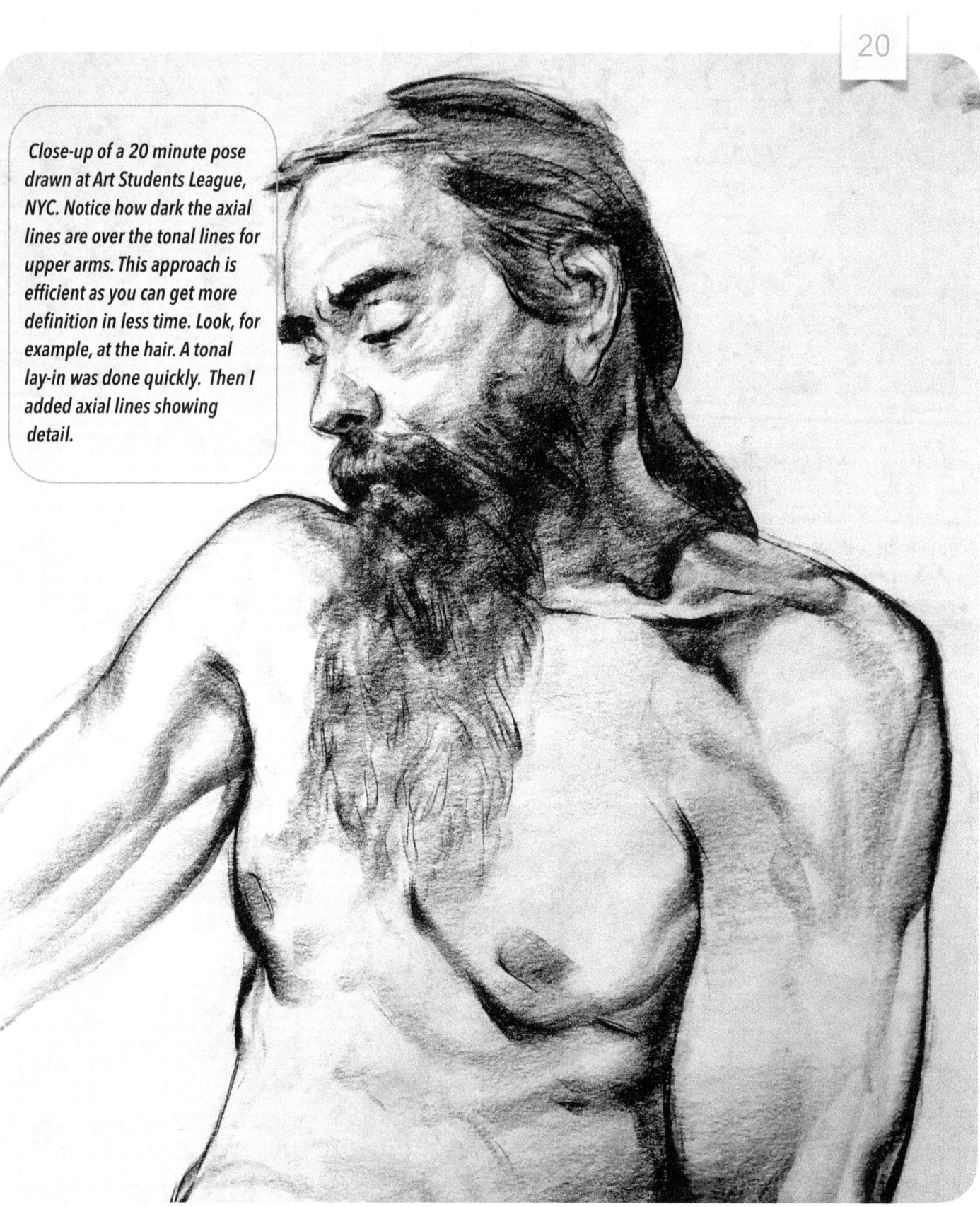

Close-up of a 20 minute pose drawn at Art Students League, NYC. Notice how dark the axial lines are over the tonal lines for upper arms. This approach is efficient as you can get more definition in less time. Look, for example, at the hair. A tonal lay-in was done quickly. Then I added axial lines showing detail.

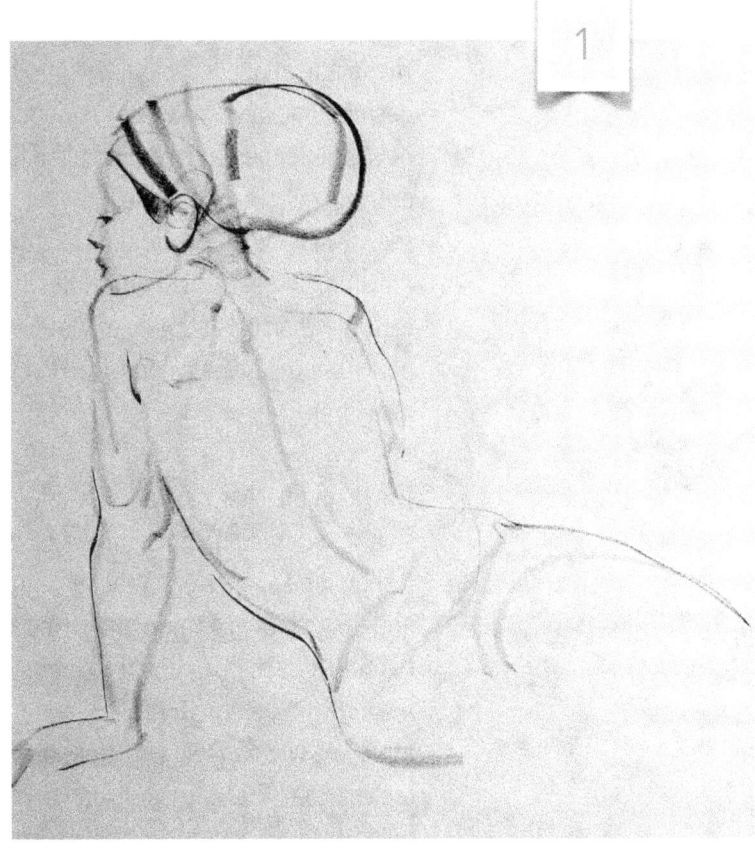

A one minute pose on the left. Initial drawing was all tone lines. I added a few axial lines for focus.

One of the disadvantages of drawing large (18" x 24") for short duration poses is that you need time for 'coverage'. If I were drawing small, hair coverage would have taken less time. But the advantage is that your hand movement is broad and originates from the elbow or shoulder.

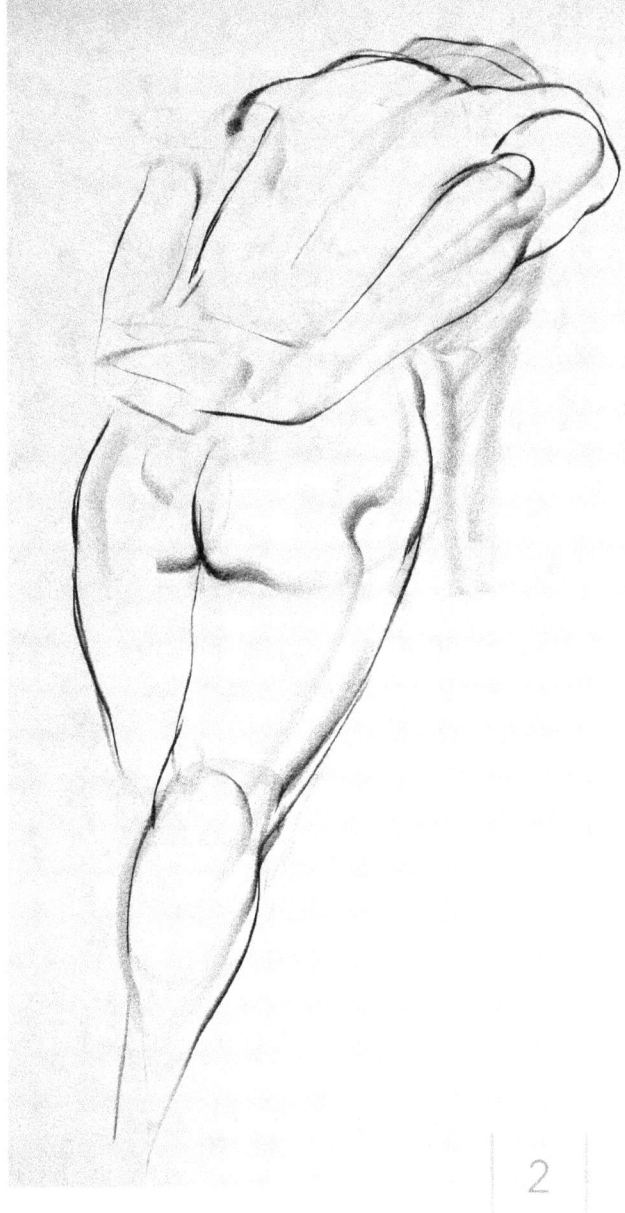

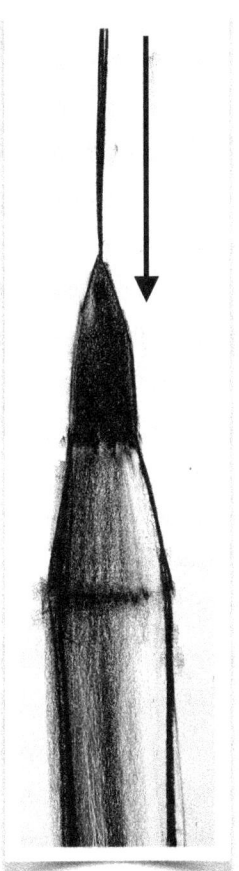

The axial line is drawn by moving the pencil along the length.

The tonal lines are drawn by dragging the pencil across the length.

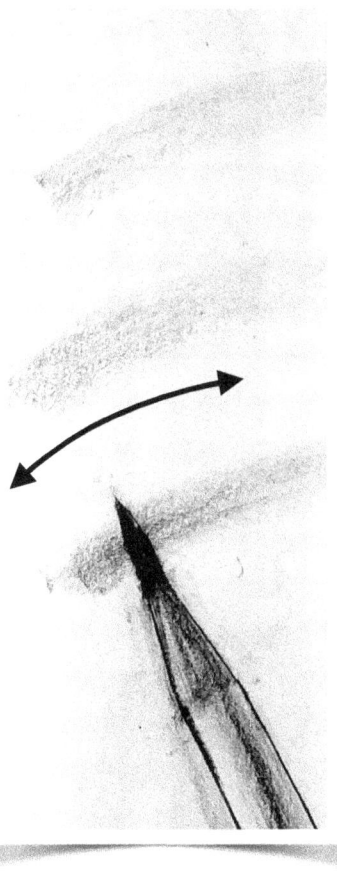

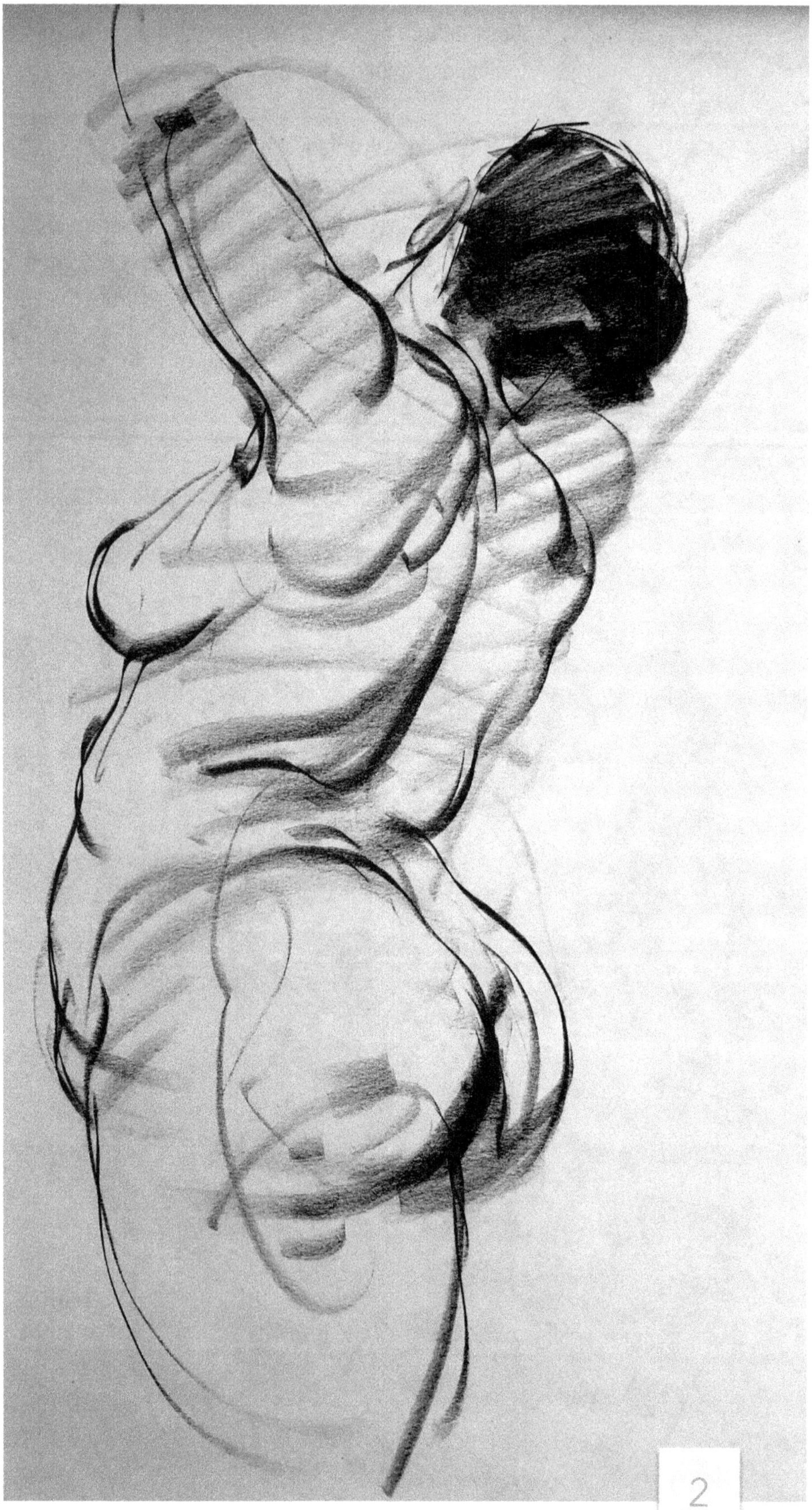

The image on the left was a two minute gesture drawing on 18" x 24" smooth newsprint paper. The drawing filled the entire sheet. The tonal lines, as you can see, have to be much wider on a large drawing. To get that kind of width, the exposed charcoal at the tip of the pencil should be between ½ to ¾ of an inch long.

The tip of the charcoal pencil, when sharpened, *shouldn't* resemble a cone. It should be a cylinder for the most part and then taper to a sharp point. The cylindrical section, denoted by (a) in the drawing below, gives a smooth tonal line when drawn with the side of the charcoal. The tapered section (b) gives the thick and thin variations to the axial lines.

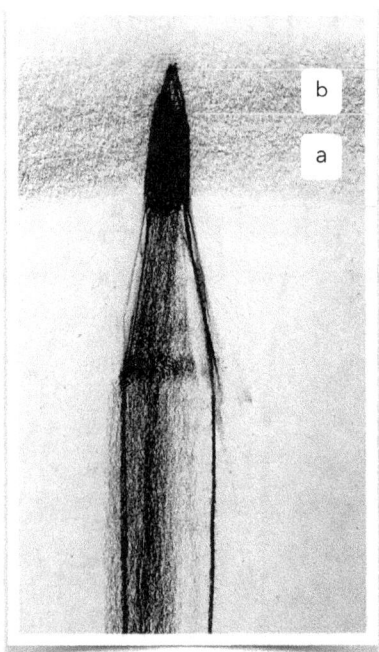

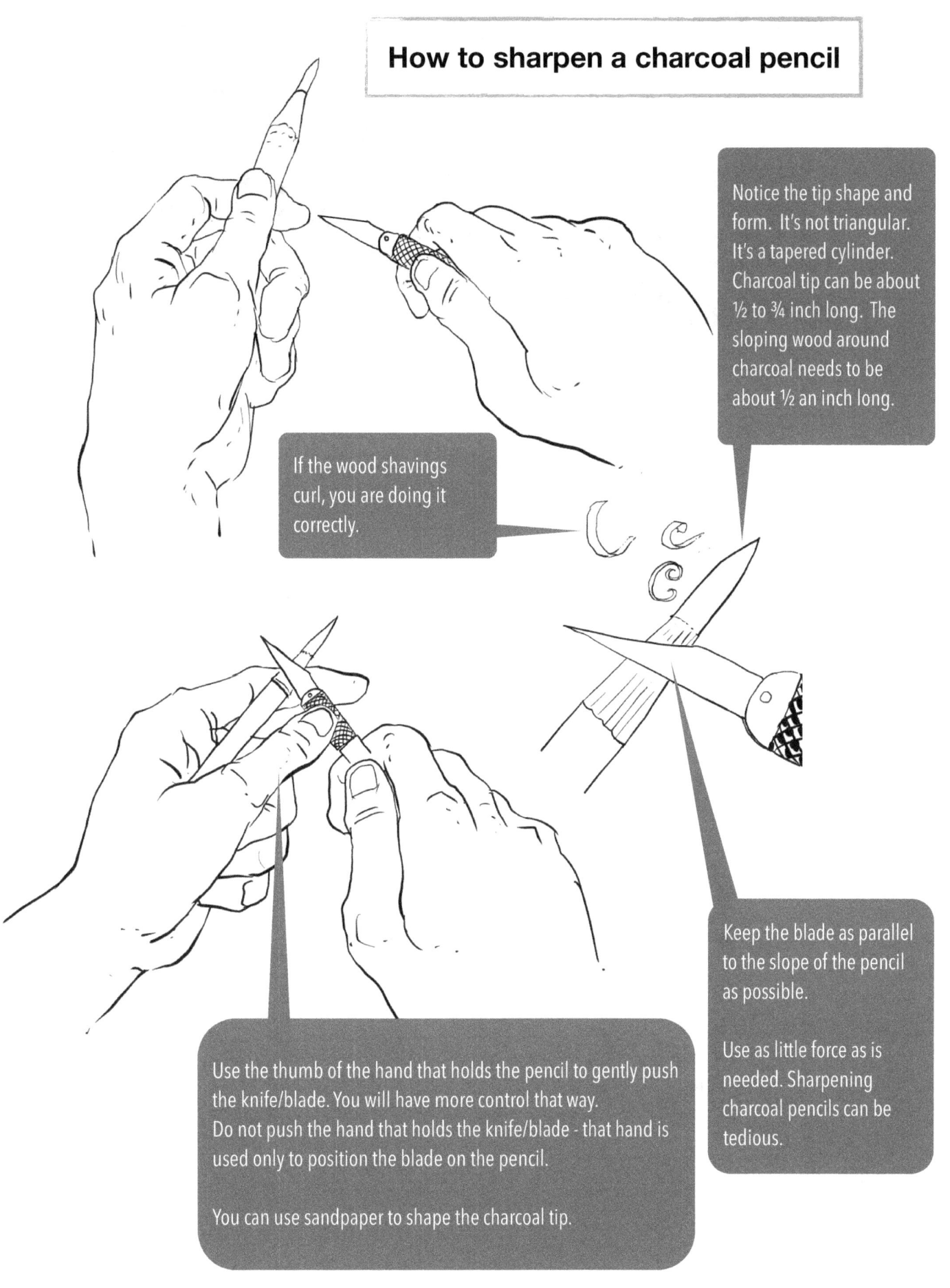

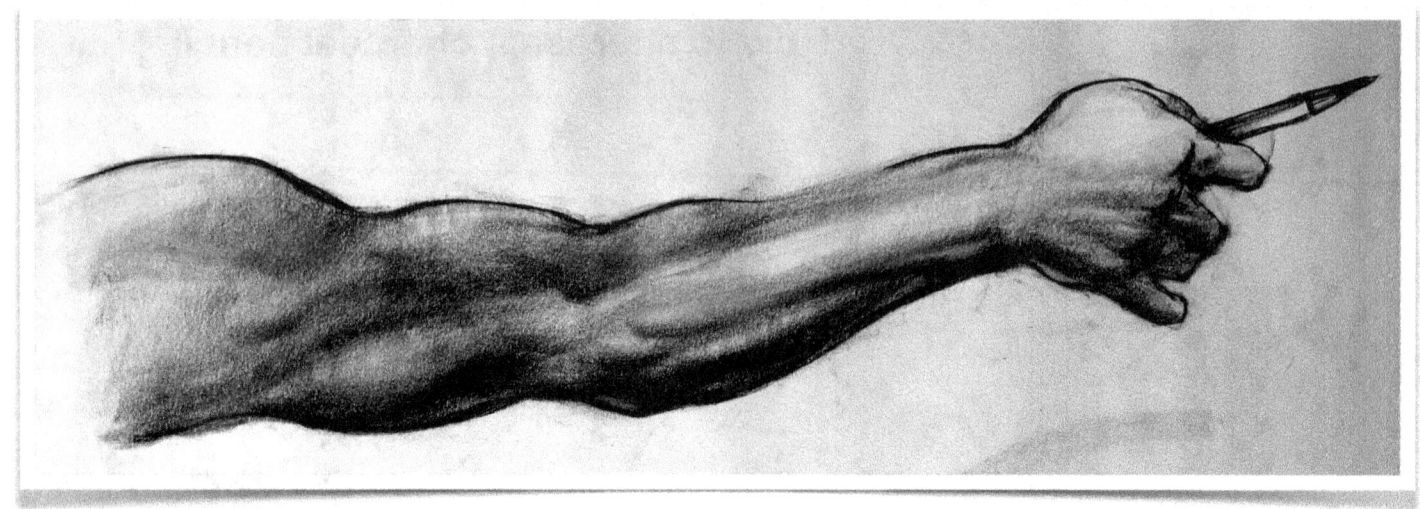

Practice holding the pencil (charcoal stick) as shown in the image above. It will allow you to use the side of the charcoal tip for tonal lines. If you hold it as a pen and use the wrist for movement, drawing big will be difficult. Use your elbow or shoulder for hand movement.

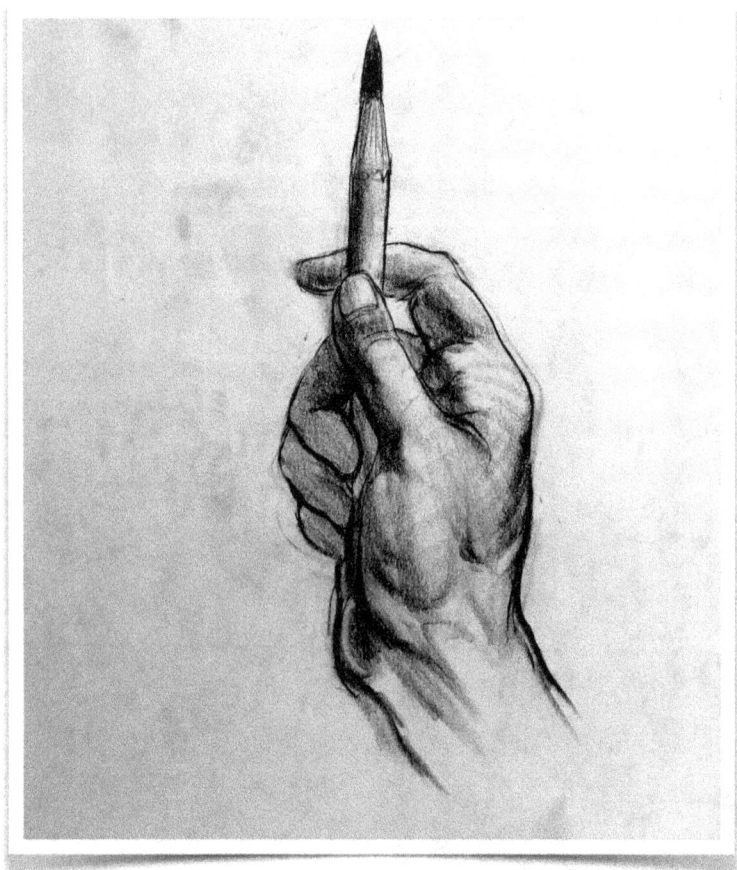

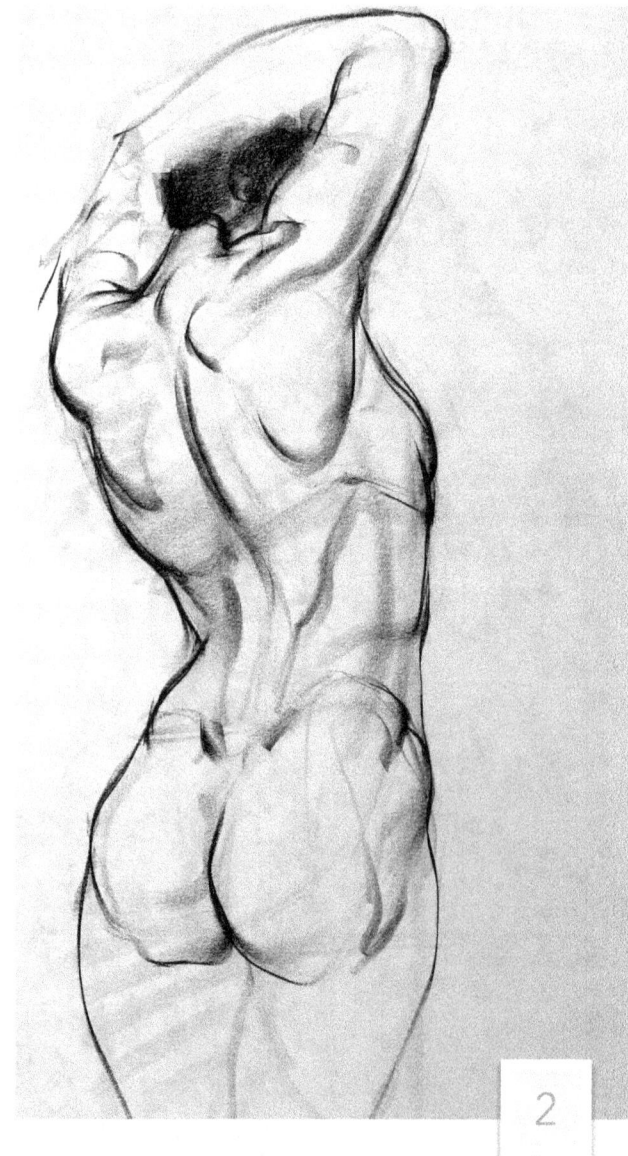

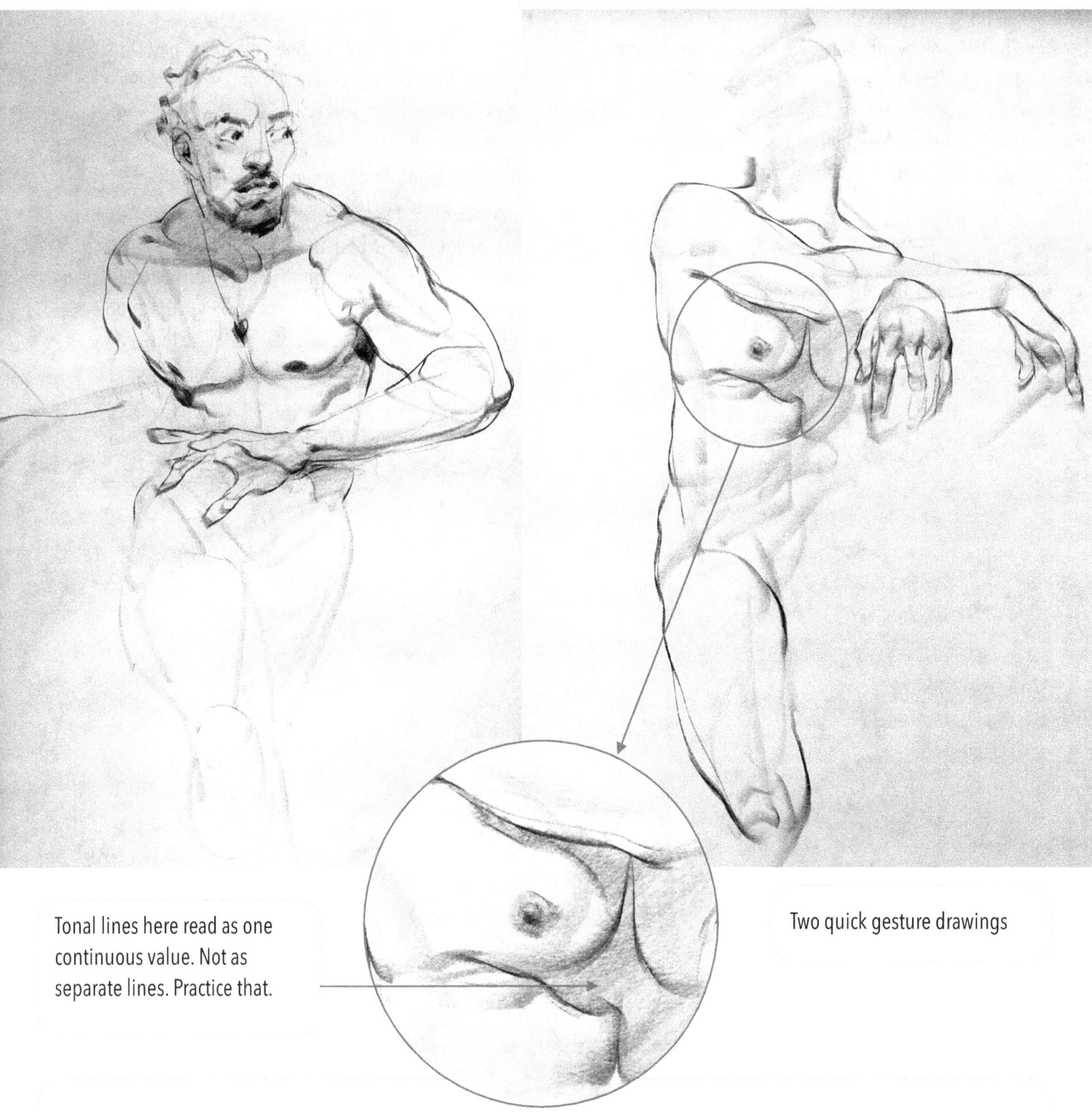

Tonal lines here read as one continuous value. Not as separate lines. Practice that.

Two quick gesture drawings

Draw as lightly as possible during the initial rough lay in phase.

Drawing along the axis (along the length) of the pencil gives you axial line. Hard to erase.
Drawing across the axis of the pencil gives you tonal line. Use them for rough lay in.

Instinct/muscle memory needs a lot mileage

Don't be seduced by other artists' methods. Draw accurately first. Do that a few thousand times, and you will learn to draw quickly *and* accurately. You will recognize that certain strokes are good for showing certain things. You will develop muscle memory for many of the strokes.

Focus on gesture

Whether it's a two, five, 10 or 20-minute pose, focus on the gesture. Gesture gives life to your drawing.

What is gesture drawing?

It's how lines/forms representing anatomical parts fit together in a pose. It shows action or movement as well as the weight and balance of the pose.

Let each drawing be a learning experience

Don't lose heart if your drawings don't look as good as you want them to be . Go back to basics (this involves drawing simple spheres, tubes etc. which we will discuss later). Spend time figuring out what's not working. The 'problem' is present in the 'bad' drawing; you just have to see it.

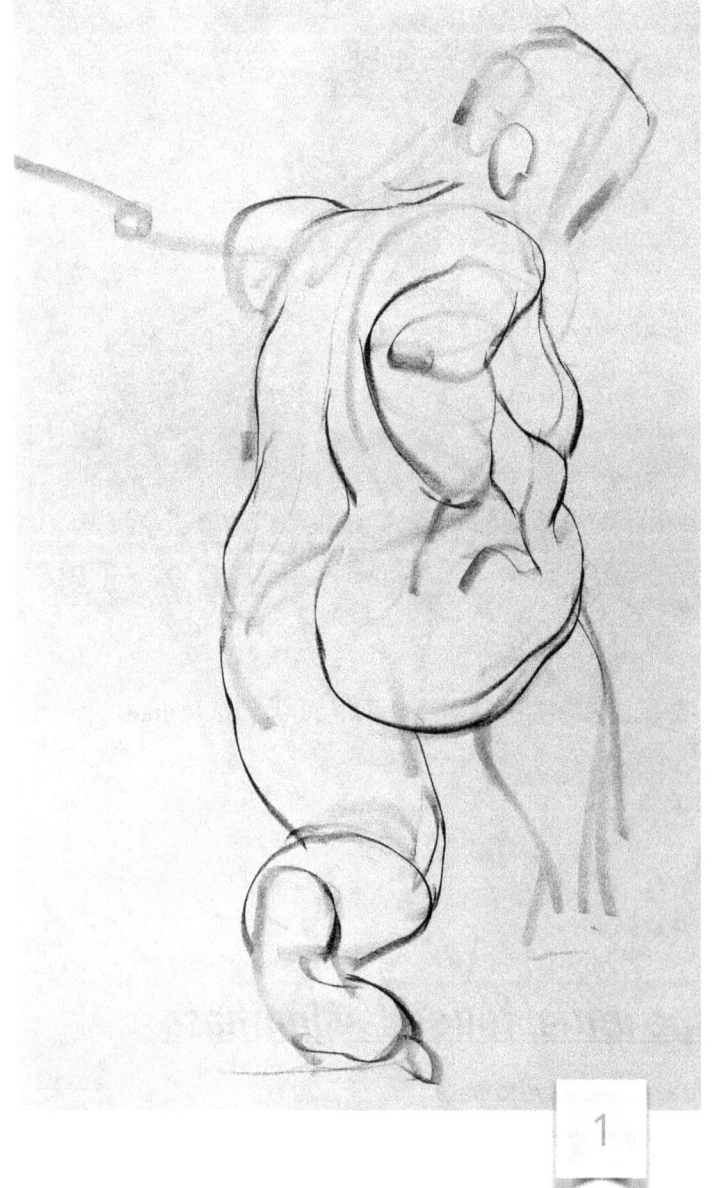

1

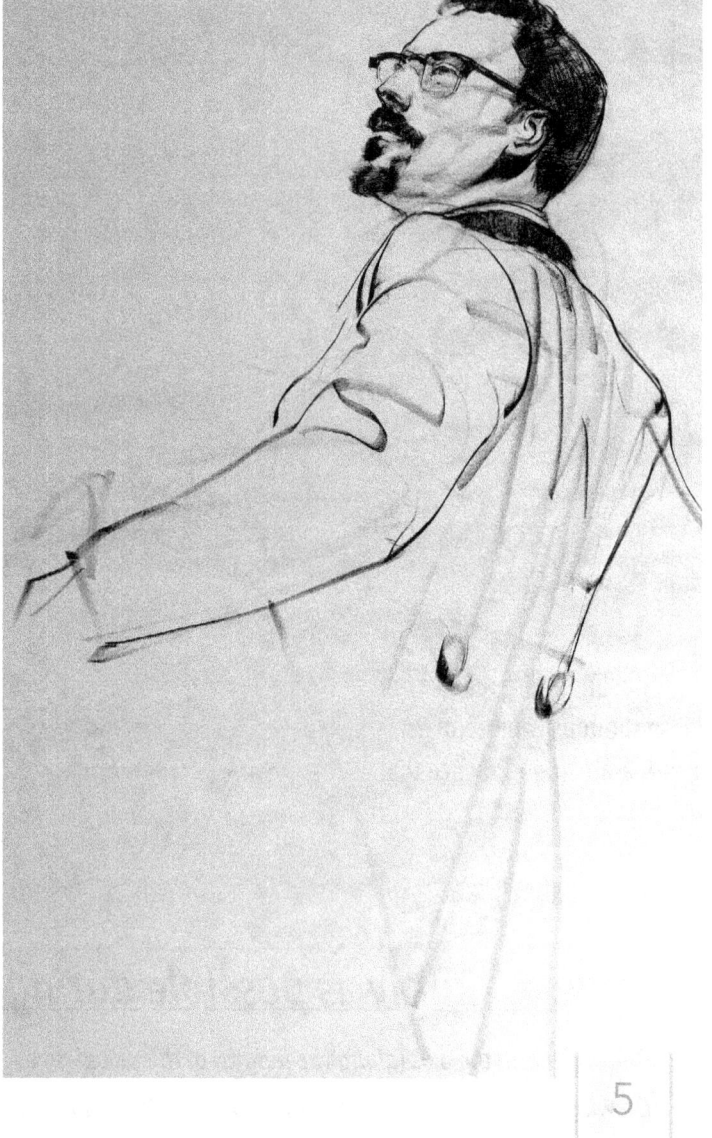

5

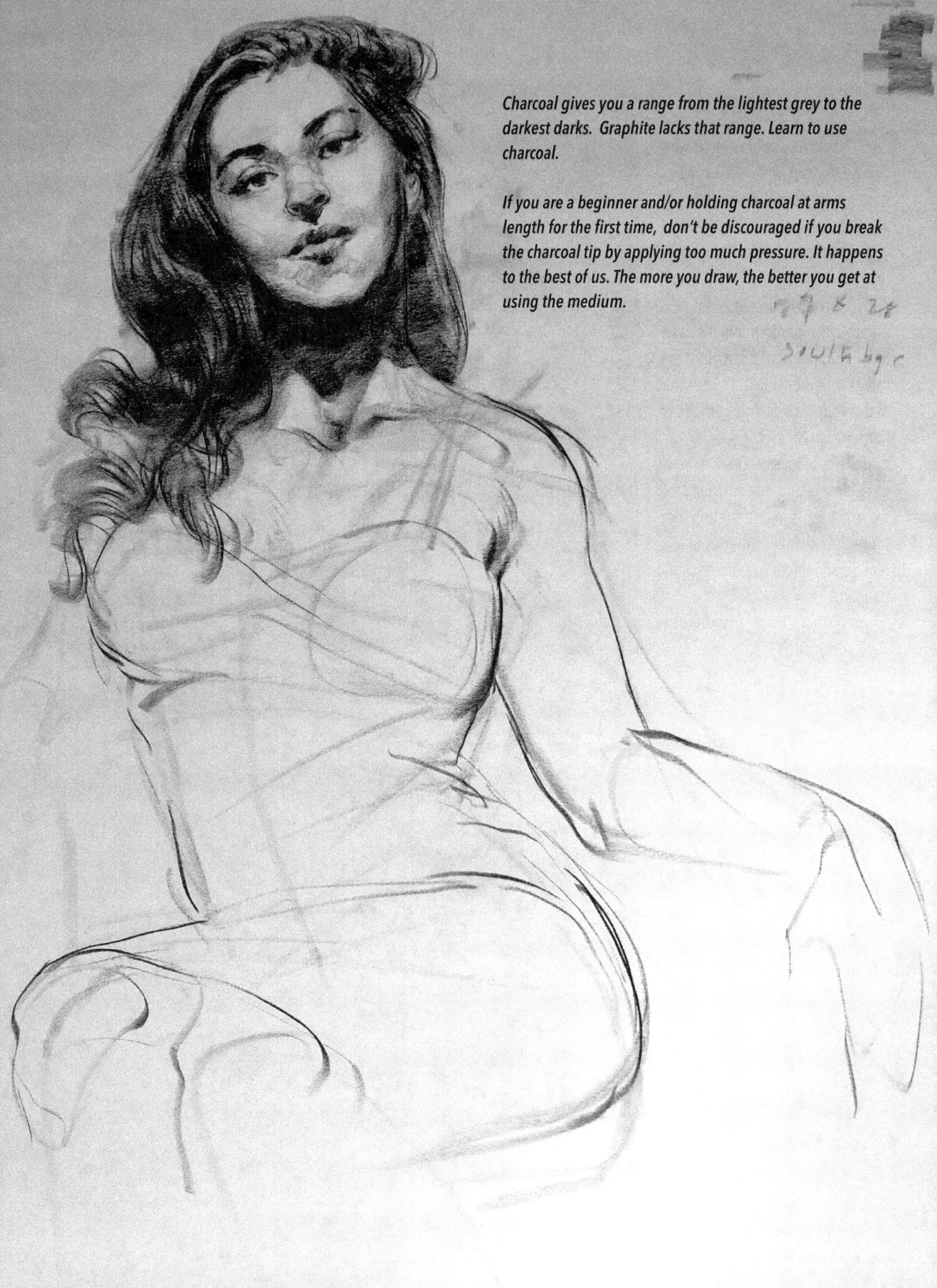

Charcoal gives you a range from the lightest grey to the darkest darks. Graphite lacks that range. Learn to use charcoal.

If you are a beginner and/or holding charcoal at arms length for the first time, don't be discouraged if you break the charcoal tip by applying too much pressure. It happens to the best of us. The more you draw, the better you get at using the medium.

If you have the opportunity, always choose to draw from life. Drawing from life helps in the analytical process. Drawing from life forces you to understand your subject first, then make your marks. If you draw from a two-dimensional image, say a photograph, it's easier to fall into the trap of 'copying' the image. In other words: the outlines of the shapes. Drawing from life is harder than copying a two-dimensional image. There is more decision-making responsibility for the artist. You are interpreting the three-dimensional volumes of a real person into a two-dimensional page.

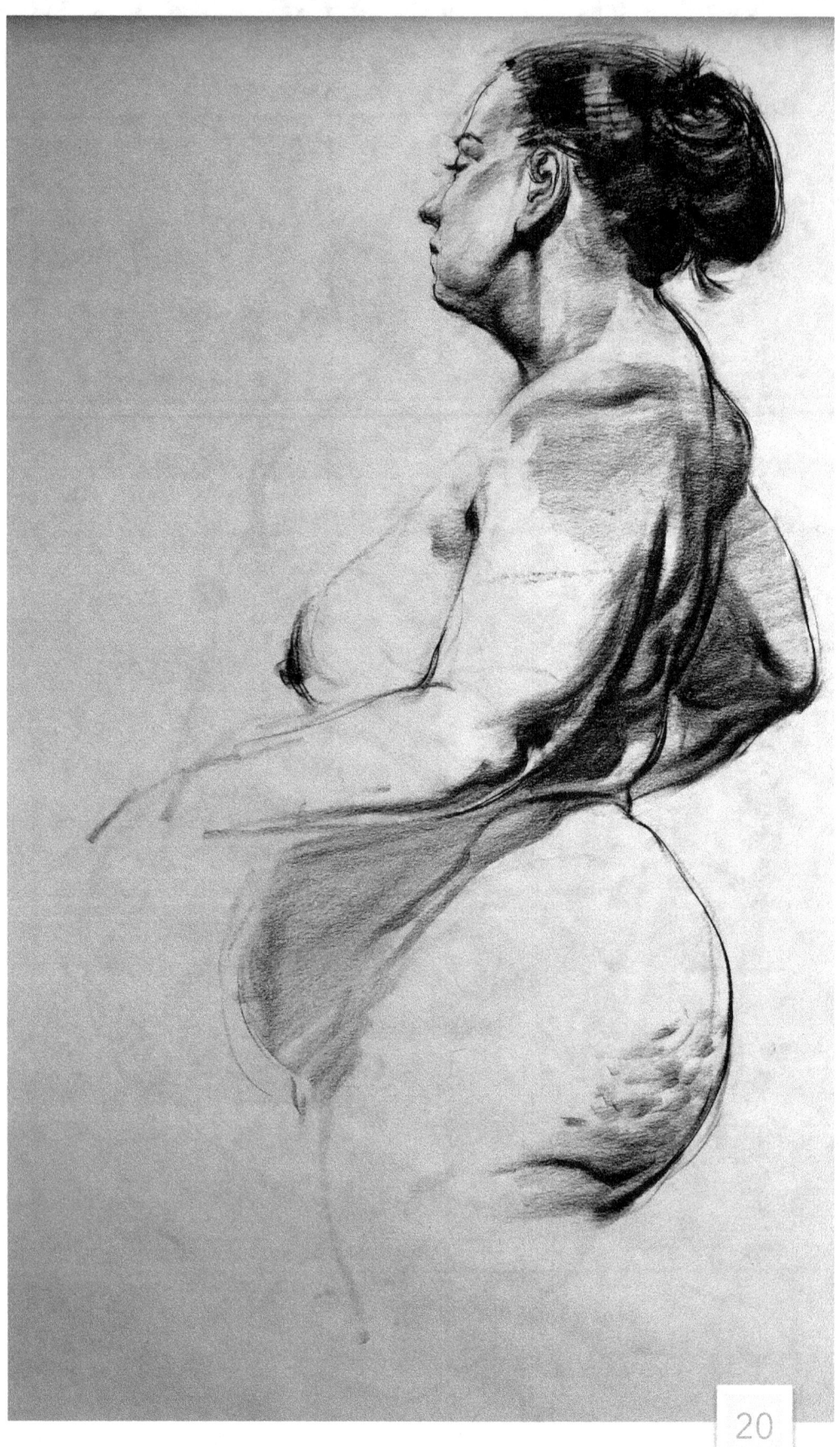

Limit the values to three or four at most in your drawing. Value is the range tones from lightest to darkest. In the drawing below, the newsprint sheet serves as the lightest value (value 1). Then the value of the rough lay in (value 2). Then the darkest value as seen in hair, clothing details and cast shadows (value 3).

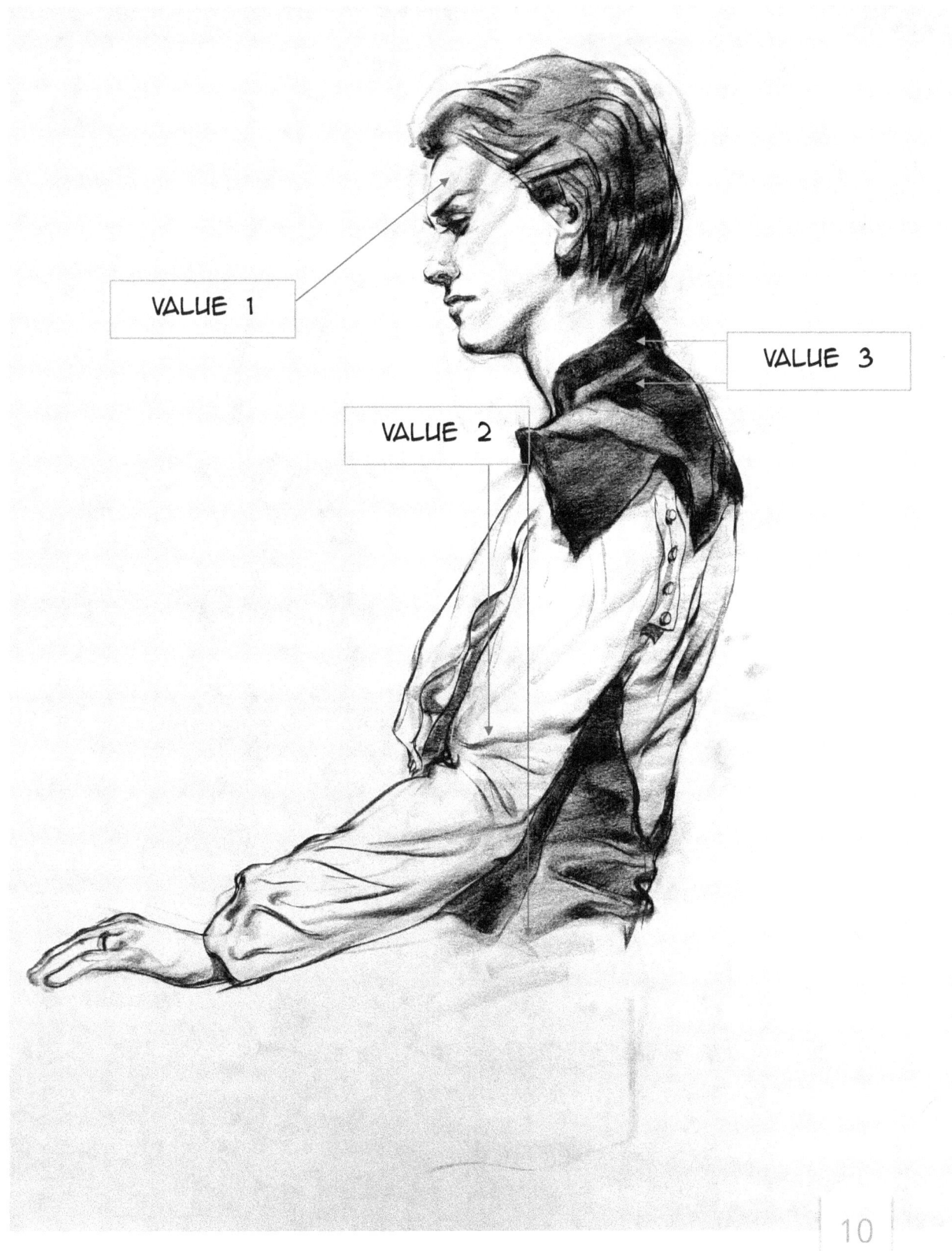

Practice drawing spheres (not circles) using three or four values. Placing these values in the right order should produce a decent sphere. Understanding value should become second nature to you. We will discuss more on this topic later in the book.

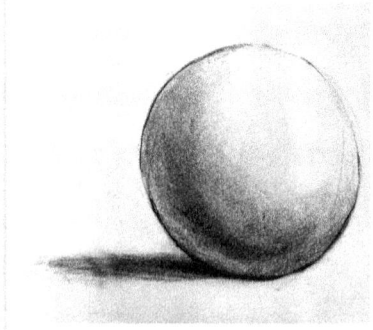

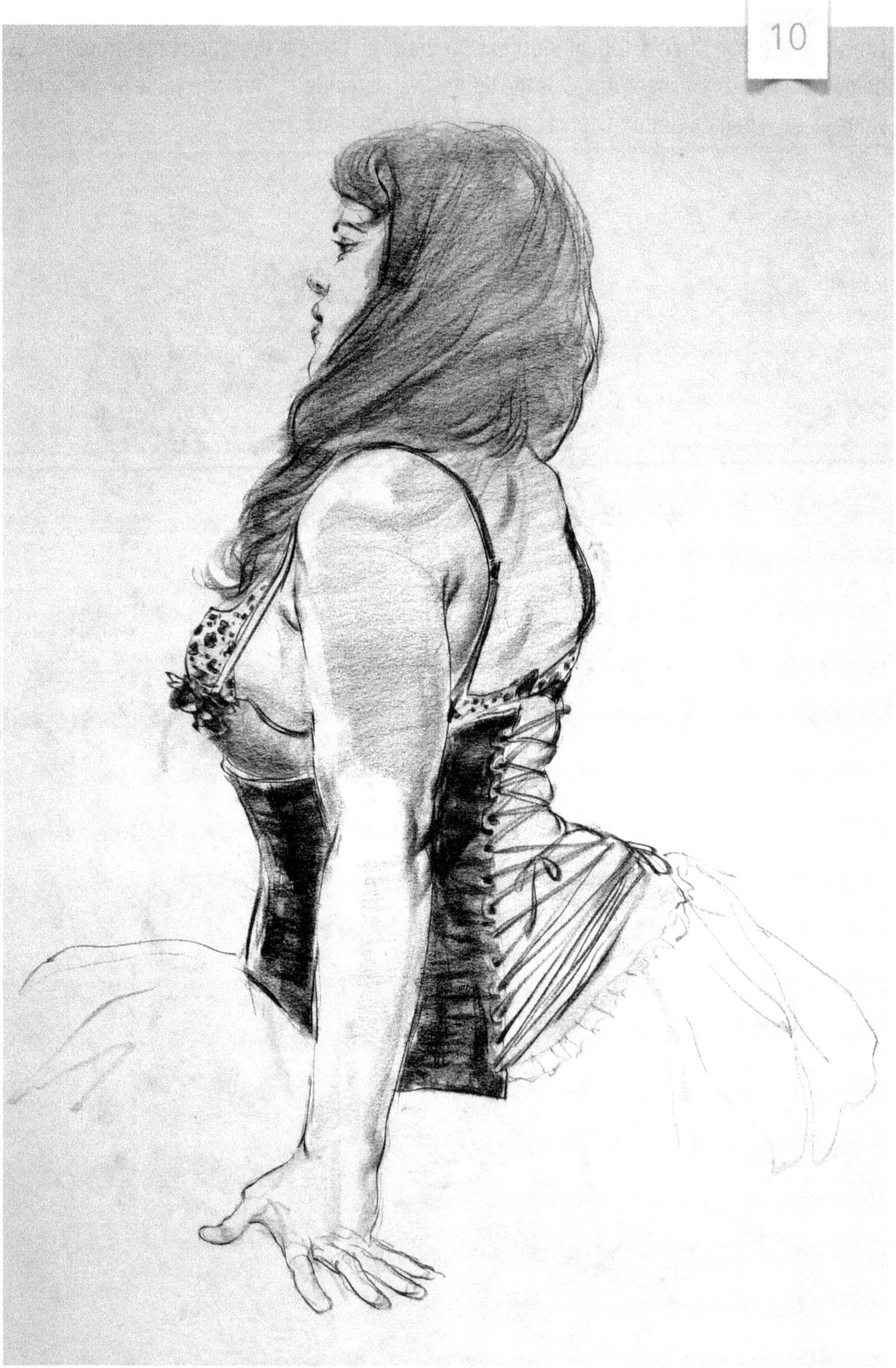

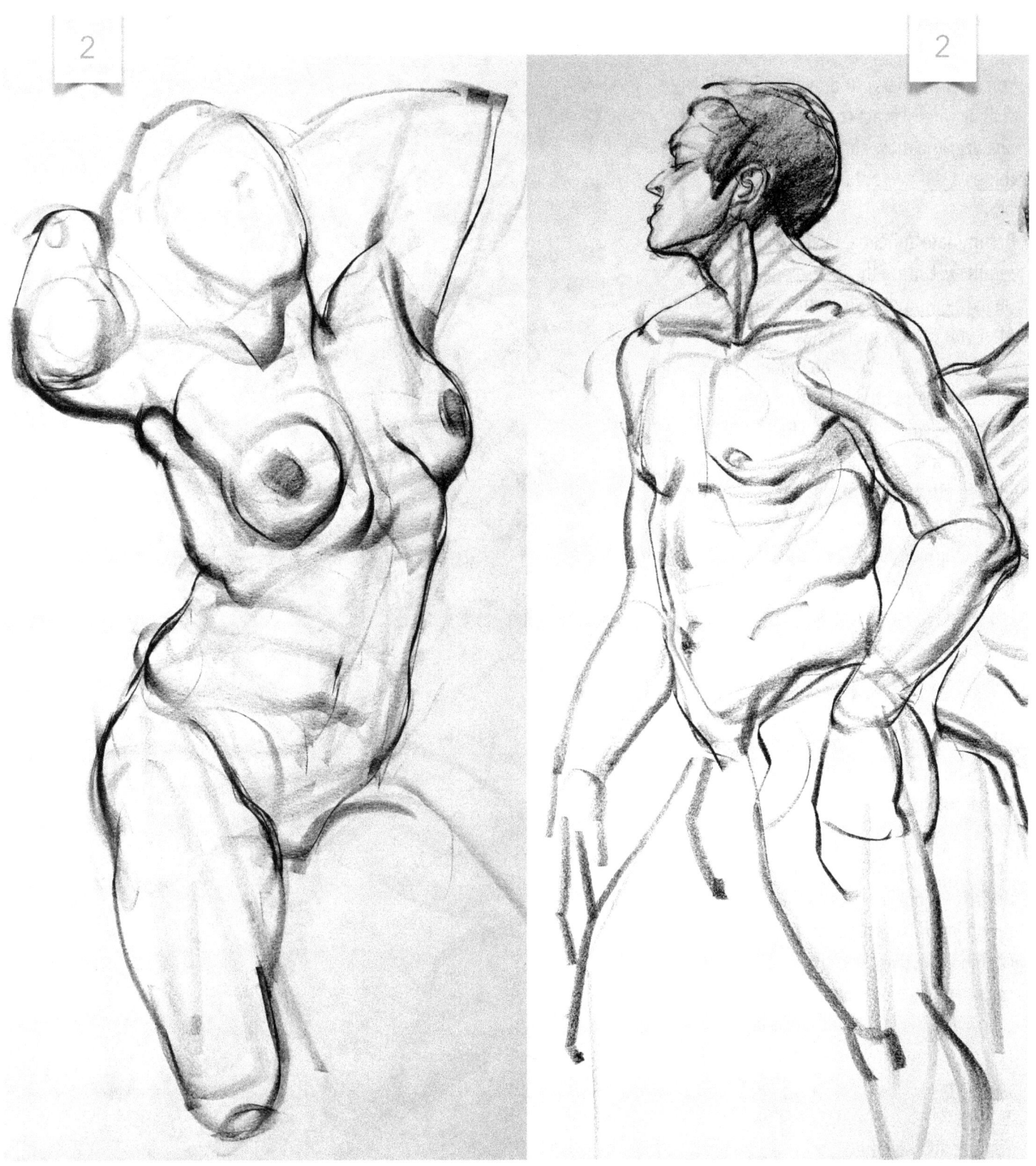

Draw three-dimensional forms as opposed to shapes. We tend to copy when we draw shapes (which are two dimensional). Instead, by studying Proportions, Anatomy, and Lighting, we are drawing the forms of underlying structure of (and lighting on) the figure.

You can improve your drawing skill by careful practice, i.e, draw, analyze, and draw again. <u>Accept this as a self-evident truth.</u>

Accumulate 'mileage' by drawing regularly. During these sessions, be <u>in the moment</u> when drawing. After you make a mark on your sheet, say an elbow of the model's left arm, analyze the drawn elbow's position in relation to neighboring body parts on the model. How far is the elbow sticking out from the torso? Is the hand aligned properly with the line of the hip? Is the upper arm too short? Too long? As I mentioned, drawing is an analytical process. <u>Do not hurry to put the entire figure on paper.</u> Take your time. It's important that what you draw is thought through and accurate.

See the incorrectly placed elbow drawn in tonal line. It was the rough lay in. A second look clarified that there was no negative space between the left elbow and the torso on the model. I corrected my drawing in the second pass.

You can also see the foreshortening on the upper left arm.

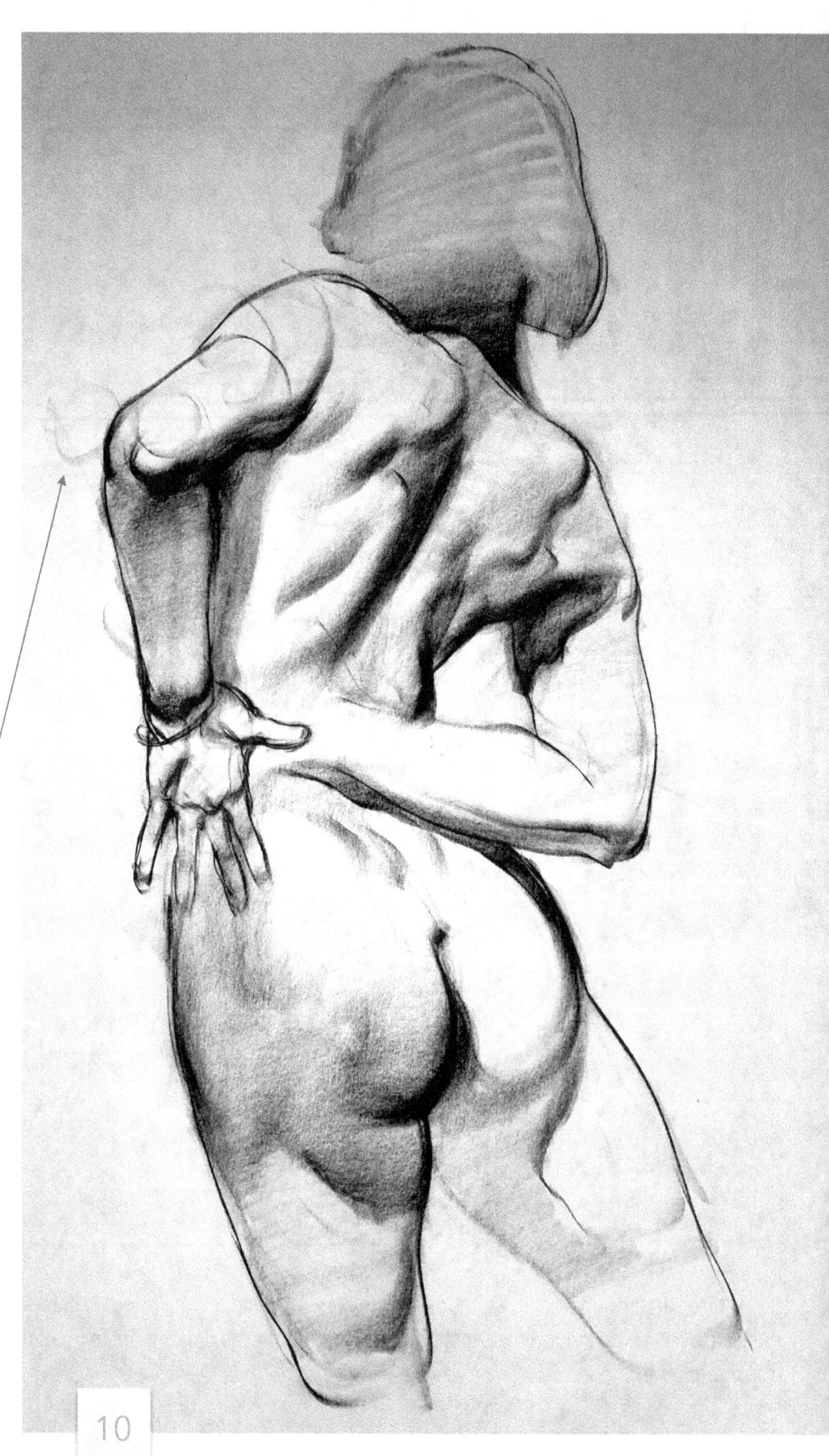

10

Focus on accuracy. Learn to distinguish between 'realism' vs. 'accuracy' in a drawing.

Notice how simple the hand is - it's not realistic but is reasonably accurate.

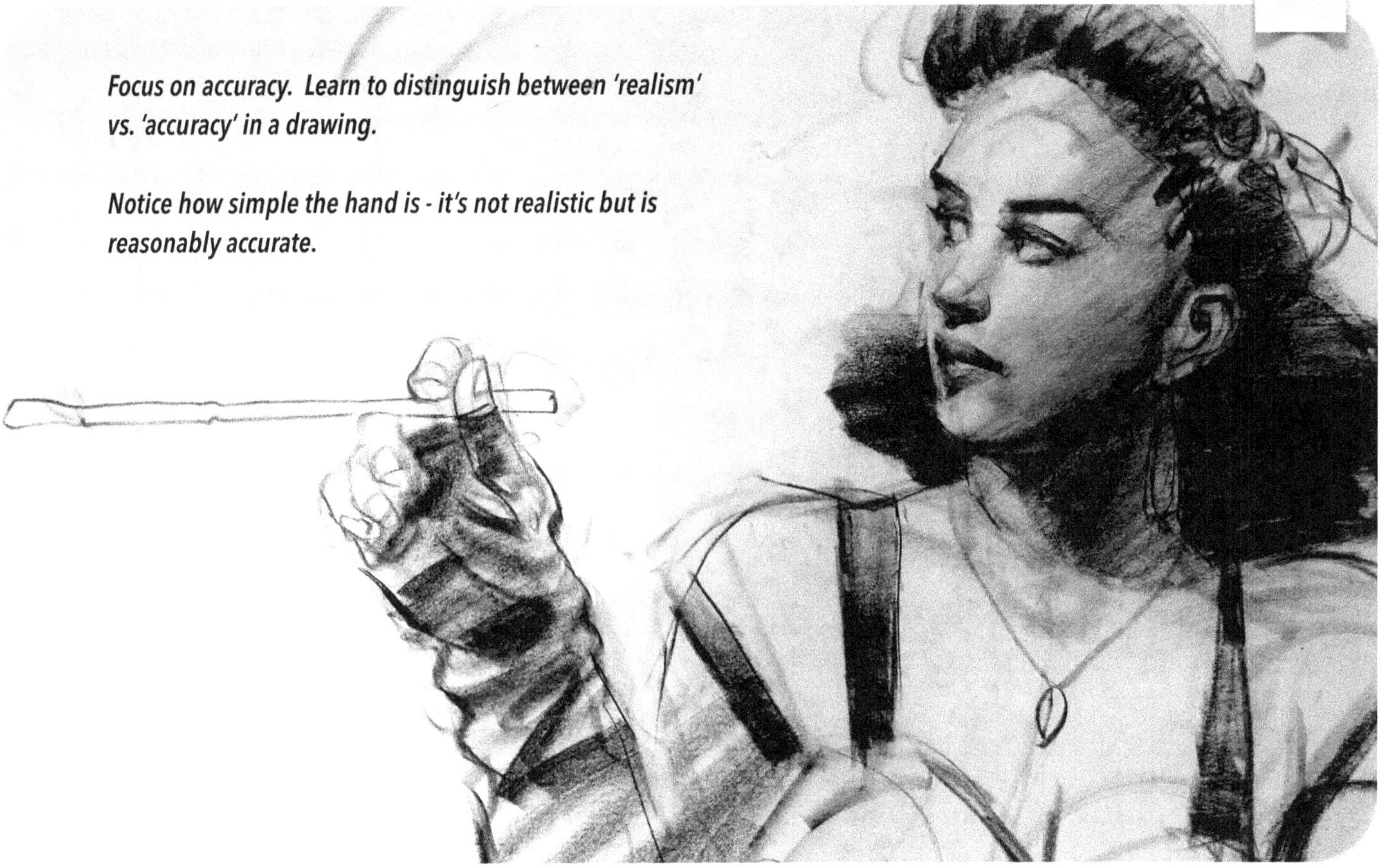

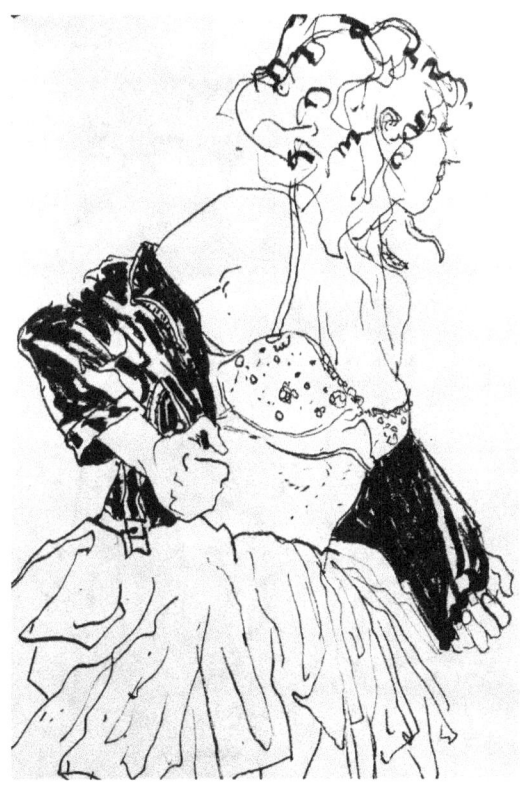

These short pen & ink life-drawings are not realistic but are 'reasonably accurate.' This is a distinction you will have to understand. Learning to draw accurately will require you to understand the subject - their proportions, anatomy, lighting, among other things.

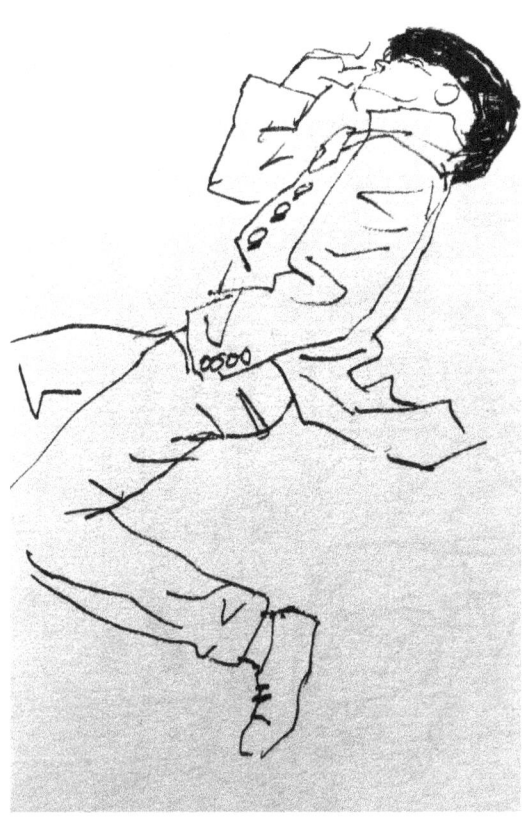

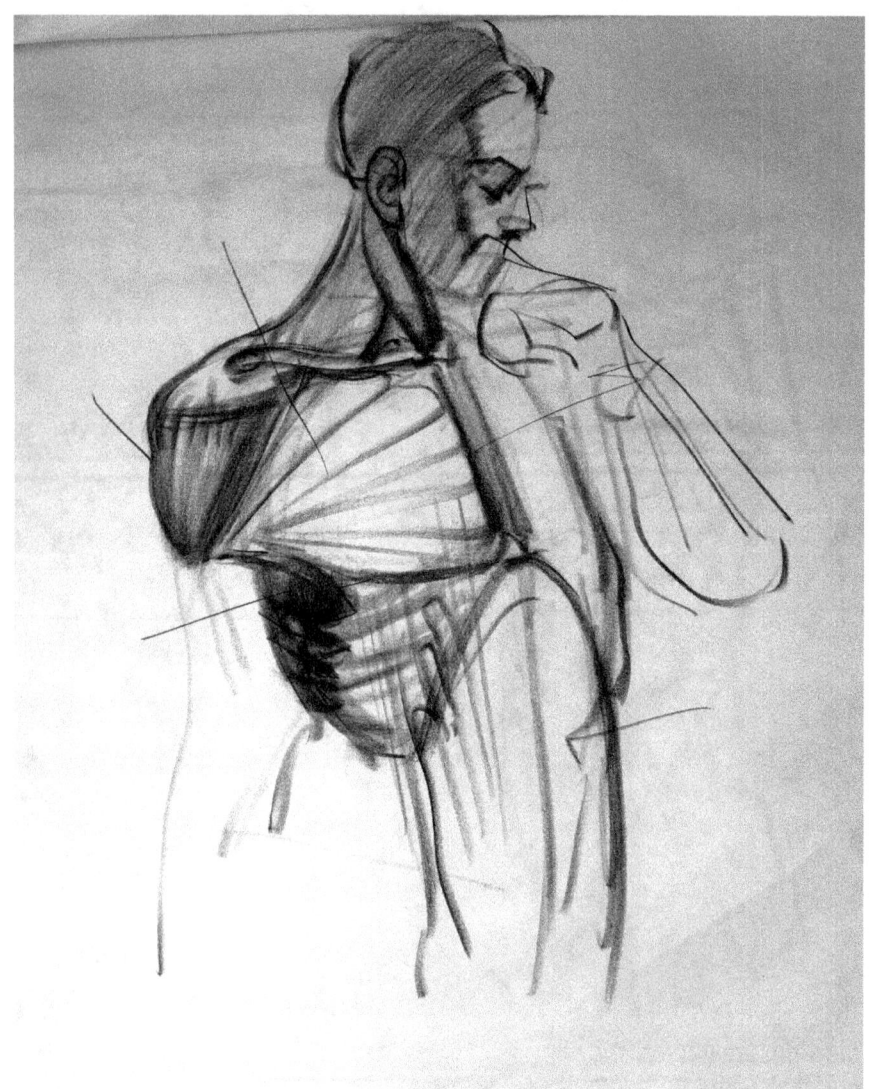

Draw big. The image on the left was done on packing paper for a class. The sheet was 3 feet long by 2 feet wide. I used a charcoal stick. Drawing big helps us initiate hand movement from the elbow or shoulder. When you draw from the wrist, you tend to get bogged down in picky stuff. Don't forget to analyze your big drawing by standing a few feet away. If you can, keep a mirror behind you so you can view the flipped drawing.

If you need practice learning to draw by holding the charcoal pencil at arms length, try drawing on a large white board with Dry Erase Markers. Hopefully, markers will force you to draw big. Below are a couple of examples from my class, drawn on a whiteboard using markers.

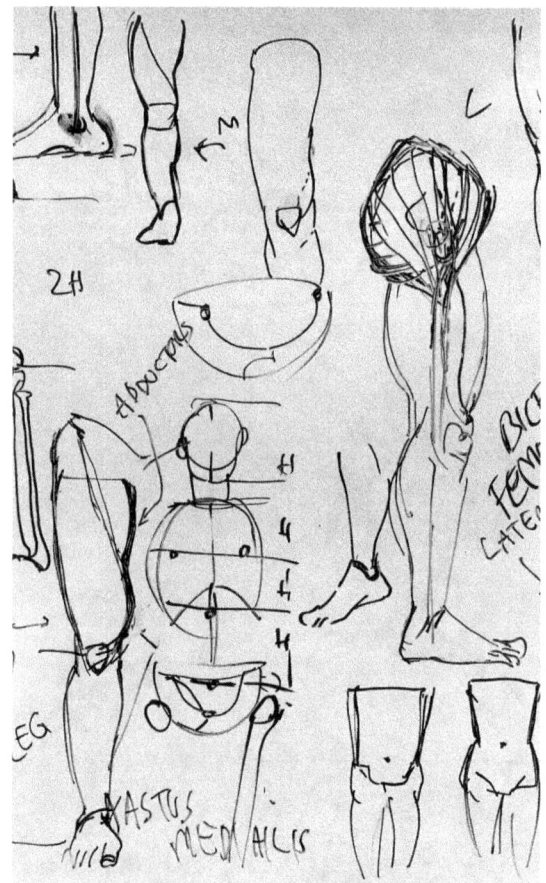

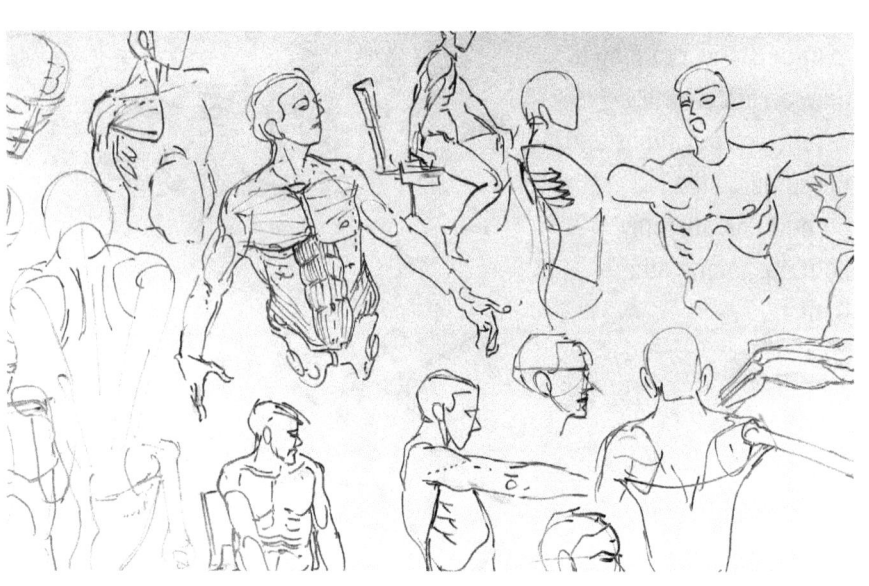

<u>Draw what you see.</u> It took me a long time to learn the significance of this simple idea. It's hard to get rid of our preconceived notions - how the eye looks in a profile drawing, for example. Remember those ancient Egyptian drawings where they drew the eyes in a front view when the head was in profile? They had philosophical reasons for doing this, but in life drawing, it's best to draw what you see.

The drawing on the right was done at a Society of Illustrators sketch night. It was a twenty minute pose. I was practicing to 'see' the muscles under the skin.

If you are drawing a motorbike, first get a rudimentary understating of how a motorbike is built. It will inform your drawings.

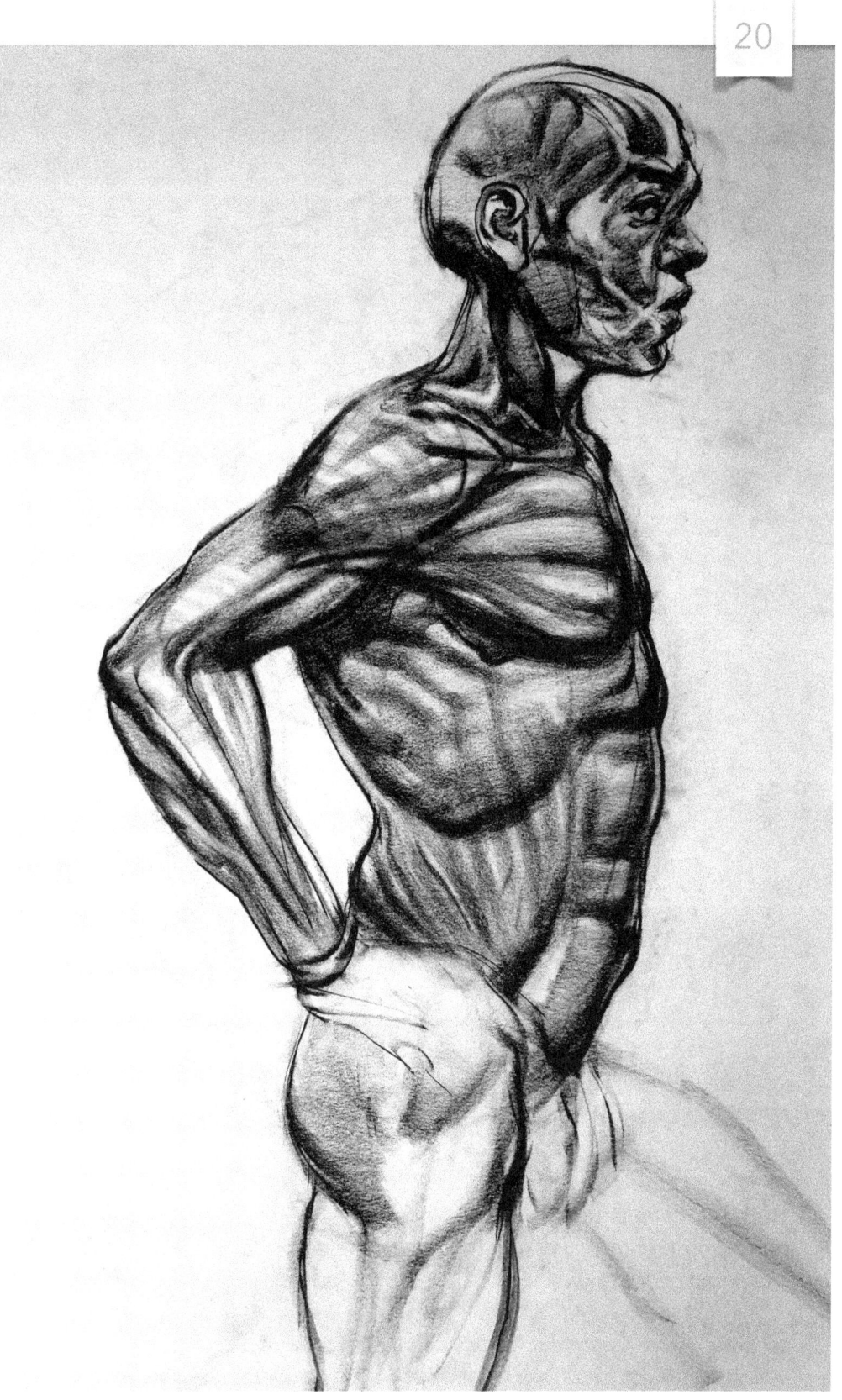

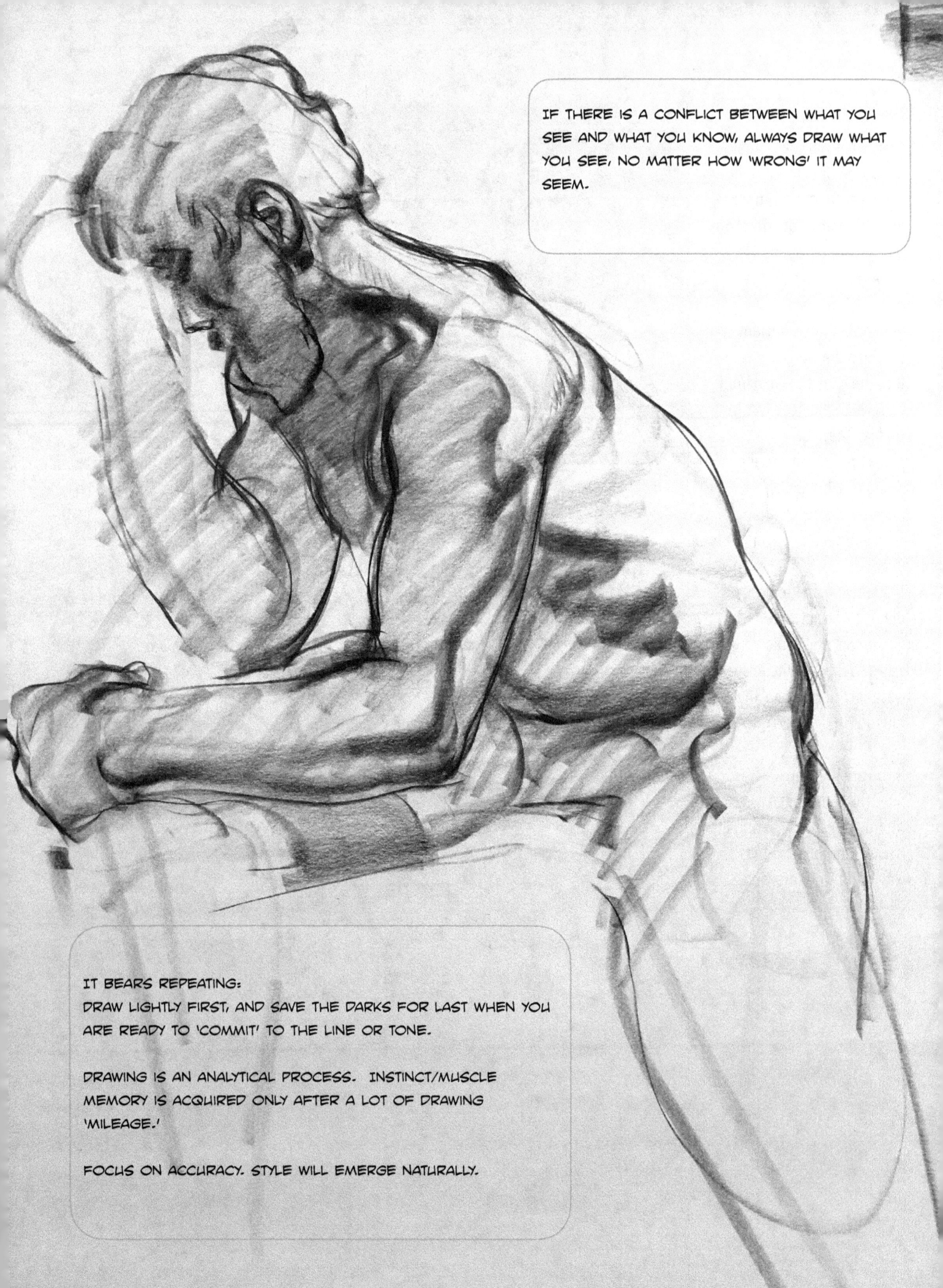

IF THERE IS A CONFLICT BETWEEN WHAT YOU SEE AND WHAT YOU KNOW, ALWAYS DRAW WHAT YOU SEE, NO MATTER HOW 'WRONG' IT MAY SEEM.

IT BEARS REPEATING:
DRAW LIGHTLY FIRST, AND SAVE THE DARKS FOR LAST WHEN YOU ARE READY TO 'COMMIT' TO THE LINE OR TONE.

DRAWING IS AN ANALYTICAL PROCESS. INSTINCT/MUSCLE MEMORY IS ACQUIRED ONLY AFTER A LOT OF DRAWING 'MILEAGE.'

FOCUS ON ACCURACY. STYLE WILL EMERGE NATURALLY.

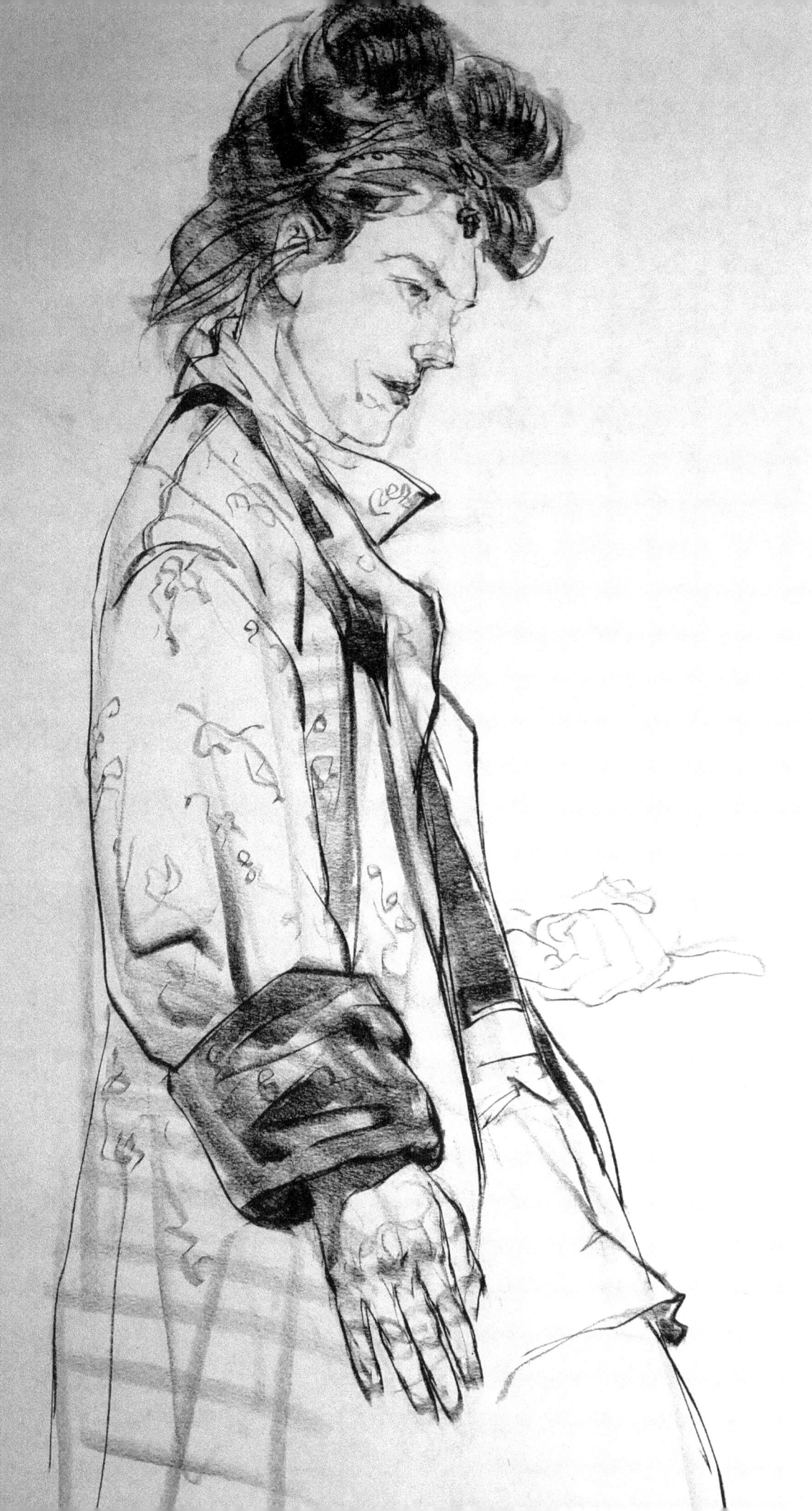

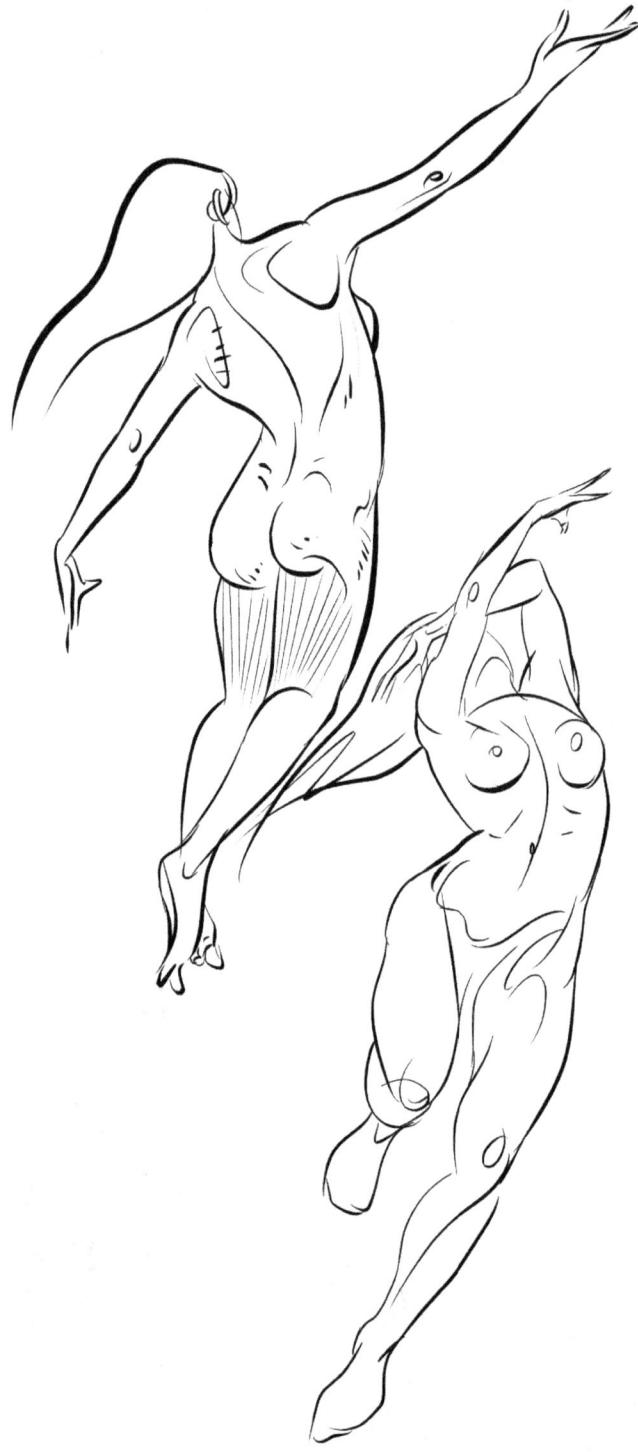
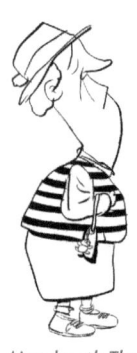

Umakanth Thumrugoti — A few Basics

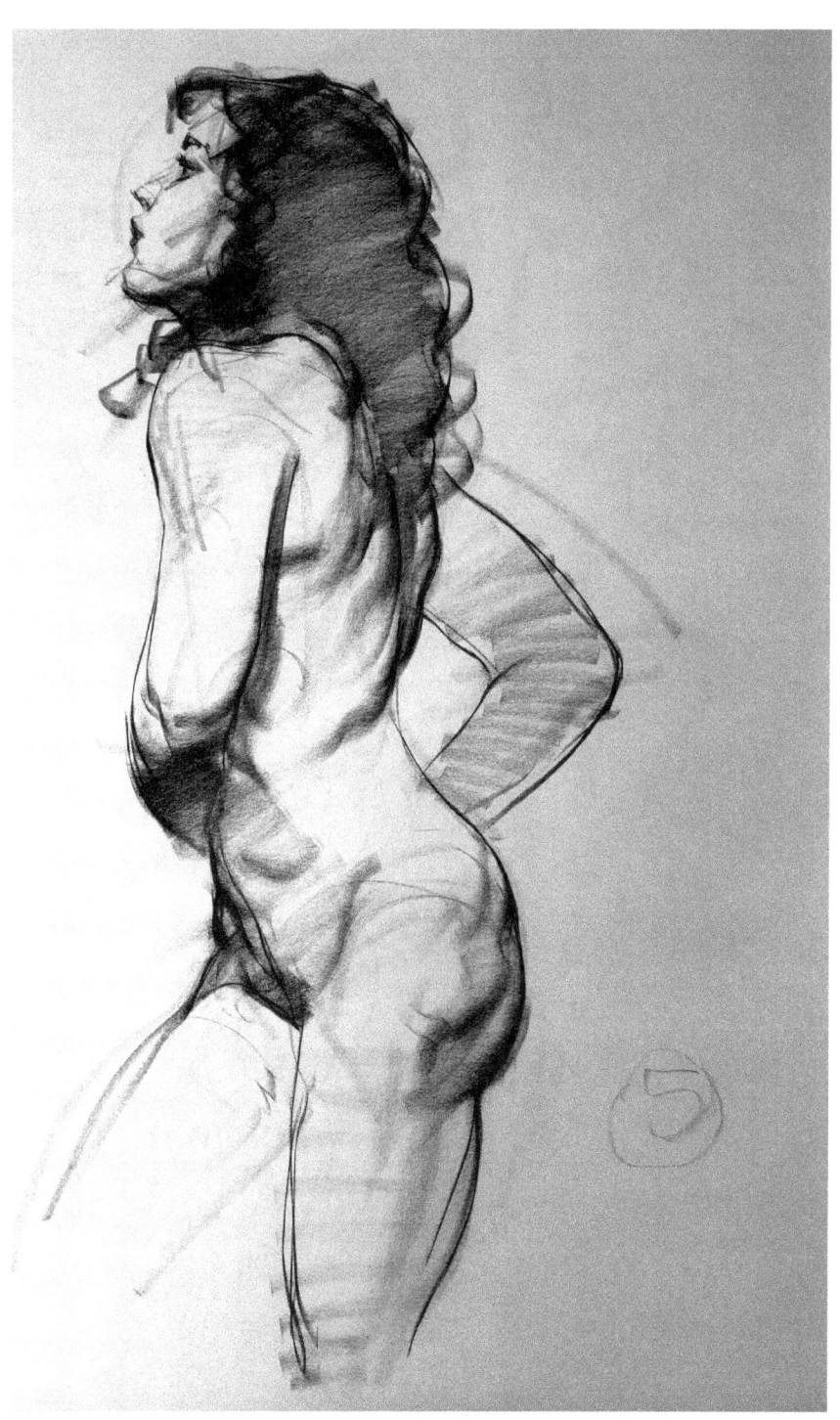

PROPORTIONS

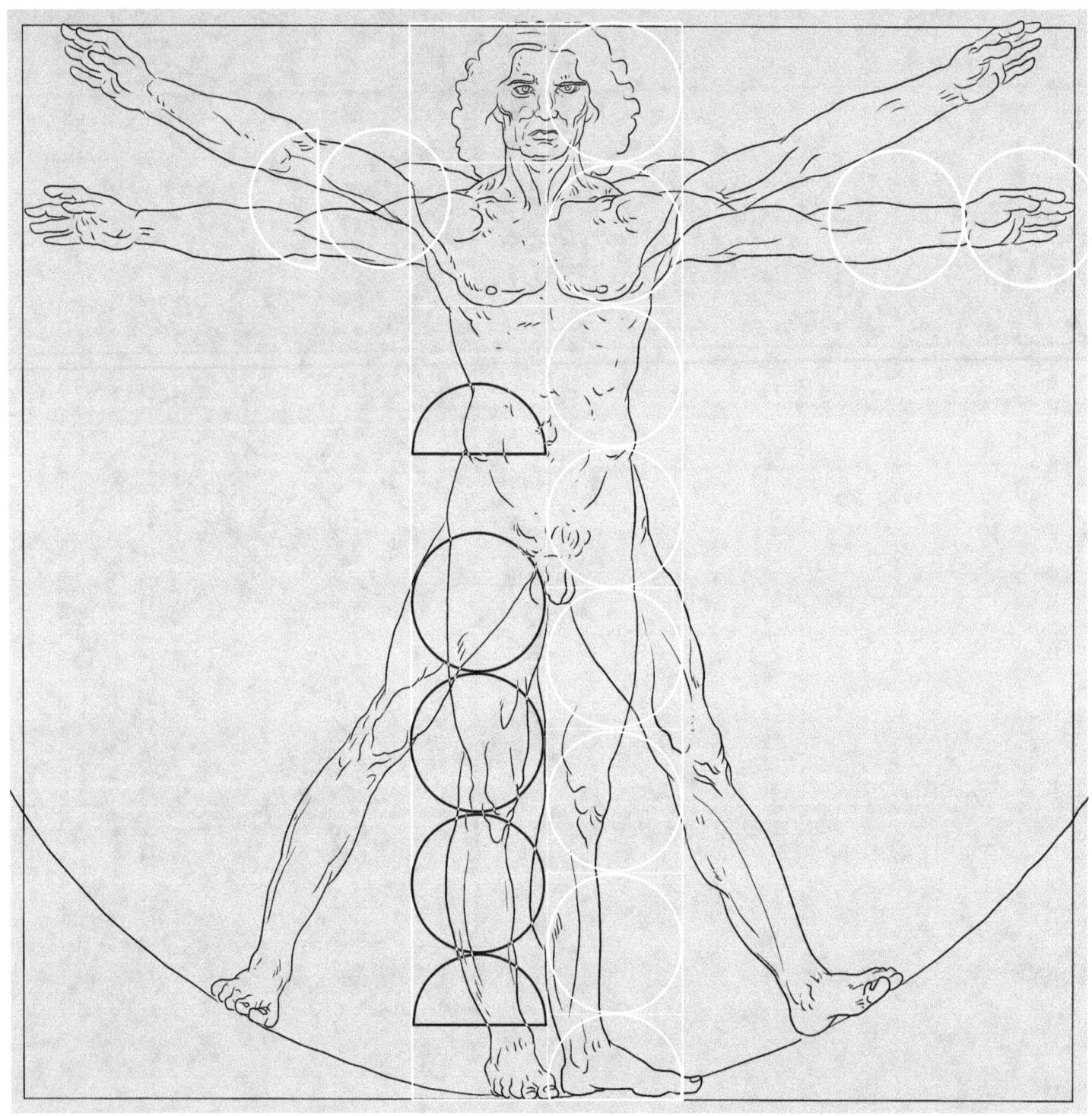

A few guidelines for the proportions of a human body. Specific proportions for individuals will vary, but this is a good starting point. Original drawing 'Vitruvian Man' by Leonardo da Vinci (about C1490).

- Using the head as a unit of measurement for the human body is a very old technique.
- The circle on the previous page represents one head length.

- The figure is seven and half heads tall.
- The neck is one third of a head.
- At the shoulders, the torso is two heads wide.
- The upper arm (Humerus bone) is one and half heads long.
- The lower arm (Radius bone) is slightly longer than one head.
- The hand is about three quarters of the head.

- The upper leg (Femur, the thigh bone) is two heads long. See the dark grey circles on the upper leg.
- The lower leg (Tibia) is one and half heads long (dark grey circles).
- Distance between the lower edge of the rib cage and top of the pelvis is about half a head long (dark half circle at the waist).

- The foot is slightly longer than a head.
- The ribcage is a bit less than one and three quarters of a head.
- The male pelvis is about one head wide. A female pelvis is slightly wider than that.

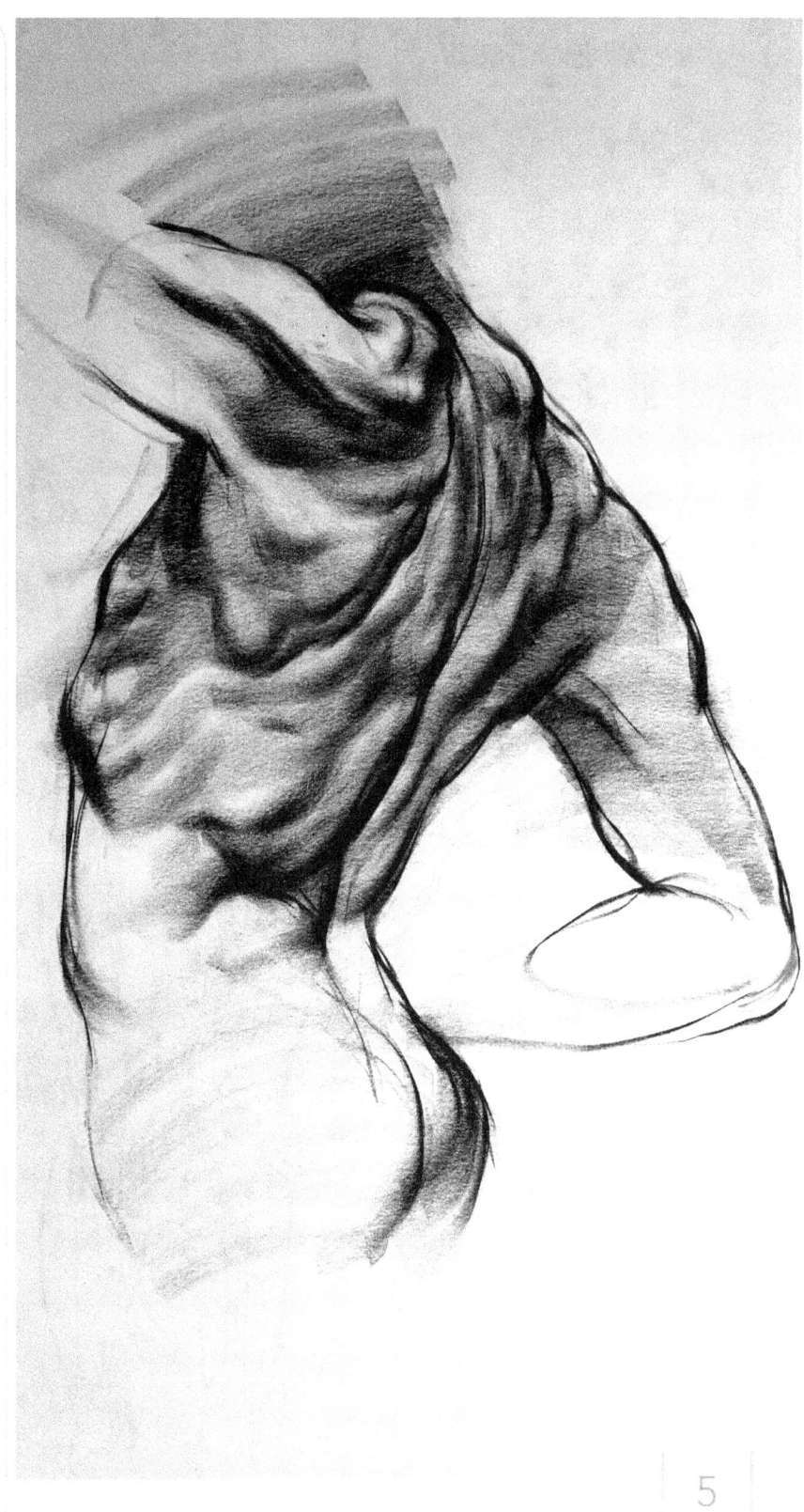

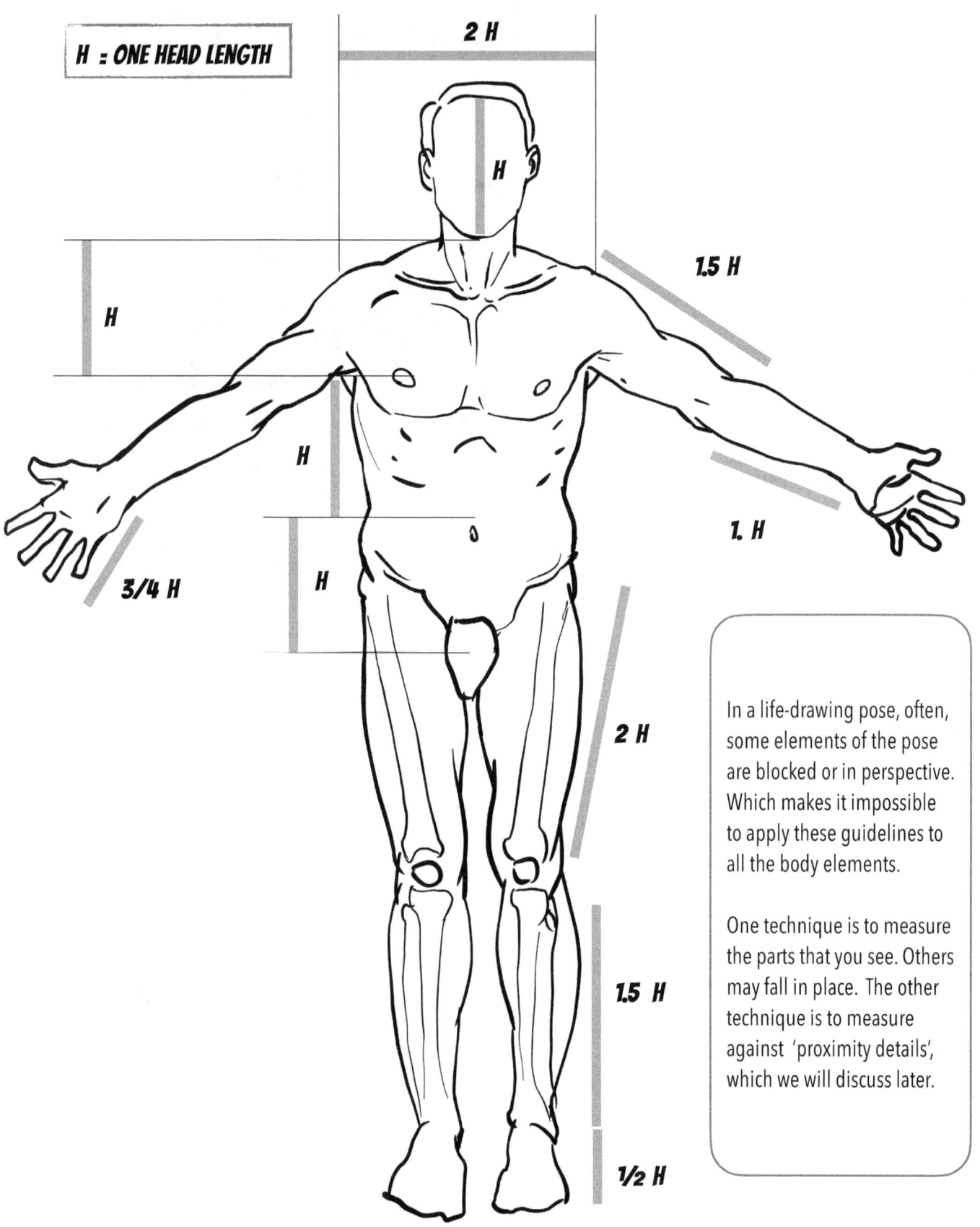

In a life-drawing pose, often, some elements of the pose are blocked or in perspective. Which makes it impossible to apply these guidelines to all the body elements.

One technique is to measure the parts that you see. Others may fall in place. The other technique is to measure against 'proximity details', which we will discuss later.

Umakanth Thumrugoti   Proportions

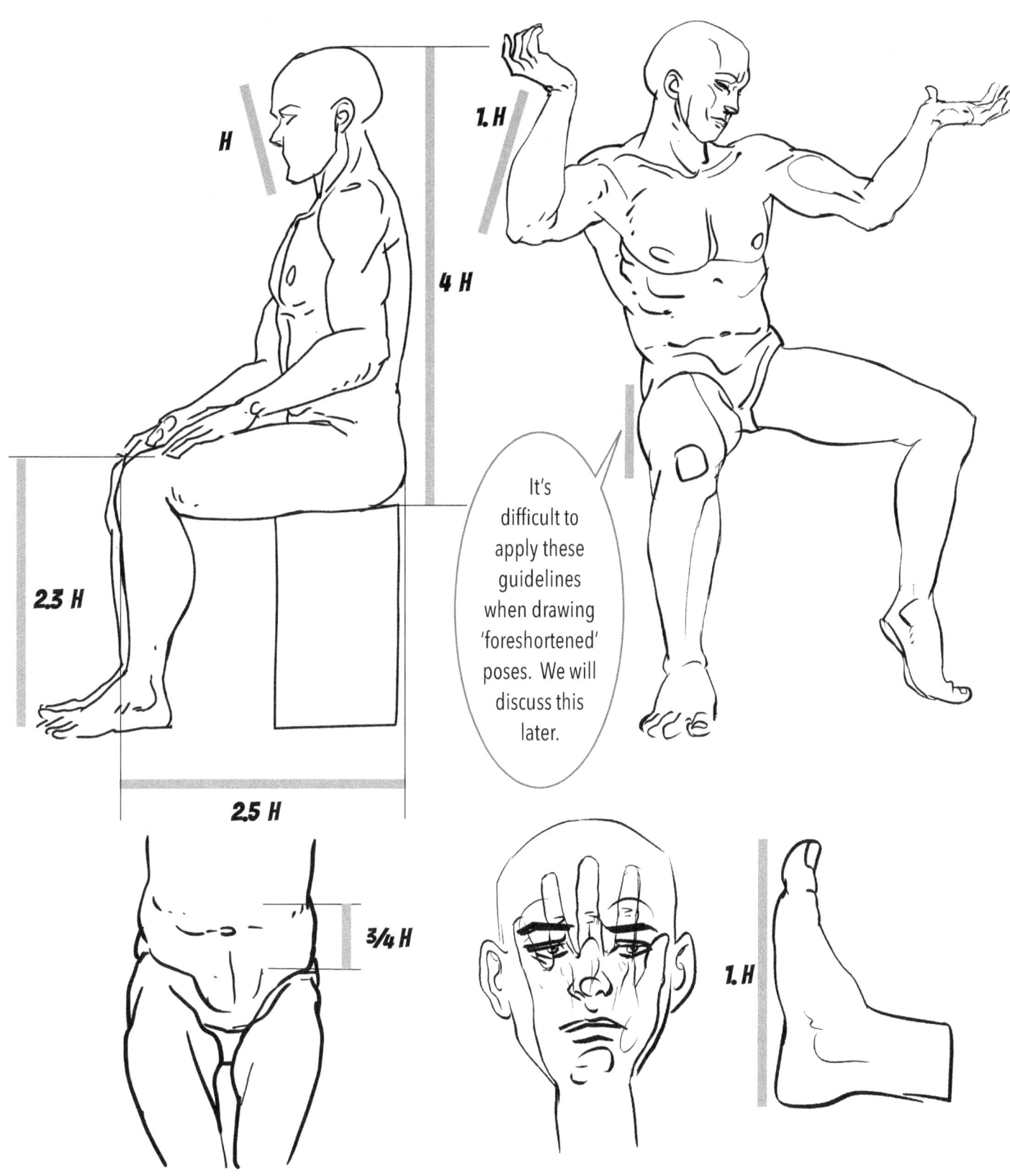

THESE ARE <u>APPROXIMATE</u> MEASUREMENTS USING THE HEAD AS A UNIT OF MEASUREMENT

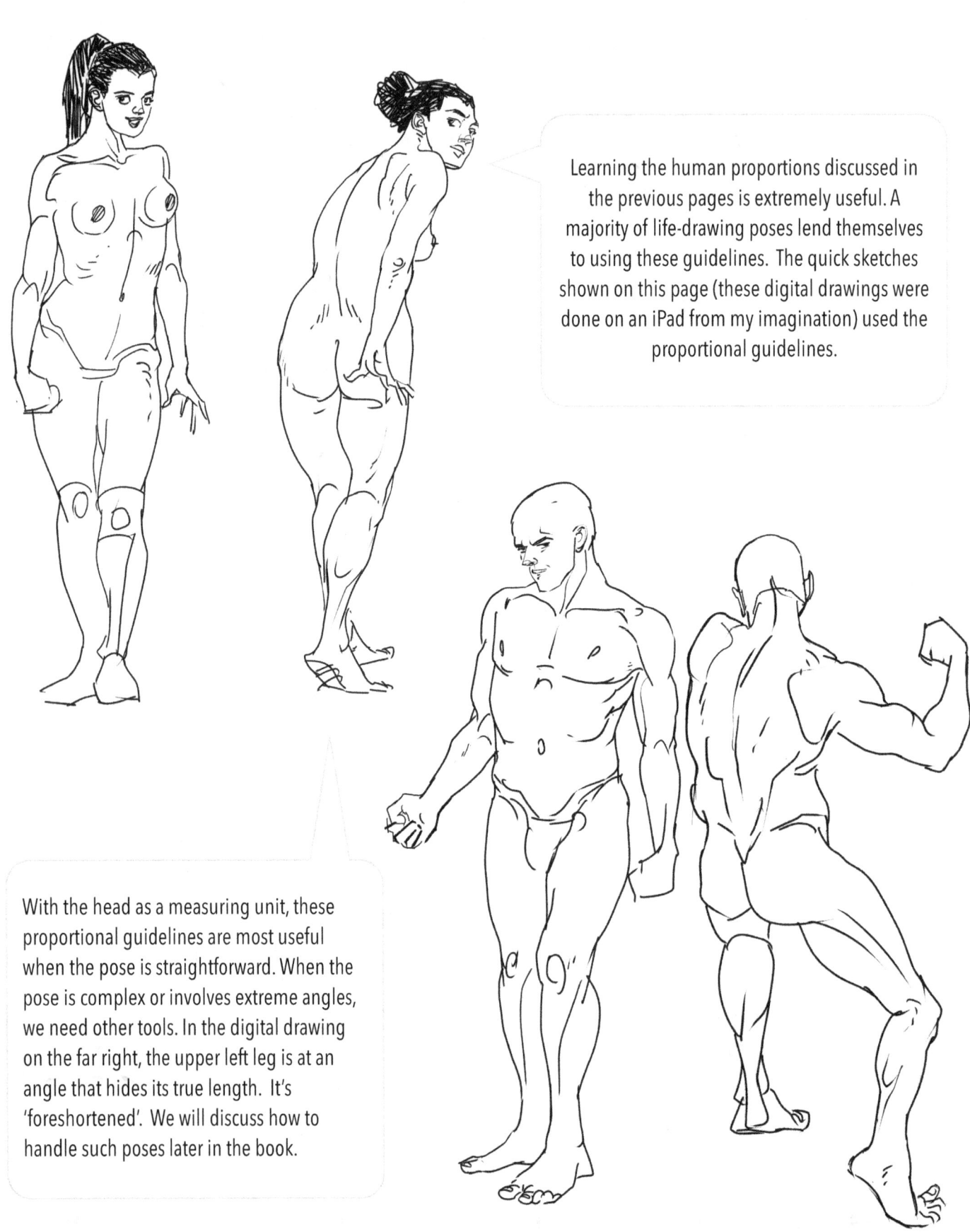

Learning the human proportions discussed in the previous pages is extremely useful. A majority of life-drawing poses lend themselves to using these guidelines. The quick sketches shown on this page (these digital drawings were done on an iPad from my imagination) used the proportional guidelines.

With the head as a measuring unit, these proportional guidelines are most useful when the pose is straightforward. When the pose is complex or involves extreme angles, we need other tools. In the digital drawing on the far right, the upper left leg is at an angle that hides its true length. It's 'foreshortened'. We will discuss how to handle such poses later in the book.

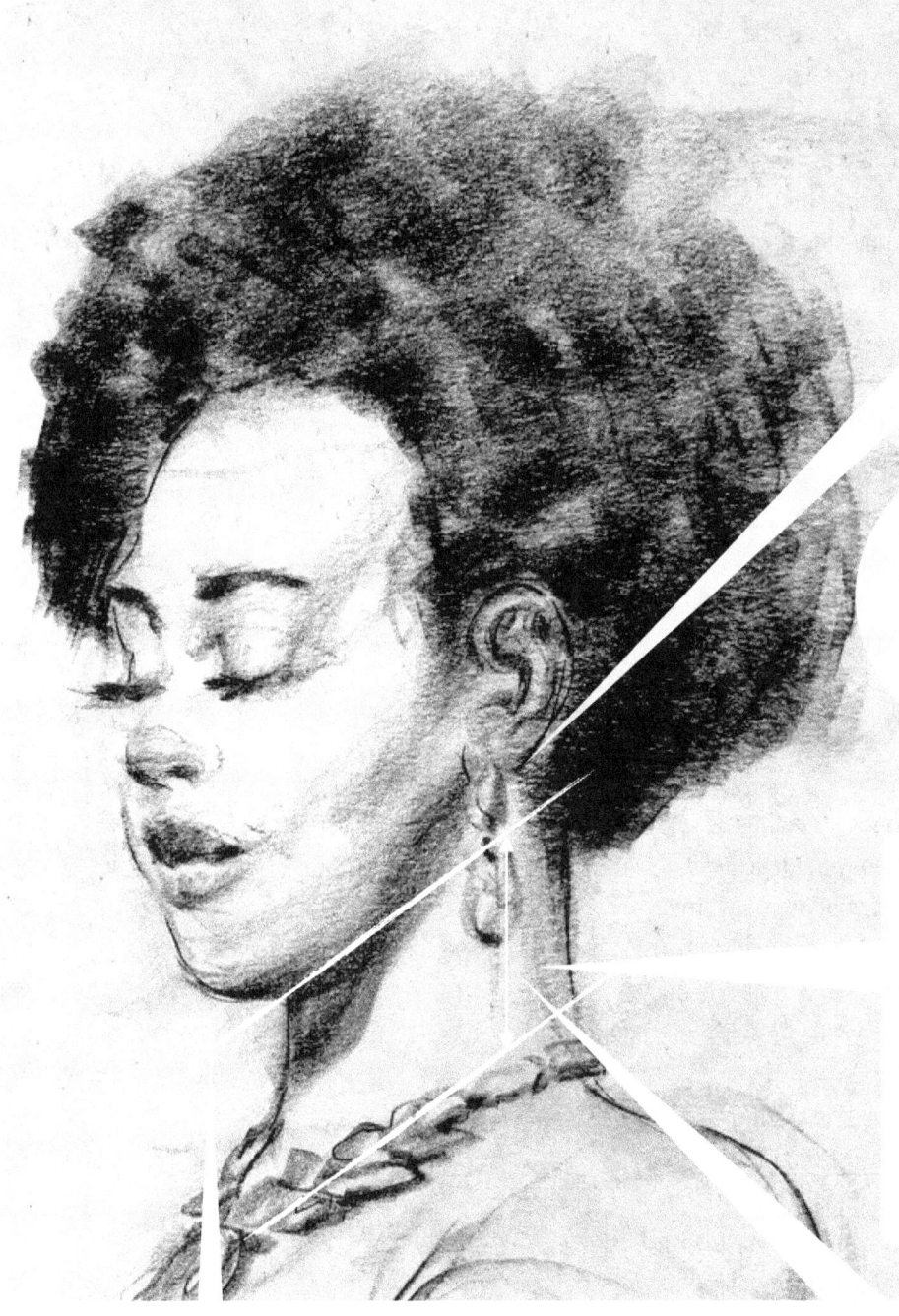

The head connects to the neck in the back at a higher point as compared to the chin.

The point where the neck connects to the torso is also higher in the back than at the front. That's why shirt collars are higher in the back and slope down to the front for the top button.

Think of the neck simply as a tube, or a tapered tube to be more precise. The top end of the neck is narrower where it connects to the head. The bottom end widens when it connects to the upper torso.

Learn to think in terms of volumes instead of shapes. Shapes are two dimensional, and volumes are three dimensional. Draw the neck as a tube. Tonal lighting will help you create the impression of volume. In the drawing above, the head is casting a shadow on the neck and tonal darks in the back of the neck help convey neck's form.

Length of the neck is roughly one third the length of the head.

The upper arm is one and half heads long. Even when drawing quick poses, pay attention to proportions. This was a five-minute pose. Don't worry about details until you have the gesture articulated.

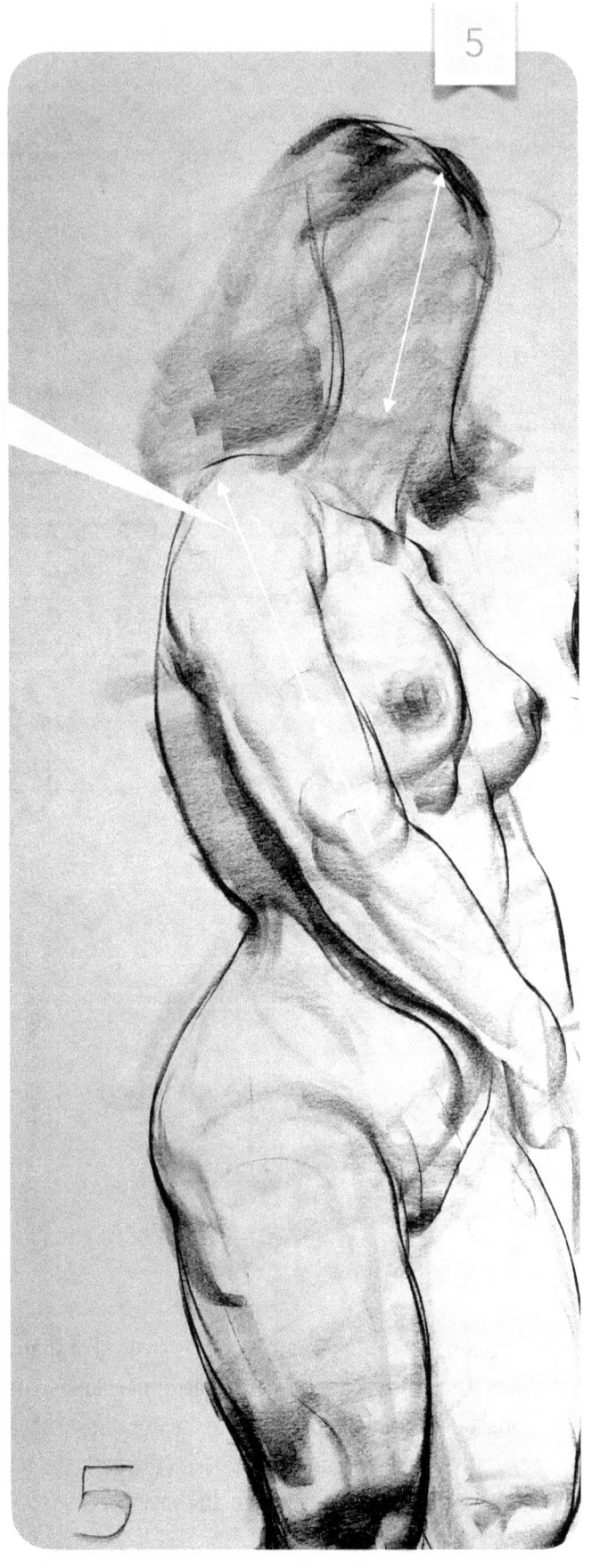

I start my rough lay-in by drawing the form that represents the head. Sometimes, it's simply an egg shaped form. I use that form as a measuring unit for drawing the rest of the body.

The inevitable question - how do I know if the upper arm I drew is one and half times the head without actually measuring? One technique is to hold your pencil at arms length against the model. Mark the length of the head with your thumb on the pencil. Keeping that "mark," measure other parts.

I learned to measure the hard way by visualizing and approximating on the paper. <u>Train your brain to measure things without actually measuring, and make your marks.</u> However, after making marks lightly, you can measure on your paper and also check for 'proximity' details.

In this case, where is the elbow in relation to the bend in the back, or the right nipple? By making sure all the body landmarks nearby in the proper relationship to the elbow (both on the model and in your drawing), you can confirm that the position of the elbow mark is reasonable.

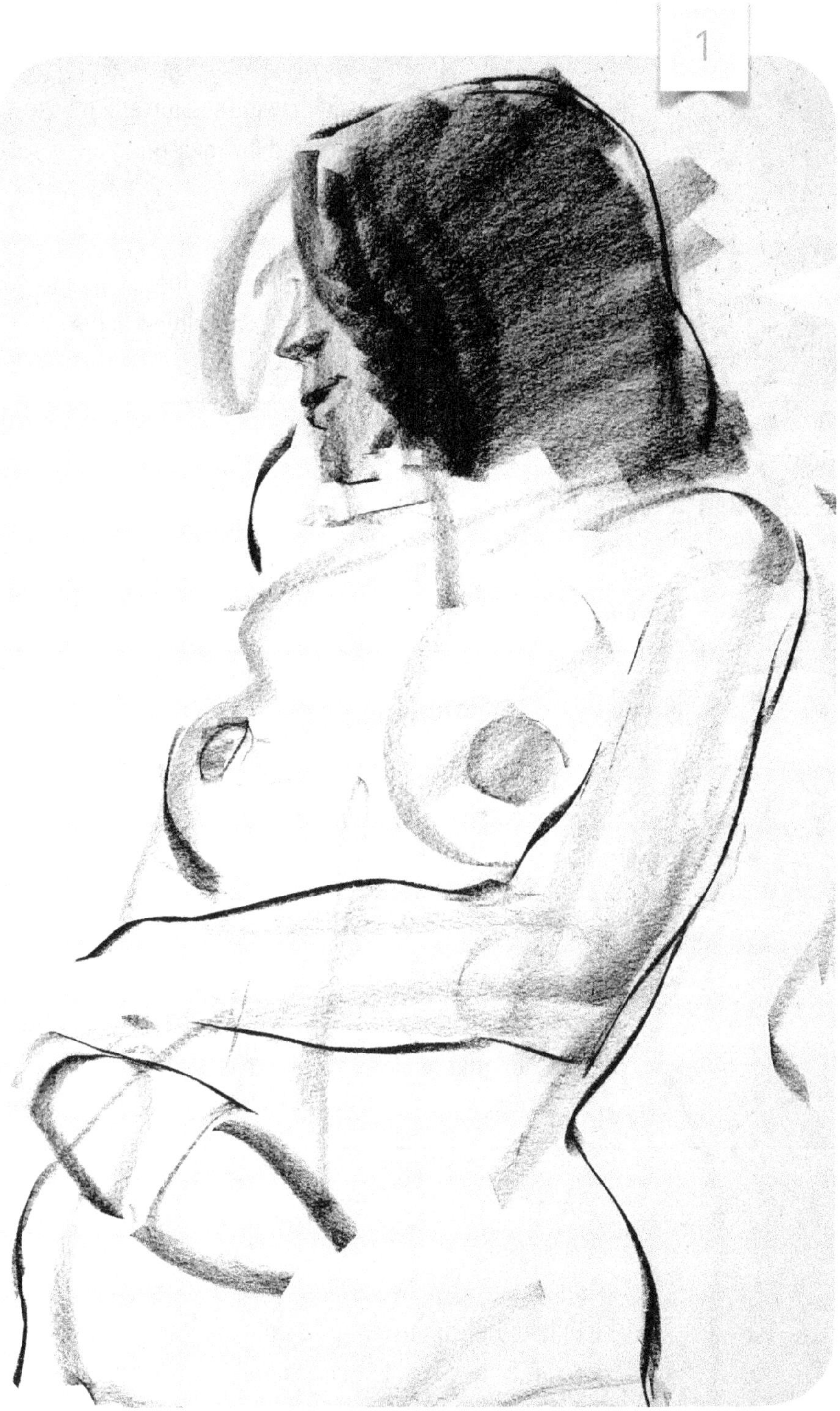

1

A quick one minute gesture drawing. The rough lay-in tonal lines and a few axial-lines are easy to see - and about all you have time for. Drawing this way requires practice - the cycle of seeing, drawing, evaluating, correcting errors, and continuing drawing.

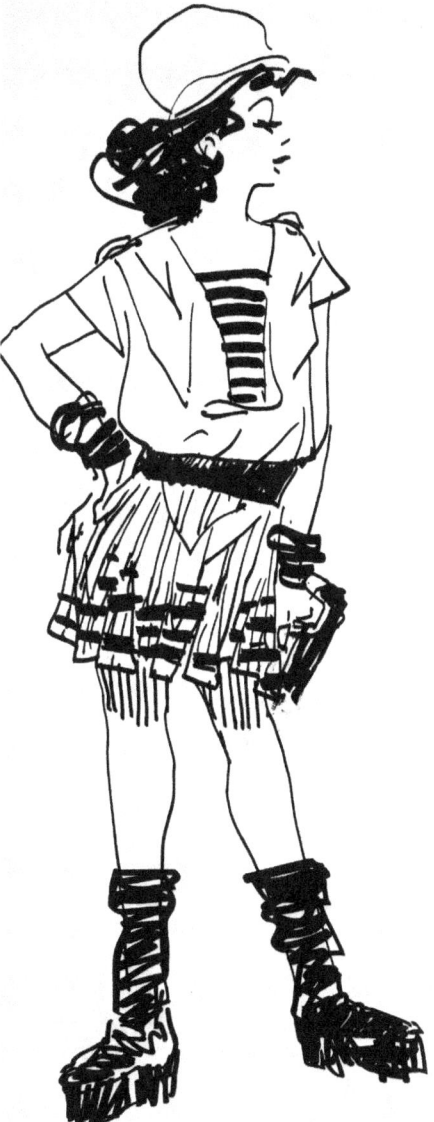

An example of a doodle drawn without a model. Practice measuring anatomical distances in your mind.

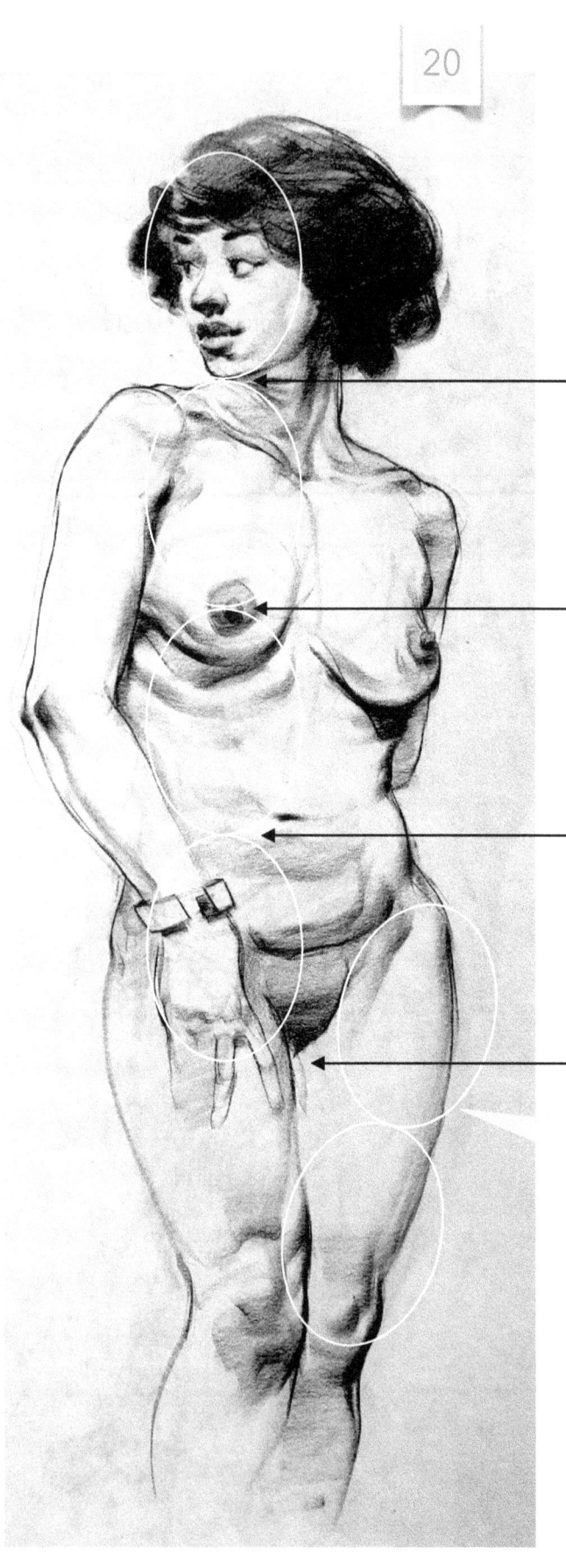

This drawing was done at a life-drawing session at the Society of Illustrators, NYC. I placed the measuring units (ellipses) later digitally.

As you can see, the height of the ellipse (it doesn't have to be a circle) is one head long. The eyes are almost at the center of the head in an adult.

One head length from the chin is the location of the nipples.

One head length from the nipples is the approximate location of the belly button.

One head length from the bellybutton is the crotch.

The upper leg is two heads long. It's actually the length of the thigh bone, or the femur. It's the longest bone in the human body. We will discuss more on anatomy later.

These guidelines for using the head as a measuring unit fall apart when the model is bending/tilting away from or toward the viewer, i.e., when foreshortening is evident.

Another technique worth learning is to visualize the elements of a human body as a collection of simple forms - spheres, tapered cylinders/tubes, boxes, etc. These forms are inherently volumetric, so your drawings will look three dimensional. We already approximated the neck as a tube. Let's continue the thought process - can we approximate the head as a sphere? Perhaps the pelvis as a bowl?

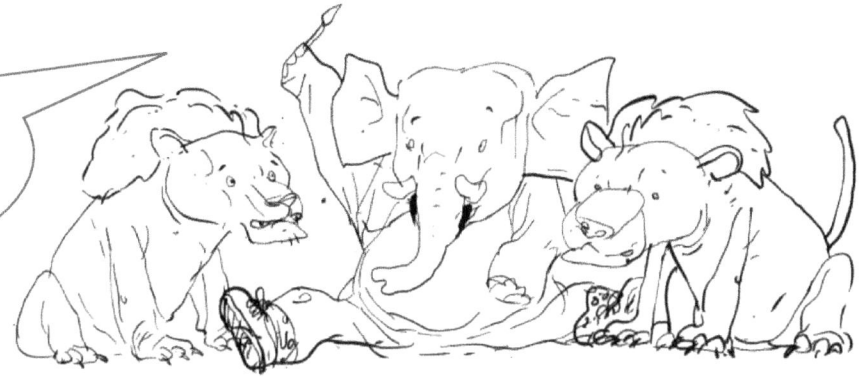

The origin of the word 'pelvis' is from Latin - it means *a basin or a bowl*.

Do you see the arms as tapered tubes in the drawing on the right? How about the entire torso as a slightly bent tube?

Drawing the limbs as tubes is a very useful simplification.

The head can be a sphere with an extended chin. We will discuss drawing the head in detail in the Head Drawing section.

For the first rough lay-in, do <u>not add any fat or muscles to the limbs. In drawing the tube, find the narrowest part of the limb. Use that as width of the tube</u> (with no fat or bulging muscles). After you get the overall proportions right, you can add the muscles and/or fat.

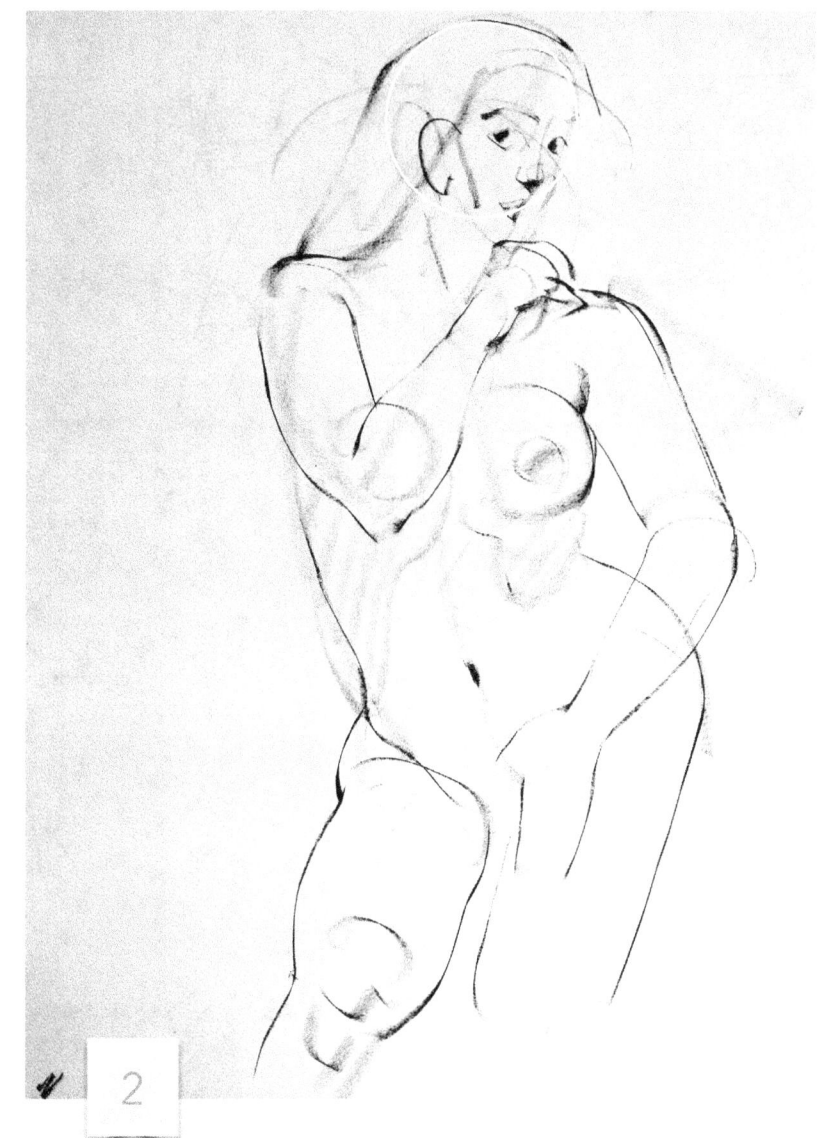

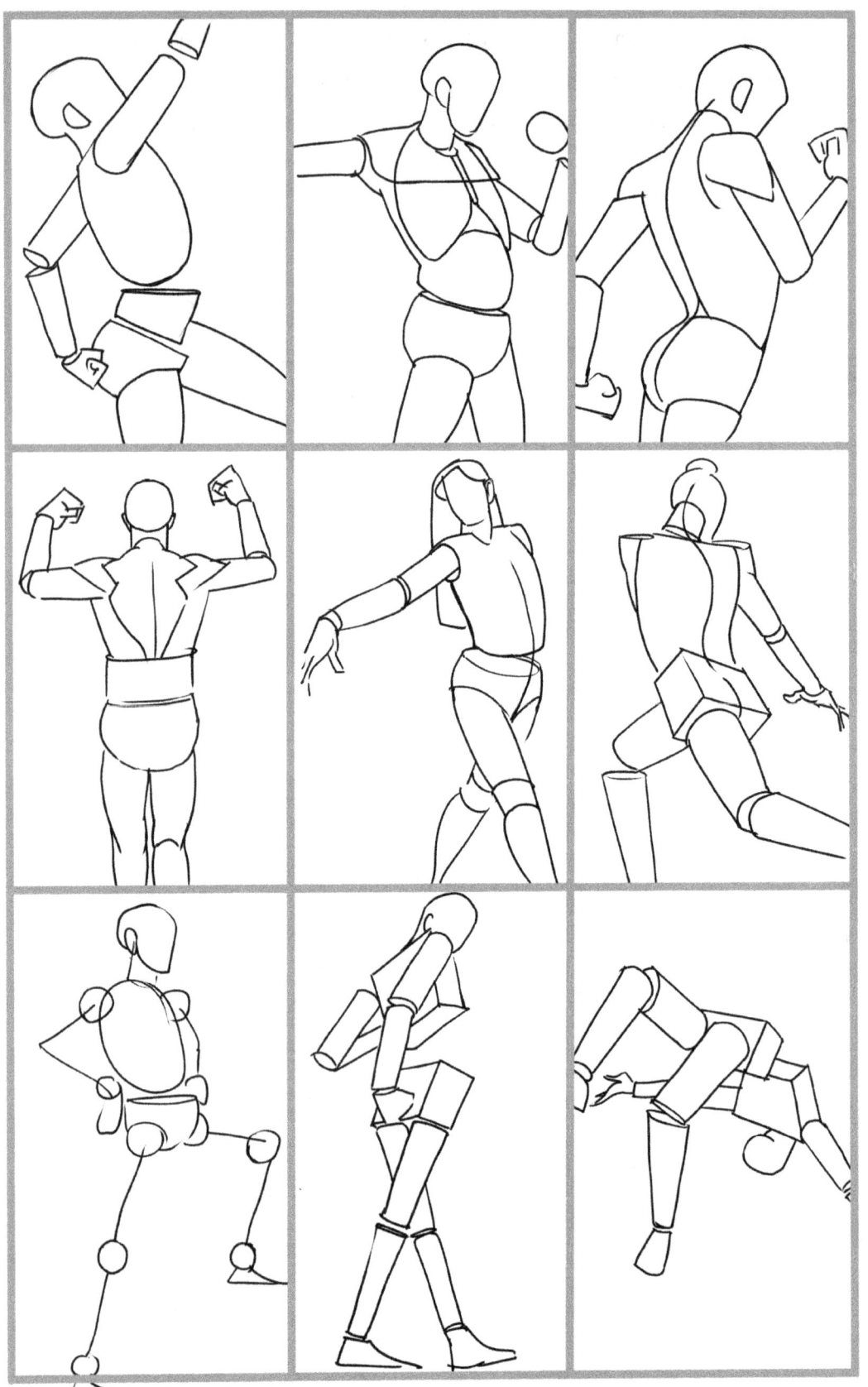

SIMPLE FORMS – *TUBES, SPHERES, BOWLS (PELVIS) EGG FORMS (RIBCAGE),* ARE USED FOR APPROXIMATING ANATOMICAL ELEMENTS.

DRAW THE FIGURE WITH THESE SIMPLE FORMS FIRST, CONCENTRATING ON CORRECT PROPORTIONS.

THEN DO ERROR CHECKING. ARE THE SURFACE LANDMARKS – KNEES, ELBOWS, COLLAR BONE, PELVIS, NIPPLES, ETC. IN THE RIGHT PLACE? IS THE UPPER ARM ONE AND HALF HEADS LONG? IS THE WRIST PLACEMENT CORRECT ON YOUR DRAWING AS YOU SEE IT ON THE POSE?

THE SIMPLER, THE BETTER. THE DRAWING ON THE BOTTOM, FAR LEFT IS MOSTLY LINES AND SPHERES.

When the life-drawing session is over, you can review your work with these simple analytical breakdowns. On the right, you see the one-minute sketches and their analytical breakdowns.

A few suggestions:

- The lines of the 'tubes' will have a curvature, however slight. Rarely are they straight lines.
- Make the tube width at elbow wider than at the wrist. Similarly, the tube width at the knee is wider than at the ankle. Follow the same idea for upper legs and arms.
- Pay attention to how narrow you draw the wrist/ankle. Beginning artists usually make them too narrow.
- The torso and the pelvis can be drawn as a long cylinder that is rounded at the base (pelvis).
- Draw through - as in make the tubes 'transparent'. This helps you think in volumes as well as see the connections completely.

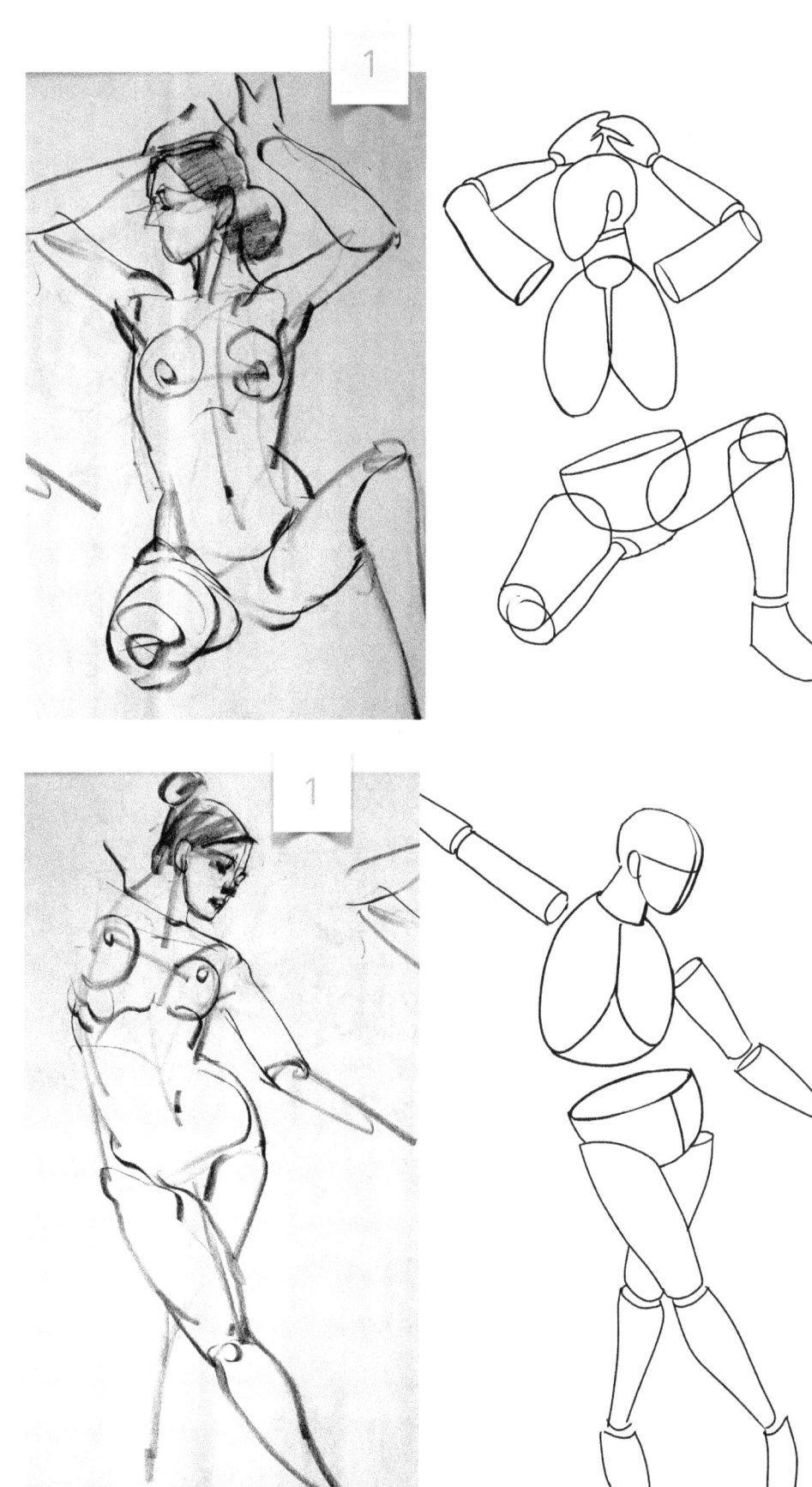

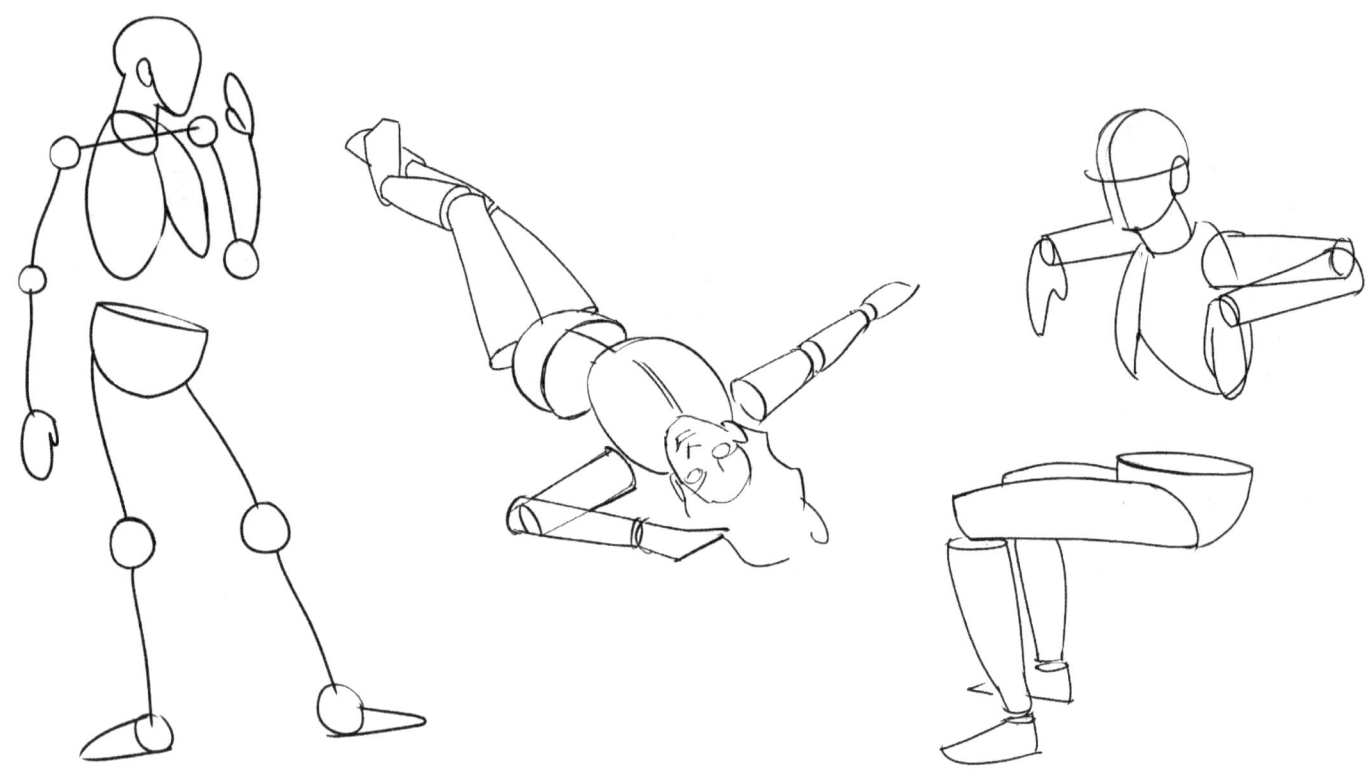

- IN THE DRAWING ON THE RIGHT, DO YOU SEE THE LIGHTLY DRAWN SPHERES AT THE SHOULDER AND ELBOW (ELBOW SPHERE WAS CORRECTED FOR LOCATION), AND THE EGG FORM FOR THE RIBCAGE?

- WHEN YOU DRAW DARKER LINES ON TOP OR NEXT TO LIGHTER CONSTRUCTION LINES, LIGHTER CONSTRUCTION LINES TEND TO 'DISAPPEAR.' DON'T BE AFRAID TO MAKE MISTAKES, AS LONG AS YOU DRAW THEM VERY LIGHTLY.

- AT RIGHT ARE EXAMPLES OF INITIAL LAY-IN <u>DRAWN THROUGH</u>. THE OBSTRUCTED PART OF THE RIBCAGE BEHIND THE ARMS IS DRAWN LIGHTLY.

- SIMILARLY, THE ANALYTICAL DRAWINGS ABOVE SHOW TRANSPARENT LIMBS. IT HELPS EVALUATE YOUR PROPORTIONS WHEN YOU DRAW 'THROUGH' AND SEE THE WHOLE BODY. JUST REMEMBER TO DRAW THE INITIAL LAY-IN VERY LIGHTLY.

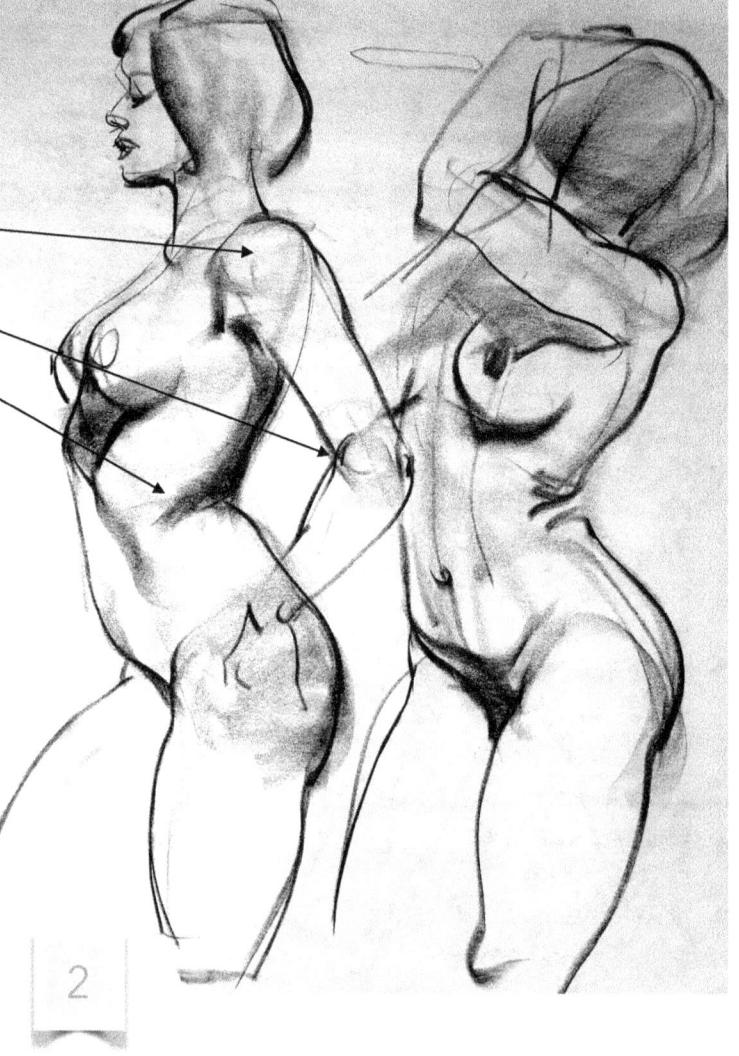

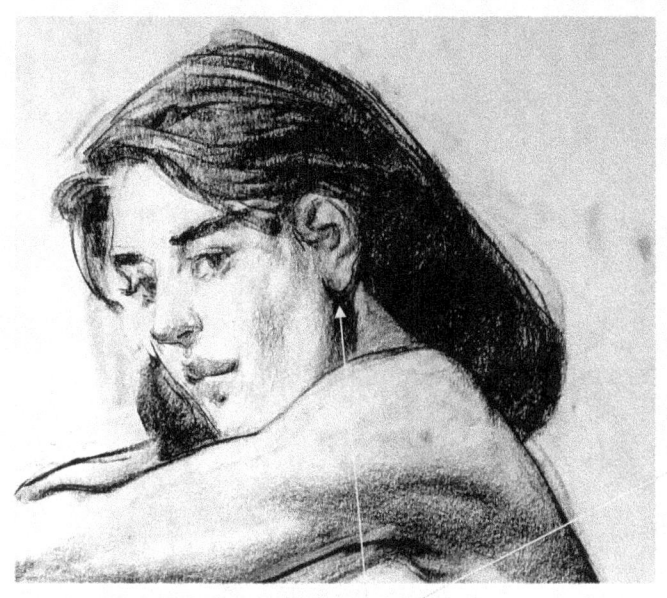
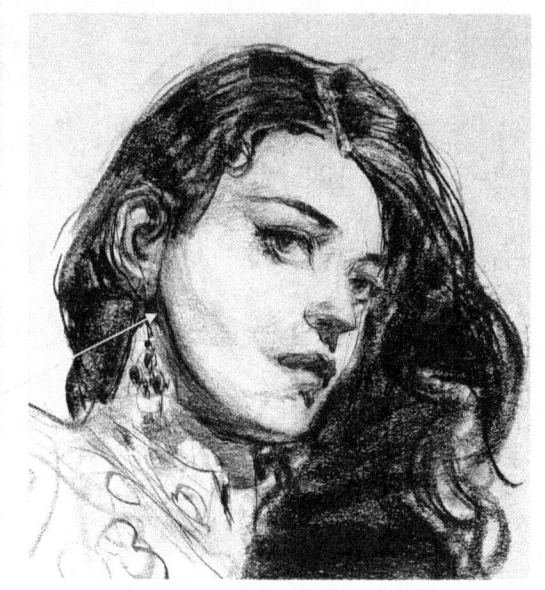

Connecting anatomical parts places them firmly on the figure. The ear in the head drawings above is 'connected' to the head with the help of the jawline and the cast shadow under the ear. This dark tone under the ear helps reinforce the connection between the ear and the face.

Notice the tone under the nose and the contact line of the nasal wings. The tone and the wing lines are important to connecting the nose to the face. In general, avoid floating body parts - attach them with either strong lines of contact or tone. It also helps add volume to your drawing.

The placement of the ear is important, as it helps us define head rotation. In the drawings on the right, the head shape is exactly the same. It's the ear placement that is different and informs us of the head turn. Also, notice the jaw line that connects the ear to the face.

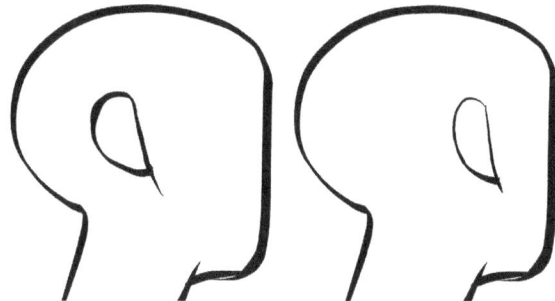

Jaw line is always *in front* of the ear.

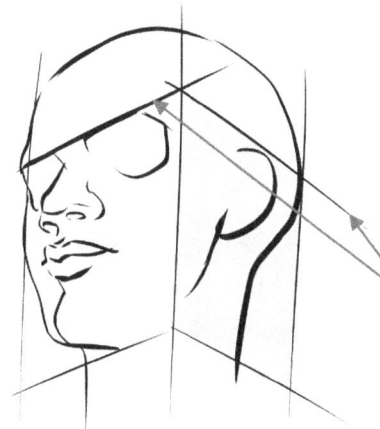

The ears and the rest of the facial features are on two different planes that are approximately at right angles to each other. Identify those planes on the model when you are drawing.

The eyebrow line and the ear line are at right angles to each other. Drawing those two constructional lines will help define the tilt of the head.

Volumes illustrate three dimensionality.

You can suggest volume by overlapping the lines when connecting body parts.

Shapes illustrate only outline but not volumes.

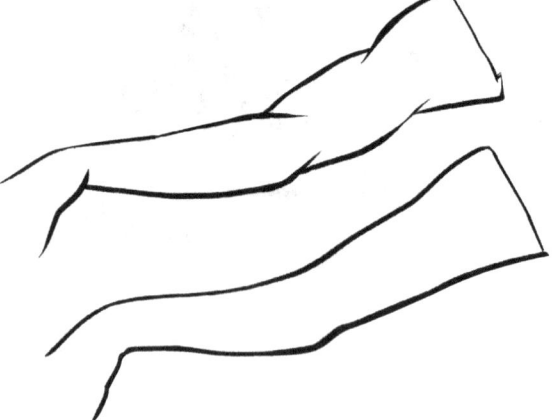

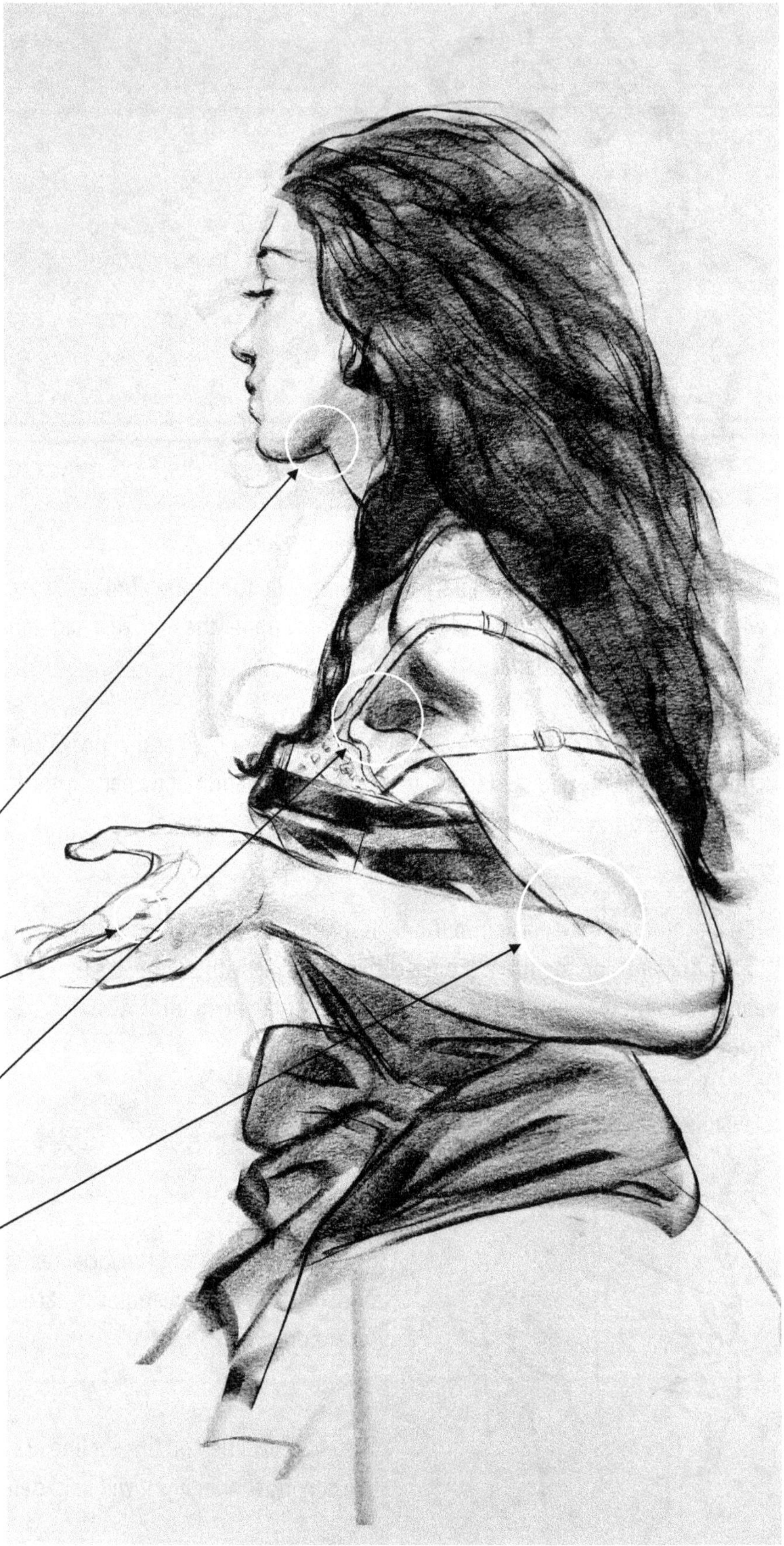

Look closely. The neck line is in front of the jaw line to show that the jaw wraps around the neck.

Finger lines overlap.

Upper arm connects in front at the chest.

The forearm volume overlaps in front of the upper arm.

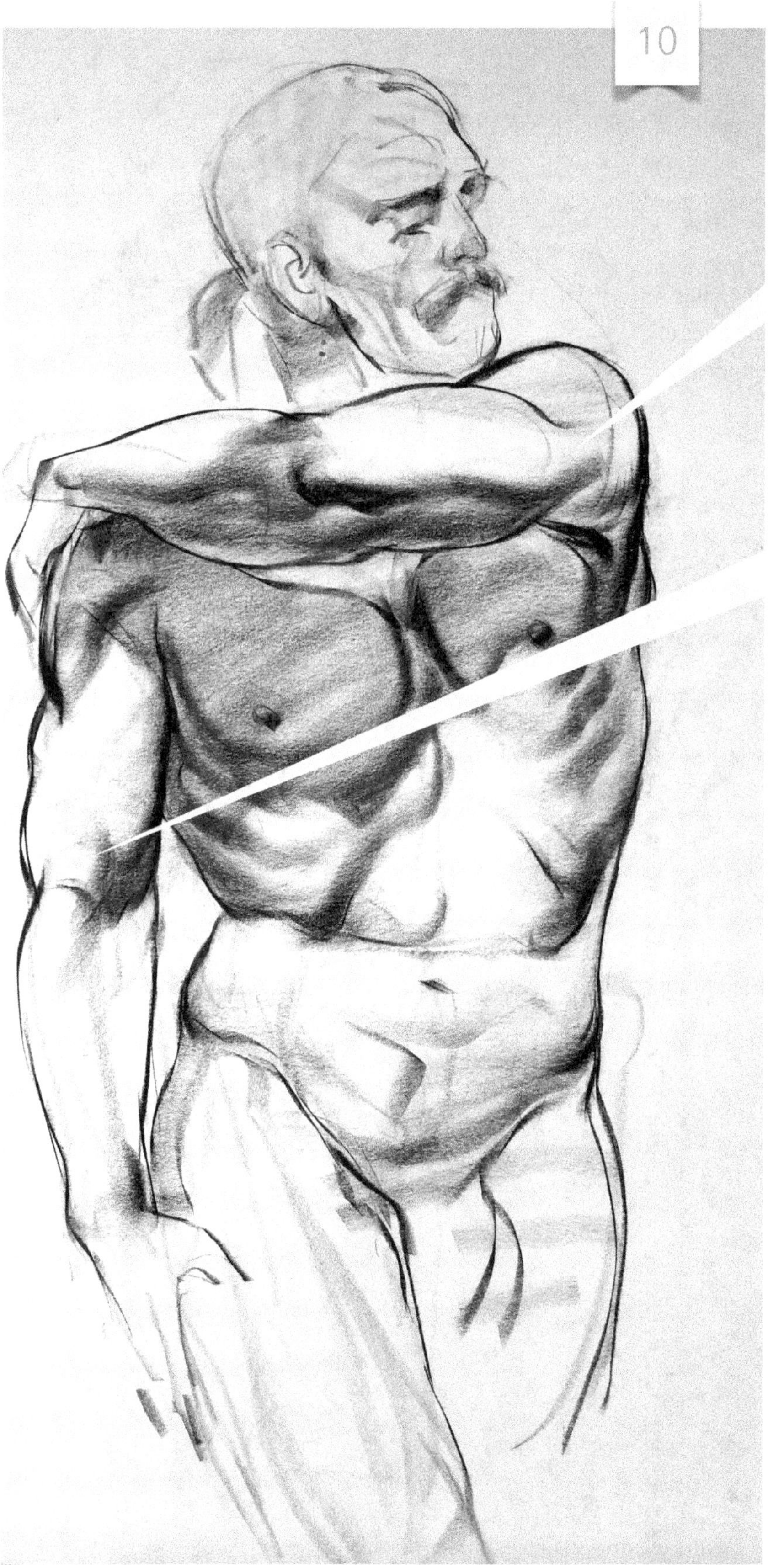

The overlap of the upper arm in front of the shoulder suggests the volume, and the foreshortening of the upper arm.

The forearm overlaps the upper arm. Upper torso overlaps the pelvic region. Both lines give three dimensionality to the form.

The setup below clearly shows the circle <u>in front</u> of the square.

We do not assume that the square is broken as shown below.

OVERLAPPING FORMS SUGGEST DEPTH AND DIMENSIONALITY.

In the pen & ink drawing on the right, the lines describe many overlapping volumes. This enhances the dynamics of the pose. This was a two-minute pose drawn at a Society of Illustrators sketch night.

Below is a charcoal drawing of the same model on the same night. This was a longer pose. Notice the overlapping lines of the upper arm to the chest and the forearm to the upper arm.

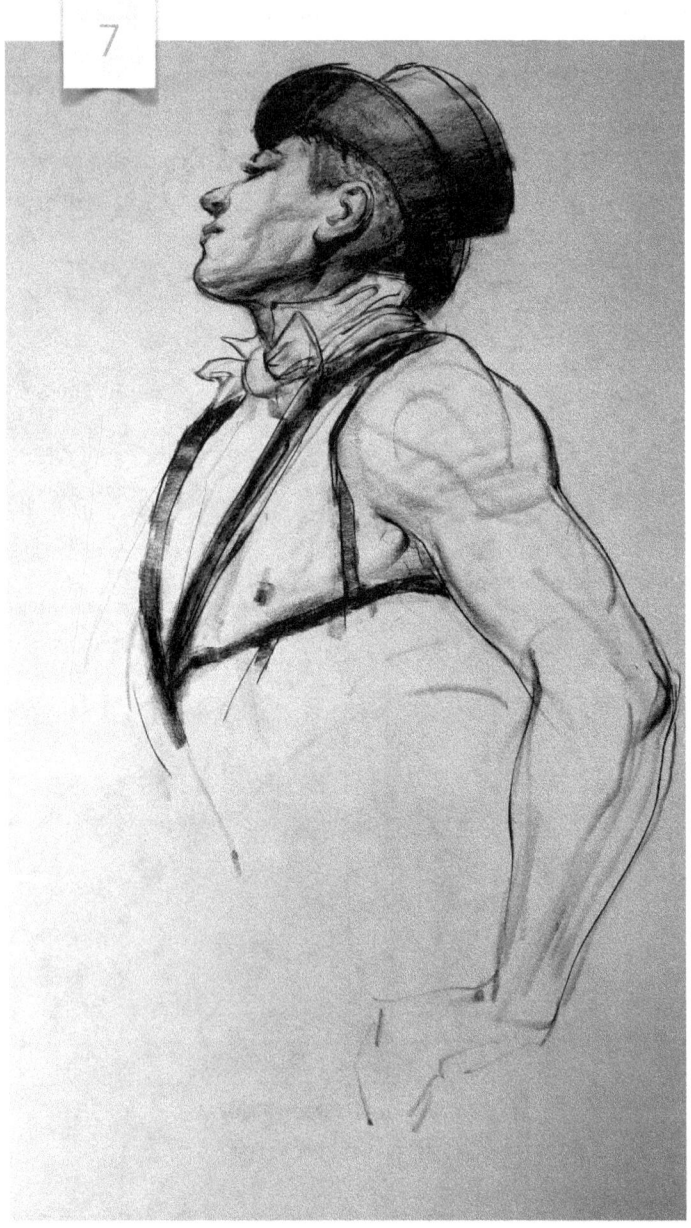

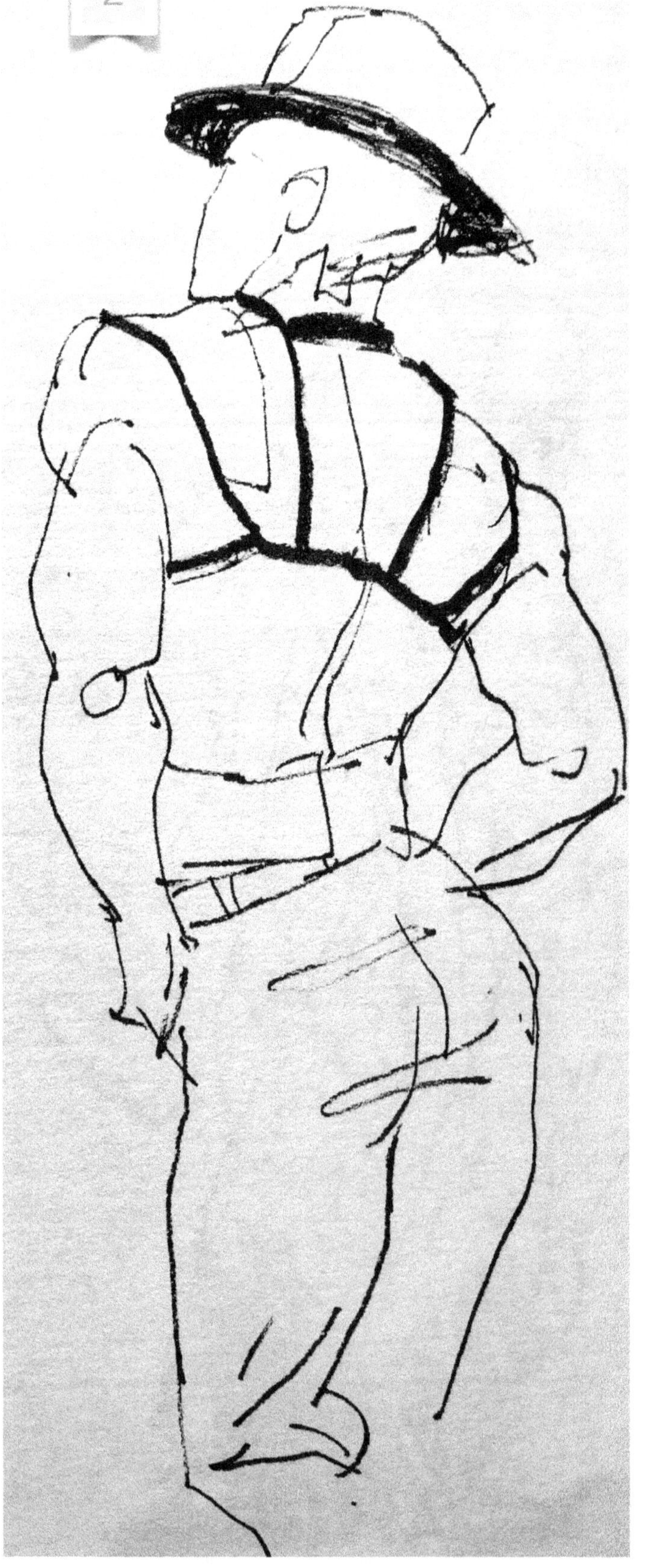

Connections help reinforce perspective and three dimensionality. Volumes approximating the body parts go 'in' and 'out' of their neighboring volumes.

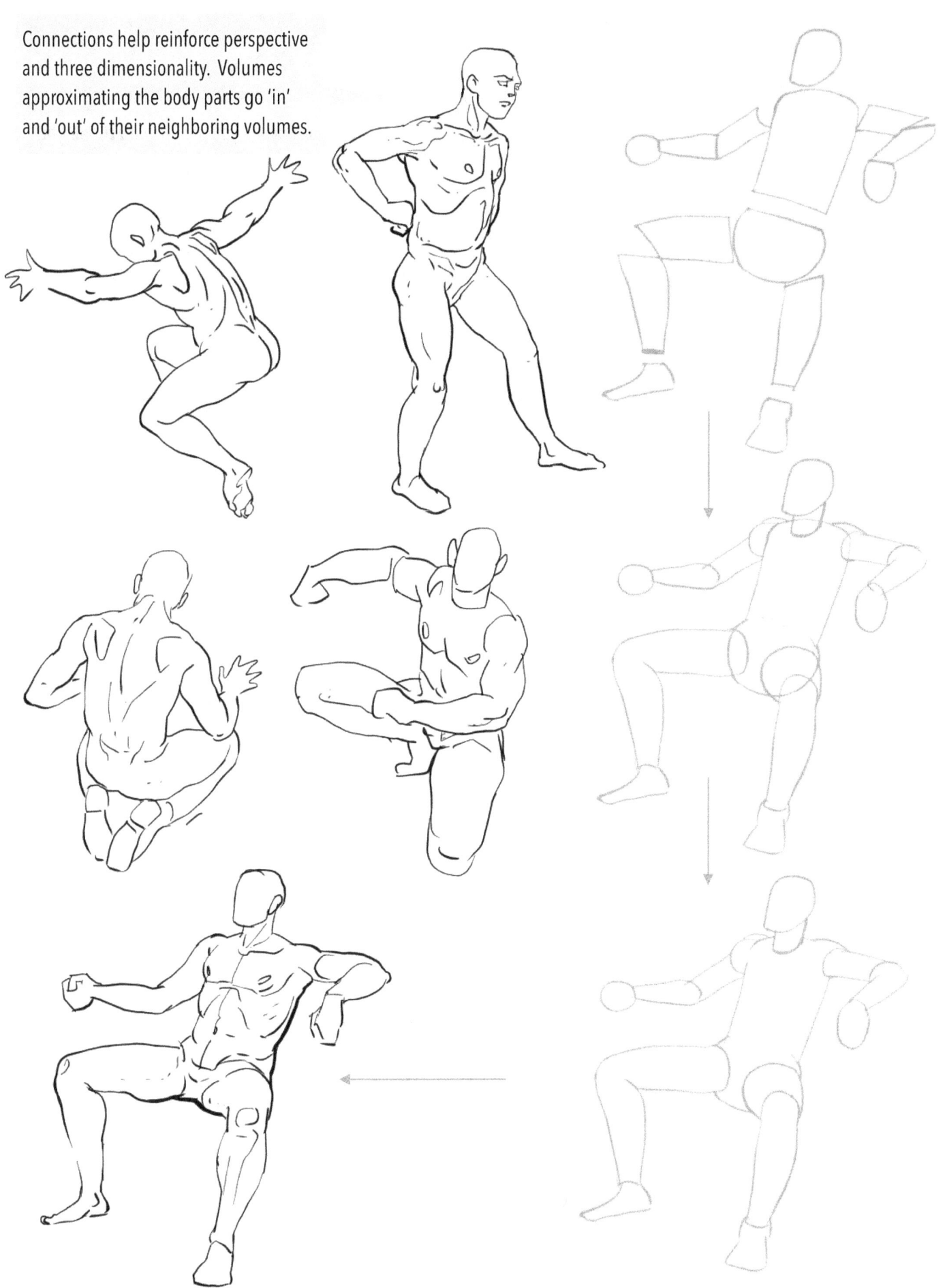

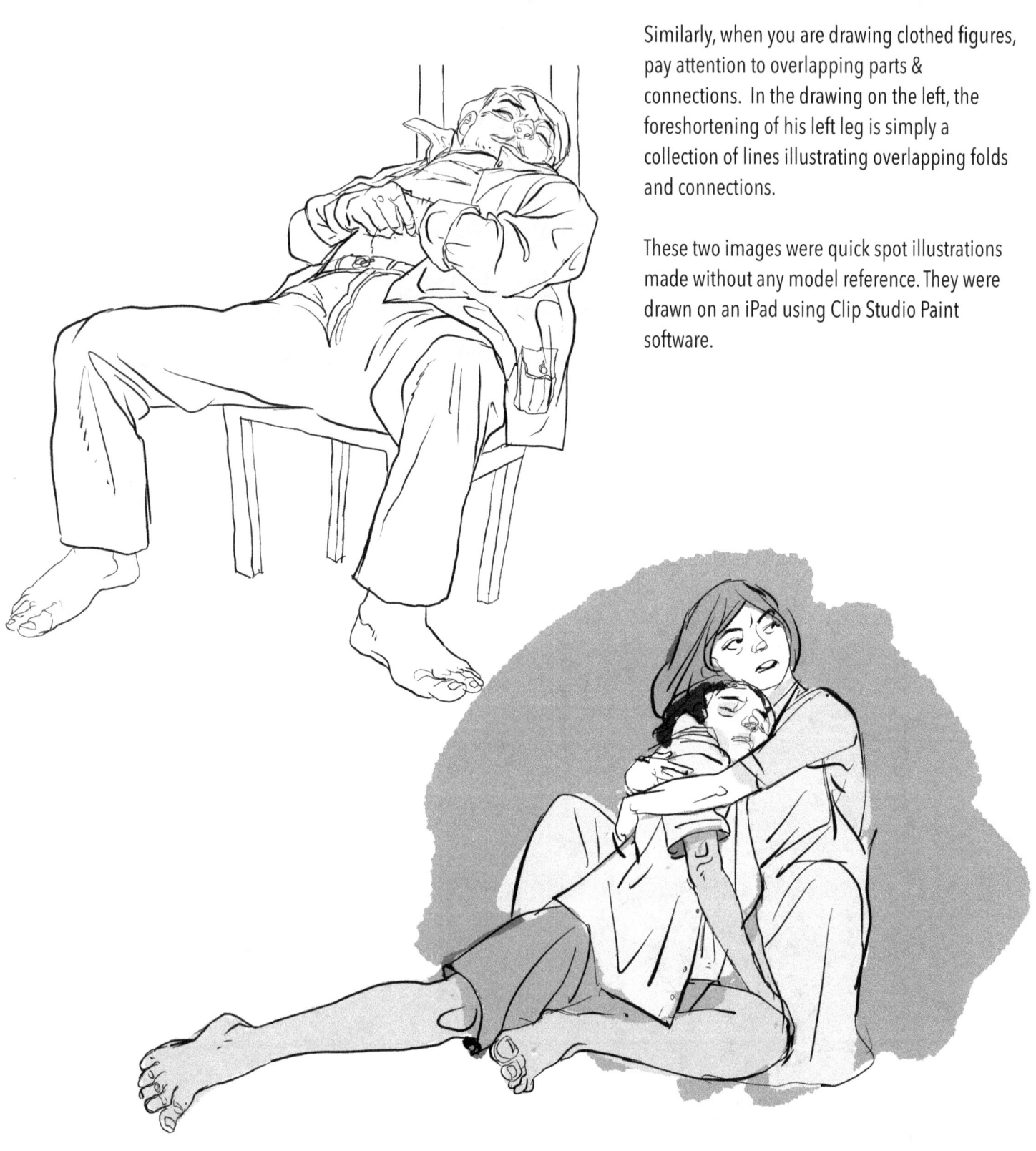

Similarly, when you are drawing clothed figures, pay attention to overlapping parts & connections. In the drawing on the left, the foreshortening of his left leg is simply a collection of lines illustrating overlapping folds and connections.

These two images were quick spot illustrations made without any model reference. They were drawn on an iPad using Clip Studio Paint software.

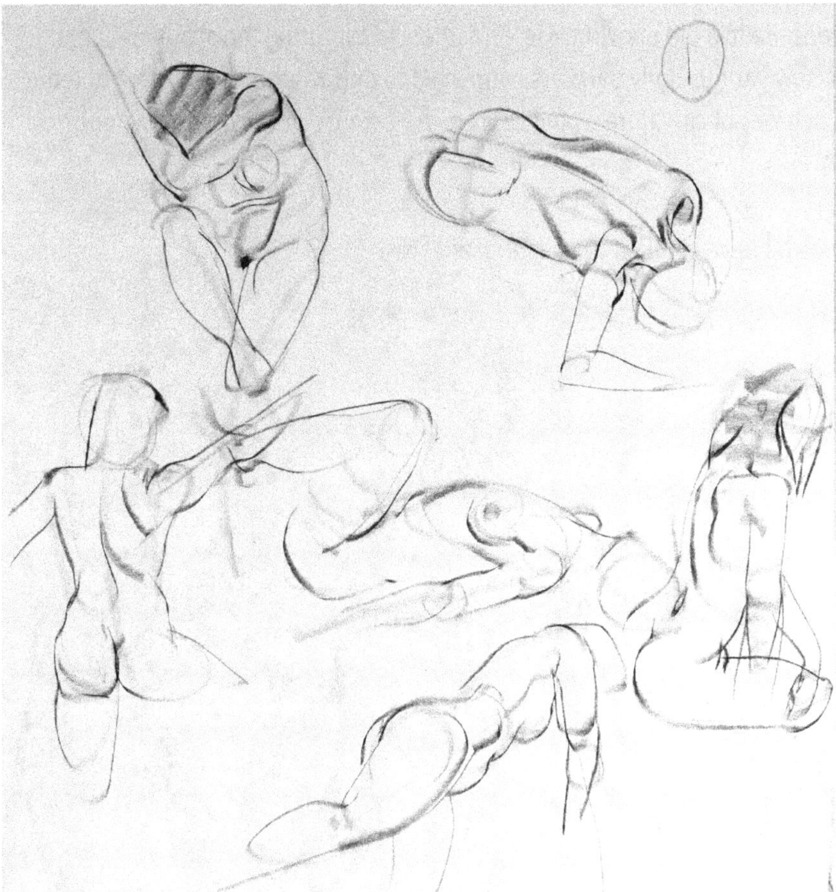

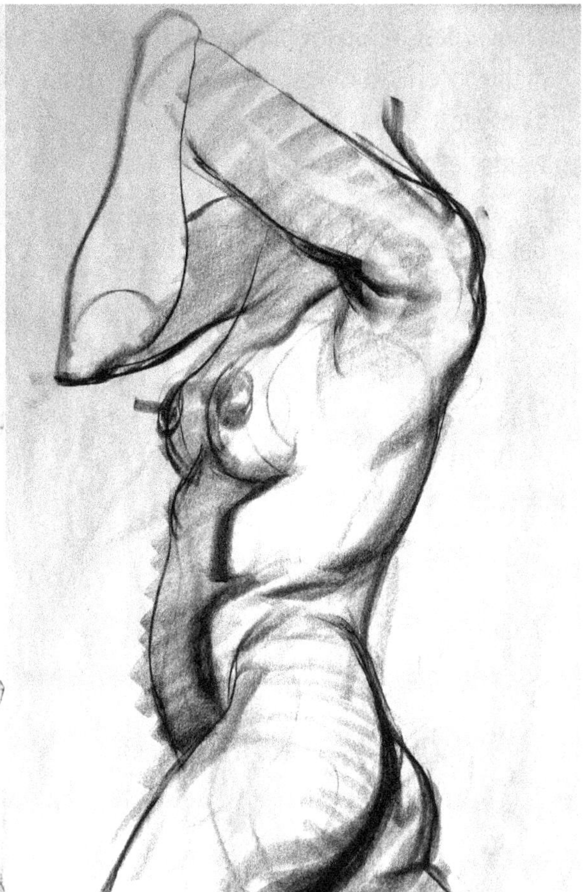

GESTURE IS THE KEY!

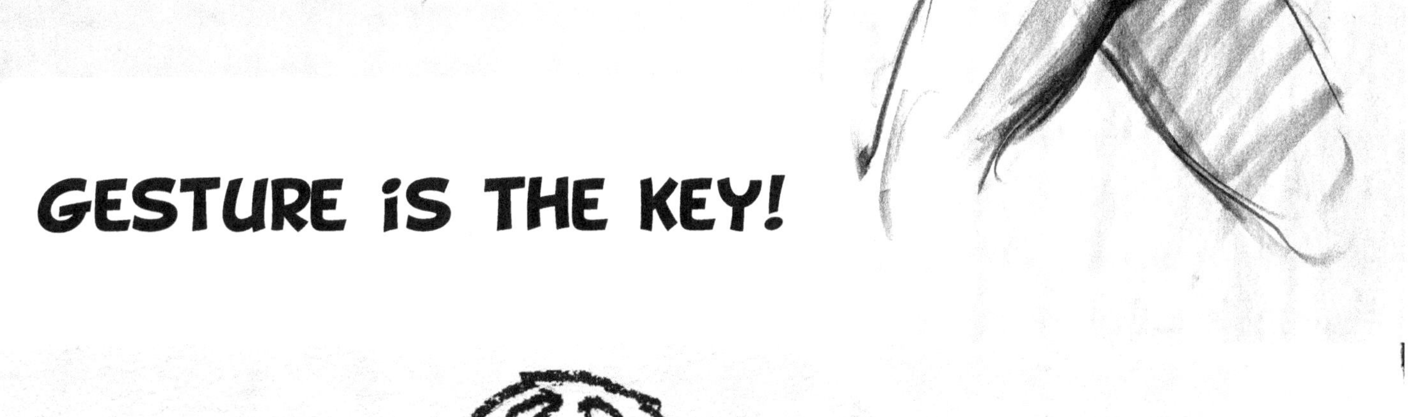

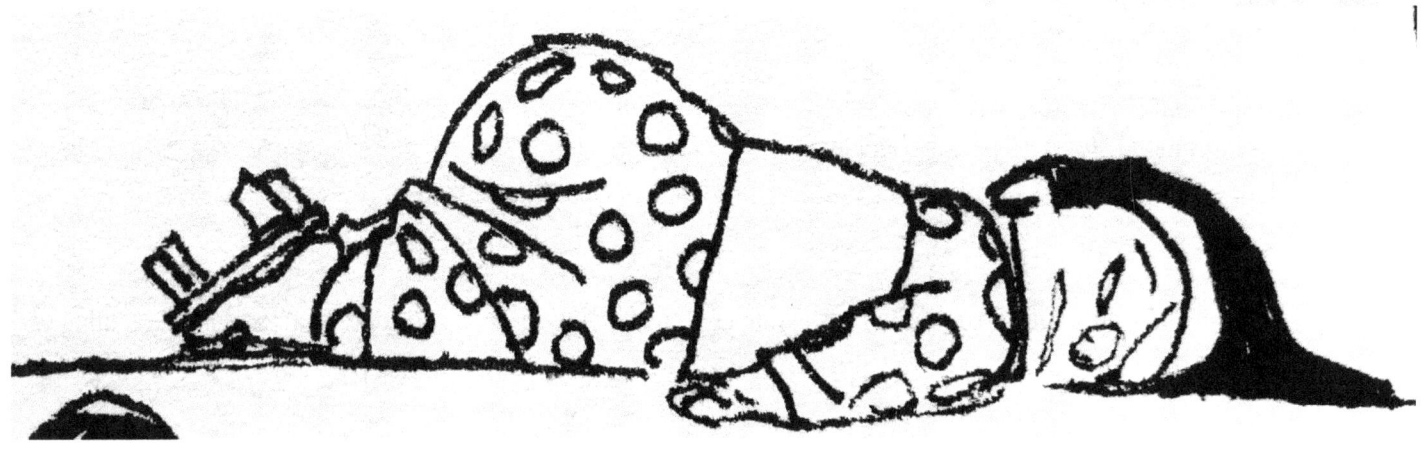

What is gesture? In my humble opinion, it's what adds life to a life drawing. Gesture refers to capturing the action or dynamics of the pose. Practically speaking though - gesture is how various body parts are connected to one another. If you were to reduce a pose to a group of lines, their relative angles and degrees of curvature would capture the essence of the gesture. Enough words; let's look at the pictures.

Below we have two, five, and ten-minute poses in which I have overlaid the gestural analysis.

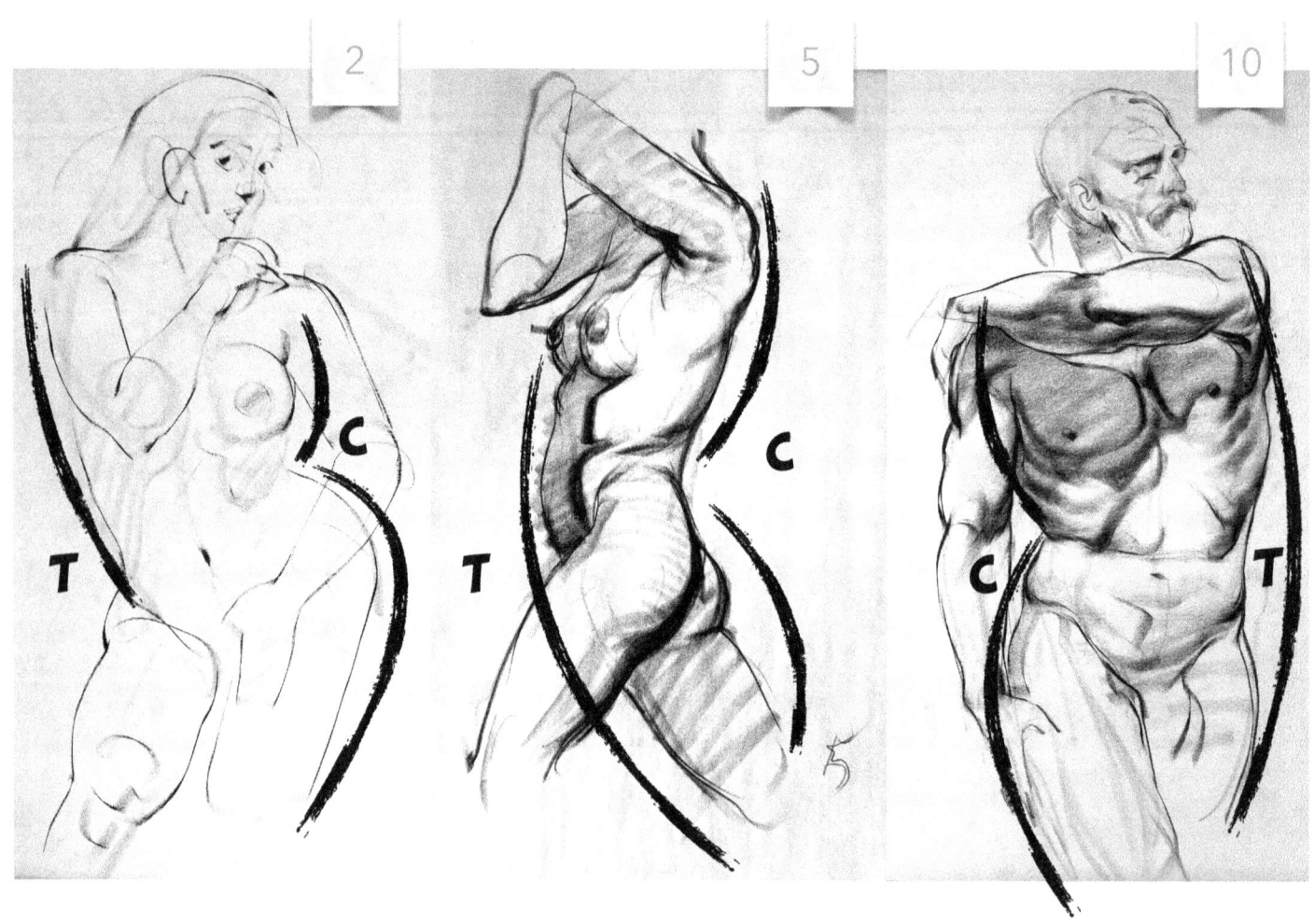

Do you see a pattern in the gestural lines (T for tension & C for compression)? Seek out these imaginary gestural lines in the model's pose before you make your first mark.

In a good gesture drawing, there are contrasting gestural lines. Look for tension (**T**) and compression (**C**) complementing each other in the pose.

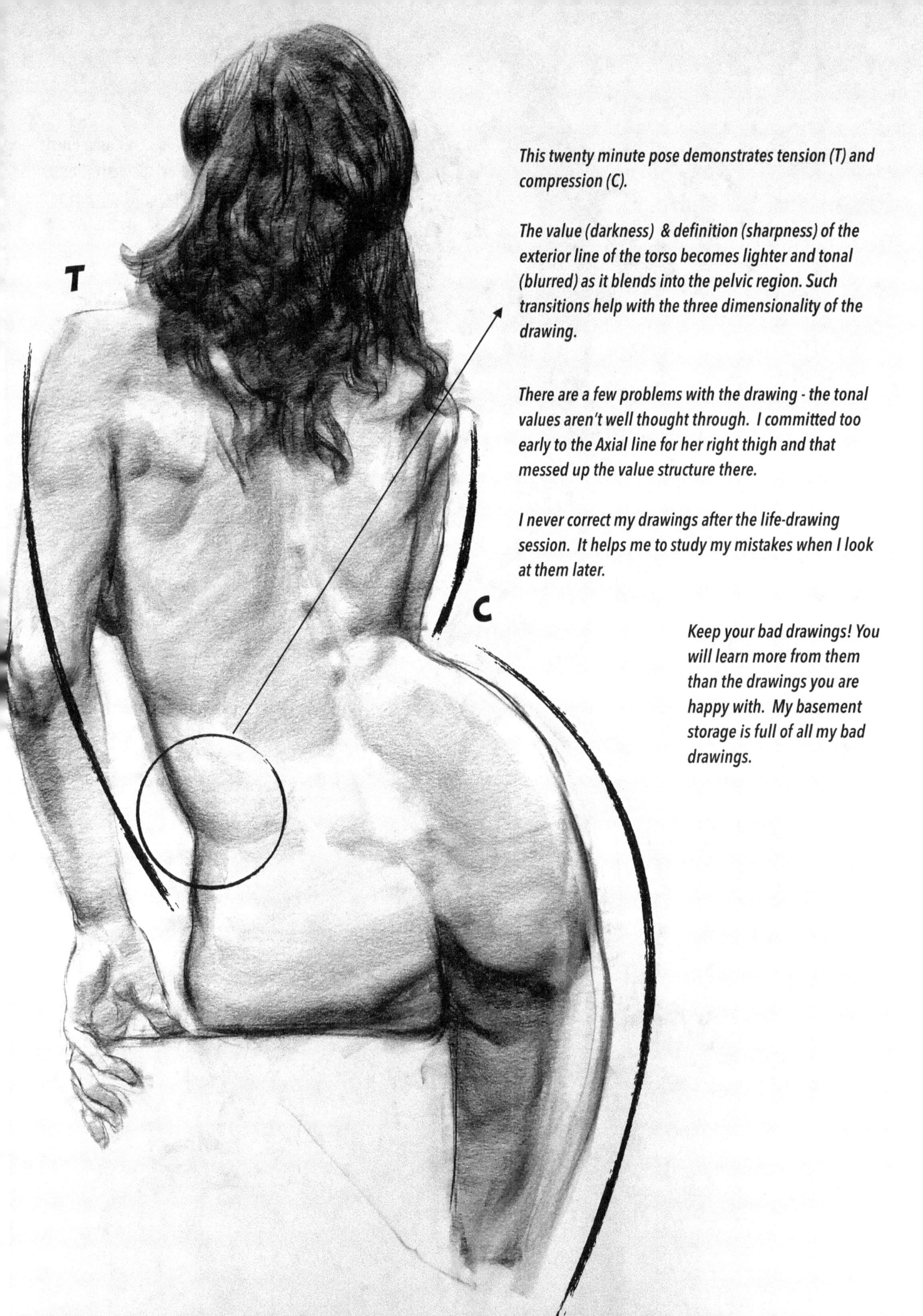

This twenty minute pose demonstrates tension (T) and compression (C).

The value (darkness) & definition (sharpness) of the exterior line of the torso becomes lighter and tonal (blurred) as it blends into the pelvic region. Such transitions help with the three dimensionality of the drawing.

There are a few problems with the drawing - the tonal values aren't well thought through. I committed too early to the Axial line for her right thigh and that messed up the value structure there.

I never correct my drawings after the life-drawing session. It helps me to study my mistakes when I look at them later.

Keep your bad drawings! You will learn more from them than the drawings you are happy with. My basement storage is full of all my bad drawings.

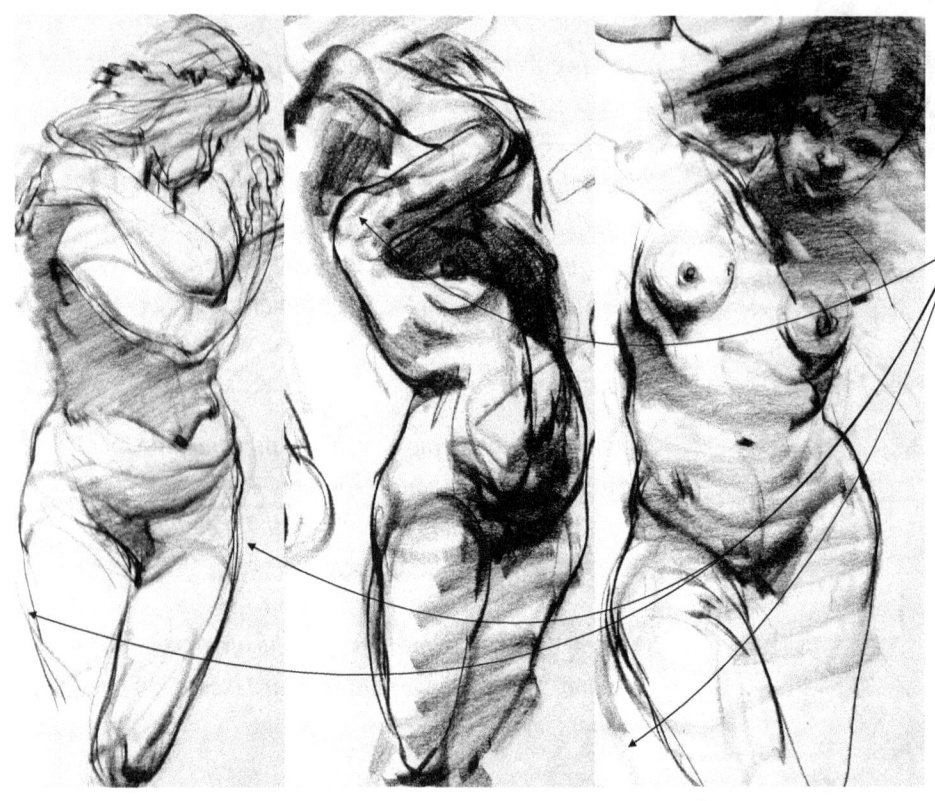

A common trait among beginning artists is the tendency to draw too many lines in an attempt to find the figure. <u>Draw those 'noodly' lines as lightly as possible.</u> All you have to do is darken the one line that you think is the most accurate.

With practice, you will get better and you will need fewer and fewer noodly lines.

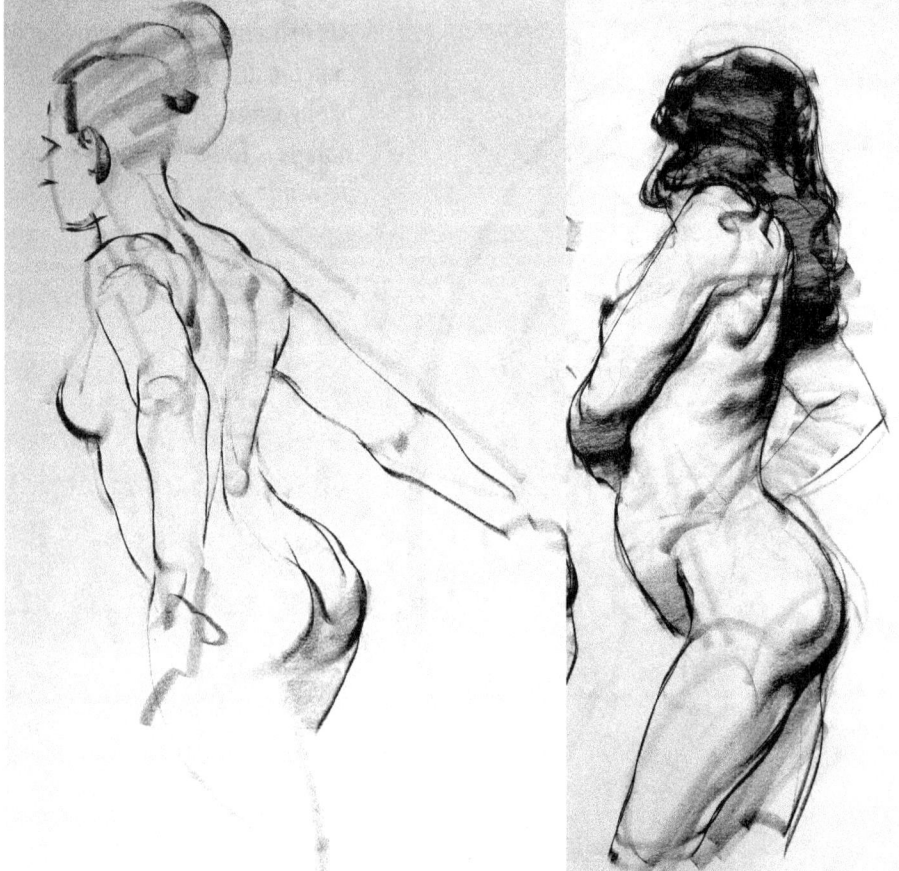

PEOPLE ATTRIBUTE 'DRAMA' (OR 'DYNAMISM', 'POWER' AND OTHER ADJECTIVES RELATED TO 'FEELINGS') TO DRAWINGS AND PAINTINGS. A DRAWING OR A PAINTING IS SIMPLY VALUE AND COLOR ON A PAPER OR CANVAS. THEY DON'T HAVE ANY FEELINGS IN THEMSELVES.

IN GENERAL, ANY DRAWING THAT EXHIBITS CONTRAST SEEMS TO INVOKE A FEELING OF 'DRAMA' IN THE VIEWER - DARK VS. LIGHT, STRAIGHT VS. CROOKED/CURVED, THICK LINES VS. THIN LINES, MORE DETAILS VS. LESS, ETC.

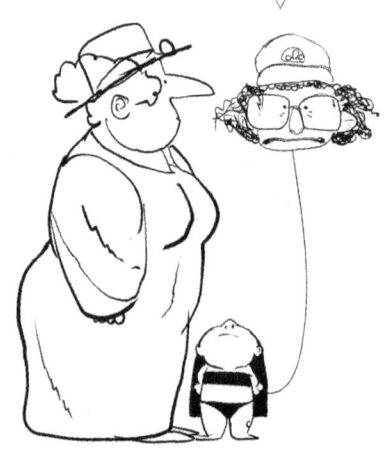

A few more examples of one-minute poses. I tend to draw the head tilt first to get the gesture drawing underway. Even if I don't draw no further details, i.e., draw no facial features, I still need to make a light mark for the head. It is one of the most important parts of showing the dynamics of the pose.

Poses that are strong gestures will be inherently dramatic. They will include strong compression and tension, which provide contrast in the pose. Before you make any marks, study the pose for this dynamic. Once you establish the compression and tension, plan your drawing to emphasize the contrast.

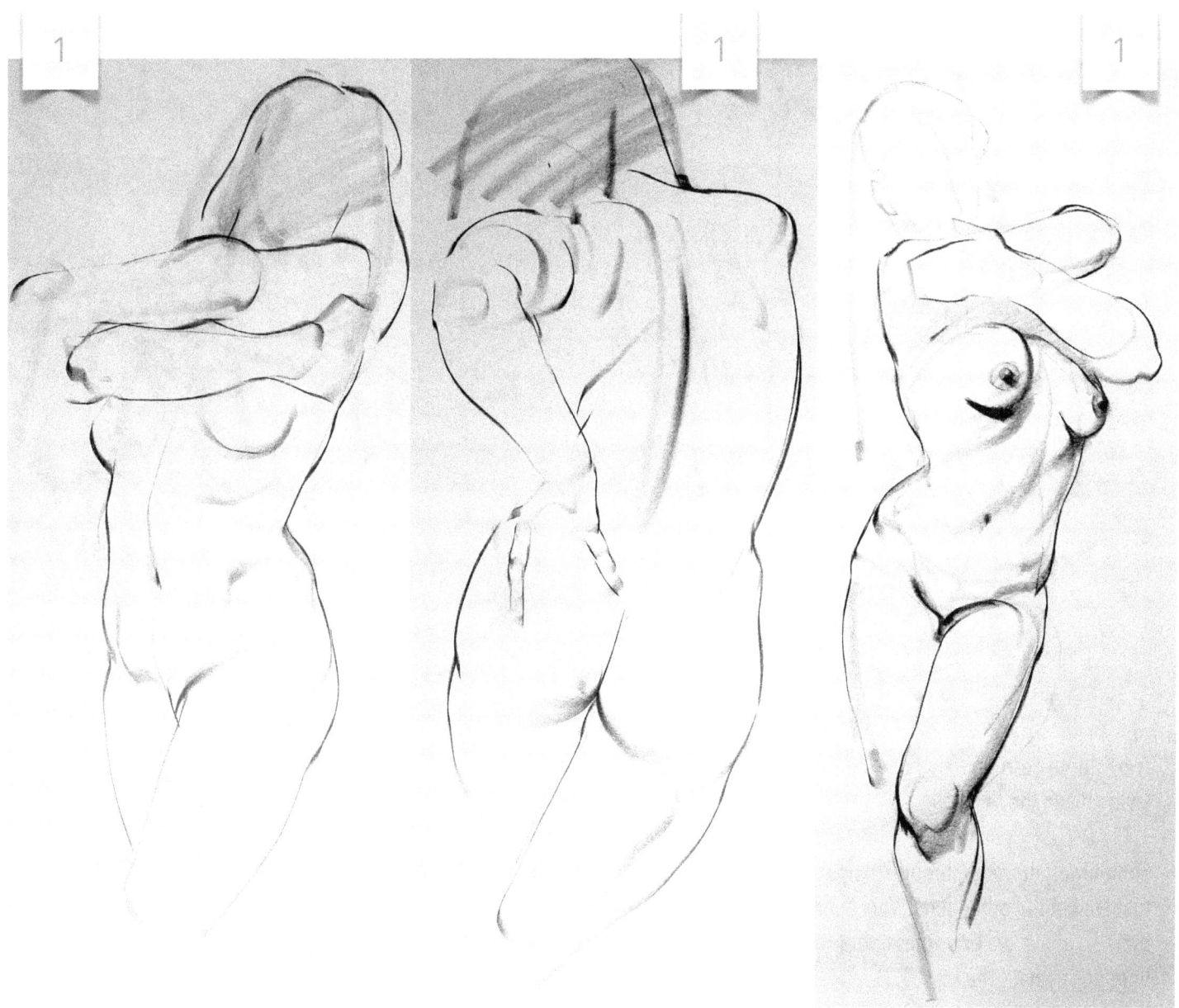

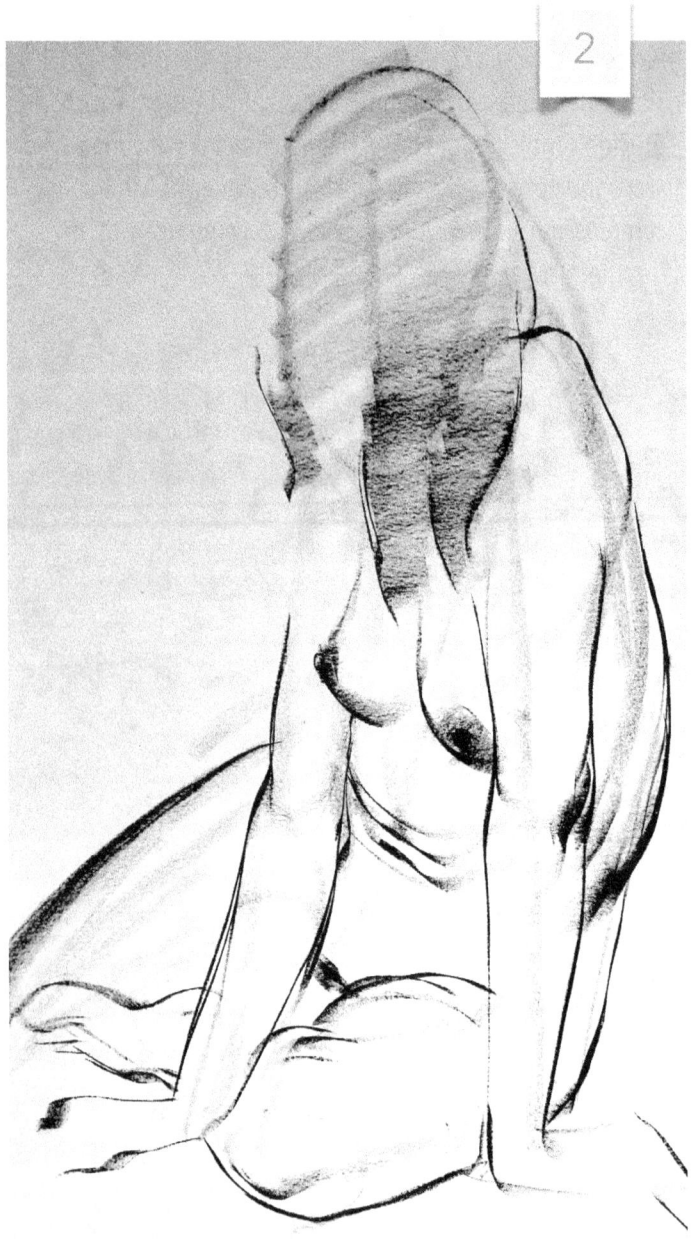

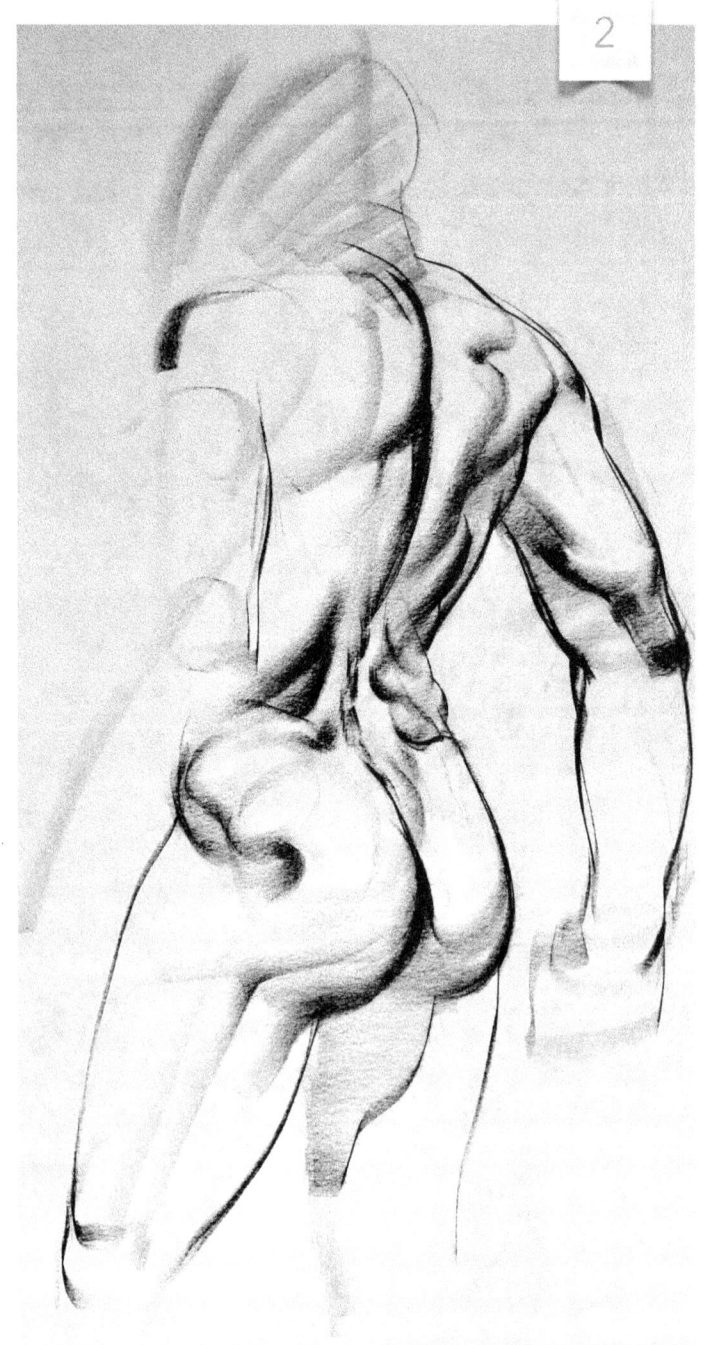

Two minute gesture drawings - the drawings started with laying down the head tilt.

Sometimes, drawing 'through' helps when drawing the parts that are behind other parts. Very light tonal lines in the drawing above are examples of drawing through. <u>Keep the lines light - that's the key.</u>

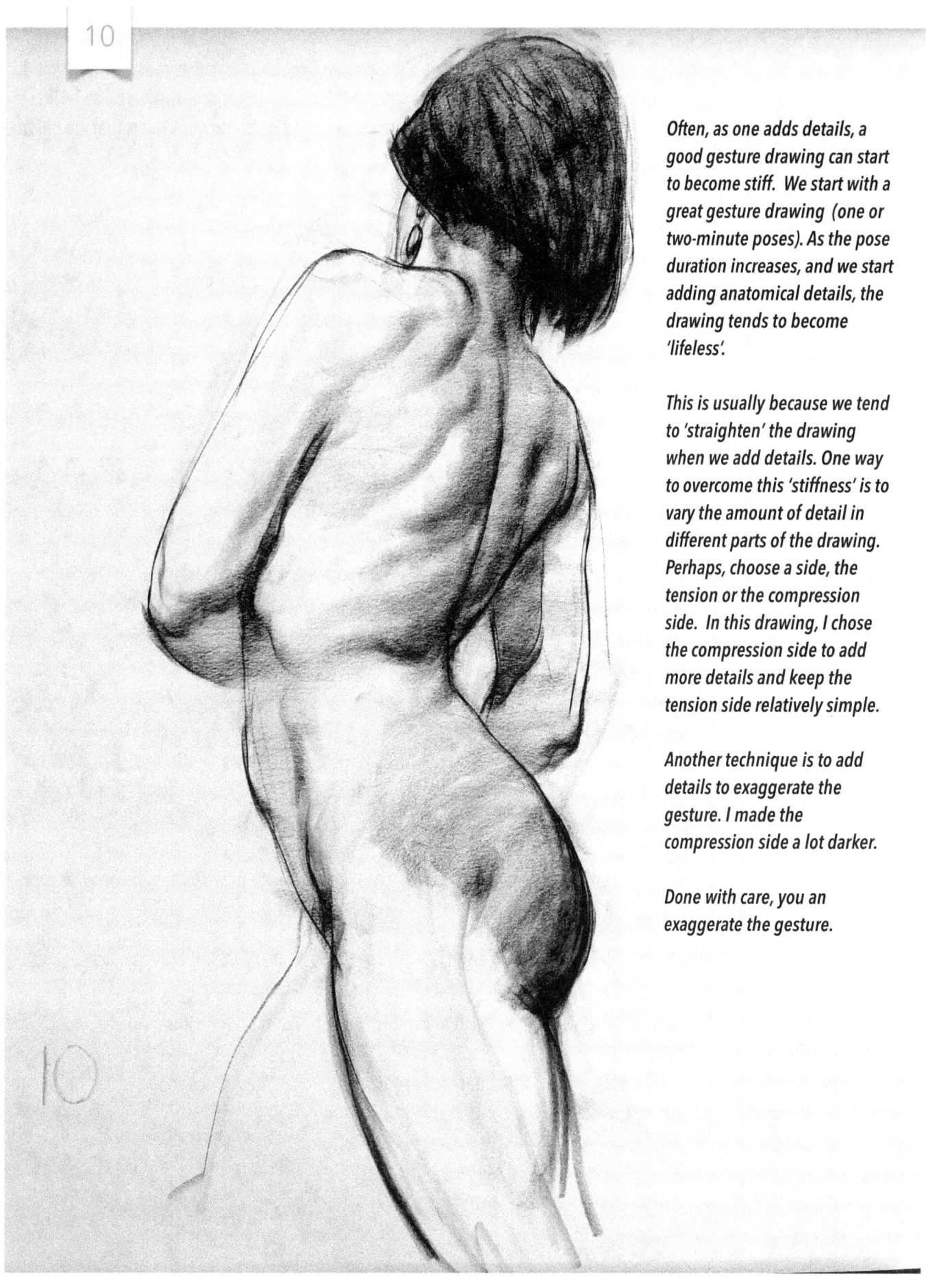

Often, as one adds details, a good gesture drawing can start to become stiff. We start with a great gesture drawing (one or two-minute poses). As the pose duration increases, and we start adding anatomical details, the drawing tends to become 'lifeless'.

This is usually because we tend to 'straighten' the drawing when we add details. One way to overcome this 'stiffness' is to vary the amount of detail in different parts of the drawing. Perhaps, choose a side, the tension or the compression side. In this drawing, I chose the compression side to add more details and keep the tension side relatively simple.

Another technique is to add details to exaggerate the gesture. I made the compression side a lot darker.

Done with care, you an exaggerate the gesture.

Given a choice between style or accuracy, I always prefer accuracy. Style shouldn't be a choice one makes consciously. If you do something, whether it's drawing, painting, cooking, or making furniture, after ten thousand times, you will have a style. It's inevitable. Style grows out of mileage. As you perform a task many times, you develop insights into the subject that are unique and special to yourself; and that learning process helps your develop your style.

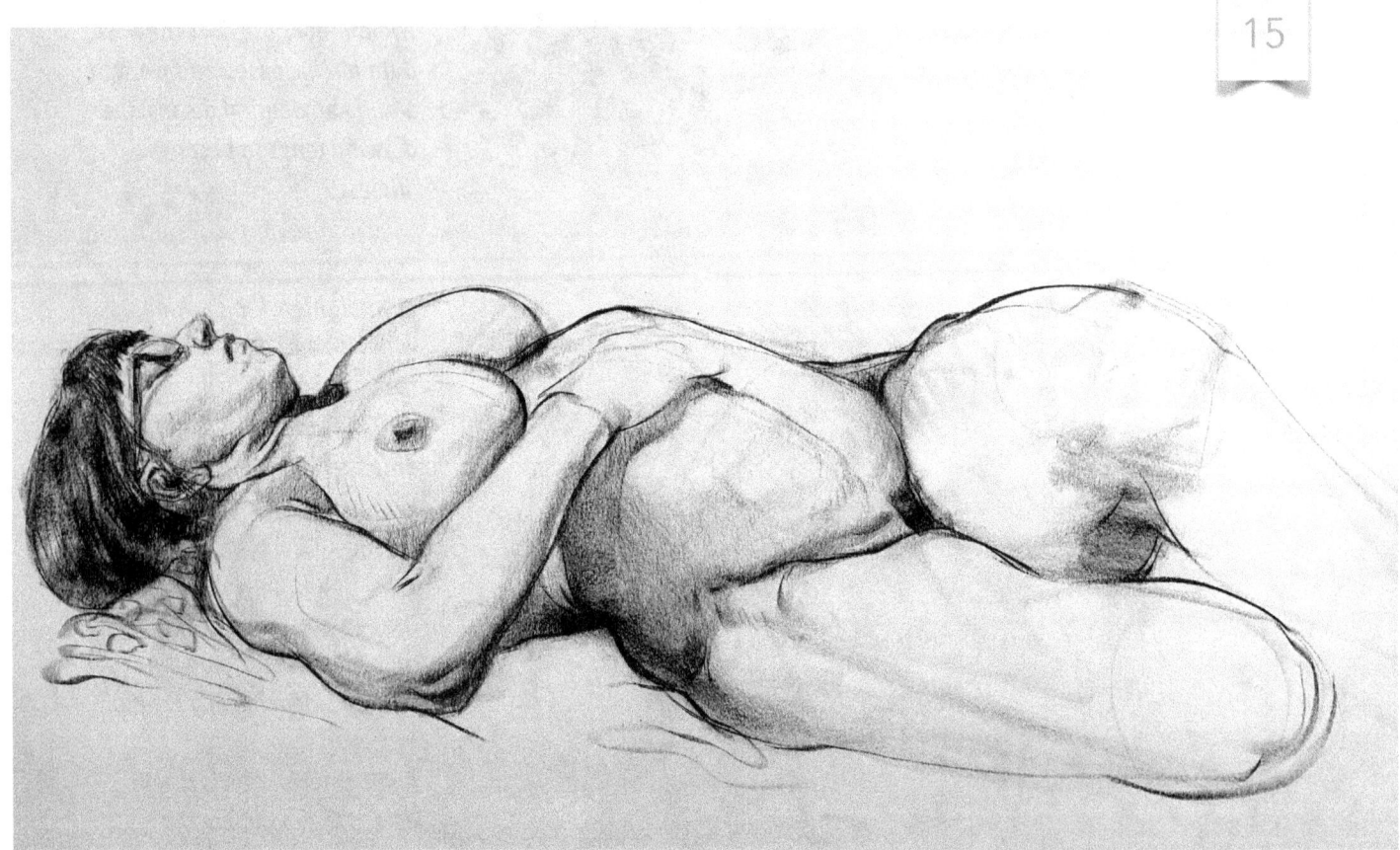

15

While drawing, it's a good idea to fix any mistakes, such as an inaccurate head tilt or head size in relation to the body, as soon as you notice them. If you continue drawing without making adjustments, the inaccuracies will accumulate.

Drawing facial features, hands (especially if the fingers are doing something specific), and feet usually takes longer. In short poses, I tend to omit such details. I'm okay with not having an entire figure on the page, as long as whatever *is* on the page looks accurate and true. The unfinished parts of the drawing show my thinking process, which can itself be interesting.

Having said that, it helps to have a rough lay-in of the entire figure using very rough tonal lines. Once you have established the gesture, you can refine and add details as time permits.

How do the ideas of proportion, such as using the head as unit of measurement, apply when the model's pose involves elements bending either away or towards you (foreshortening)? In the left hand drawing below, the arm is raised and held straight towards the viewer. In the right hand sketch, the model is seated so that the knee is facing the viewer head-on. How do we measure these elements when their true length is not displayed?

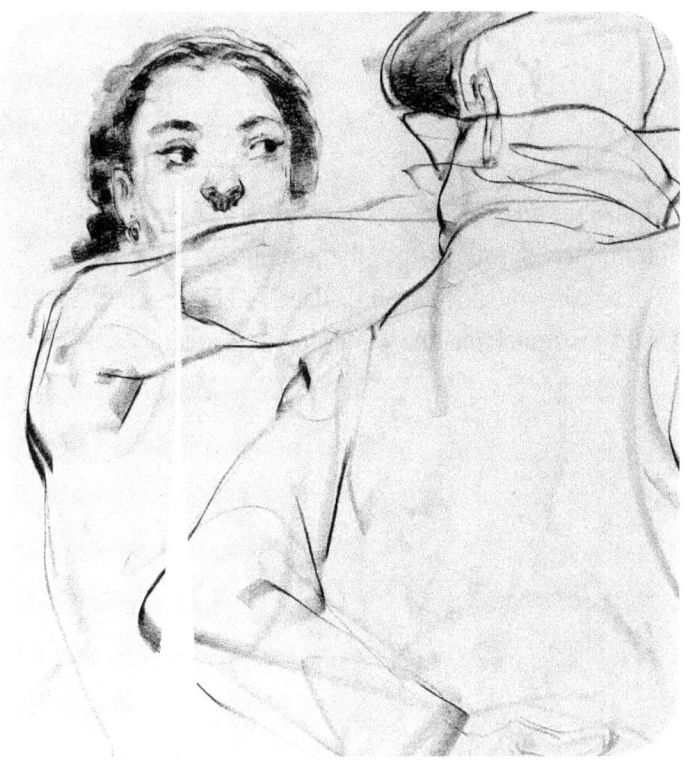
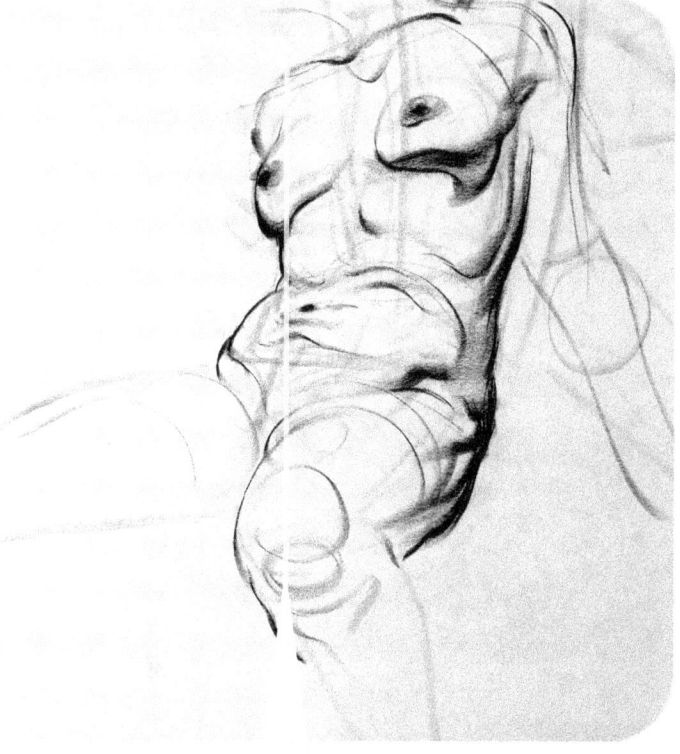

When we can't use the head as a measuring unit, use _proximity alignments._ Proximity alignments involve visualizing imaginary vertical and horizontal lines. In the drawing on the left, the elbow needs to be placed correctly in relation to the shoulder, as her upper arm is foreshortened. After establishing the head, make a light mark for the elbow where you think it should be. Then imagine, on the model, vertical and/or horizontal lines from the elbow, seeing what other features those lines intersect. In this case, a vertical from the elbow lines up with model's right eye, which made my elbow mark correct. If not, examine where your elbow mark should be in relation to the _proximity surface details_ and adjust your elbow mark.

In this pose, an imaginary vertical line through the knee lines up with the model's right shoulder.

Keep in mind the discussion in the previous section on approximating various body parts as tubes or spheres. Drawing tubes, or spheres connected with lines, can be a great start in gesture drawing. See the drawing on the next page.

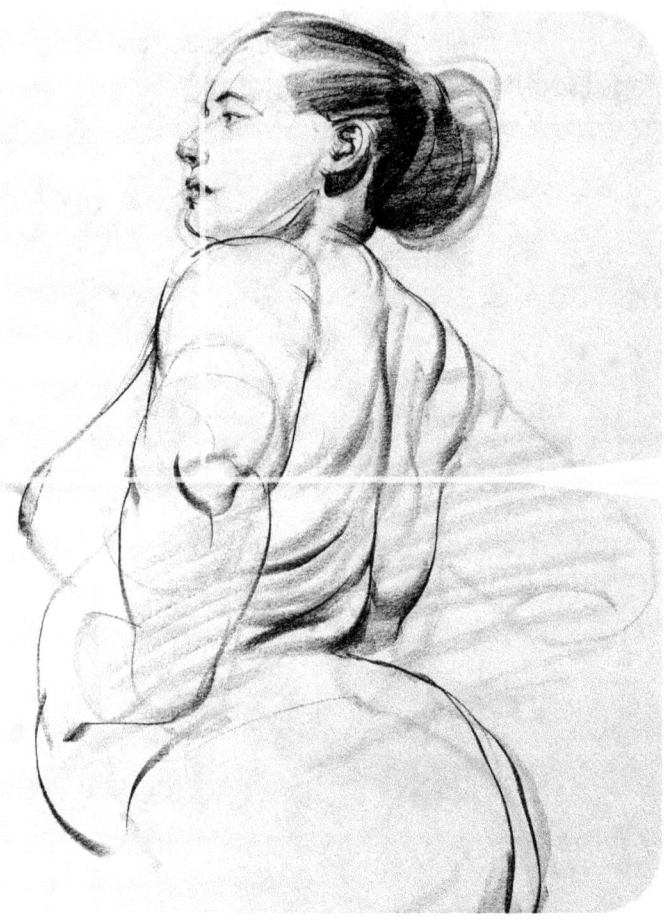

The elbow in this pose was easy to place. A horizontal line from the elbow lines up with the nipple. A vertical line establishes the position of the face. You can use both vertical and horizontal imaginary lines for more accuracy.

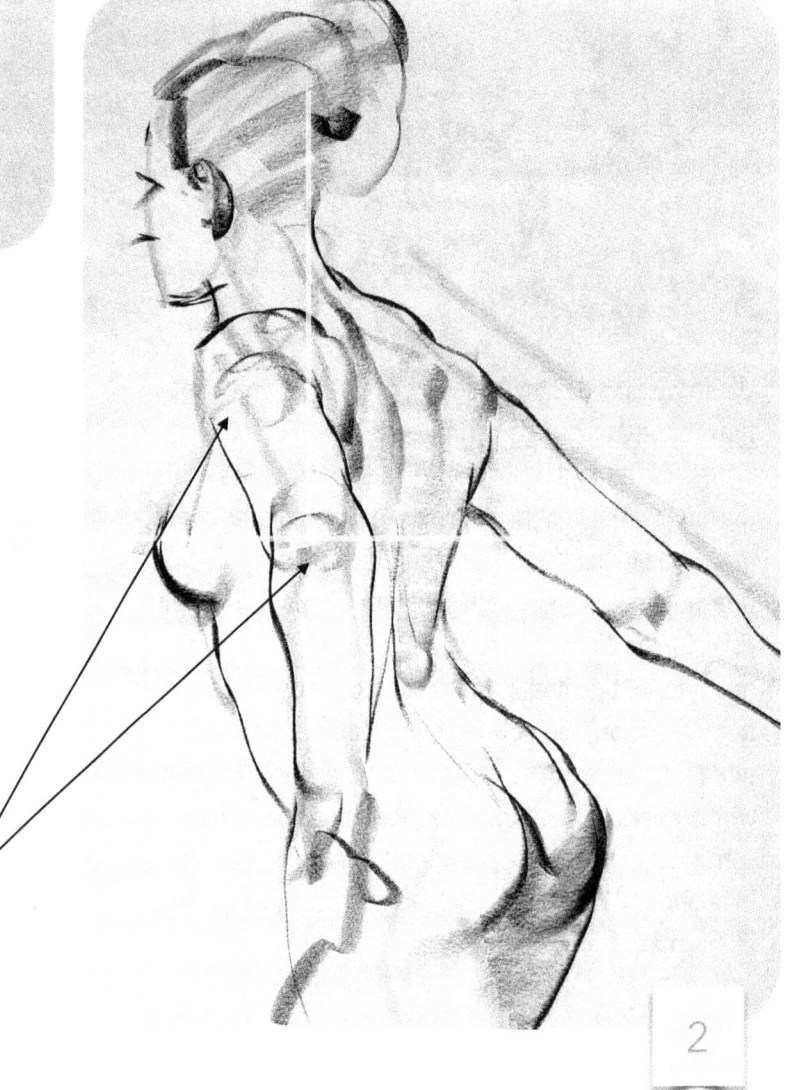

In the drawing on the right, the back of the neck lines up with the elbow. This helps to achieve the degree of lean in the pose

Using proximity alignment with imaginary horizontal and vertical lines, you can achieve proportional accuracy.

Obviously, this approach works best if you draw the non-foreshortened features first - head & upper torso in examples on this page.

NOTICE THE TONAL LINES CONNECTING 'SPHERES' MARKED FOR THE SHOULDER AND ELBOW. THESE ARE DONE QUICKLY AND LIGHTLY.

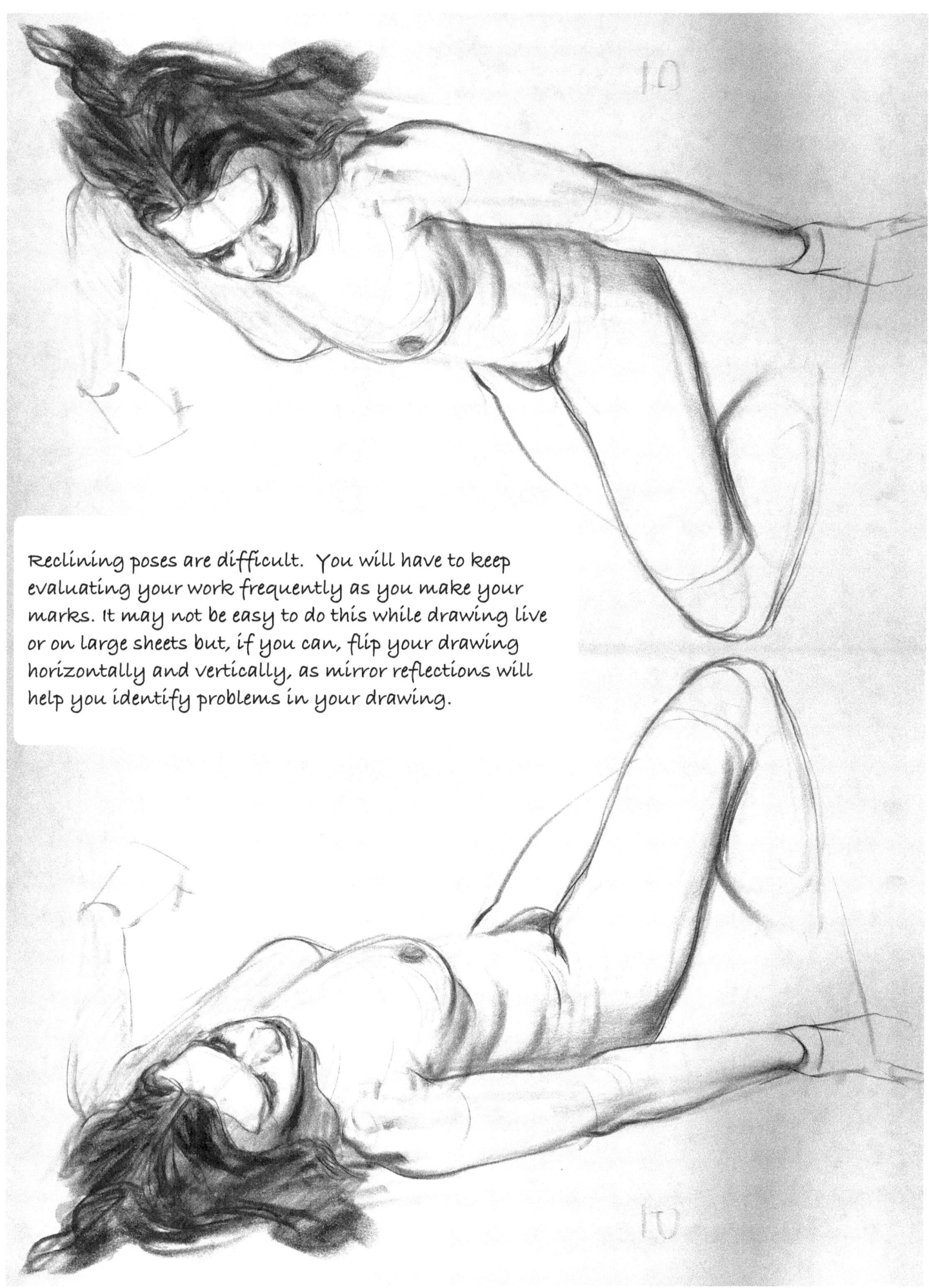

Reclining poses are difficult. You will have to keep evaluating your work frequently as you make your marks. It may not be easy to do this while drawing live or on large sheets but, if you can, flip your drawing horizontally and vertically, as mirror reflections will help you identify problems in your drawing.

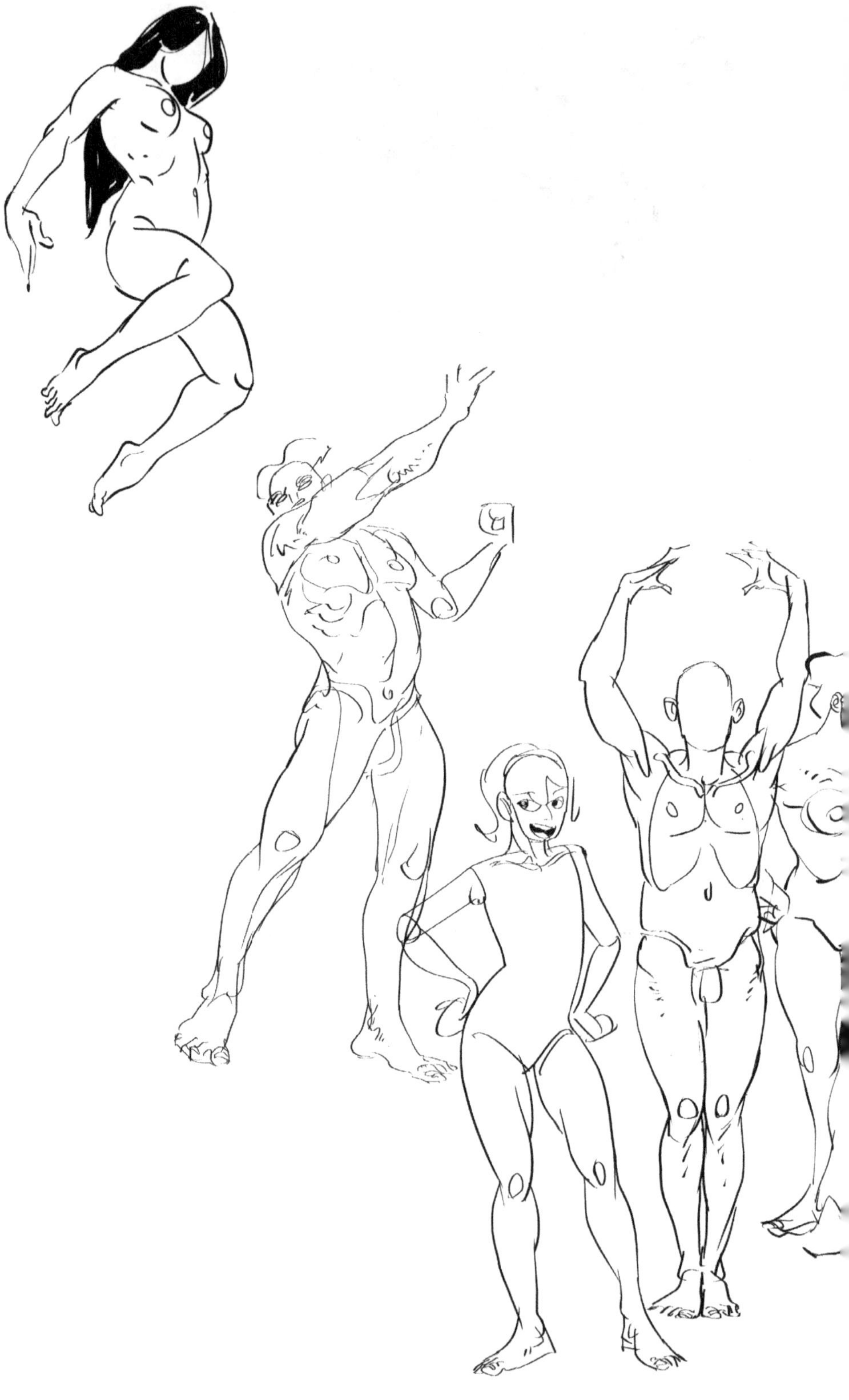

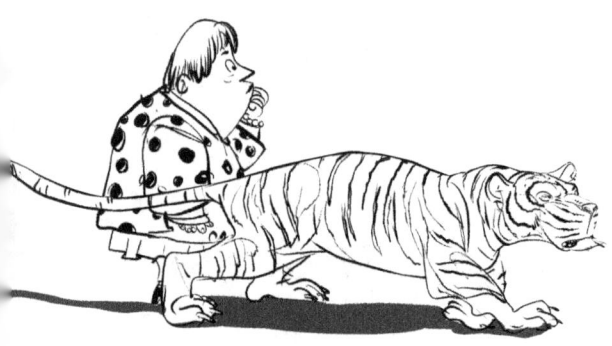

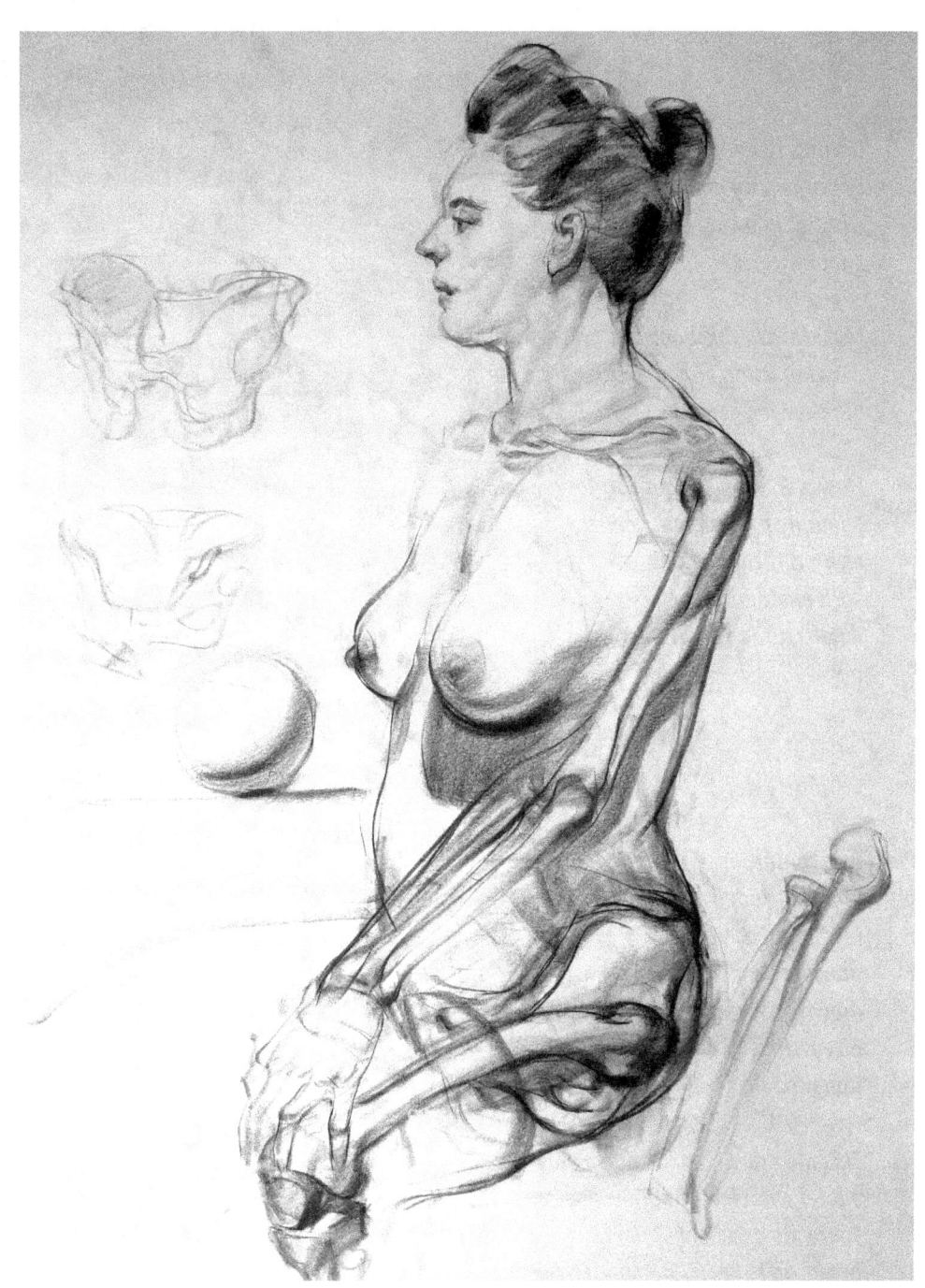

ANATOMY: BONES

It's impossible to achieve a certain level of proficiency in figure drawing, without knowing a little bit about anatomy.

My intent in this book was to discuss life drawing using only drawings done during life-drawing sessions.

However, discussing musculoskeletal anatomy presents challenges, as it's difficult to draw such anatomical details during short poses.

As a compromise, I have included a few timed charcoal drawings and iPad drawings for anatomical discussion, all drawn from imagination.

This life-drawing book offers only a brief overview of human anatomy. There are excellent books on Human Anatomy. I have listed a couple of them in the closing chapter. I suggest you look into them.

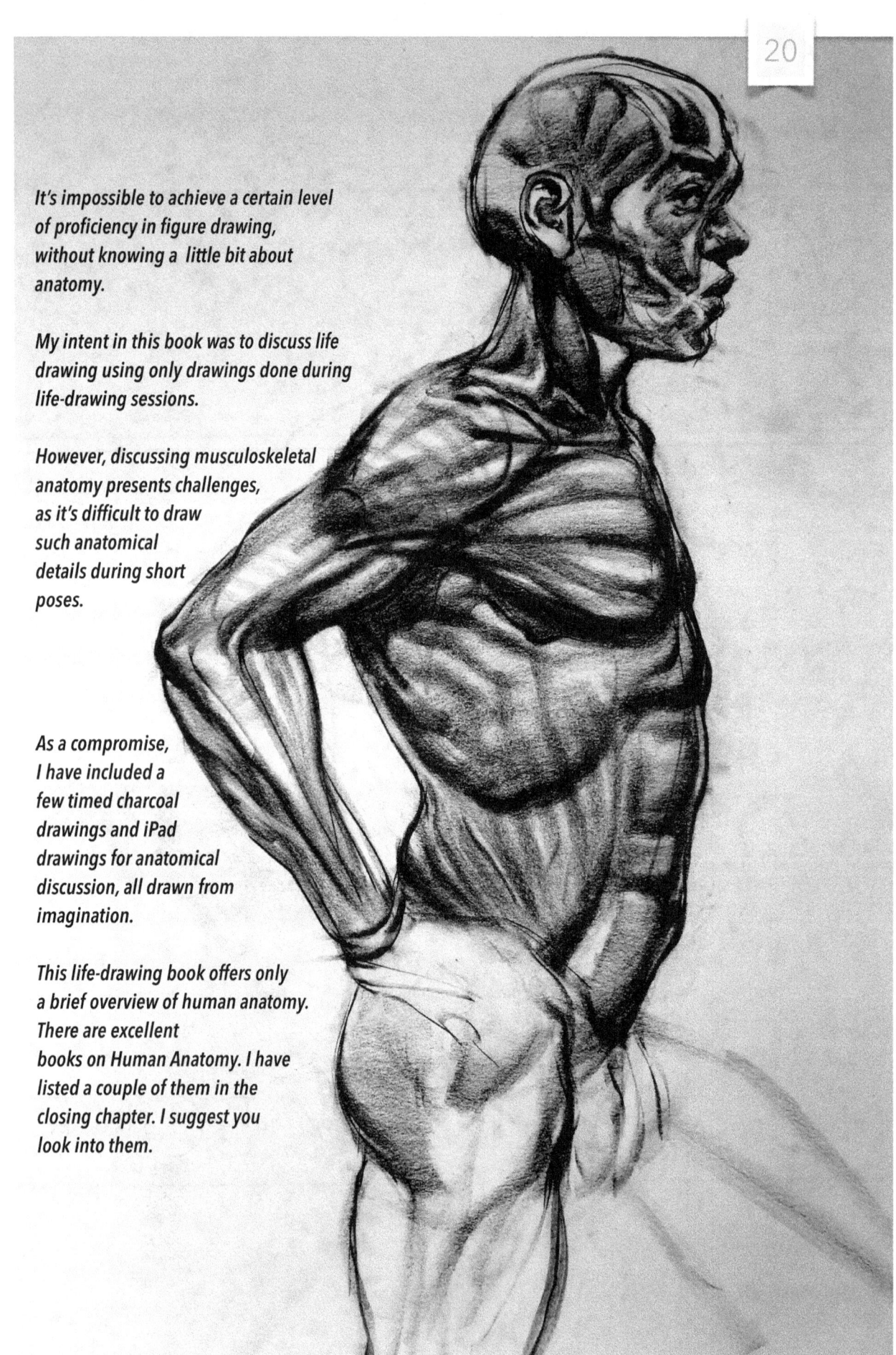

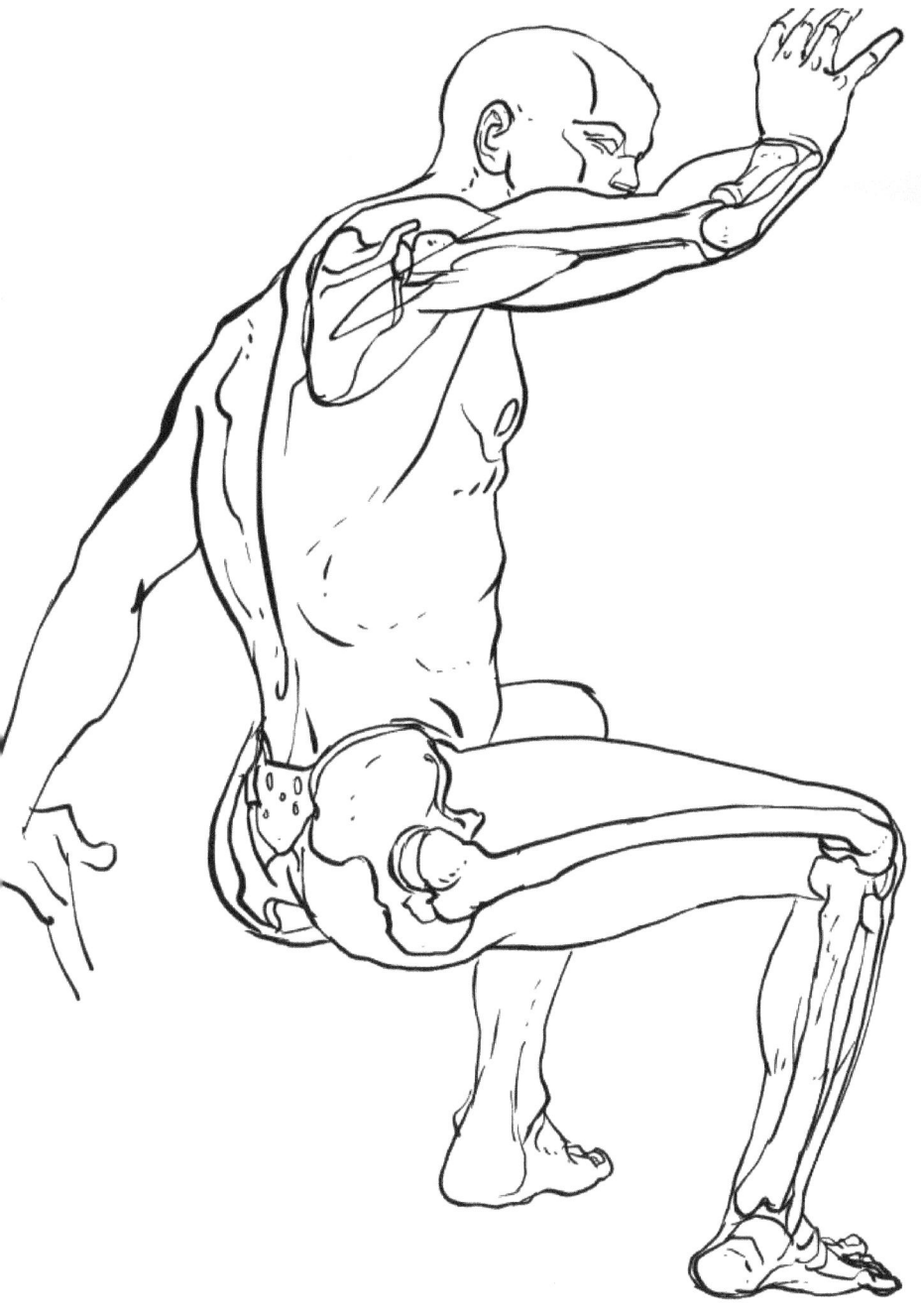

Here is a list of bones that give evidence of themselves on the surface of the body. For convenience, let's call them 'surface bones'. I have simplified some of the names so they are easier to remember. As you can see, the number of bones to remember isn't that daunting.

Skull
Backbone
Shoulder blade (scapula)
Collar bone (clavicle)
Ribcage
Breast bone (sternum)

Humerus
Kneecap (patella)
Ulna & radius

Pelvis
Iliac crest
Greater trochanter
Sacrum

Femur
Tibia, fibula

Hand bones
Foot bones

How does one go about including bony details in life drawing? Perhaps start with learning where these bones show themselves on the human body. Then look for them on the model and reproduce what you see in your drawing. Easy peasy!

Th skull is simply the head - we will save that discussion for the Head Drawing section. Let's discuss the rest of the bones.

SURFACE BONES AND MUSCLES FOR FRONT VIEW

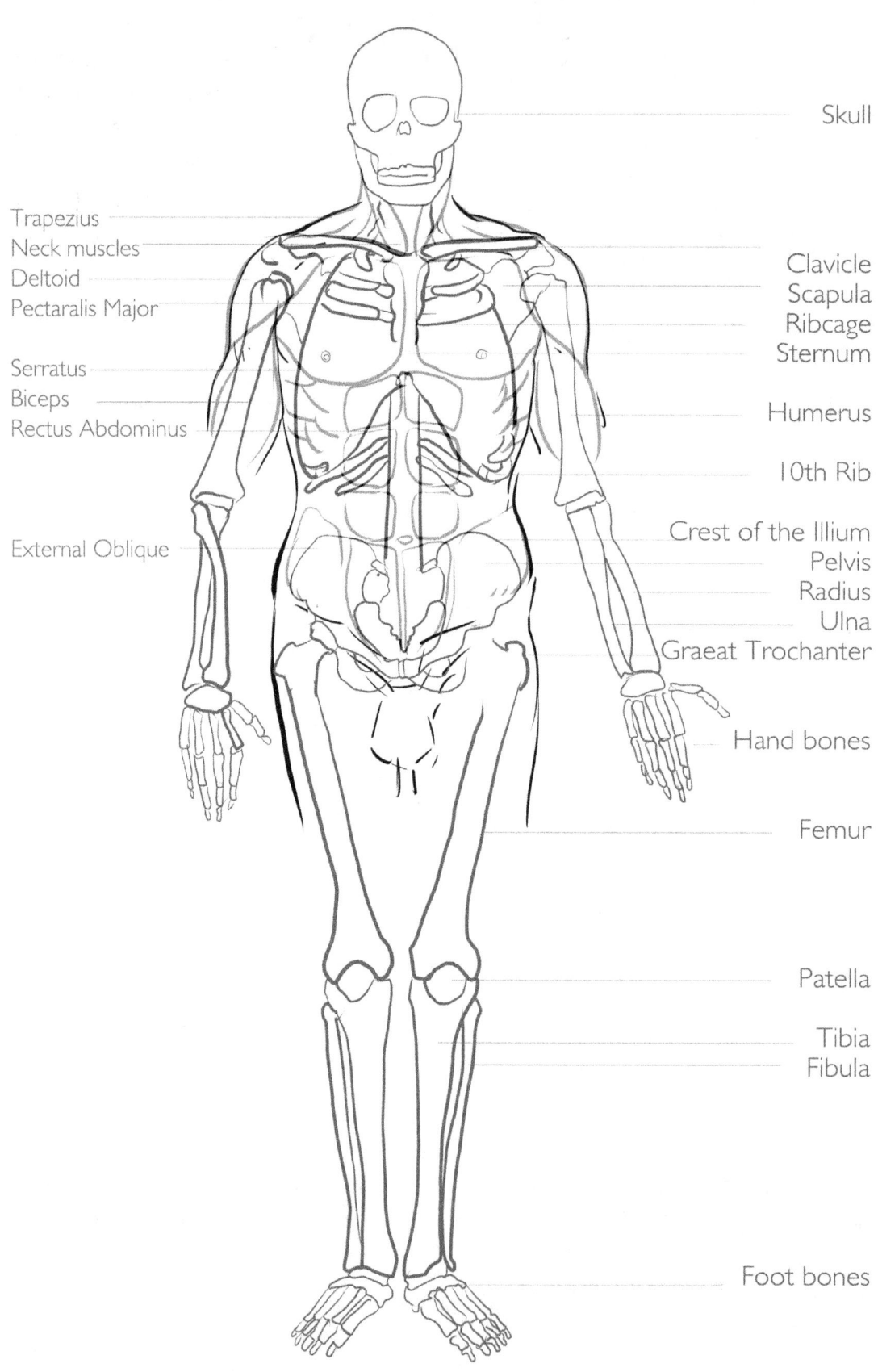

SURFACE BONES AND MUSCLES FOR BACK VIEW

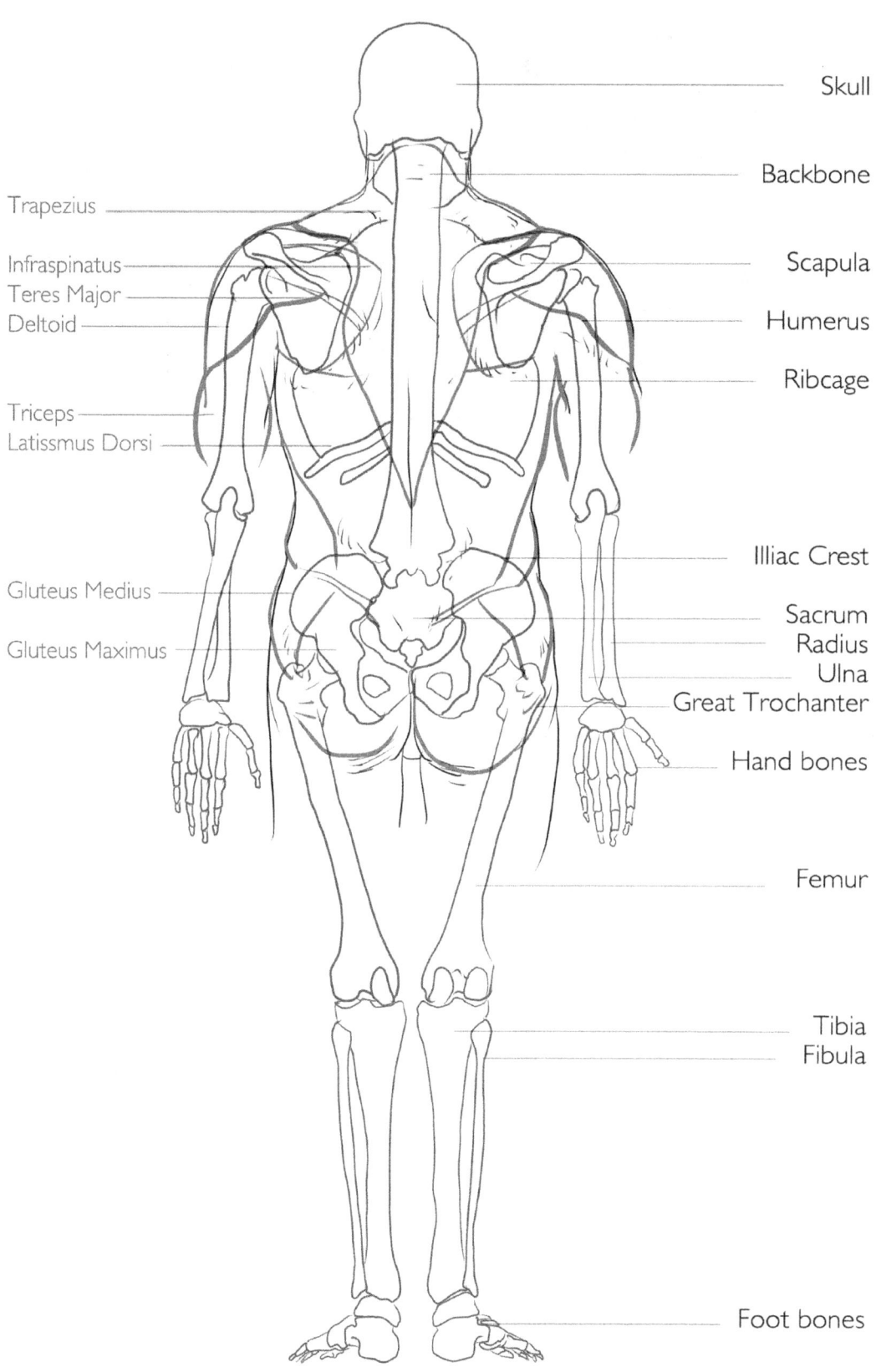

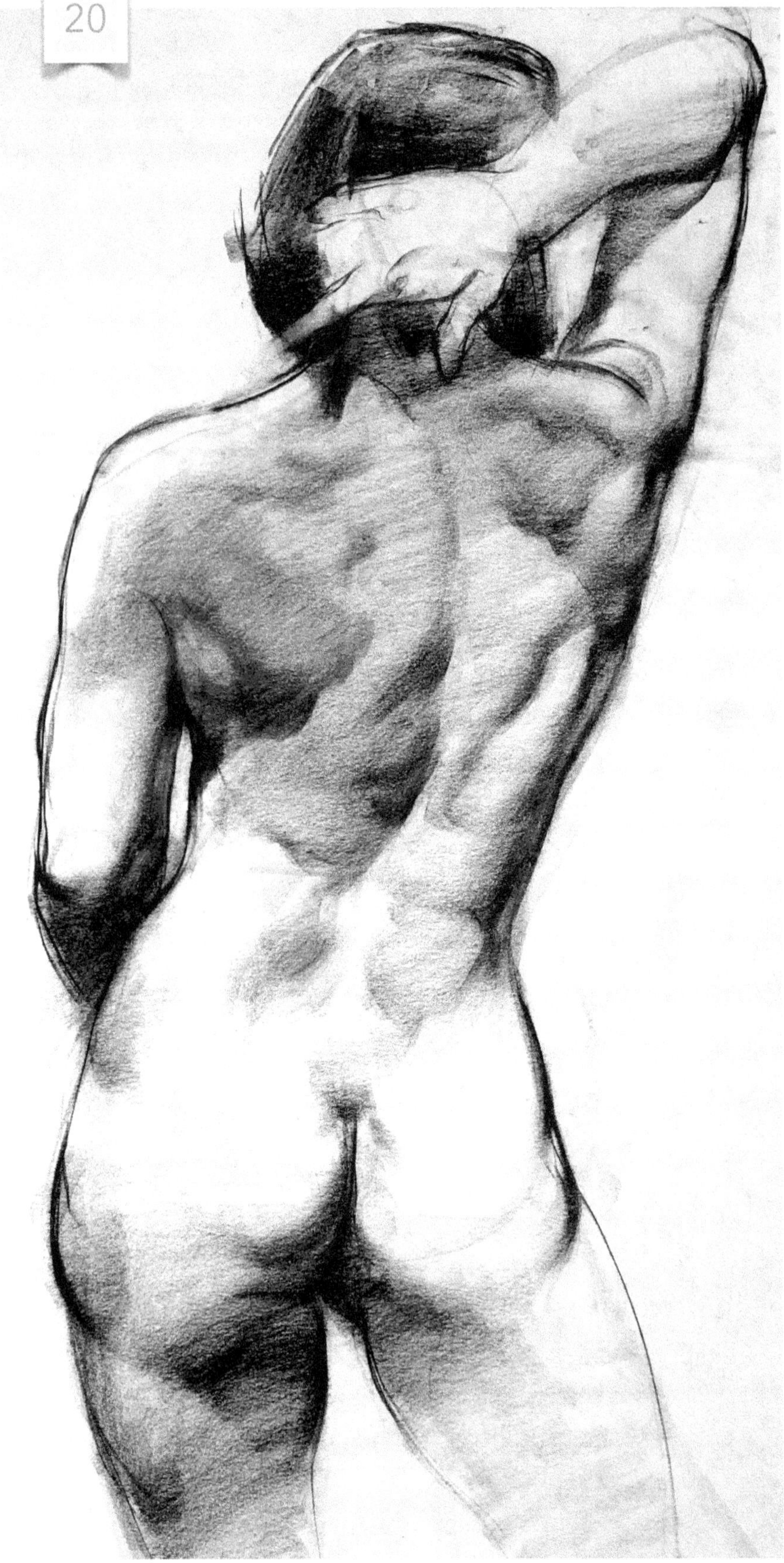

The backbone starts at the base of the skull and goes all the way to sacrum - if humans had a tail, it would start at the base of the sacrum (there is small bone there called the coccyx).

Ignoring the gnarly details of anatomy, try drawing the backbone/spine as a curved line at the center of the back. Can you see it in the drawing on the left?

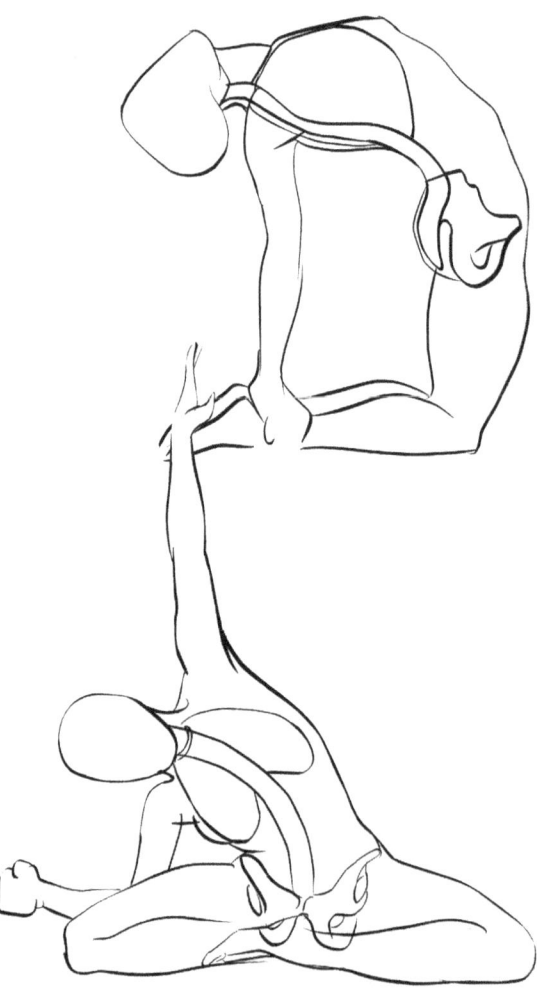

Some bones express their positions as indentation, like parts of the backbone.

See the one and two-minute drawings elsewhere in this book.

THE BACKBONE IS AN 'S' CURVE. IT IS A GREAT SURFACE BONE FOR ESTABLISHING THE GESTURE OF THE POSE.

It has four sections:
- Cervical that allows the head to tilt.
- Thoracic that supports the ribcage.
- Lumber that supports the lower back (and the pelvis hangs onto this).
- Sacrum/coccyx, the bottom bits.

The sketches below show how the cervical section (neck) of the backbone allows the head to tilt. Visualize that part of the backbone before you make a mark.

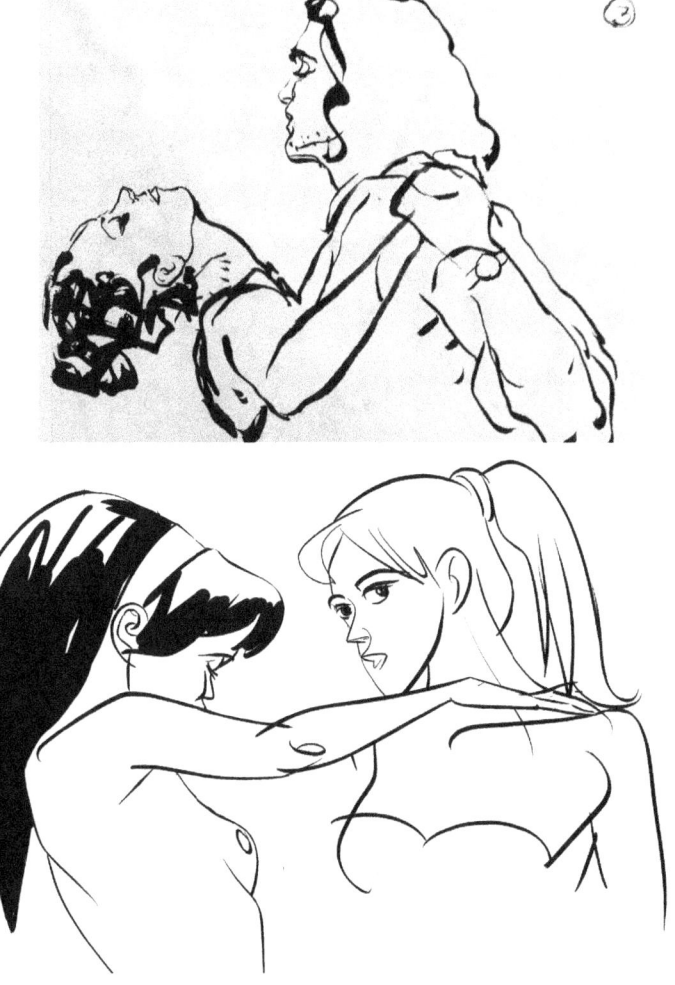

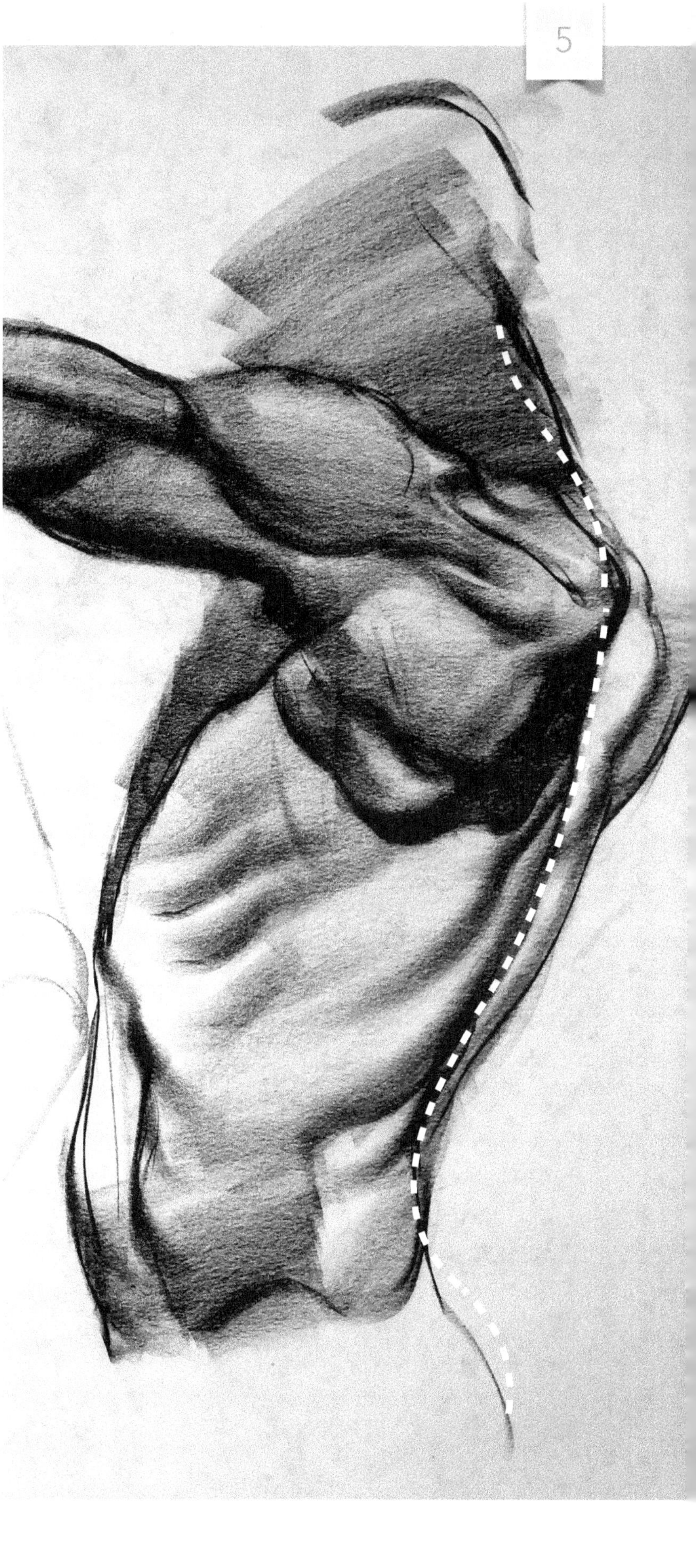

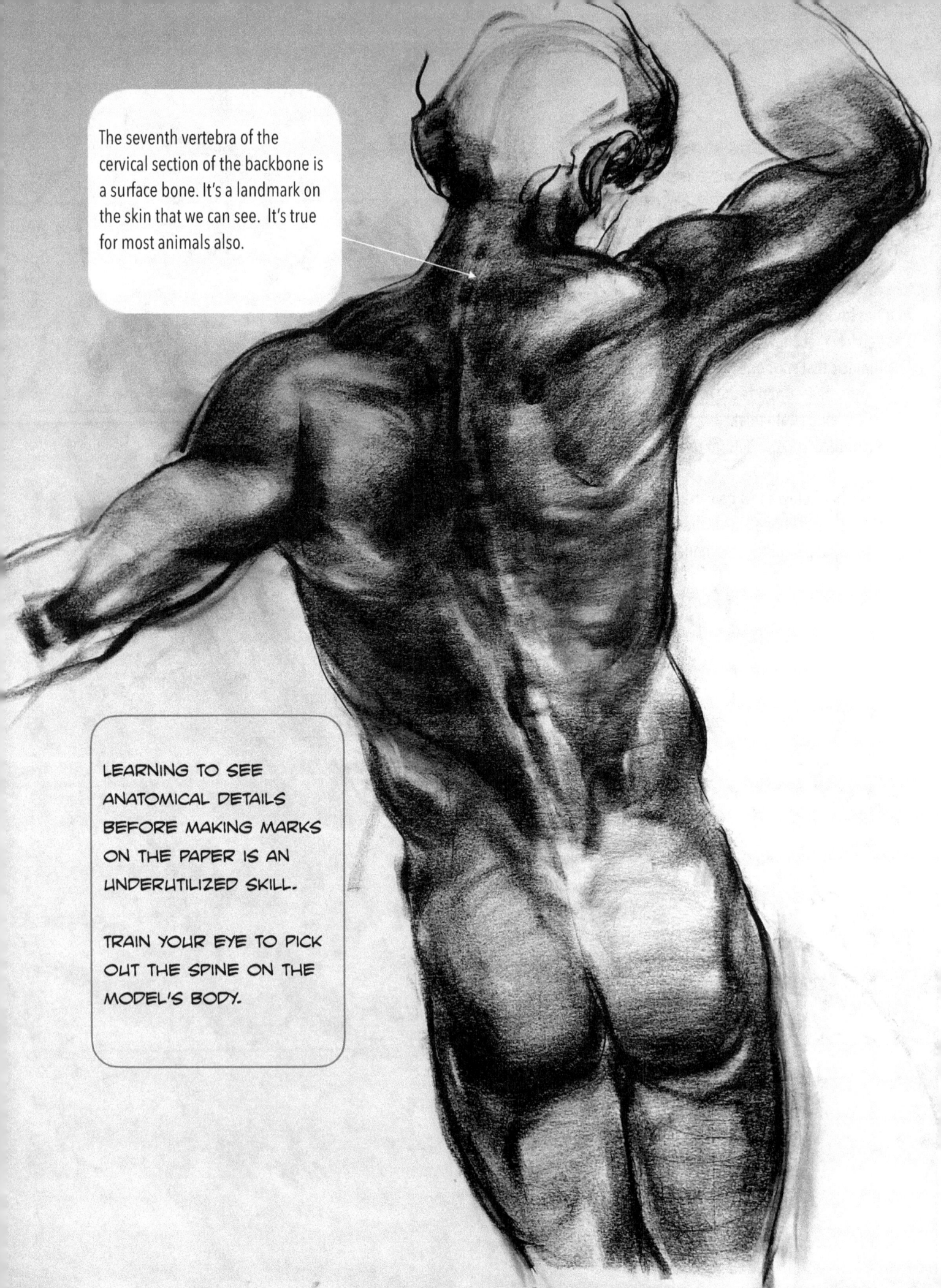

Visualizing the spine on the model is very useful - it's a great gesture line. Since it's the median line at the center of the torso, you can use that line for delineating the twist in the body.

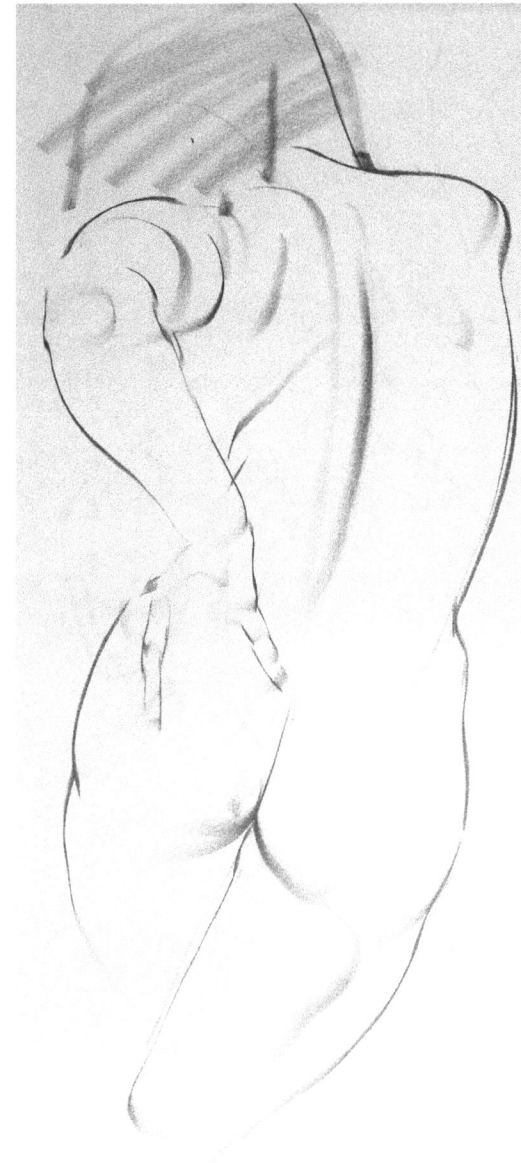

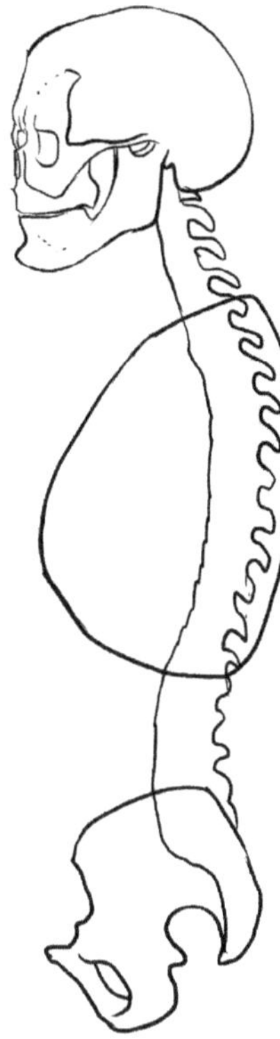

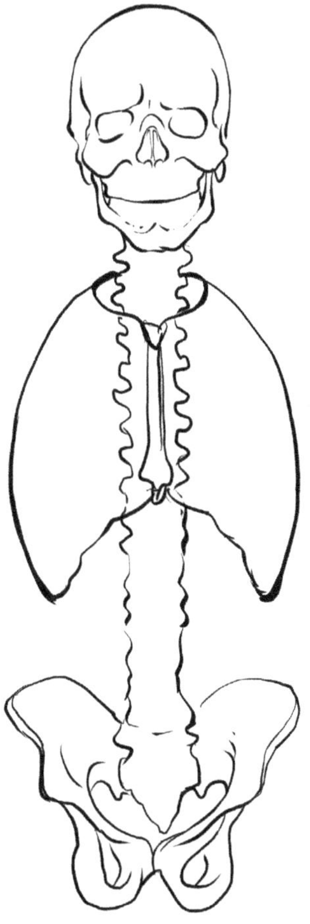

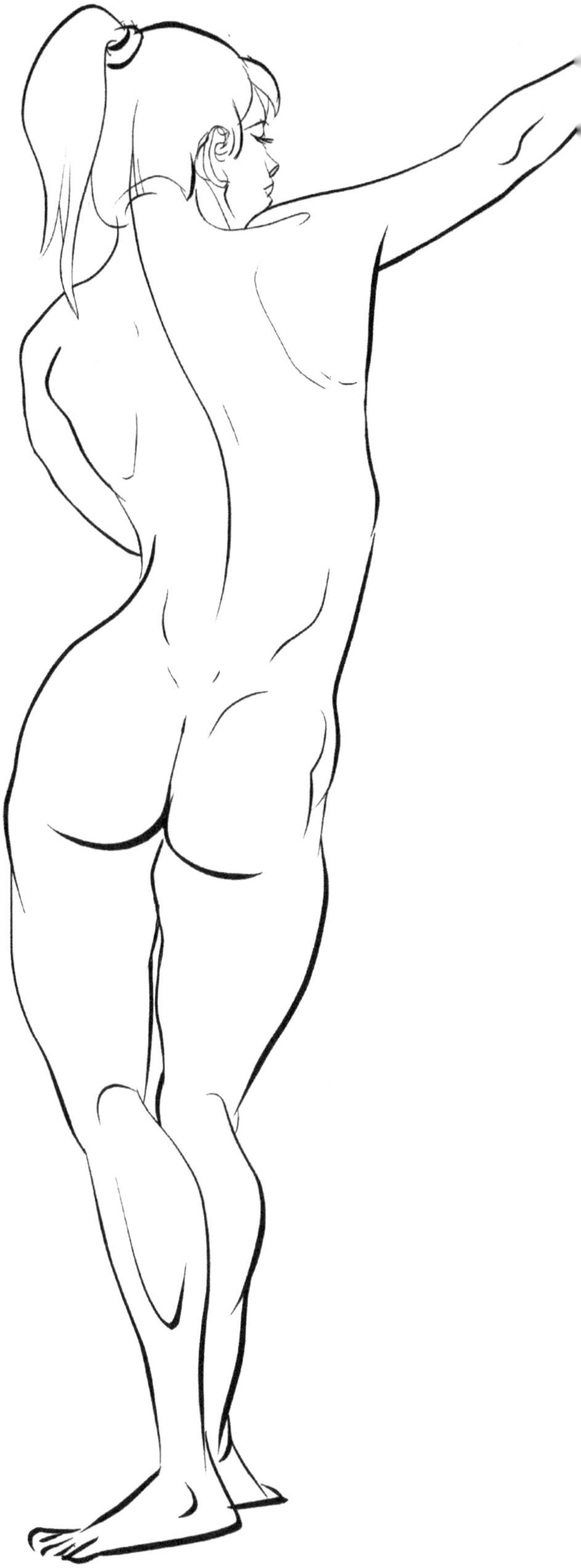

The backbone is made up of units called vertebrae, which give it such flexibility. The drawing on the far right shows those interlocking vertebrae. It also shows the four sections of the backbone we discussed earlier.

In the drawing to the right, you can see the four sections of the backbone in action. Fortunately, you don't have to draw the actual backbone. Only its surface detail as shown in the drawings below. Usually it's a line in pen and ink drawings or a tone in charcoal drawings.

Learn to visualize the backbone in any pose before making marks.

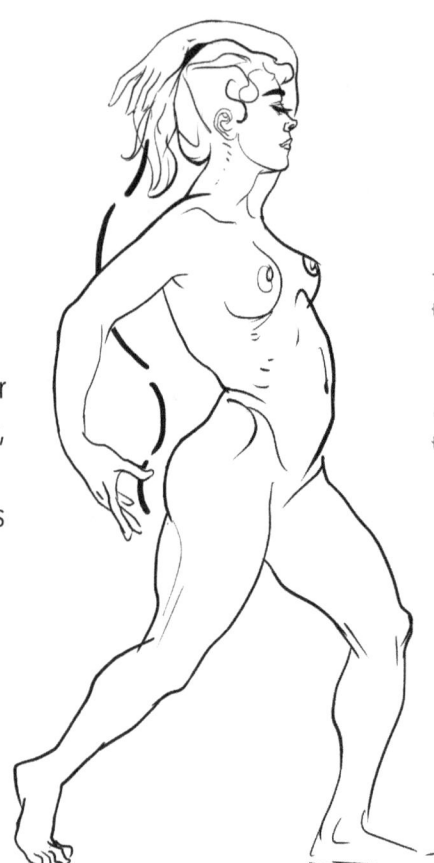

The Cervical section

Thoracic section, the upper body

Lumbar section, the lower body

Sacrum

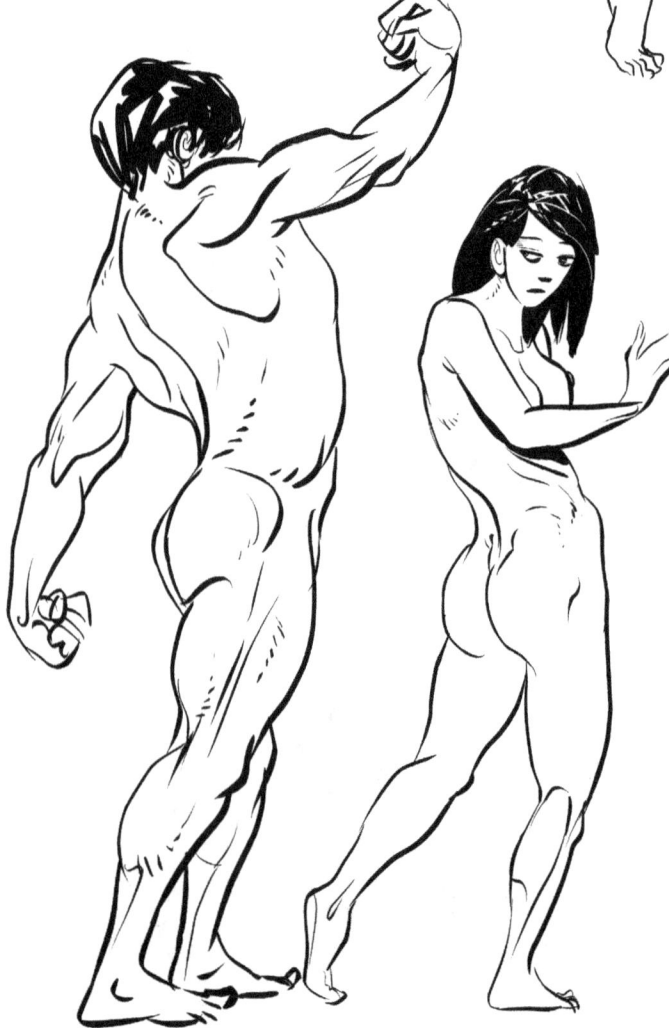

In the two examples on the left, the line delineating the backbone helps show the twist of the body.

The drawing on the right is a neutral pose. The backbone in this pose is a very strong **s** curve.

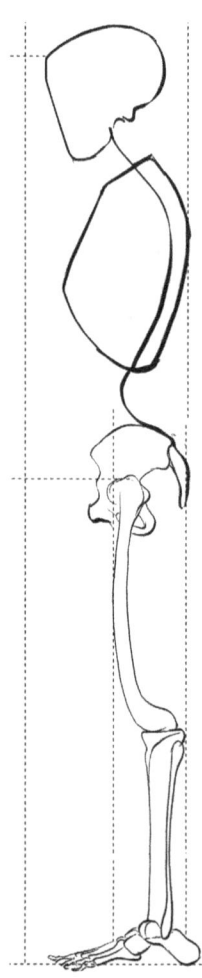

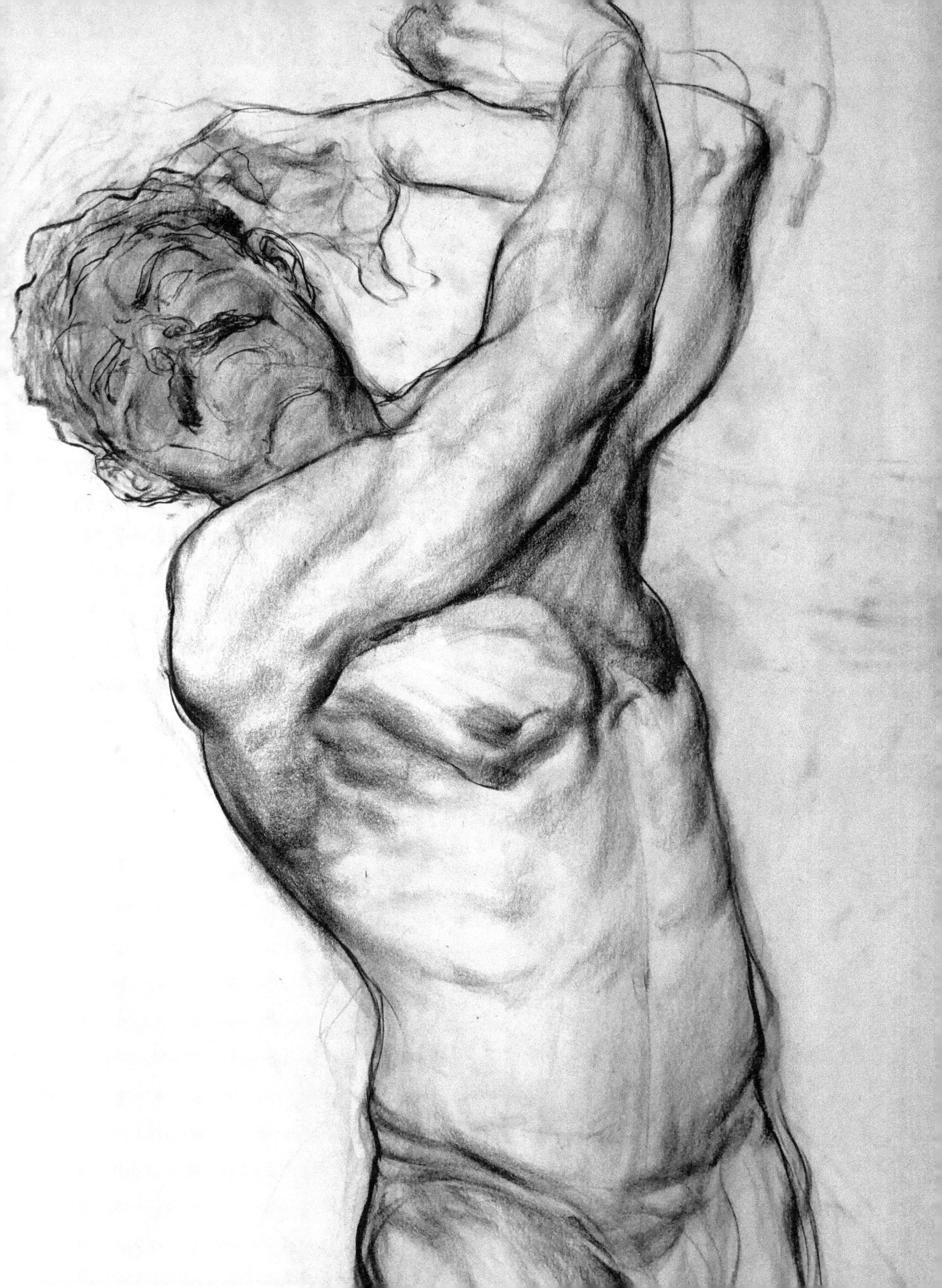

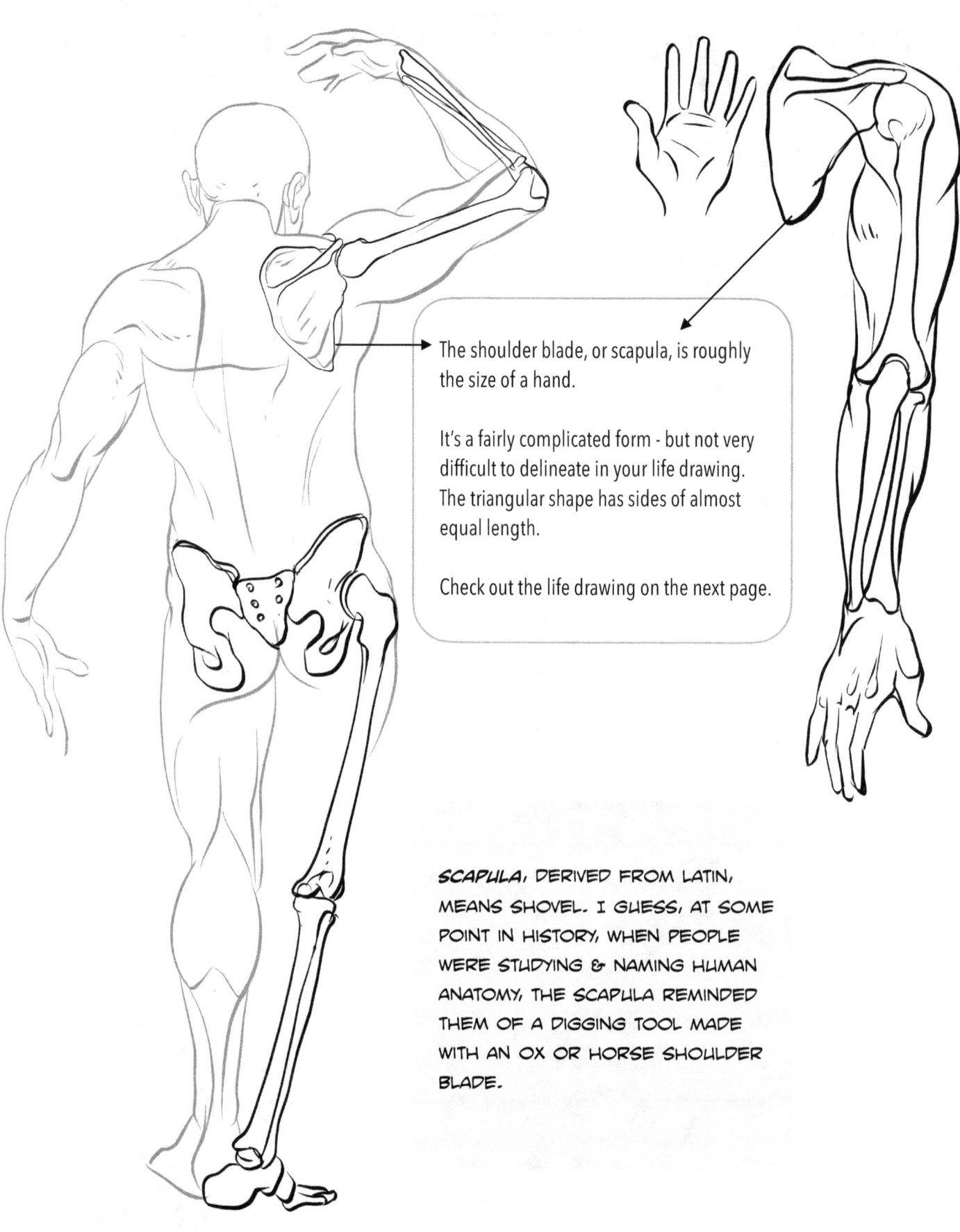

The shoulder blade, or scapula, is roughly the size of a hand.

It's a fairly complicated form - but not very difficult to delineate in your life drawing. The triangular shape has sides of almost equal length.

Check out the life drawing on the next page.

SCAPULA, DERIVED FROM LATIN, MEANS SHOVEL. I GUESS, AT SOME POINT IN HISTORY, WHEN PEOPLE WERE STUDYING & NAMING HUMAN ANATOMY, THE SCAPULA REMINDED THEM OF A DIGGING TOOL MADE WITH AN OX OR HORSE SHOULDER BLADE.

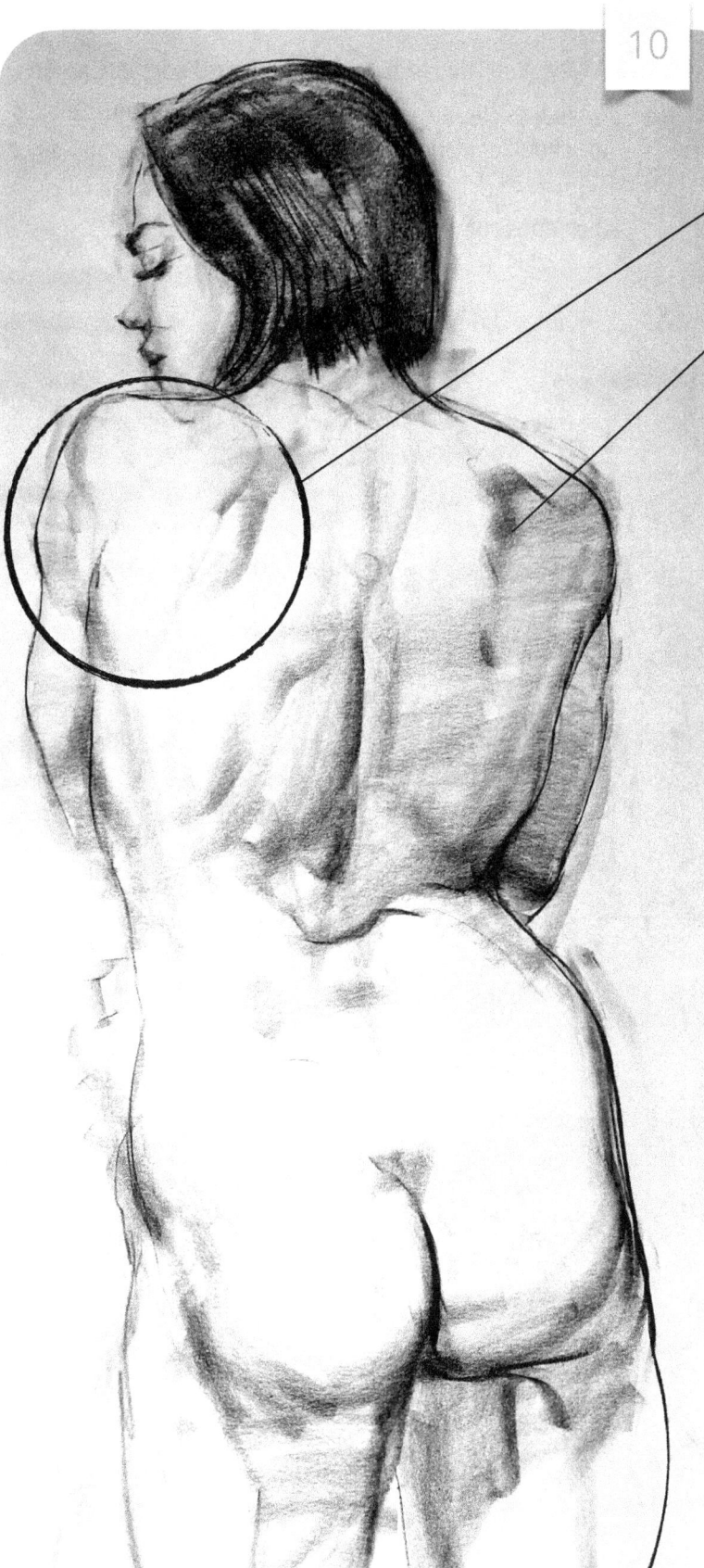

Lightly shaded marks here show the tonal definition of the shoulder blade.

You can also see the tone on her right shoulder blade. Although the anatomy of the shoulder blade is complex, drawing it in your life drawing doesn't have to be. See how her left shoulder blade seems to have slid toward the edge. That's because the scapula (shoulder blade) can slide over the ribcage.

A few useful (approximate) measurements for error checking:

- The length of breastbone (sternum) is
- equal to the length of the collar bone (clavicle), which is
- equal to each of the vertical & horizontal sides of the shoulder blade (scapula), which is
- equal to the spine of the scapula, which is
- equal to the length from top of the head to bottom of the nose, which is
- equal to bottom of the nose to pit of the neck, which is
- equal to one third of the upper leg bone, which is
- equal to half of the upper arm bone.

These tips are so useful I may revisit this list again later in the book.

The scapula (shoulder blade) isn't fused to the ribcage - it's connected with muscles. It can slide quite dramatically over the rib cage.

A very interesting back muscle (trapezius) goes into action when the arms are raised above the head. That muscle pulls the shoulder blades with it, causing them to slide up. Look at the bottom corner of the scapula when someone raises their arms above their head.

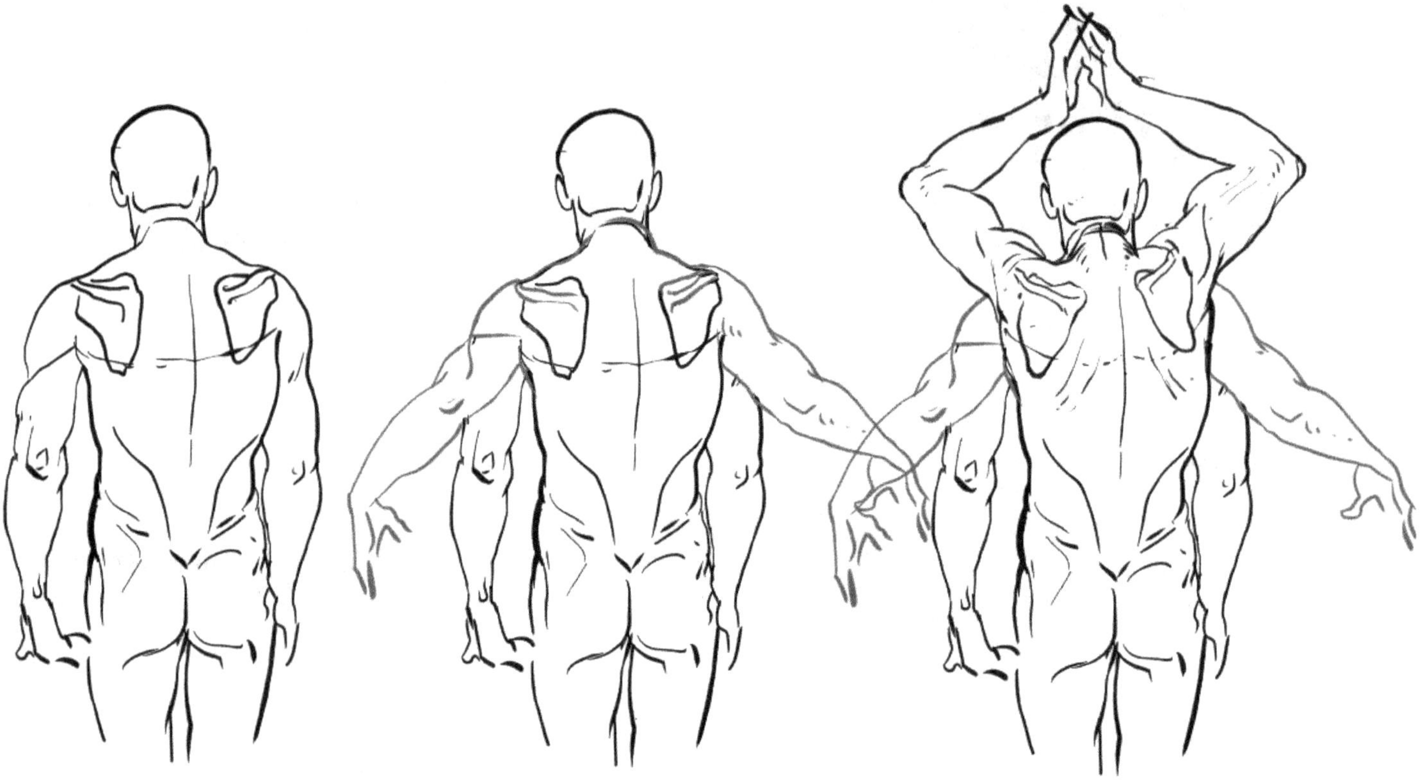

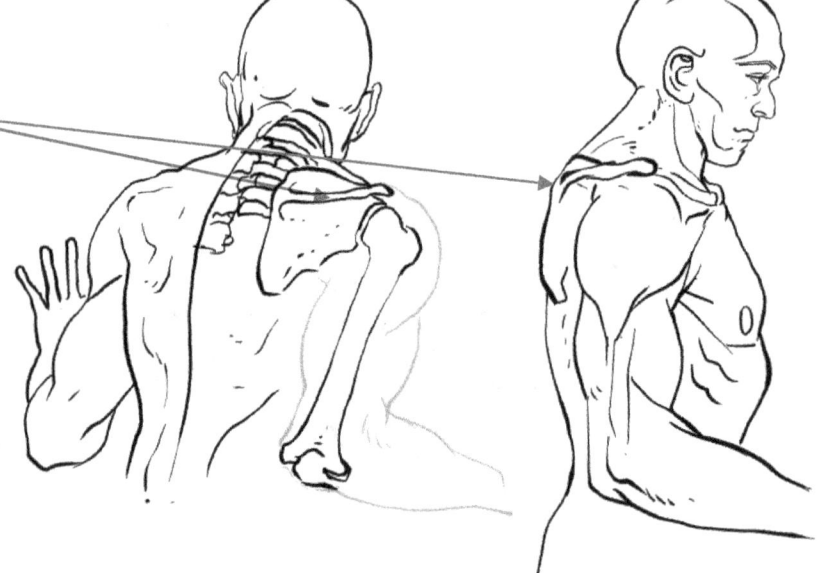

Sometimes we may see hints of the spine of the scapula on the model. It's the ridge running along the top third of the shoulder blade. Look for it on the model and if you see it on the model, make a mark on your drawing, as it can cast a tonal shadow on the shoulder.

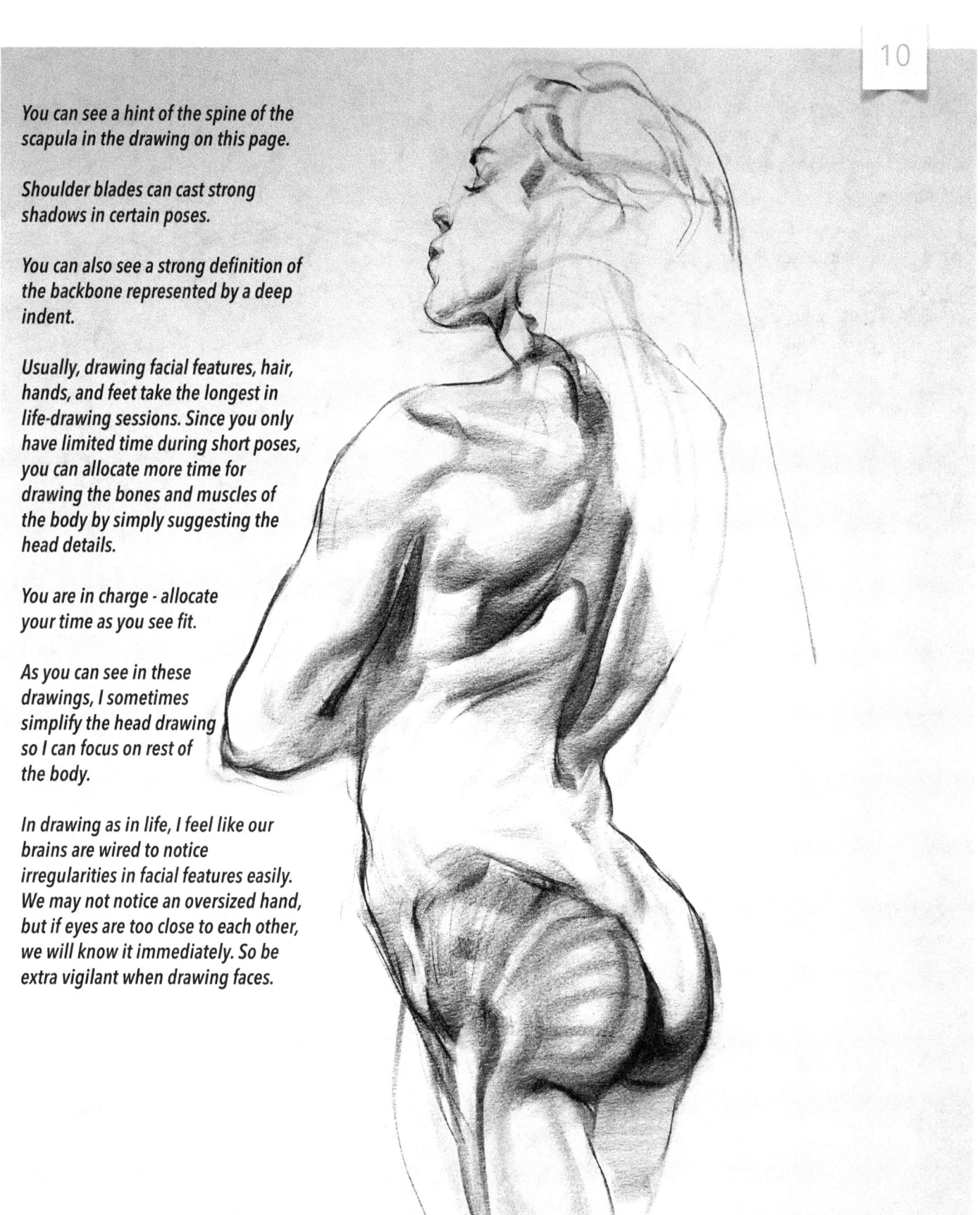

You can see a hint of the spine of the scapula in the drawing on this page.

Shoulder blades can cast strong shadows in certain poses.

You can also see a strong definition of the backbone represented by a deep indent.

Usually, drawing facial features, hair, hands, and feet take the longest in life-drawing sessions. Since you only have limited time during short poses, you can allocate more time for drawing the bones and muscles of the body by simply suggesting the head details.

You are in charge - allocate your time as you see fit.

As you can see in these drawings, I sometimes simplify the head drawing so I can focus on rest of the body.

In drawing as in life, I feel like our brains are wired to notice irregularities in facial features easily. We may not notice an oversized hand, but if eyes are too close to each other, we will know it immediately. So be extra vigilant when drawing faces.

Drawing the ribcage can be daunting - luckily we don't have to draw it in its entirety in life-drawing sessions. There are a few landmarks we should pay attention to.

If the model is facing you, look for the
. pit of the neck,
. clavicle or collar bone,
. sternum or breast bone,
. ribs with muscles on top (the zig zag shapes),
. lowest corners (10th rib) of the ribcage

Remember the discussion earlier on simplifying anatomical forms. The ribcage is almost an egg shaped form with the top and bottom cut off. Visualize that form when making marks.

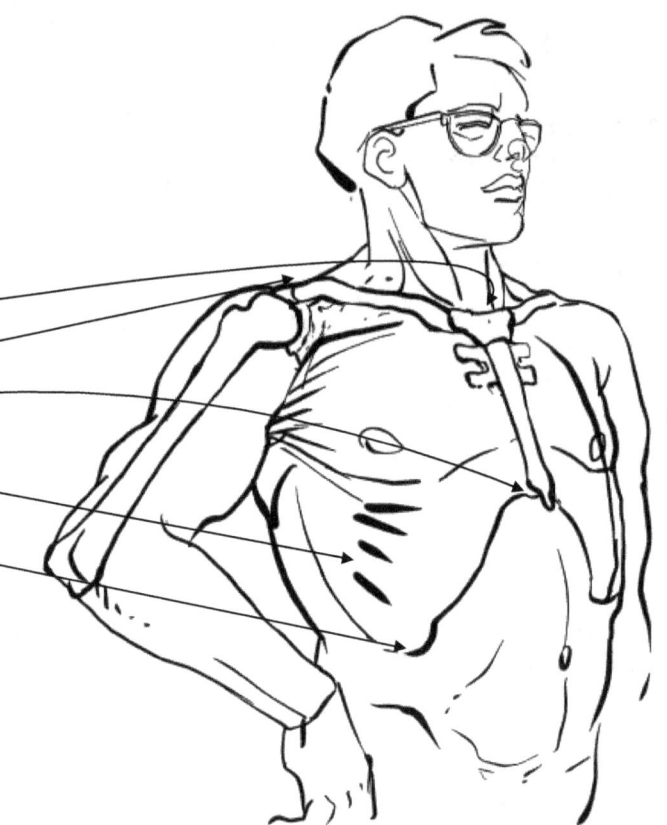

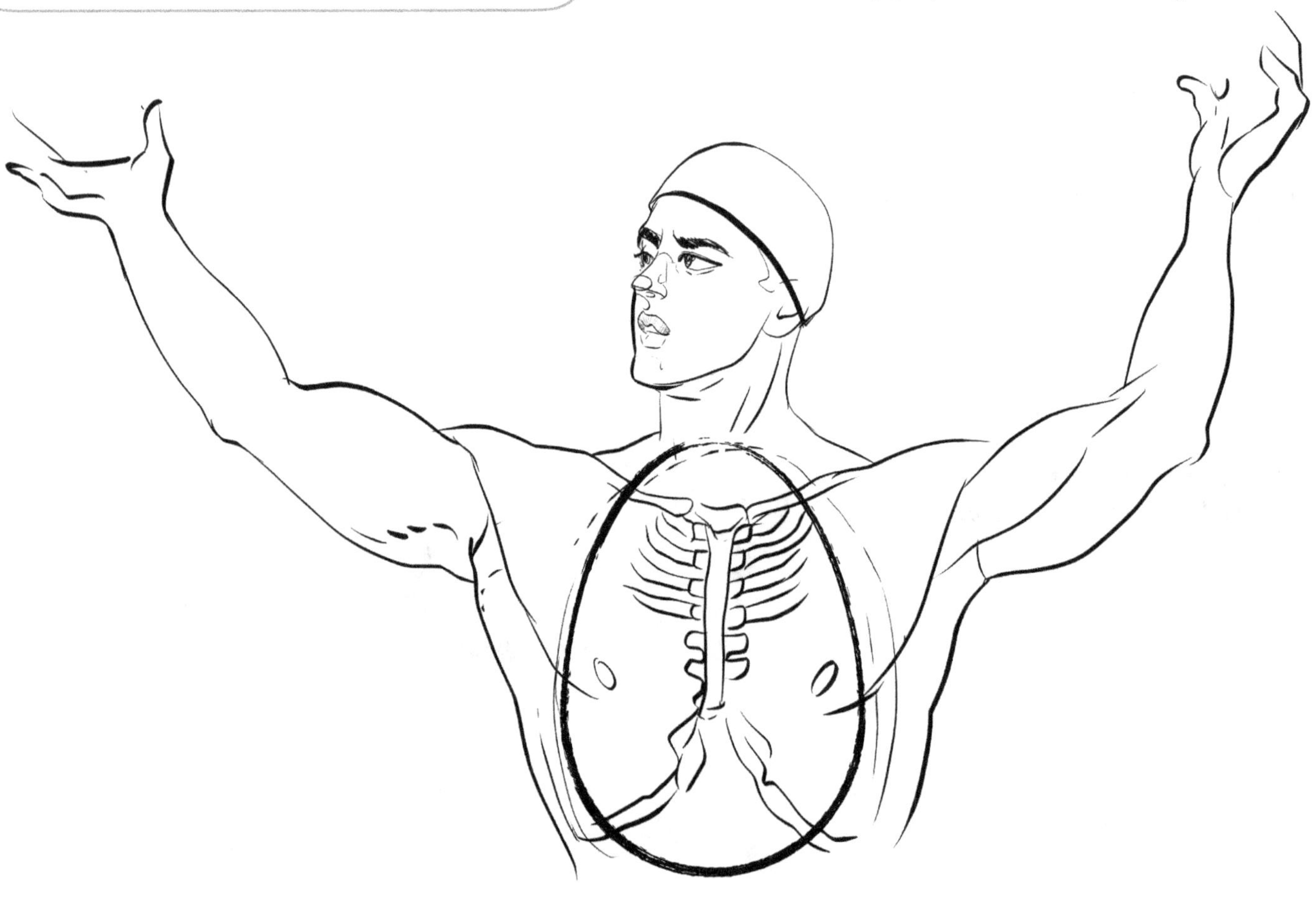

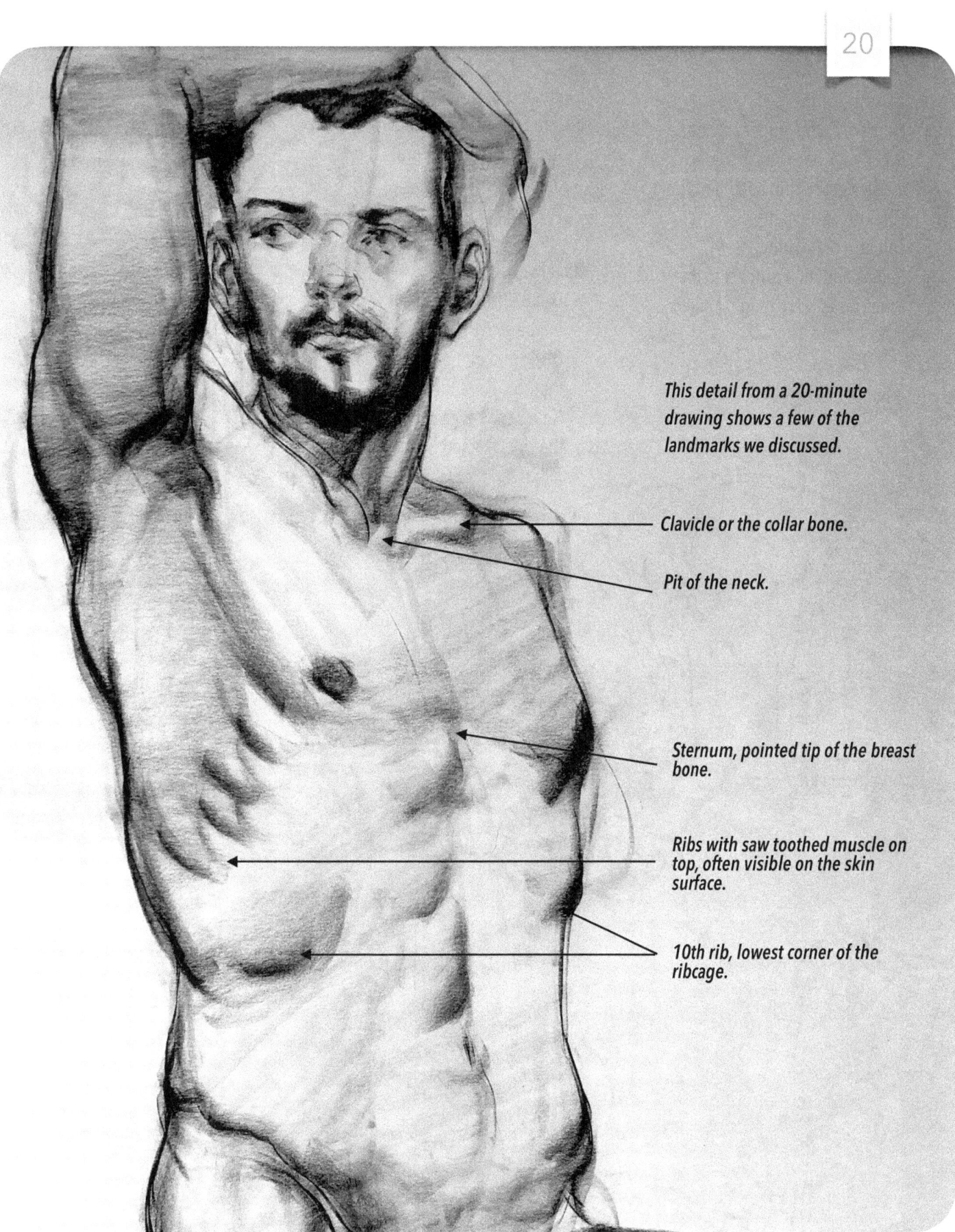

This detail from a 20-minute drawing shows a few of the landmarks we discussed.

— Clavicle or the collar bone.

— Pit of the neck.

— Sternum, pointed tip of the breast bone.

— Ribs with saw toothed muscle on top, often visible on the skin surface.

— 10th rib, lowest corner of the ribcage.

Bones of the arm :
a. Humerus is the upper arm bone that hangs from the shoulder blade. It's one and half heads long.
b. Forearm bone: radius.
c. Forearm bone: ulna.
Radius and ulna connect to the humerus and are roughly one head long.

Landmarks of the surface bones near the elbow seen from the back:
d. Two condyles (side protrusions) of the humerus
e. The head of the ulna (elbow).

Near the wrist:
f. Distal (furthest) end of the ulna, on the pinky side of the hand.
g. Distal end of the radius, on the thumb side of the hand.
h. Notice the concave alignment at the wrist formed by the ulna & radius.

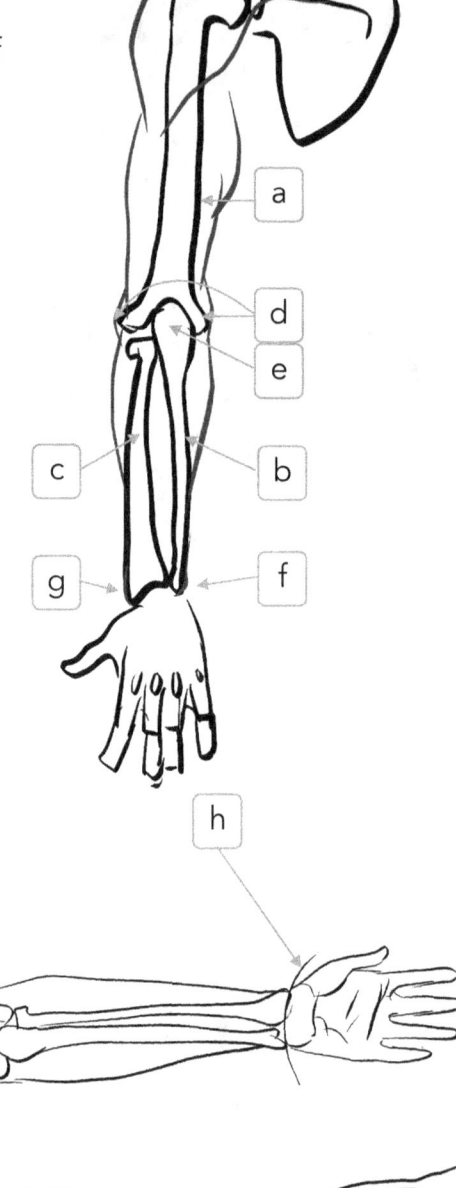

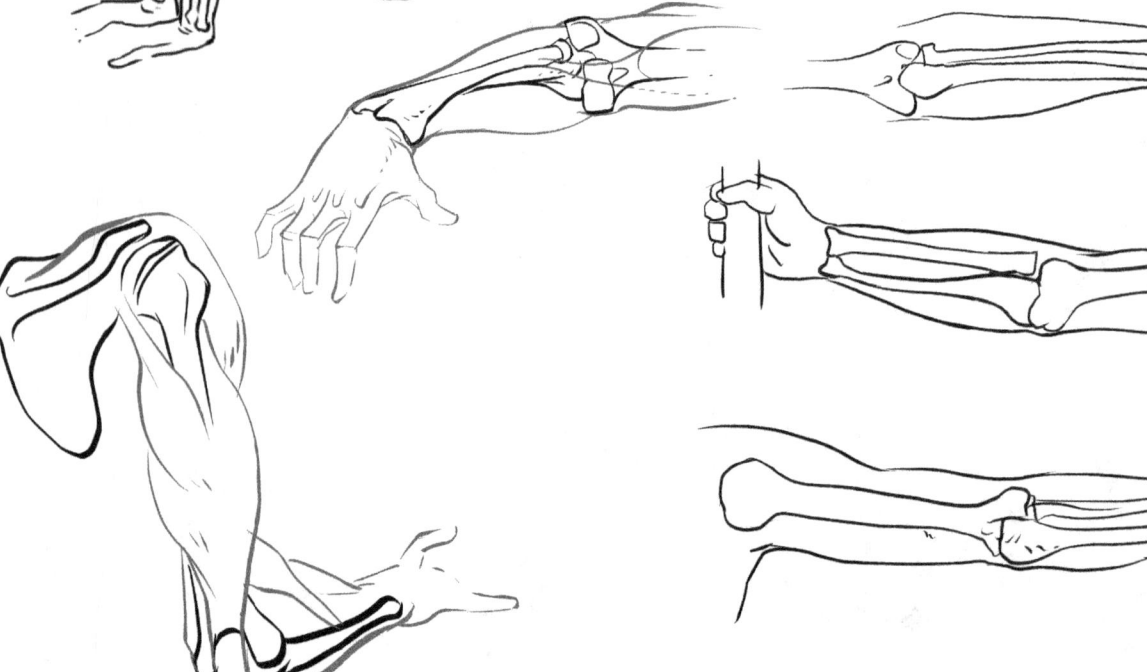

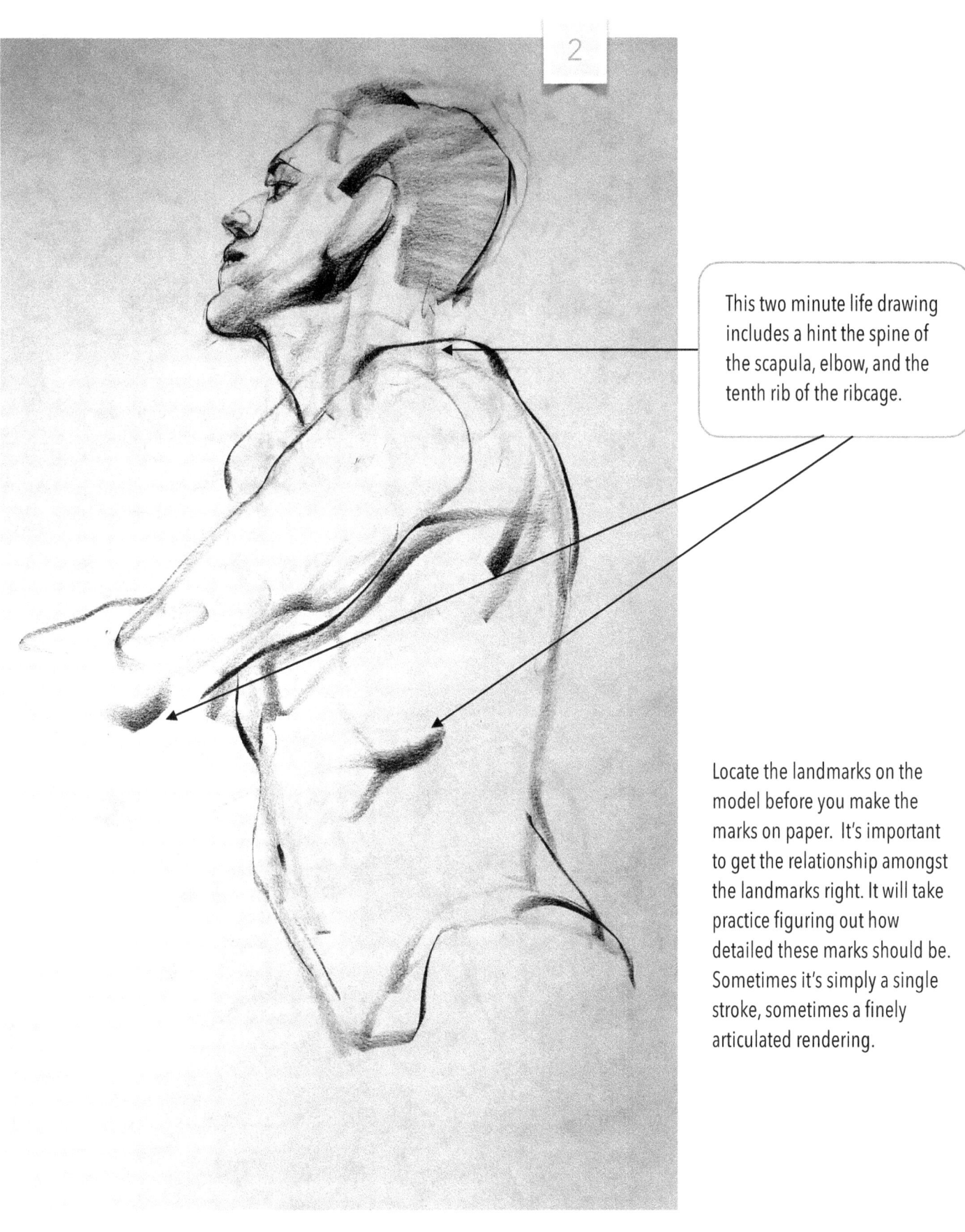

This two minute life drawing includes a hint the spine of the scapula, elbow, and the tenth rib of the ribcage.

Locate the landmarks on the model before you make the marks on paper. It's important to get the relationship amongst the landmarks right. It will take practice figuring out how detailed these marks should be. Sometimes it's simply a single stroke, sometimes a finely articulated rendering.

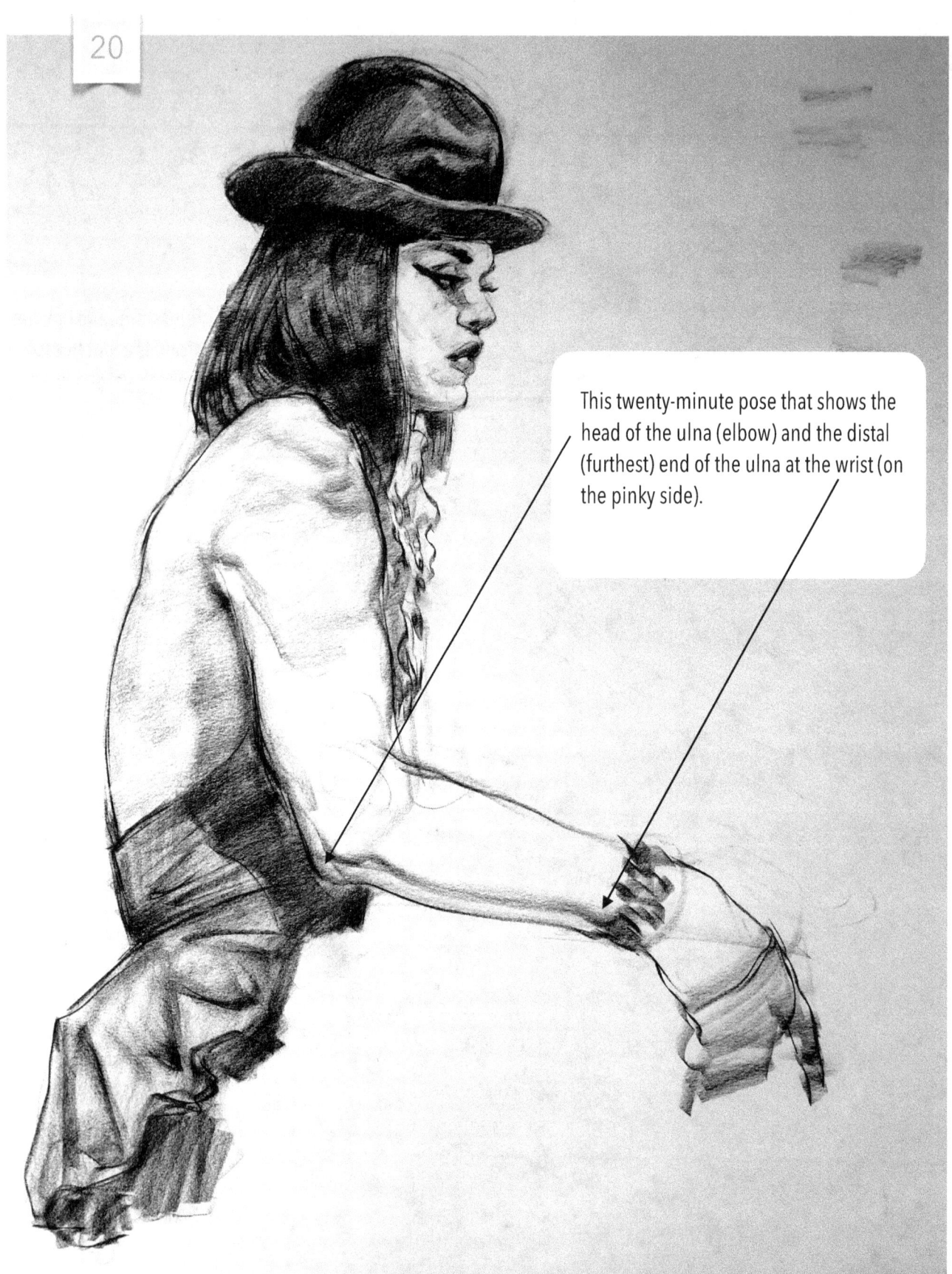

This twenty-minute pose that shows the head of the ulna (elbow) and the distal (furthest) end of the ulna at the wrist (on the pinky side).

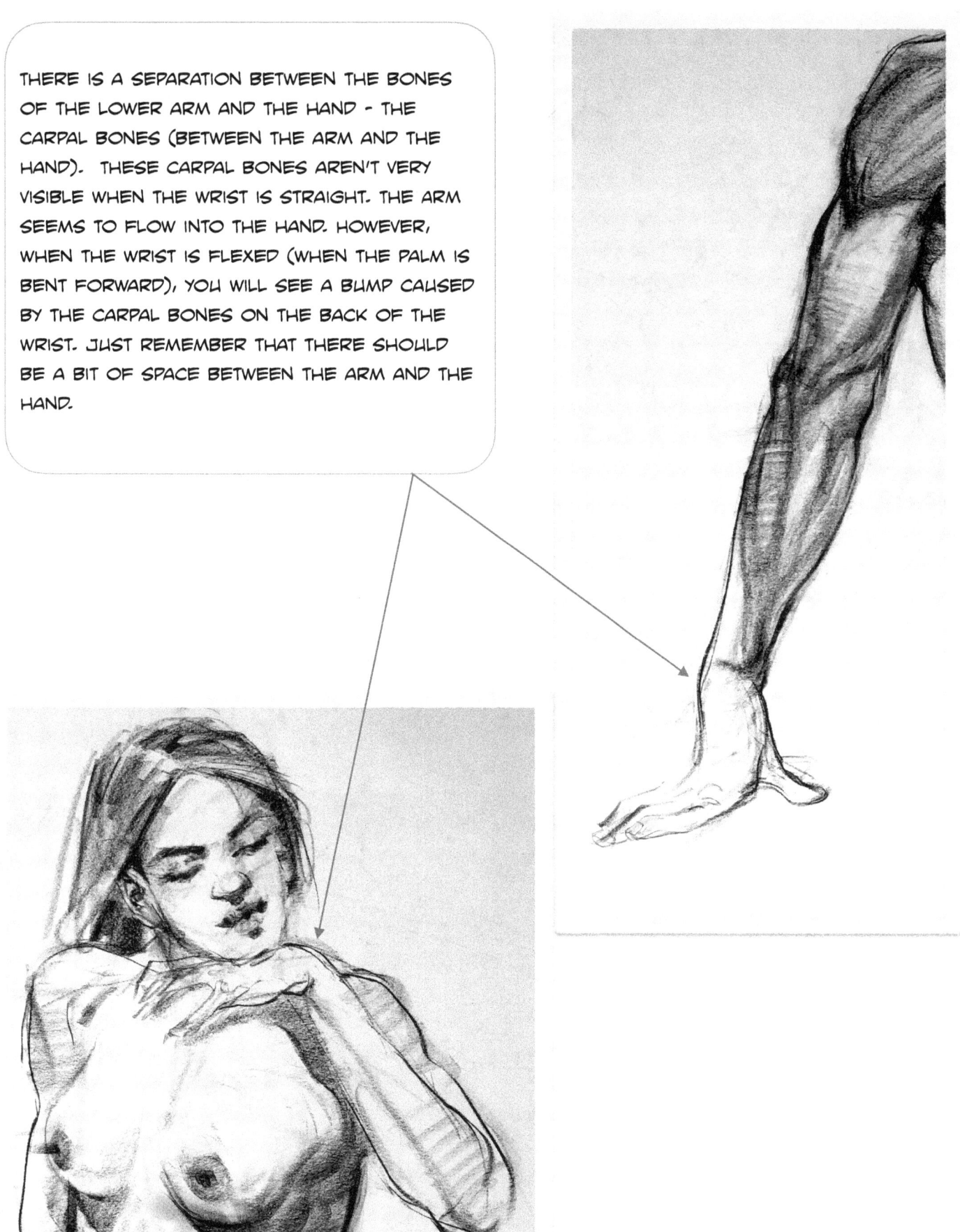

There is a separation between the bones of the lower arm and the hand - the carpal bones (between the arm and the hand). These carpal bones aren't very visible when the wrist is straight. The arm seems to flow into the hand. However, when the wrist is flexed (when the palm is bent forward), you will see a bump caused by the carpal bones on the back of the wrist. Just remember that there should be a bit of space between the arm and the hand.

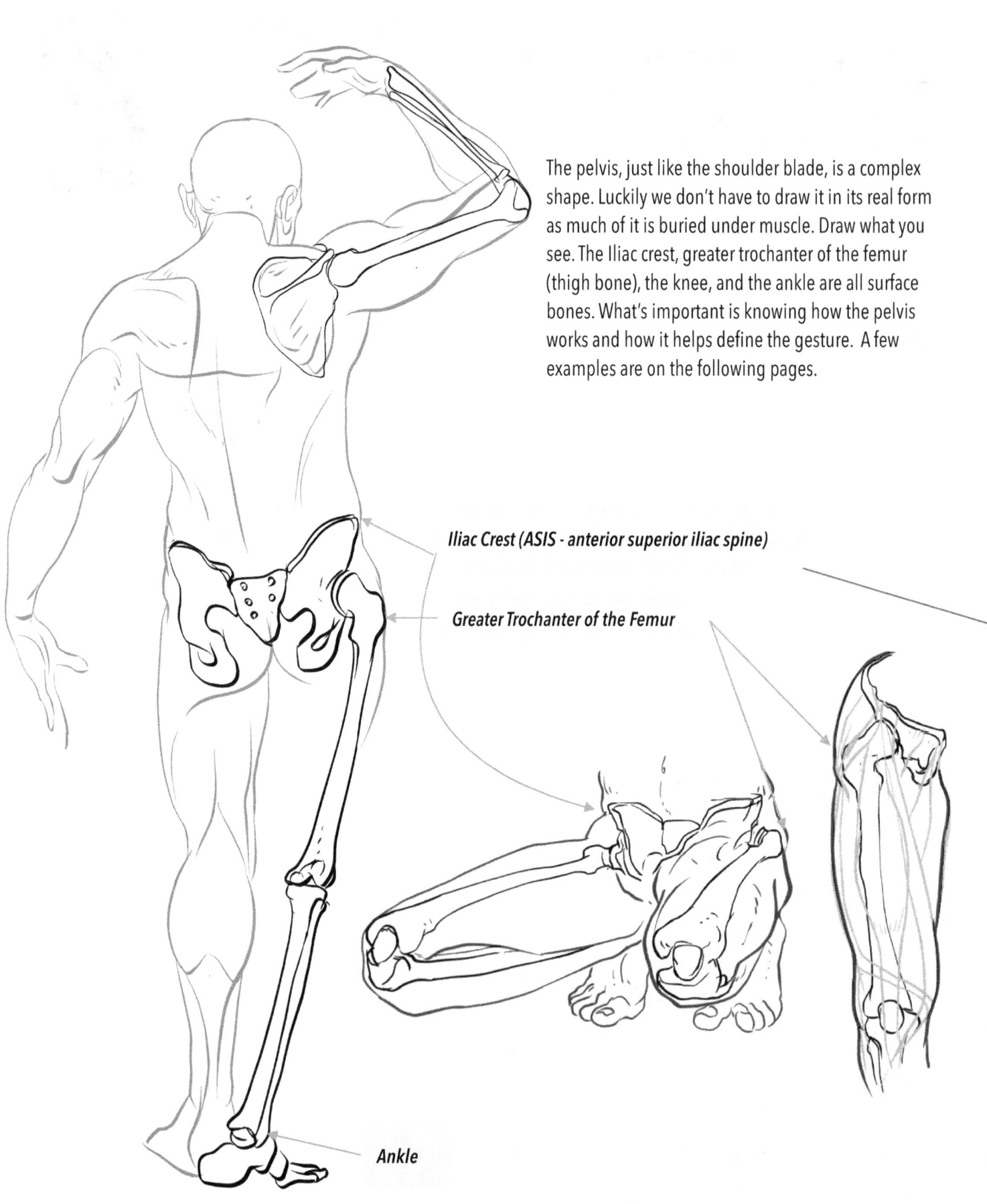

The pelvis, just like the shoulder blade, is a complex shape. Luckily we don't have to draw it in its real form as much of it is buried under muscle. Draw what you see. The Iliac crest, greater trochanter of the femur (thigh bone), the knee, and the ankle are all surface bones. What's important is knowing how the pelvis works and how it helps define the gesture. A few examples are on the following pages.

Iliac Crest (ASIS - anterior superior iliac spine)

Greater Trochanter of the Femur

Ankle

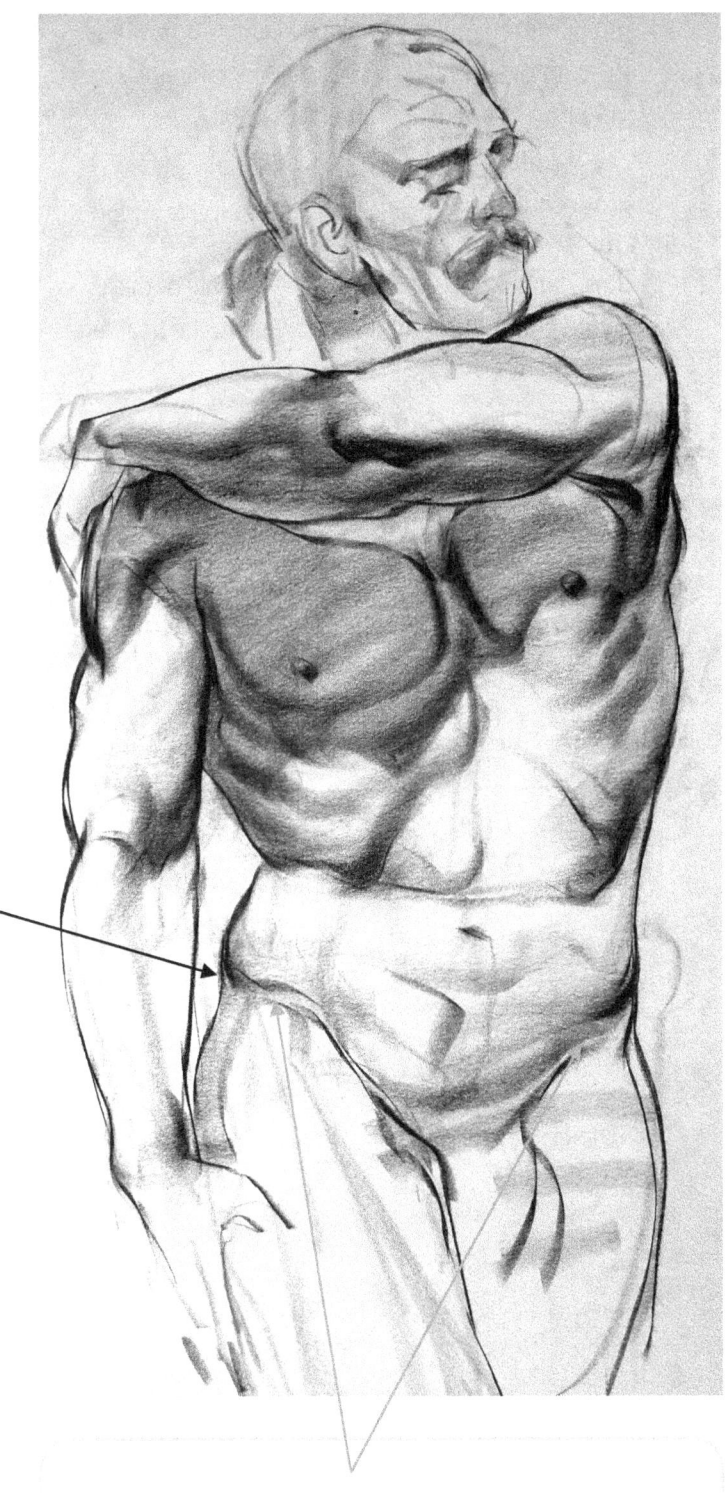

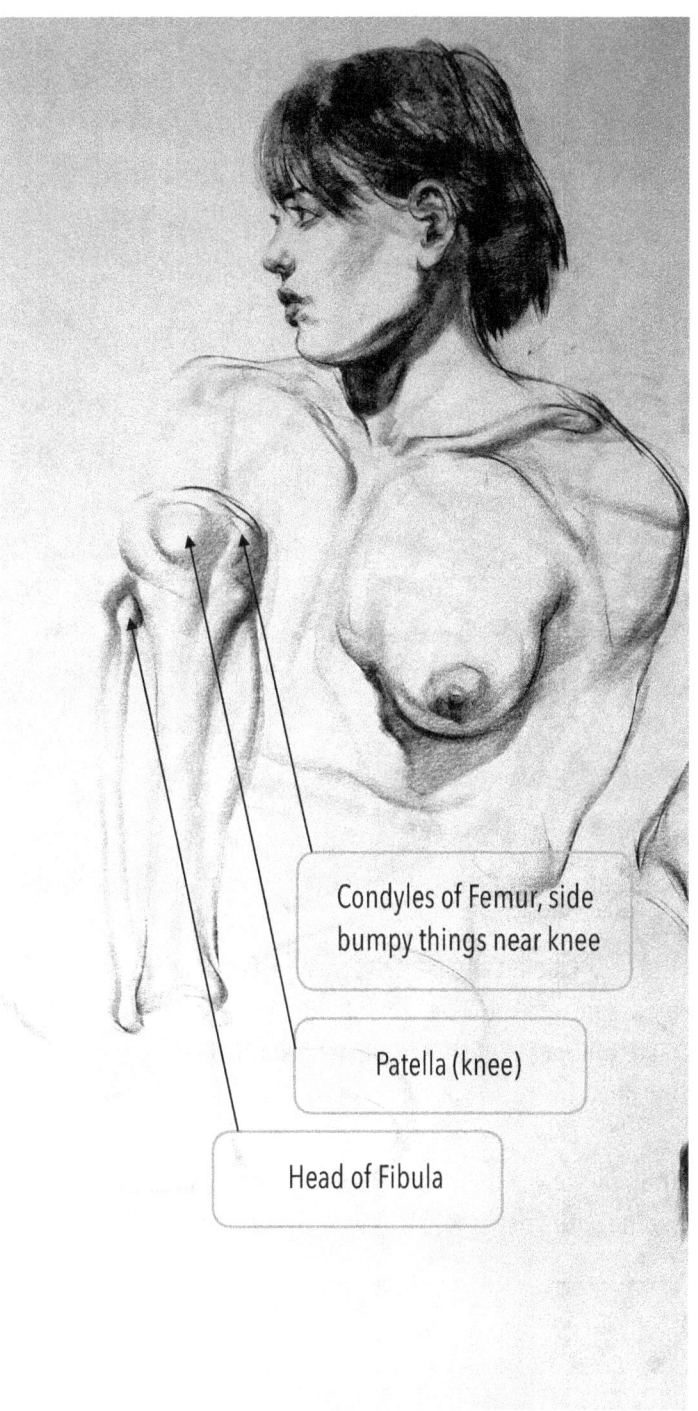

Condyles of Femur, side bumpy things near knee

Patella (knee)

Head of Fibula

You can see the top of the pelvis on almost all models. Usually, there is a bit of tone, probably a bony protrusion depending on the model's physique. Draw what you see on the model.

This seated model had her knee drawn up to her chest. I went overboard here by drawing the actual bones of the lower leg during this short pose. It doesn't hurt to train your mind to see the underlying anatomy while drawing from life. I'd recommend referring to anatomy books to confirm the accuracy of your drawing.

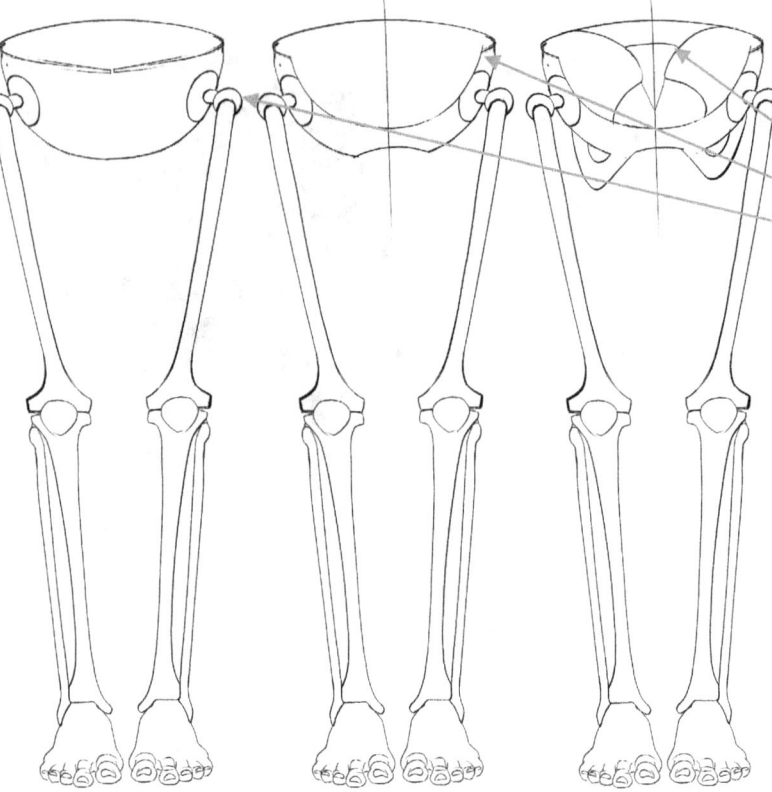

The pelvis looks like a small bowl and tilts forward. The surface landmarks you should look for are:
- PSIS (posterior superior iliac spine)
- ASIS (anterior superior Iliac spine)
- Greater trochanter

These landmarks are located on each side of the body. Look at the simplified drawing to the near left.

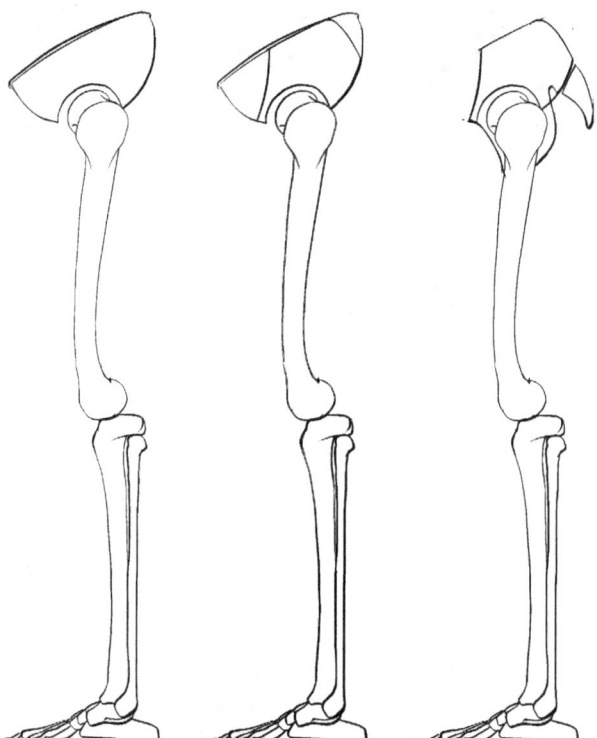

ASIS's are closer to the lateral (outer) edge of the upper thigh.

The pelvis, being a bone, can't change its shape. The two ASISs are always in a straight line. This straight line can be used to establish the tilt of the waist, which is useful in gesture drawing. Look for them on the model.

The side view and the front view of the pelvis are shown below. The profile of the pelvis is half as wide as the front view.

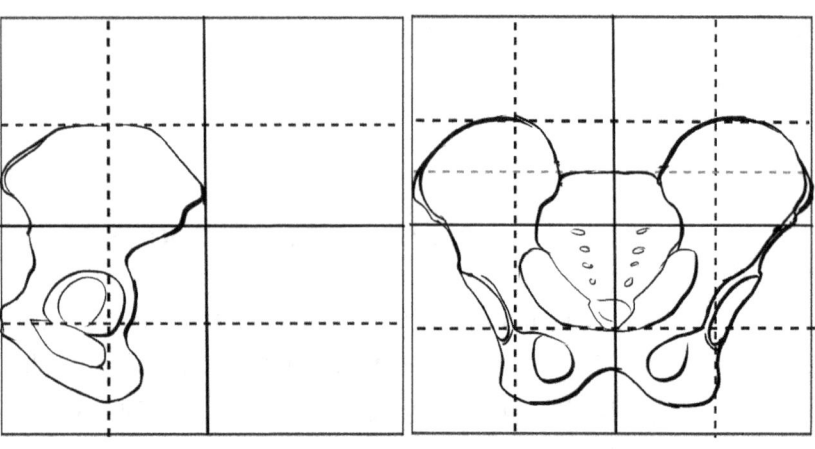

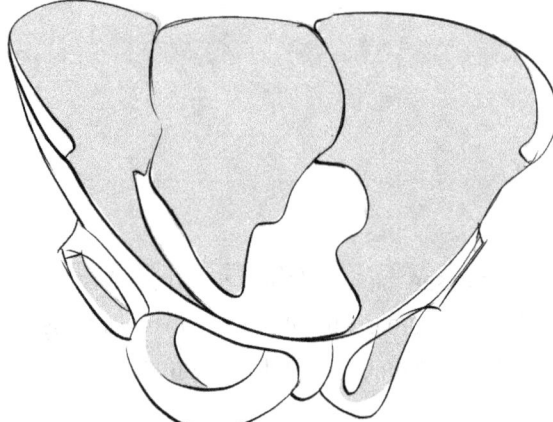

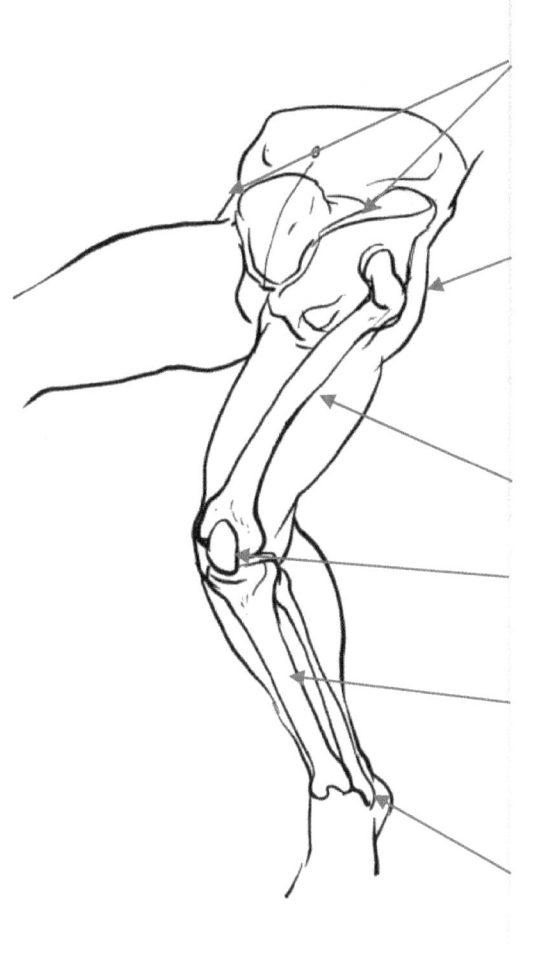

Iliac Crest, top of the pelvis in the front. These two points are ASIS (anterior superior iliac spine)

Greater Trochanter, the protrusion of the femur (upper leg bone) on the side of the thigh - usually visible on the model.

Femur

Knee and Condyles (the side protrusions of Femur).

Tibia, a very strong bone, that carries the weight of the body.

Fibula, the bone on the lateral (outside) side of the lower leg. It ends at the ankle bone which is easily seen.

LOCATE THE FOLLOWING LANDMARKS IN THE DRAWINGS ON THE RIGHT

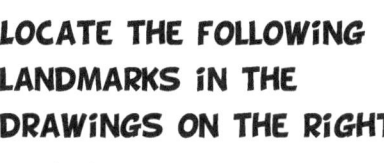

Tenth rib
Collar bone
Sternum
Knee
Femur condyles
End of Tibia
Pelvis (ASIS)
Greater trochanter

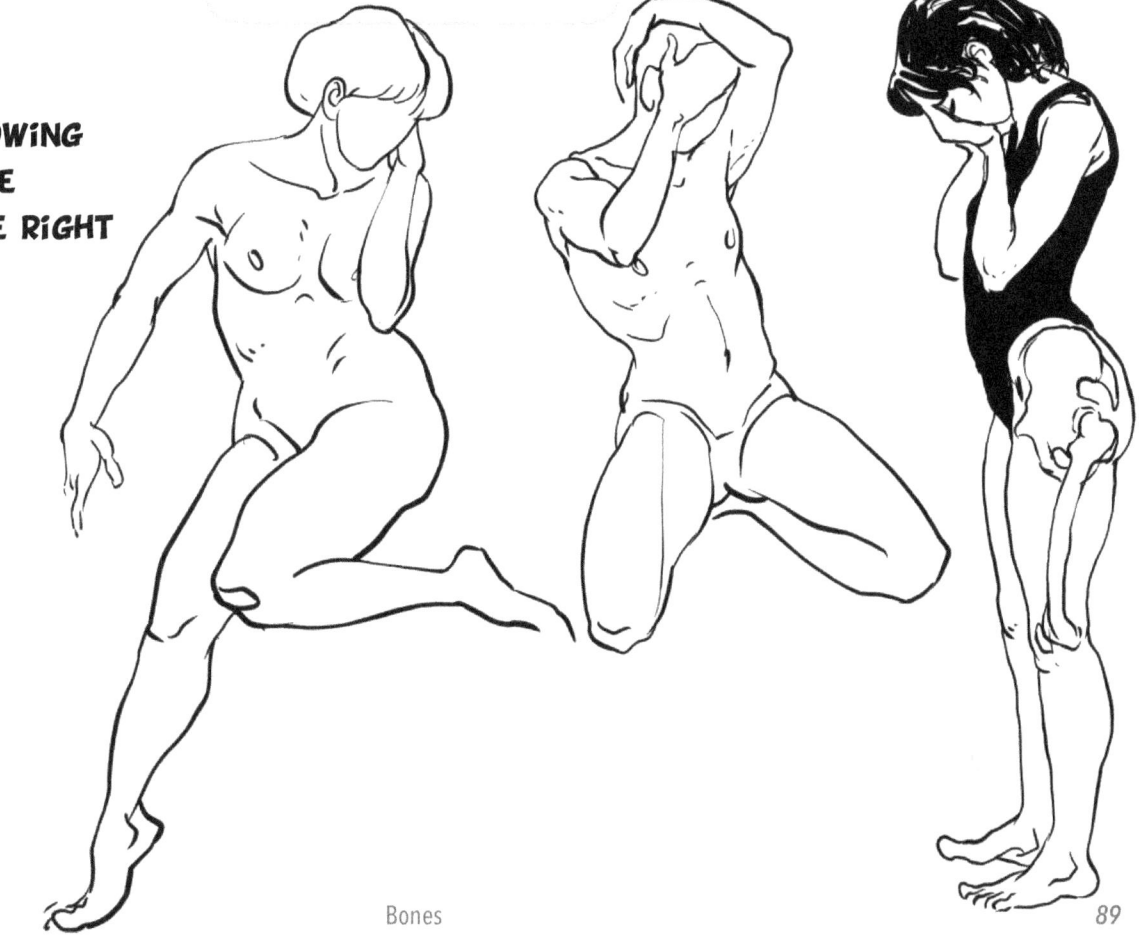

Umakanth Thumrugoti — Bones — 89

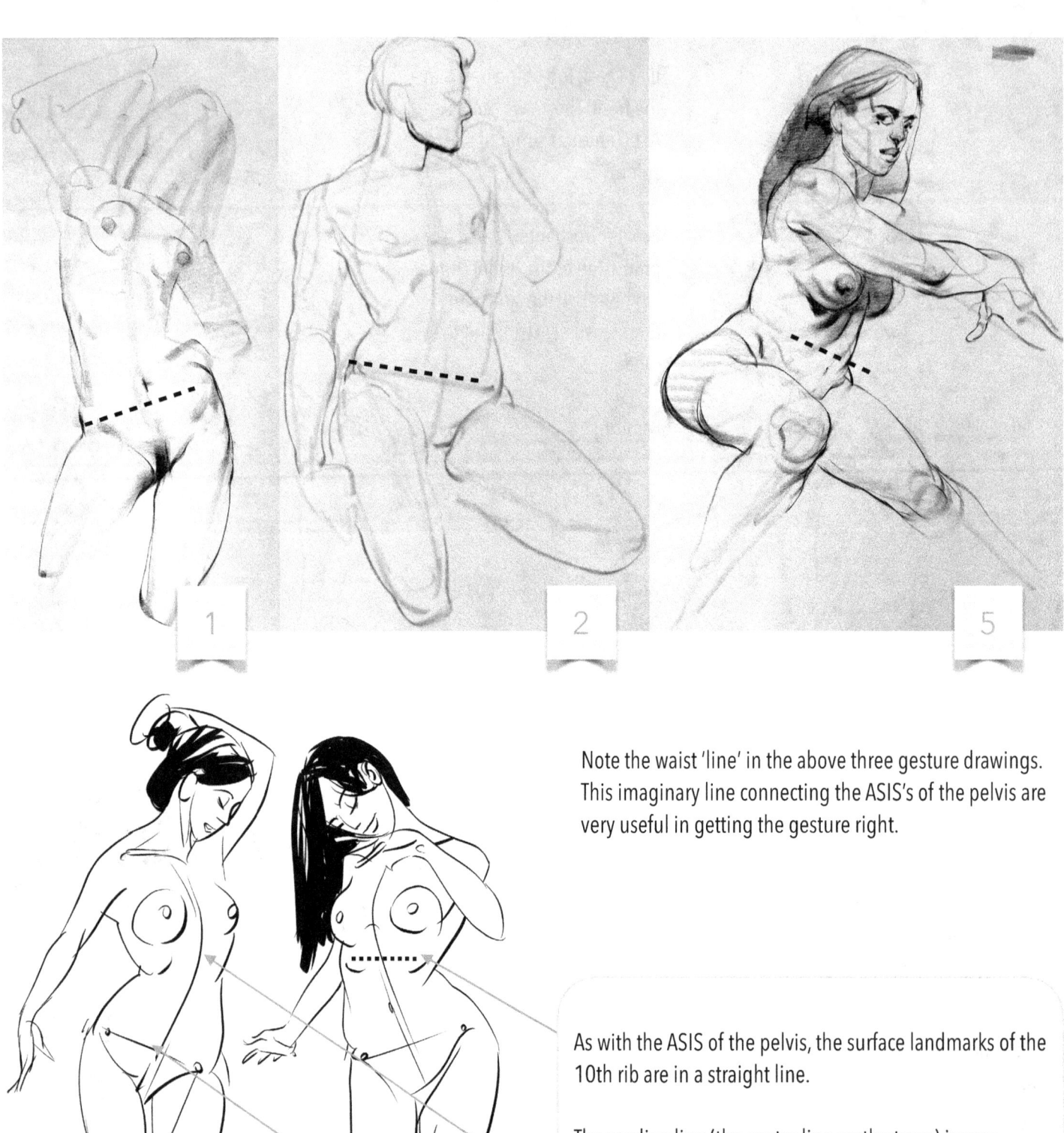

Note the waist 'line' in the above three gesture drawings. This imaginary line connecting the ASIS's of the pelvis are very useful in getting the gesture right.

As with the ASIS of the pelvis, the surface landmarks of the 10th rib are in a straight line.

The median line (the center line on the torso) is very useful in getting the gesture working. The median line in both drawings on the left favors one side at the top, then settles at the center of the body near the pelvic area clearly marking the gestural twist of the pose.

Notice the waist line.

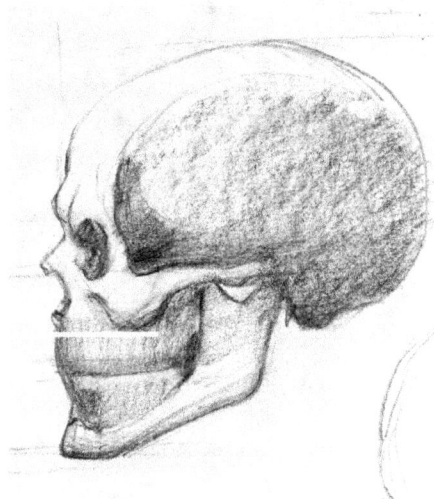
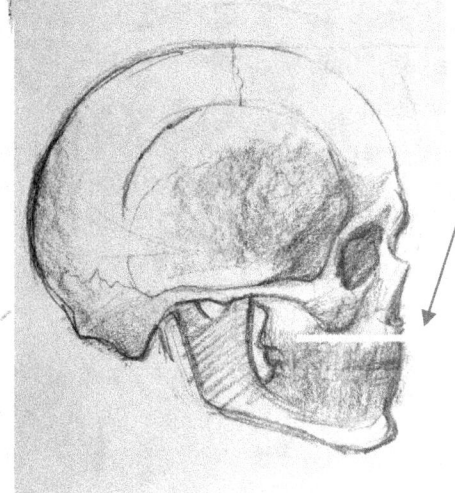

The slope of the cheek bone is visible and is in line with where the nose meets the upper lip.

However there are muscles overlaying the cheek bones, which often appear as a tone slightly below that cheekbone.

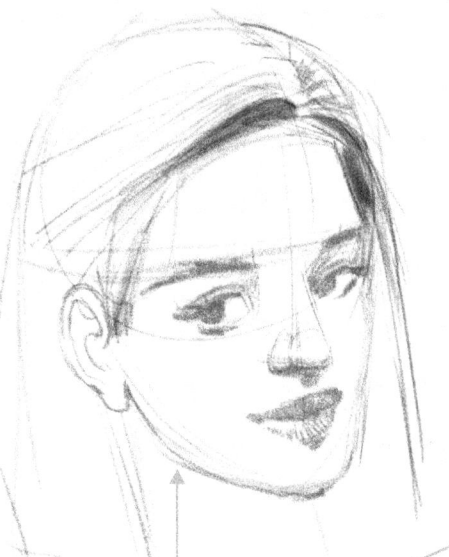
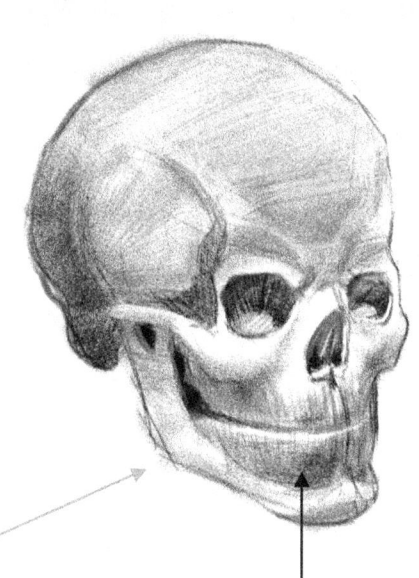
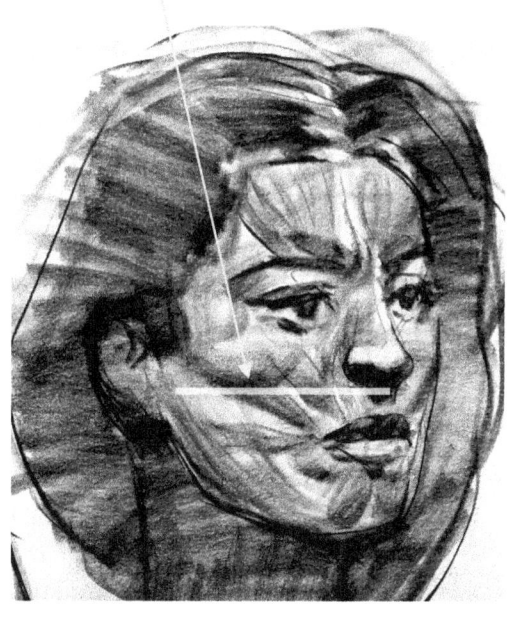

1. The jaw turns just a little below the lip line - I'm using the word 'lip line' to define the line where upper & lower lip come together. Draw that jaw turn where it belongs.
2. Notice the convex shape under the mouth - it curves 'out' like a drum. This is especially visible in profile.
3. The chin juts out. In profile view, if you draw a vertical line from the edge of the lips, it will touch the front of the chin.
4. The corners of the mouth wrap around the head - imagine drawing a line on a rounded surface like a tennis ball. This is especially important when drawing extreme tilts and angles of the head. Learning how to draw the skull will help you in the construction of the mouth.

WE WILL DISCUSS HEAD DRAWING IN DETAIL IN ITS OWN SECTION LATER IN THE BOOK.

The following are a few 'bony' landmarks on the body. Look for them on the model and if you see them, draw them. Perhaps 20 may be a few too many - start with, say, five landmarks, then keep adding the rest as you get more drawing mileage.

1. End of cervical vertebrae, seventh bone, on the back of the neck
2. Scapula (shoulder blade)
3. Acromion process (process means lever) on the shoulder
4. Clavicle (collar bone)
5. Sternum (breast bone)
6. Ribcage (especially, the 10th rib)
7. Backbone
8. Humerus condyles (the bumps on either side of the elbow)
9. Head of Ulna (elbow)
10. End of Ulna (bump on the wrist on the pinky finger side)
11. End of Radius (bump on the wrist on the thumb side)
12. Iliac crest, especially the on the front where you see ASIS (anterior superior iliac spine) - see the notation on the drawing
13. We may see PSIS (posterior superior iliac spine)
14. Greater trochanter (the bump on the side of the leg - this is the upper part of the Femur, thigh bone)
15. Condyles of the femur (boney protrusion on the sides of the knee)
16. Patella (knee)
17. Tibia (shin part of the lower leg)
18. Head of Fibula (look at the drawing on the right)
19. End of Tibia & Fibula (ankle)
20. Calcaneus (heel)

Umakanth Thumrugoti

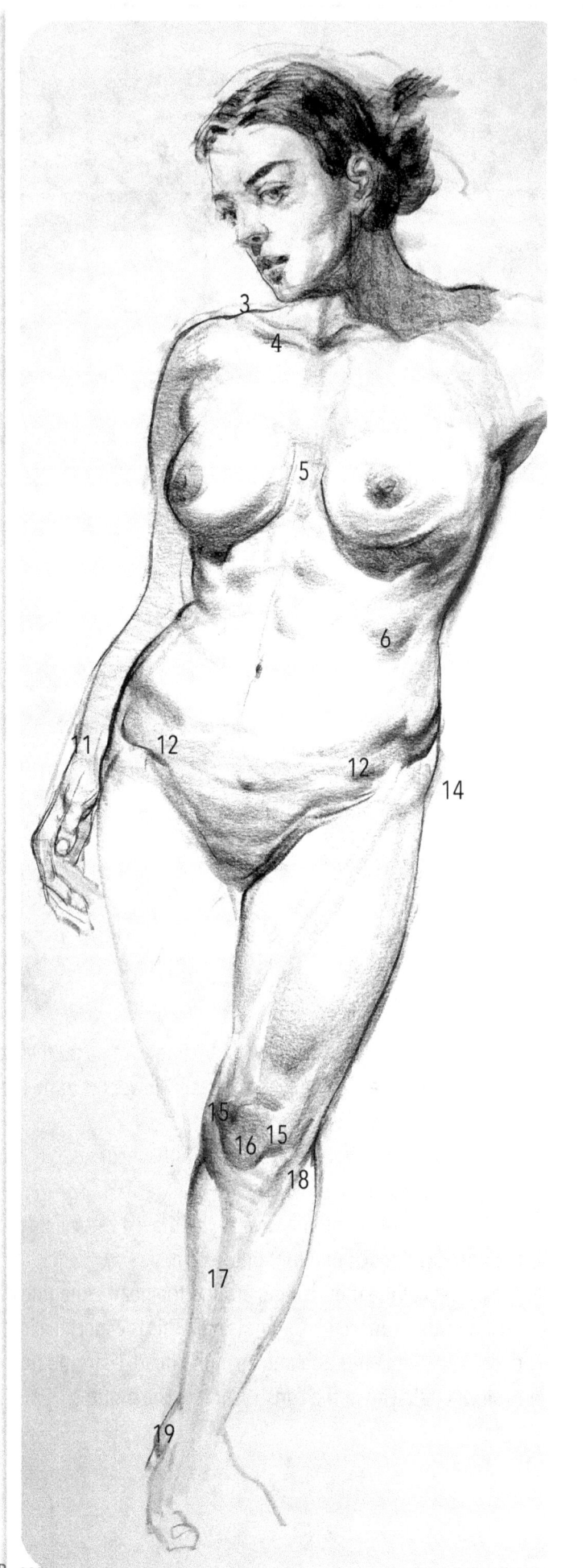

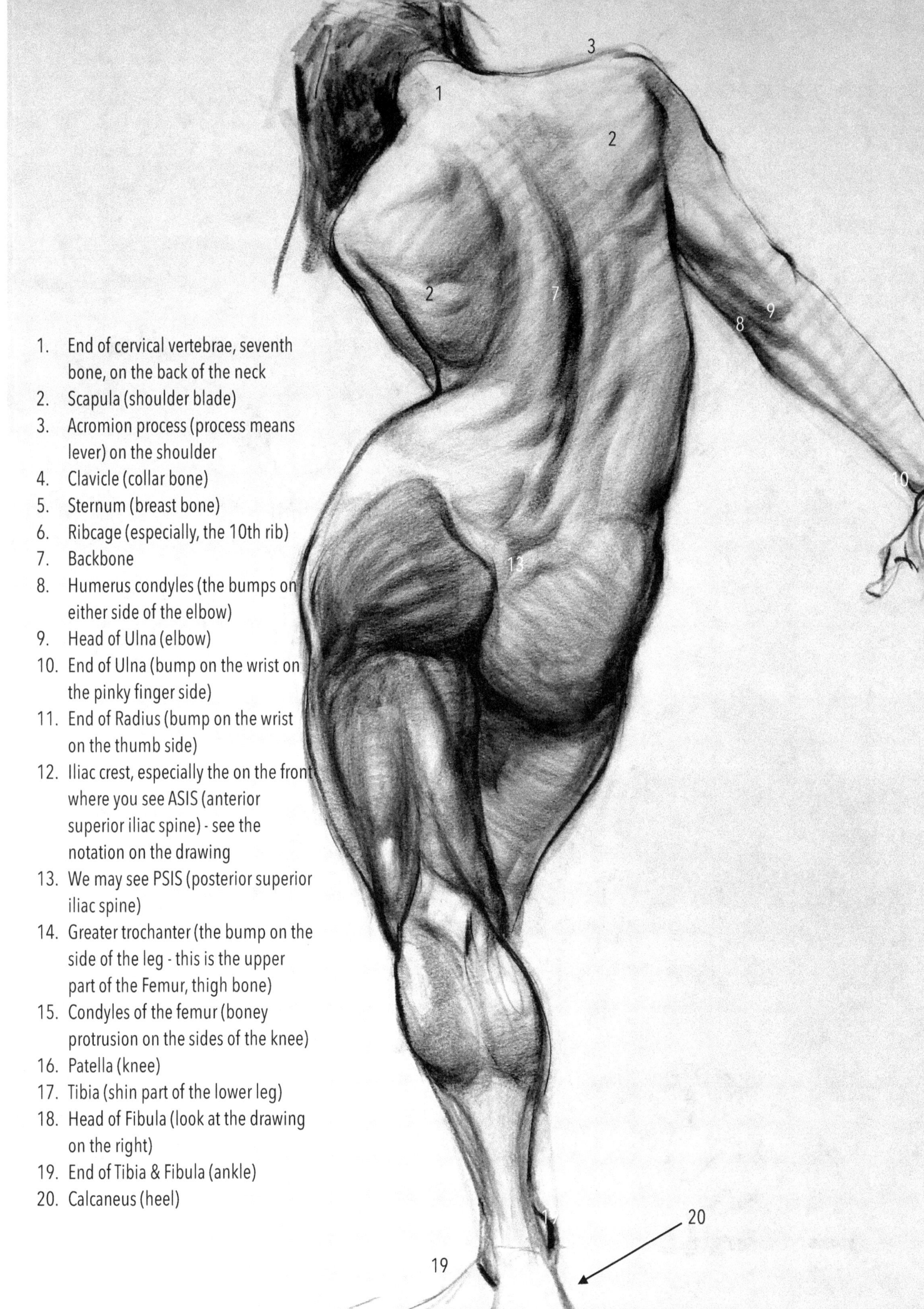

1. End of cervical vertebrae, seventh bone, on the back of the neck
2. Scapula (shoulder blade)
3. Acromion process (process means lever) on the shoulder
4. Clavicle (collar bone)
5. Sternum (breast bone)
6. Ribcage (especially, the 10th rib)
7. Backbone
8. Humerus condyles (the bumps on either side of the elbow)
9. Head of Ulna (elbow)
10. End of Ulna (bump on the wrist on the pinky finger side)
11. End of Radius (bump on the wrist on the thumb side)
12. Iliac crest, especially the on the front where you see ASIS (anterior superior iliac spine) - see the notation on the drawing
13. We may see PSIS (posterior superior iliac spine)
14. Greater trochanter (the bump on the side of the leg - this is the upper part of the Femur, thigh bone)
15. Condyles of the femur (boney protrusion on the sides of the knee)
16. Patella (knee)
17. Tibia (shin part of the lower leg)
18. Head of Fibula (look at the drawing on the right)
19. End of Tibia & Fibula (ankle)
20. Calcaneus (heel)

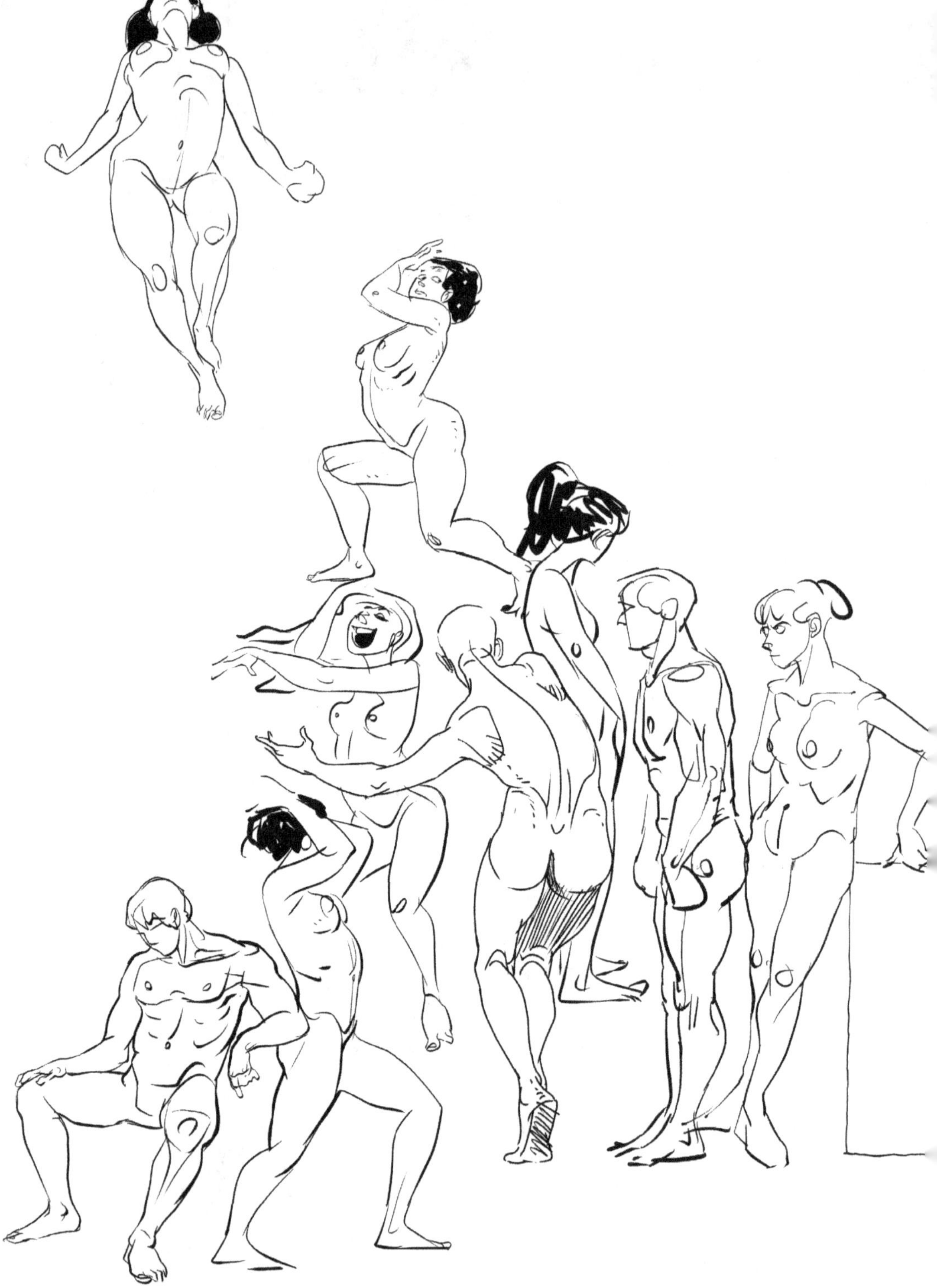

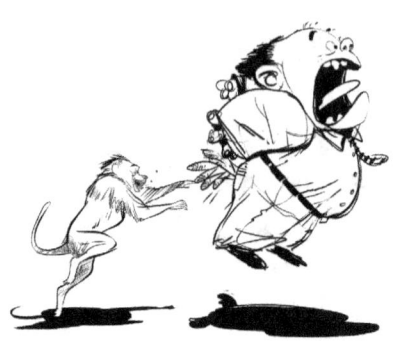

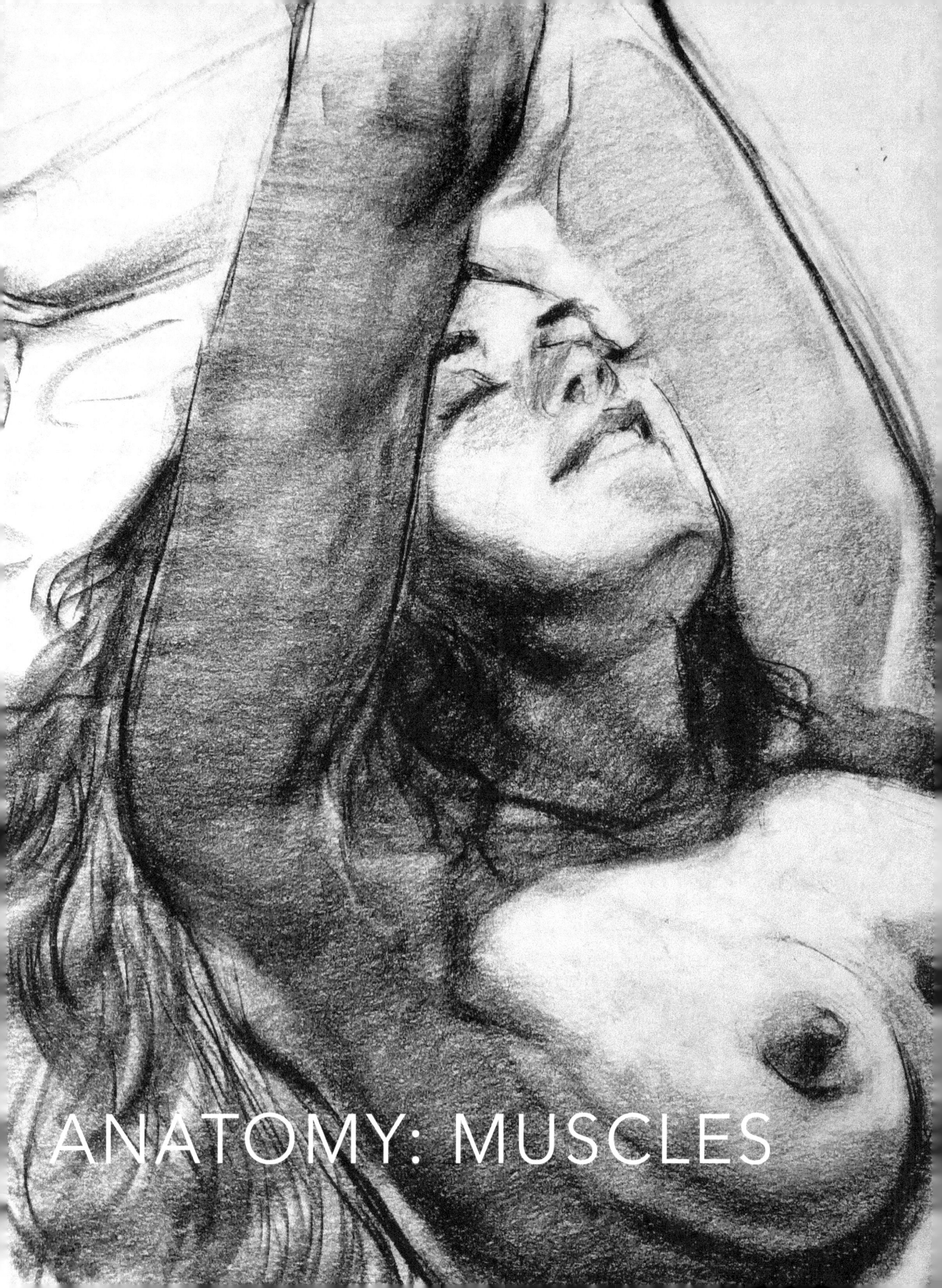
ANATOMY: MUSCLES

THE BEST WAY TO LEARN MUSCULAR ANATOMY IS TO UNDERSTAND THEIR FUNCTION, WHAT MUSCLES ACTUALLY DO.

MUSCLES CAN ONLY "PULL." THEY DON'T WORK LIKE A SPRING BUT LIKE A ROPE. YOU CAN PULL ON A ROPE TIED TO AN OBJECT TO DRAG IT TOWARD YOU. BUT YOU CAN'T PUSH THE OBJECT AWAY BY RELEASING MORE ROPE.

WHAT THIS MEANS IS THAT FOR EACH GROUP OF MUSCLES THAT DOES A SPECIFIC TASK (BICEPS : BEND THE ARM AT THE ELBOW), THERE HAS TO BE A GROUP OF MUSCLES THAT DOES THE OPPOSITE ACTION (TRICEPS: STRAIGHTEN THE ARM AT THE ELBOW).

WE WILL DISCUSS MUSCLES FROM THE TOP DOWN - FROM THE NECK MUSCLES TO THE LEG MUSCLES.

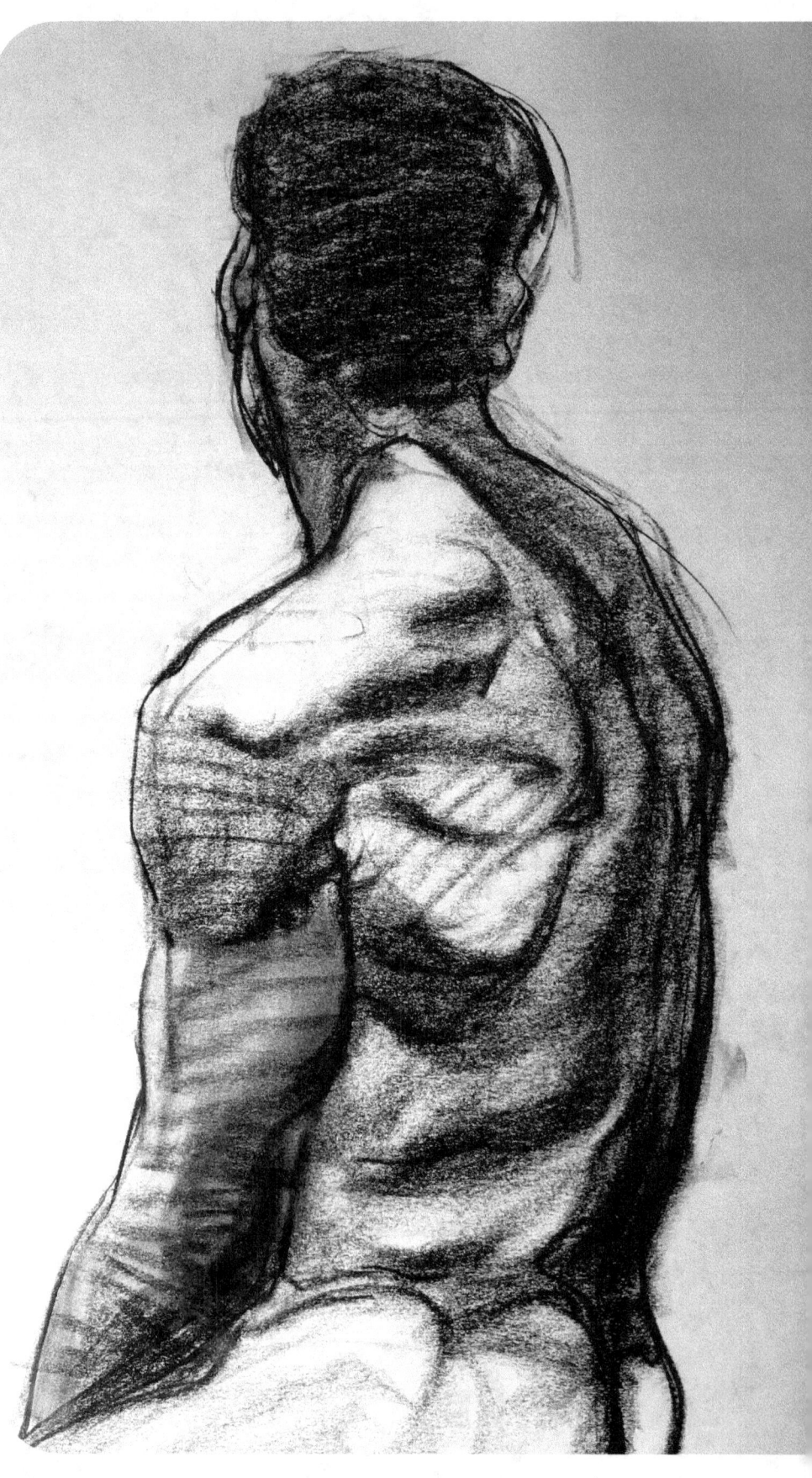

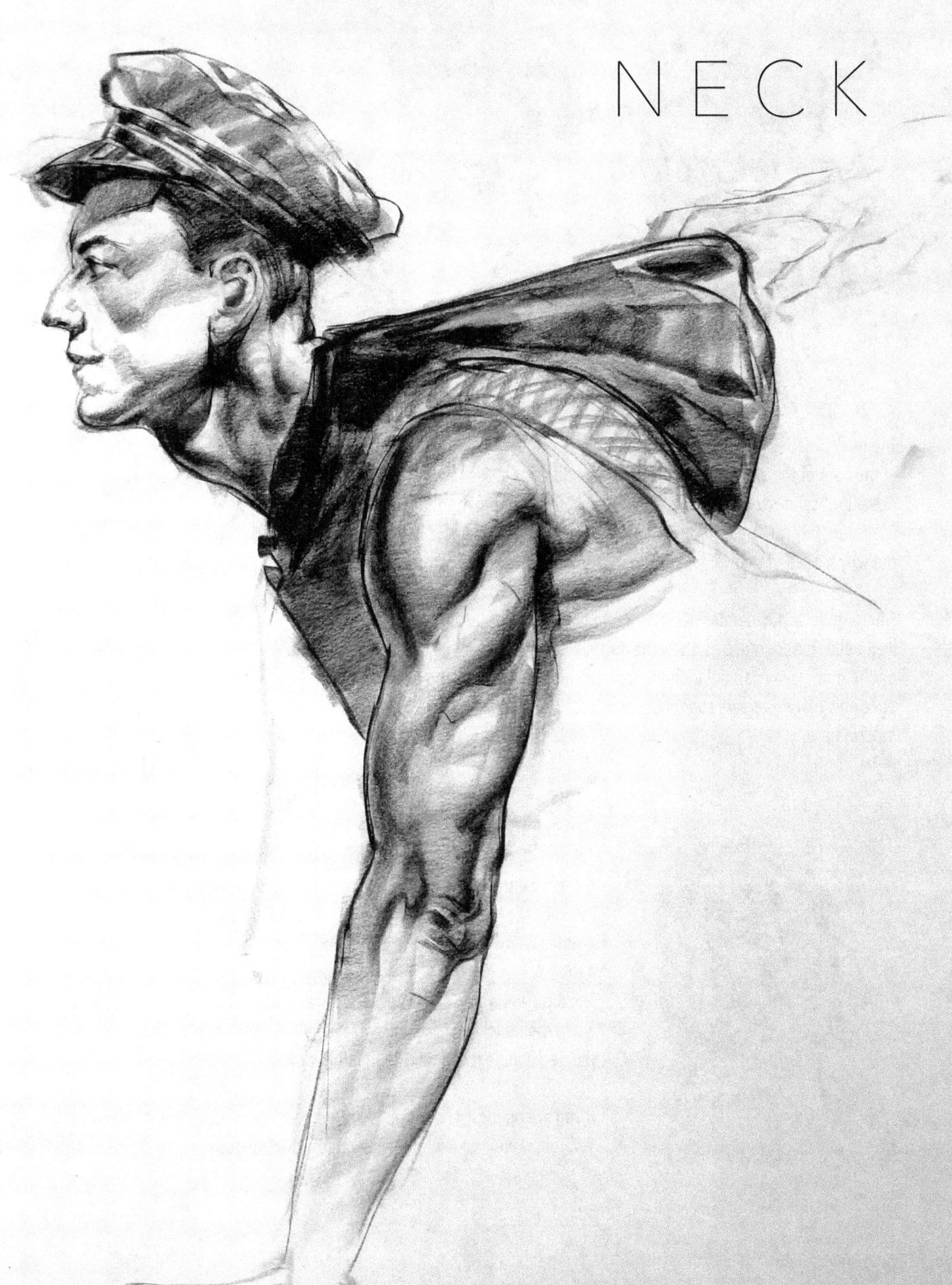

NECK

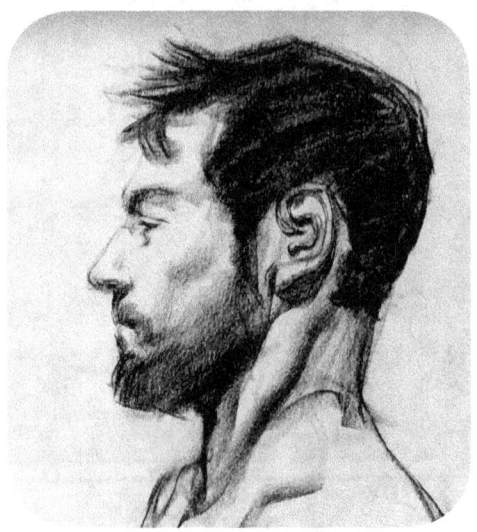 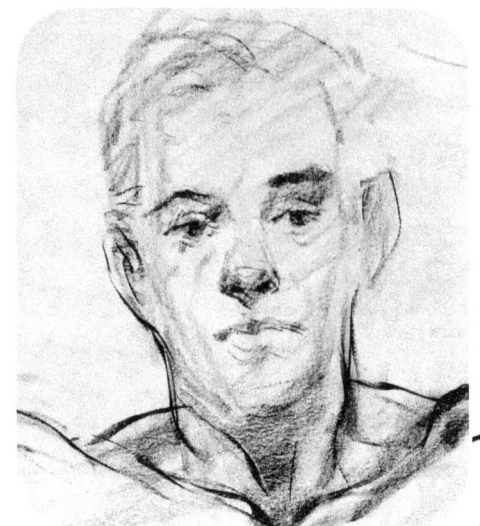 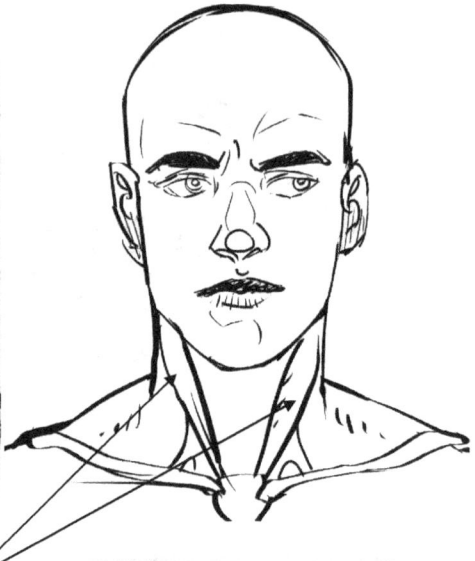

The neck muscles (one on each side of the head) start from a little bump (mastoid) at the back of the skull right behind the ear and ends at the pit of the neck. Actually, it connects to the top of the breast bone (sternum) and the collar bone (clavicle). This muscle's medical name is sternocleidomastoid (SCM) - you figure out why it's called that.

Often models with slender necks, when their head is not turned, do not show a well defined neck muscles. Draw the muscle only if you see one or both of them on the model. Pay particular attention to the head shadow on the neck. *Most lighting situations create shadows on the neck that can help define the neck's musculature.*

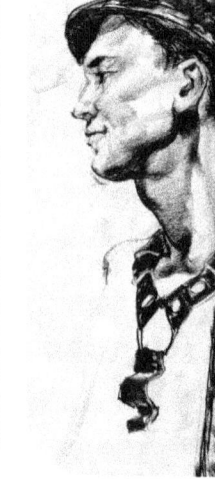

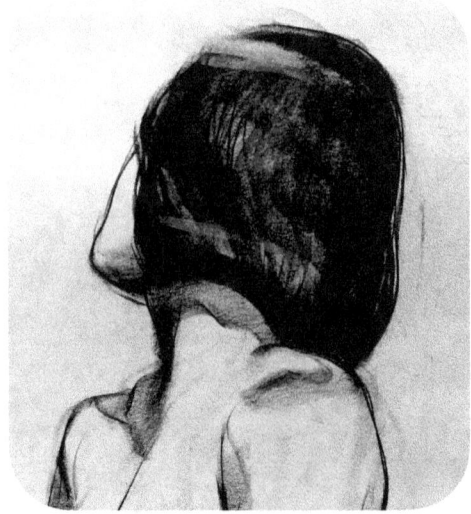

The function of the neck muscles is to turn the head - when the left side neck muscle contracts, the head turns right and vice-versa. If both neck muscles contract, the head tilts down. When the head is turned, neck muscle is more visible.

The top 7 vertebrae of the backbone are contained in the neck. In fact, often when the head is bent down, you can feel/see the seventh vertebra in the back of the neck where it connects to the upper torso.

If you are up for it, check out two more neck muscles: splenius capitis and levator scapuli, for example, in a good anatomy book.

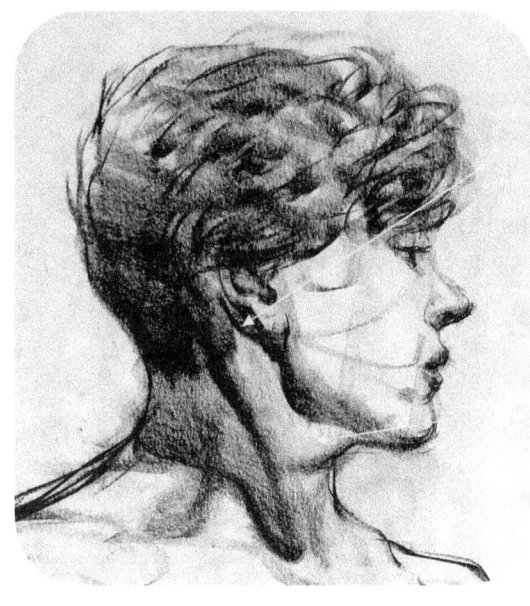

The neck muscle connects to the skull, right behind the ear. Use the lower third of the ear for your neck starting point.

Throat muscles are complex - let's ignore their details; just focus on the fact that they sit between the neck muscles. If you see throat tonal details, add them to your drawing. Most necks are fairly simple tubes with tonal shadows defining the neck muscles. Draw the tube and then add muscle definition if you see it.

The neck connects to the head just behind the ears in the back, and below the chin in the front. This means the neck starts at a higher point in the back compared to the front. There is a reason why shirt collars slope down to the front.

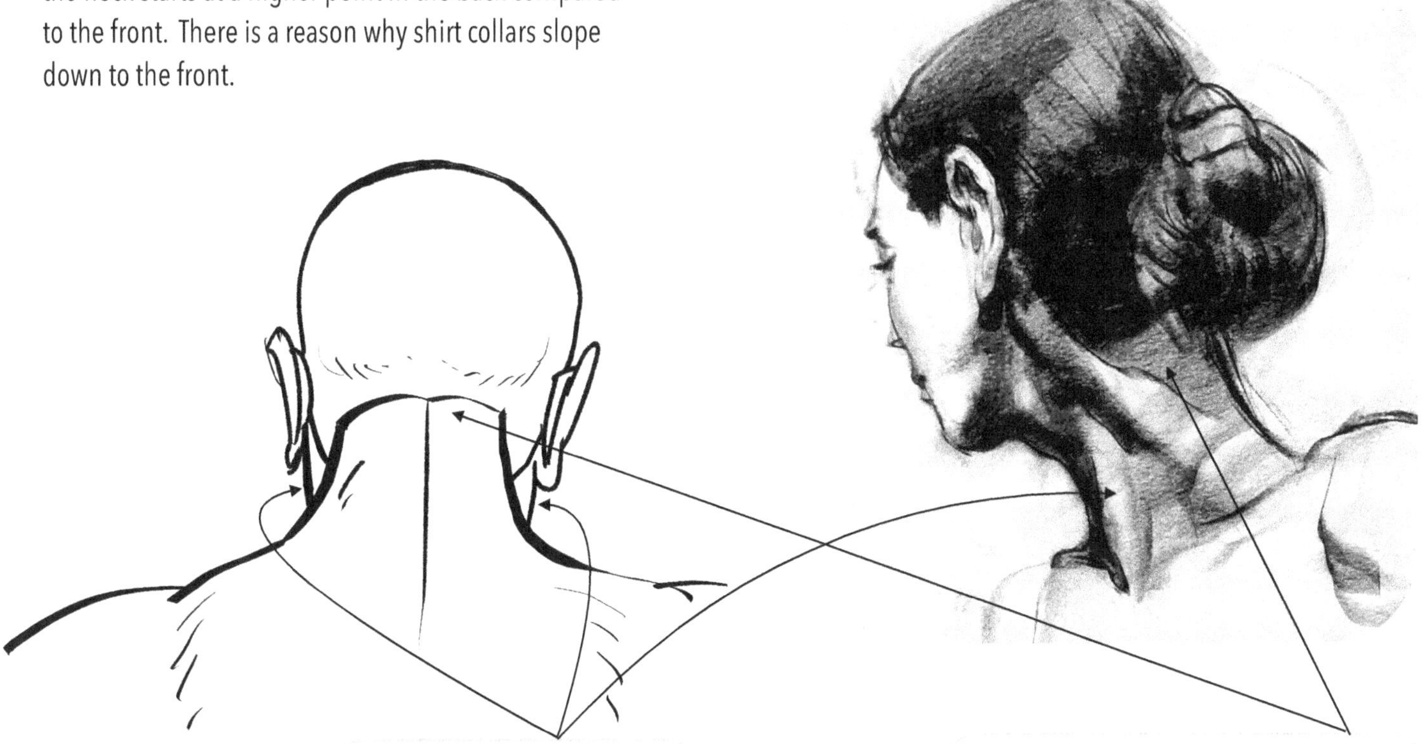

These are the neck muscles

At the back of the skull, the top of the trapezius muscle connects to the skull

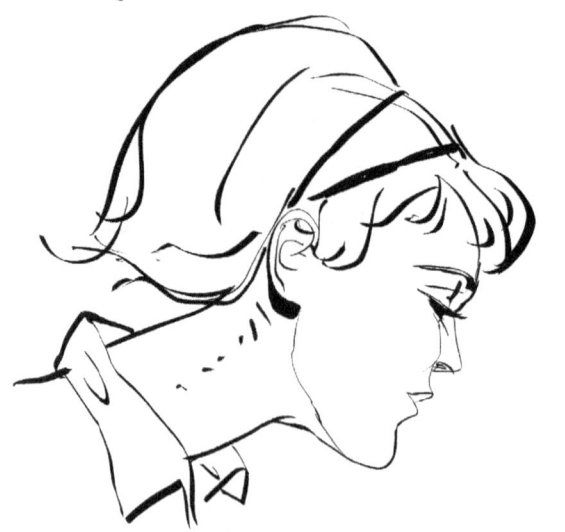

Is the neck too wide or too narrow in your drawing? Just remember that the neck starts from behind the ears; that should help you figure out the width of the neck if the model is facing you. It's a tube of uniform diameter that opens up a little when it connects to torso.

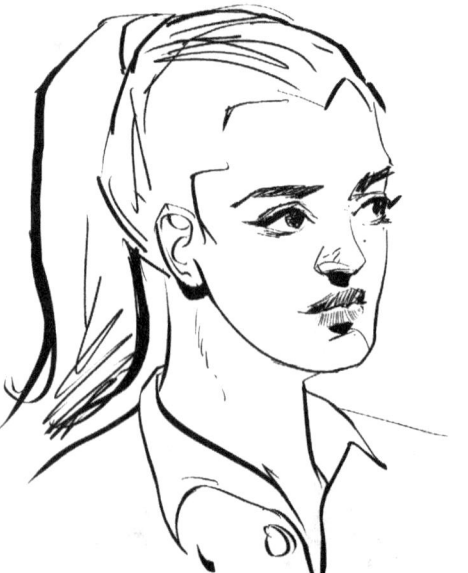

In the digital drawings on the left, see how simple the neck is - a tube with a hint of neck muscle definition. You can also look at the many charcoal drawings throughout this book for neck and throat definition at various angles.

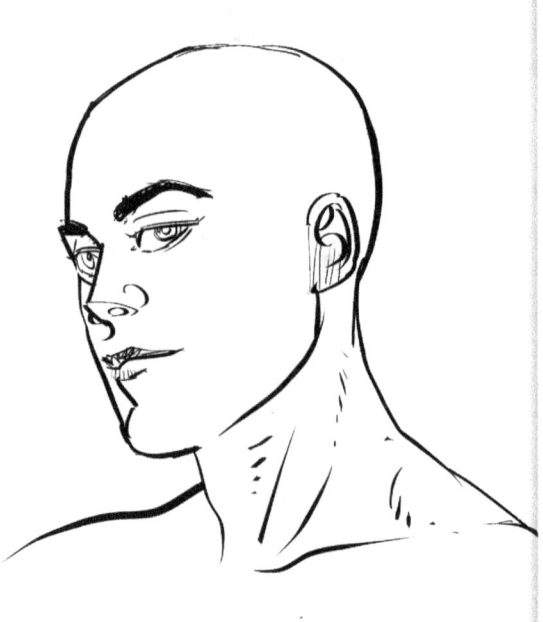

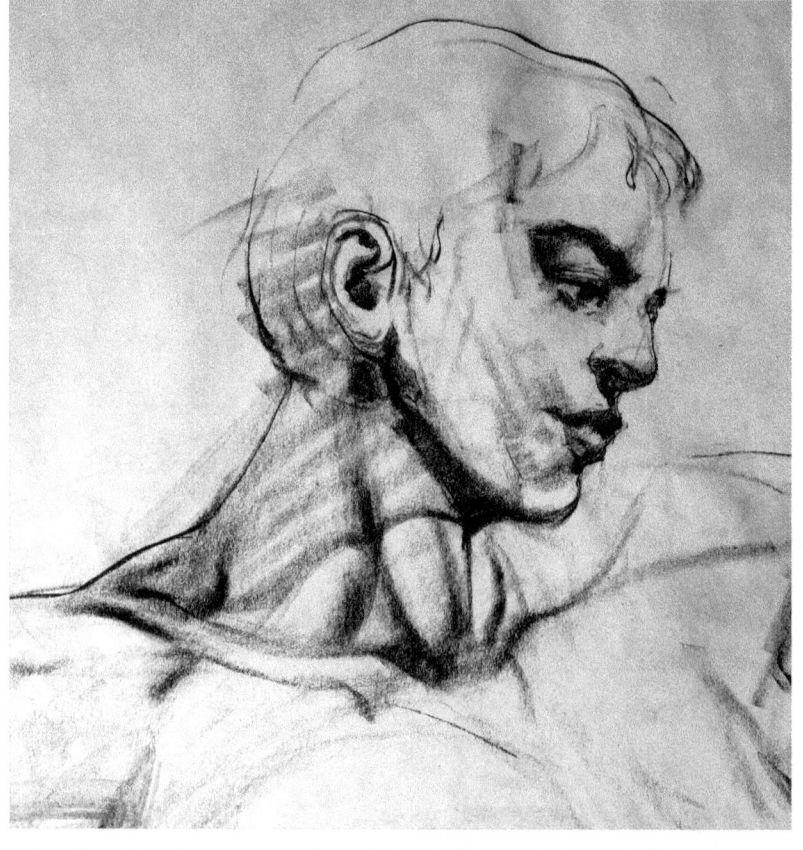

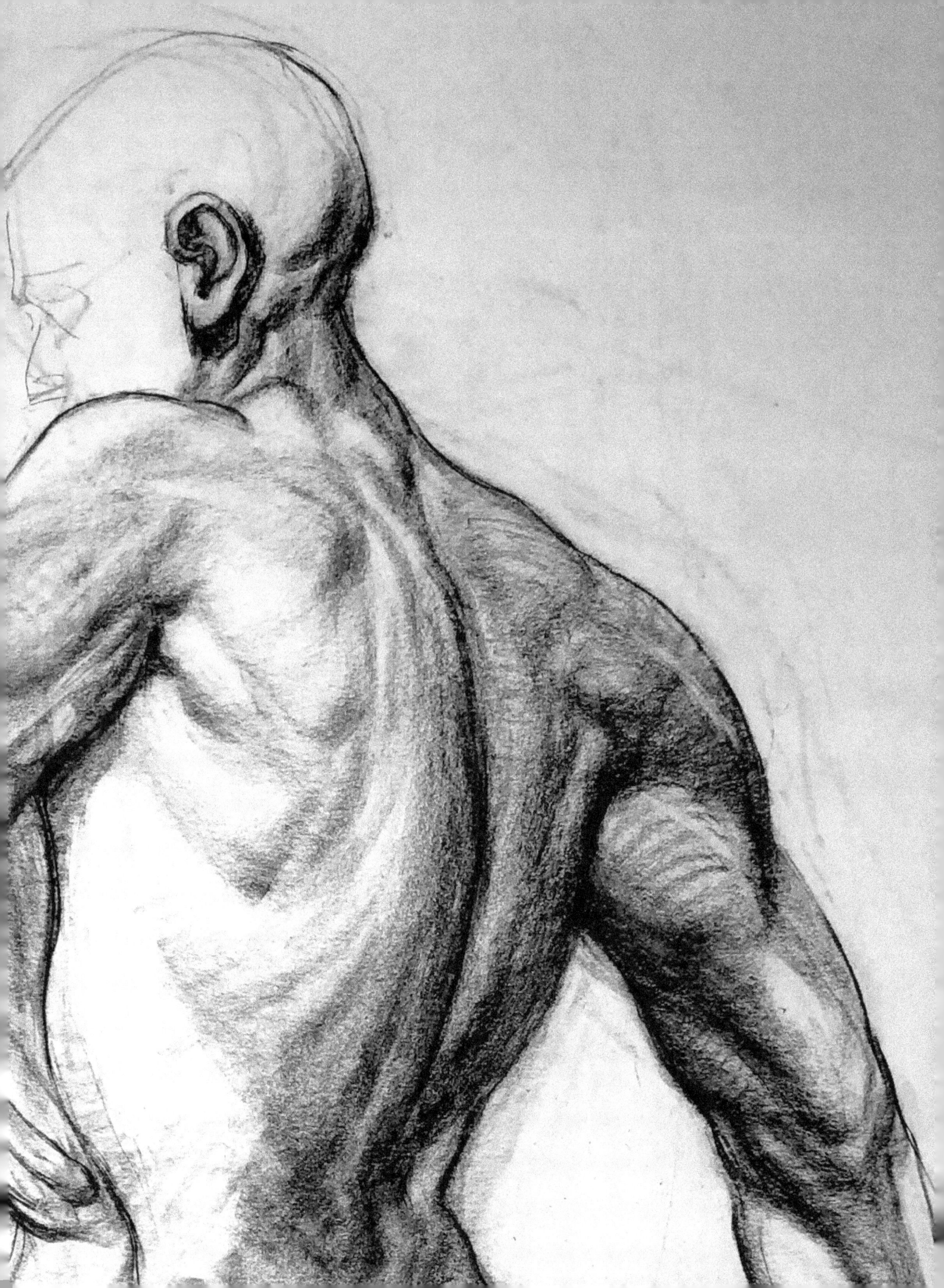

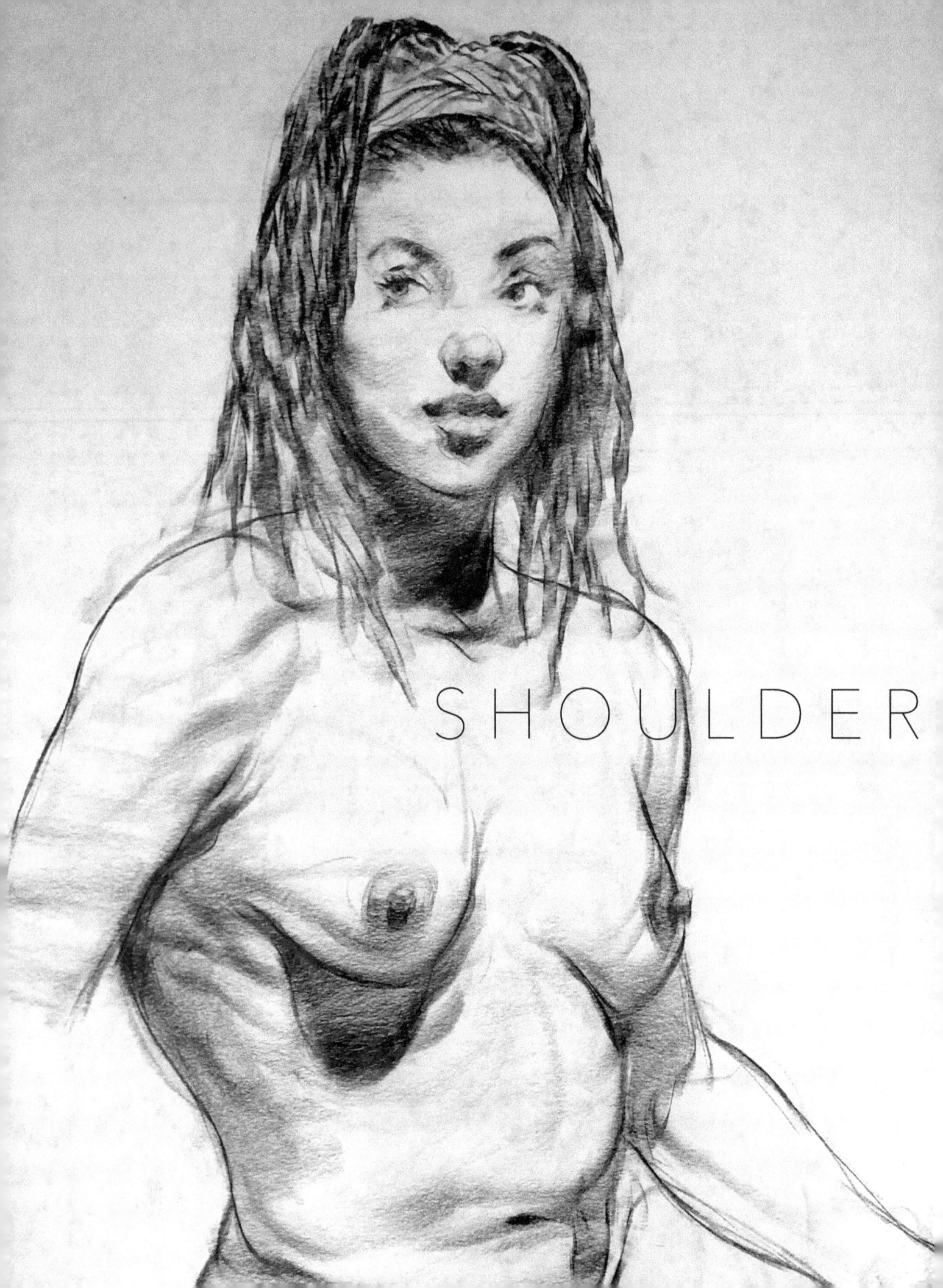

SHOULDER

I'd classify studying musculoskeletal anatomy under "Top 10 things not to do on a beautiful summer day," but to achieve proficiency in life drawing, I believe you will have to learn surface anatomy.

To make it a little less painful than, say, getting tested on Latin declension (my apologies to Latin instructors), I added a few bits of information that might make the discussion interesting.

The upper torso muscles we are interested in are listed below. Perhaps you can identify some of them in the drawing? I gave you a few hints.

- Trapezius (shrugging muscle)
- Deltoid (shoulder muscle)
- Infraspinatus (shoulder blade muscle)
- Teres major(round shoulder blade muscle)
- Teres minor
- Pectoralis major (we will discuss this later)

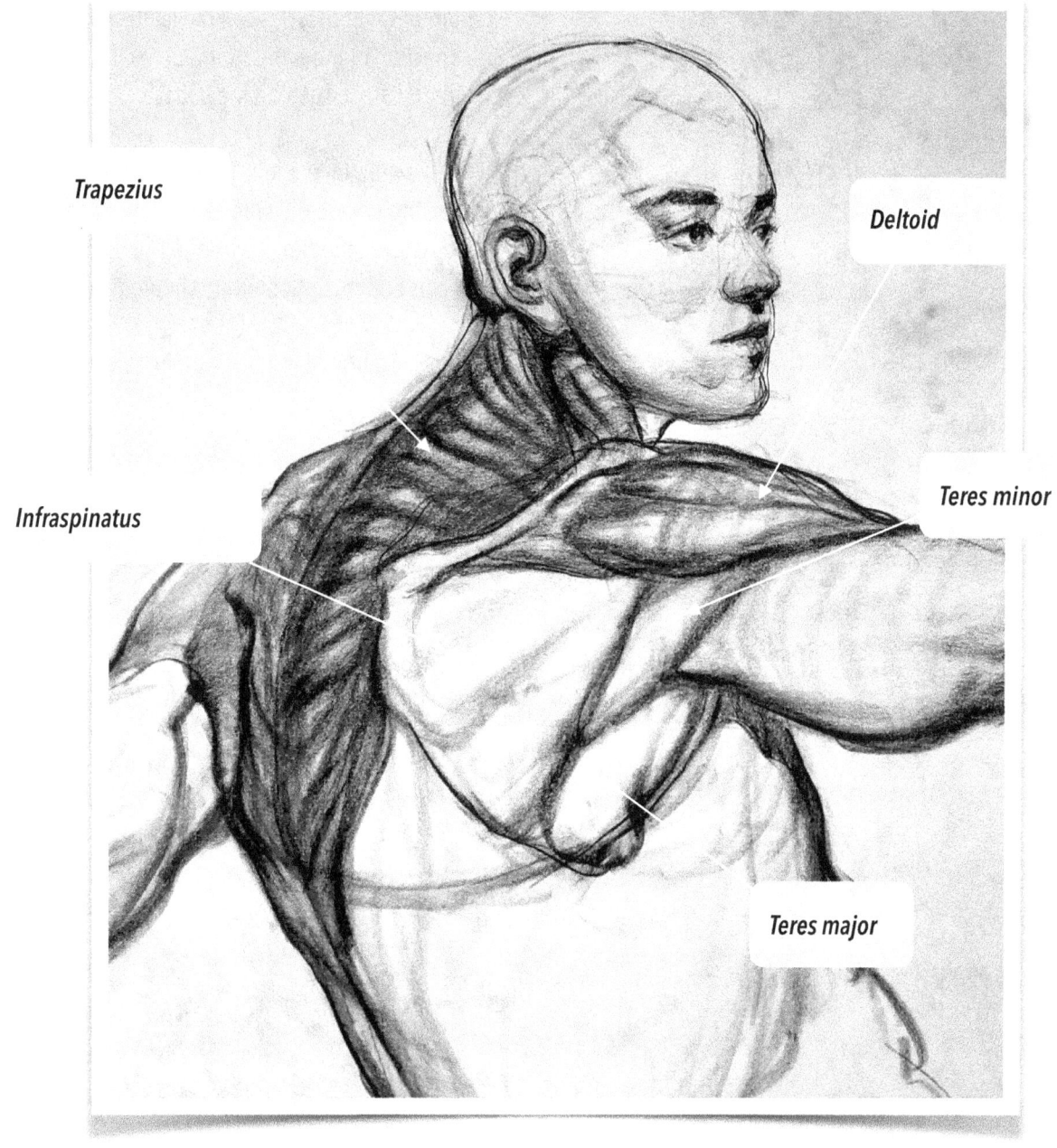

The trapezius (the shrugging muscle) is a great muscle - it performs more functions than simply helping us shrug. It helps us raise our arms above our heads, for example. Swimmers have a strong Trapezius muscle.

If you ever watched a film when sitting in the first row and experienced a pain in your neck the next day, it's because you stressed your trapezius. This muscle starts at the back of the skull, connects to the collar bone in the front, spine of the scapula, and finally to the vertebra down the spine. Its shape is a trapezium (see your high school math book - not the Latin book) and has four sides.

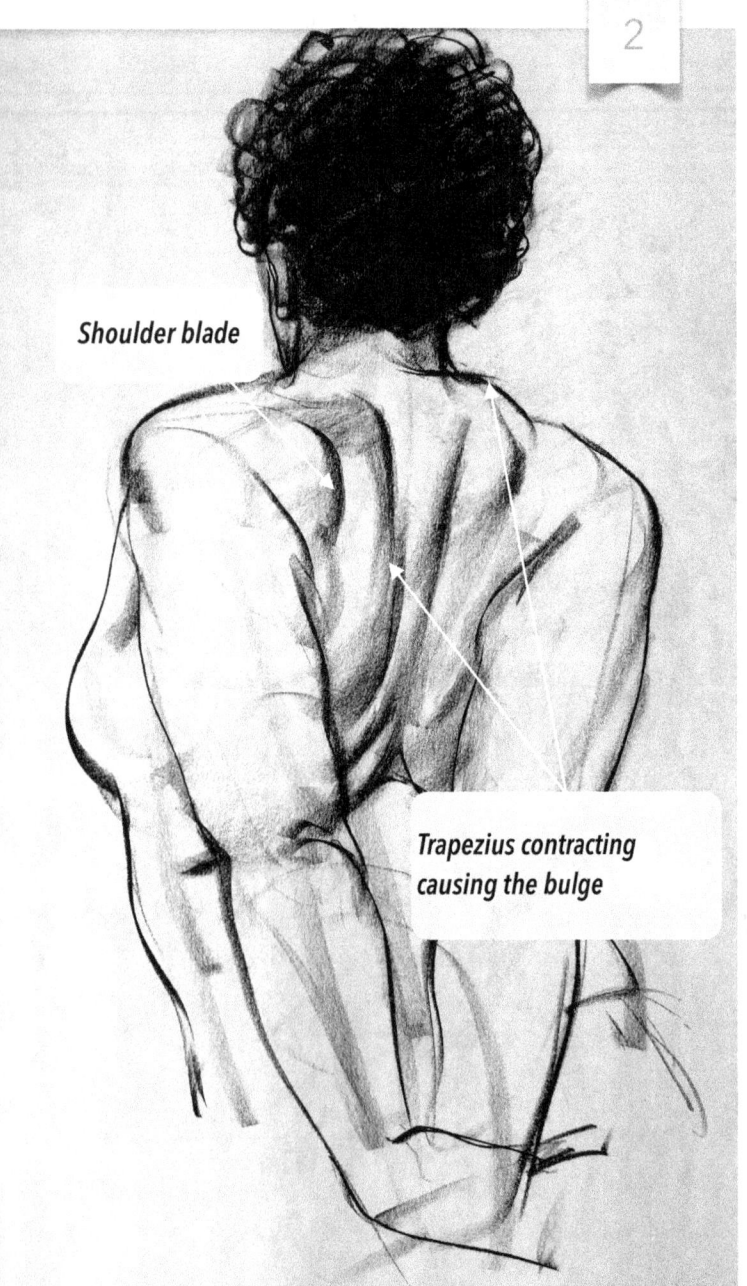

Shoulder blade

Trapezius contracting causing the bulge

Remember that muscles can only pull. And they pull in the direction of the fibers. Sometimes the definition of the fibers can be seen on the surface.

In the drawing on the left, the trapezius muscle is contracting toward the spine - which pulls the shoulder blades closer together. Hence the two lines, one for the trapezius and the other for the shoulder blade.

Do you see a hint of trapezius in the drawing below?

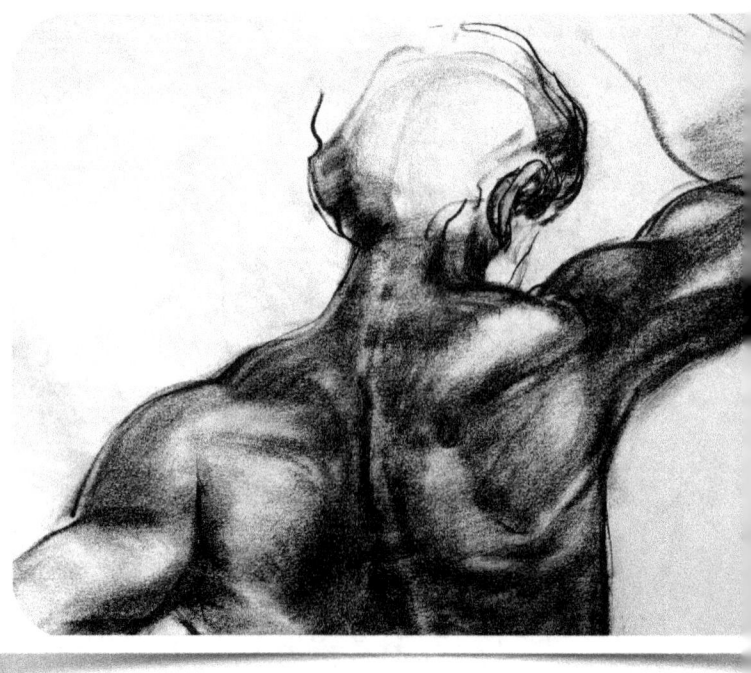

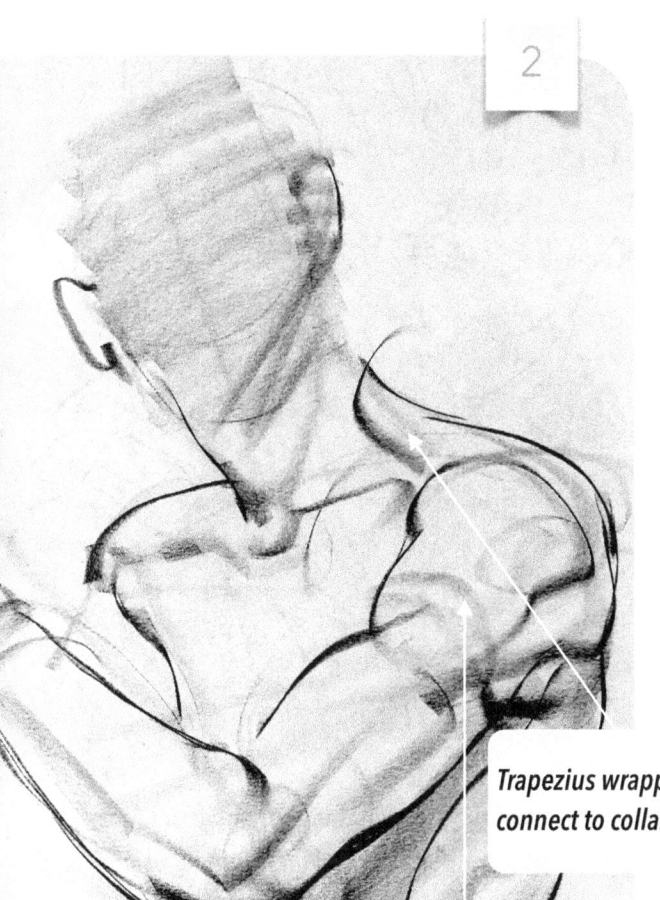

Learning the proportions, connections, function, and forms of the muscle makes for more dynamic drawings. (Is that too much to ask?)

The two-minute drawing on the left hints at the deltoid and the trapezius. The deltoid covers almost one half of the upper arm (proportion). When the arm is raised over the head, the trapezius bulges between the shoulder and the neck (function). The deltoid is triangular in shape (form). The trapezius connects to the back of the skull, one third of the collar bone in the front, the entire length of the spine of the shoulder blade, and about the length of the ribcage on the backbone (connection).

Trapezius wrapping over to connect to collar bone

Deltoid (shoulder muscle)

The chest muscles, pectoralis major, are the 'throwing' muscles. There are three connections for this muscle. The collar bone (clavicle) and the entire length of the breast bone (sternum) are fixed connections. The third and 'mobile' connection is to the upper arm bone (humerus).

When you throw things at your latin instructor because you failed your declension test, you are using the chest muscle. What happens when this muscle contracts at the sternum (*origin* of the chest muscle)?

Please don't throw things at your Latin instructor.

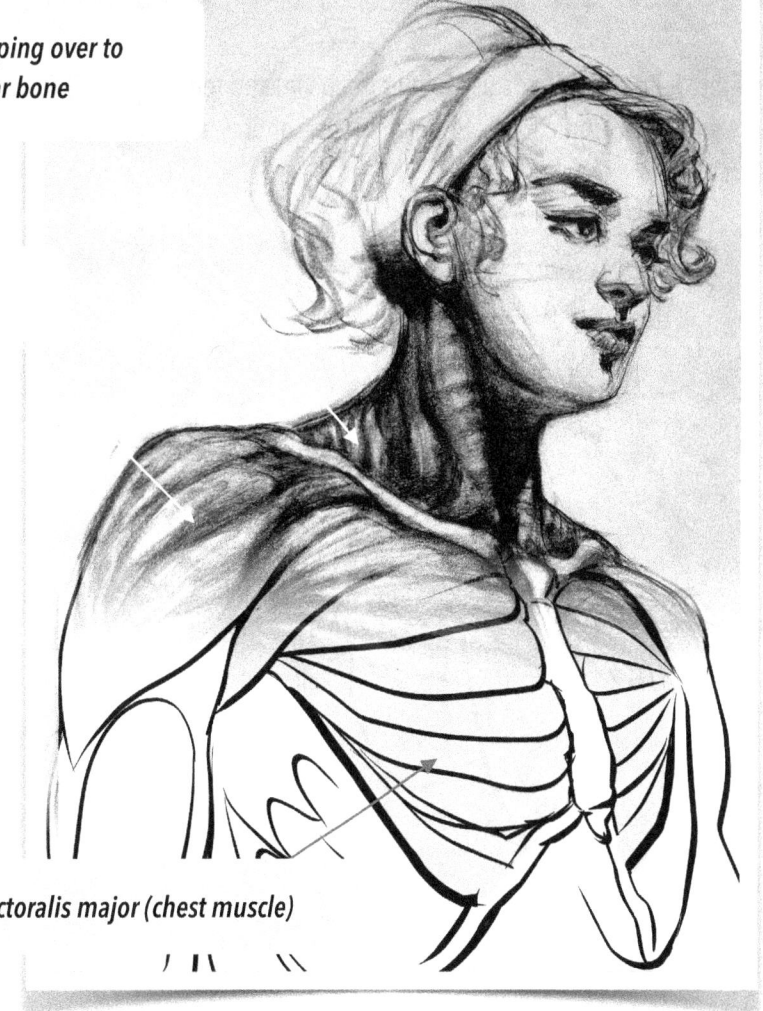

Pectoralis major (chest muscle)

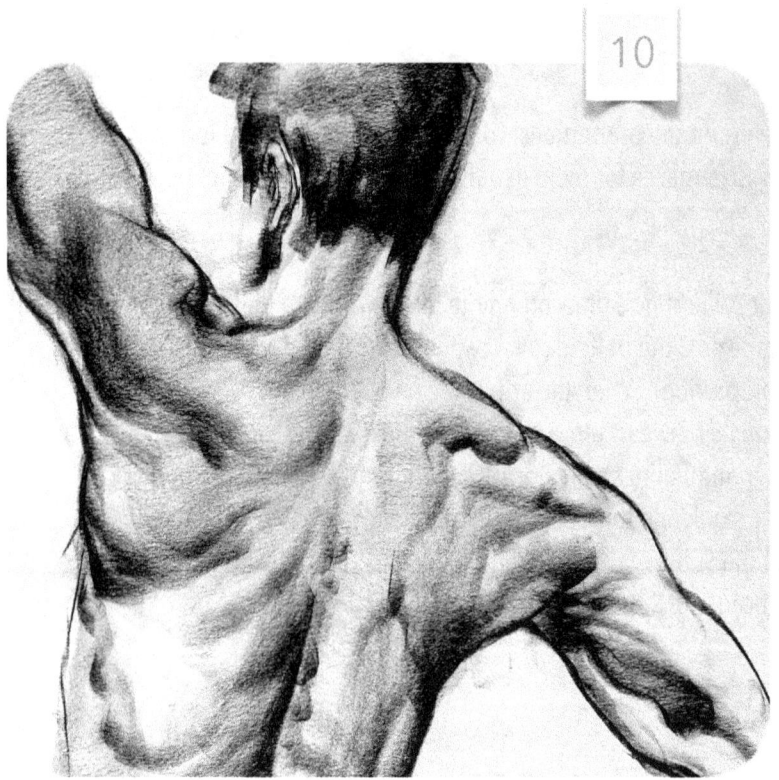
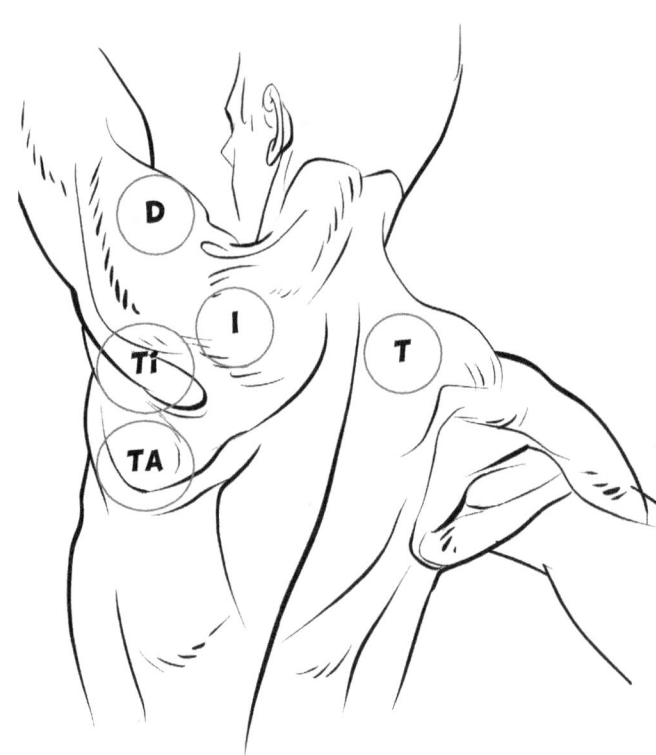

See the deltoid(D), trapezius(T), teres major(Ta) and teres minor(Ti), infraspinatus(I), and the shoulder blade. Start your life drawings with simple forms (tapered tubes, spheres, etc). Add details after you get your proportions working. Limit tonal values to three or four.

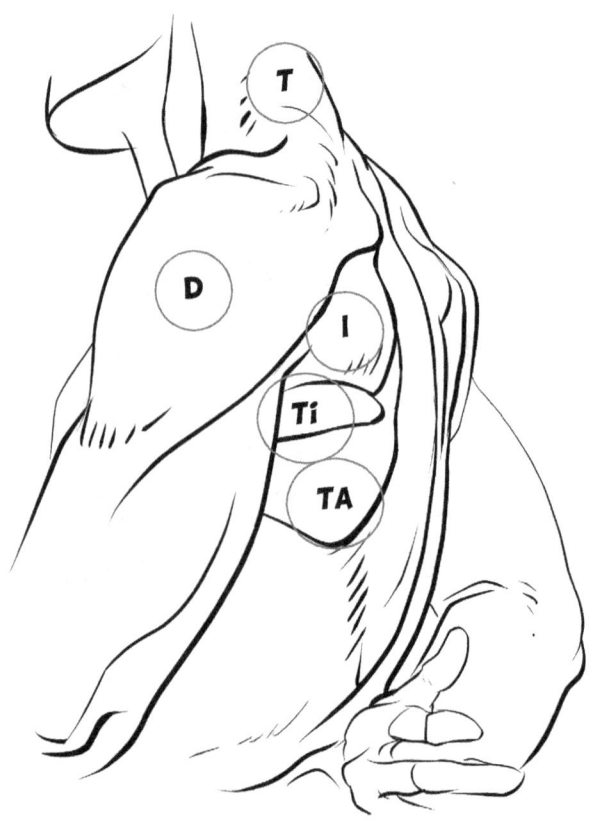
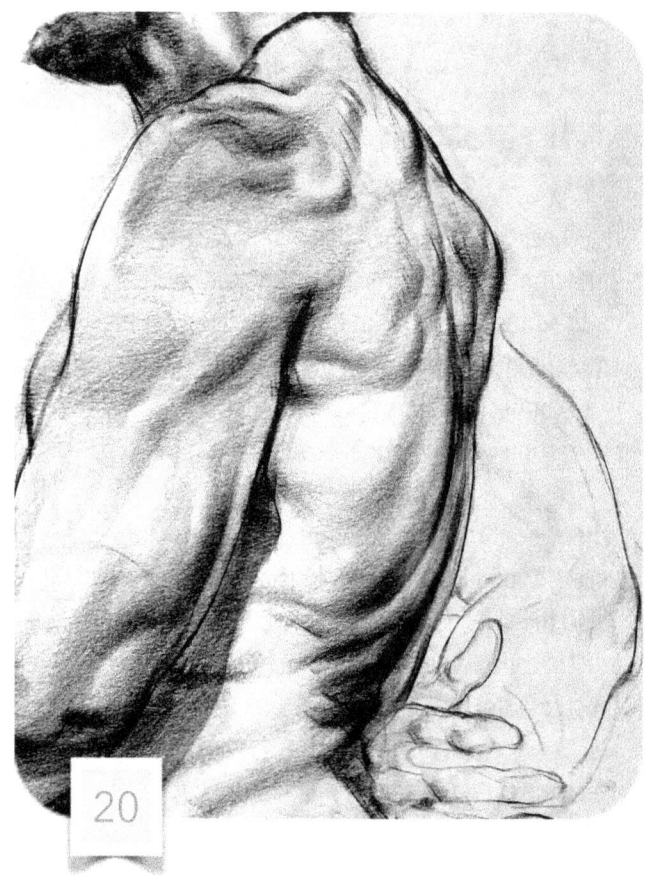

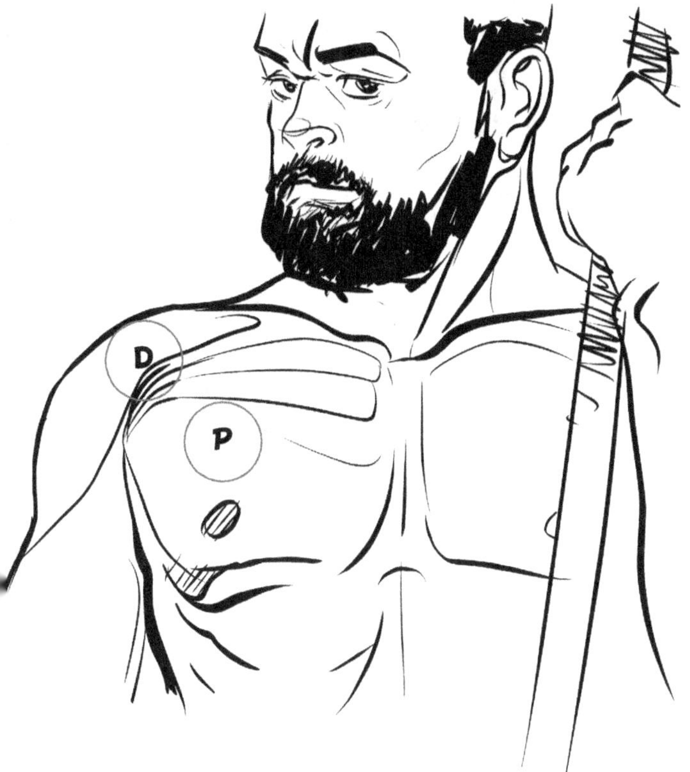

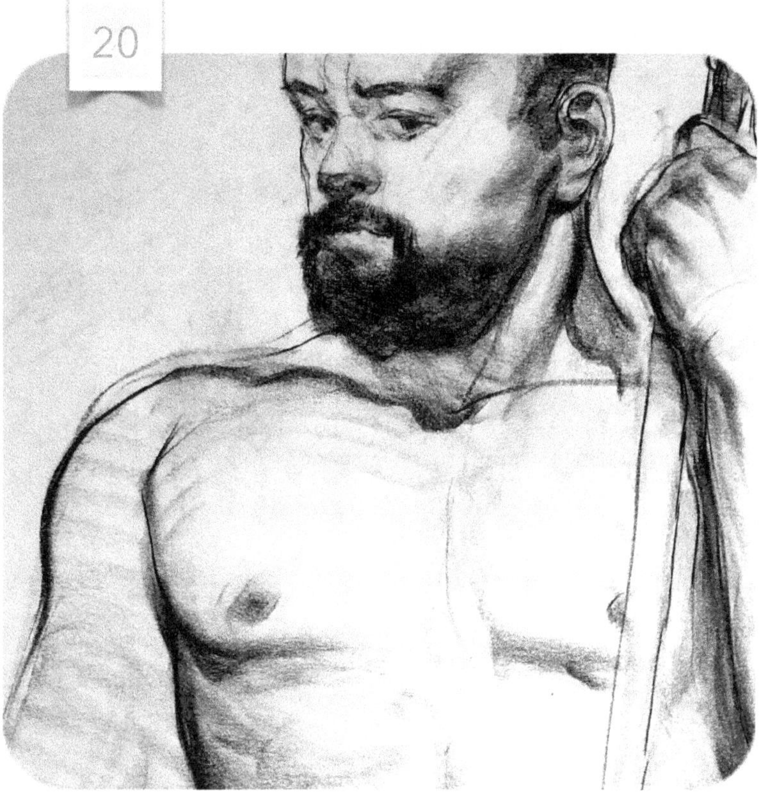

The pectoralis major (chest muscle) is connected to the upper arm bone (humerus), almost at the top. The model above turned his head to his right, which works his left neck muscle. It is worth repeating: Draw only what you see.

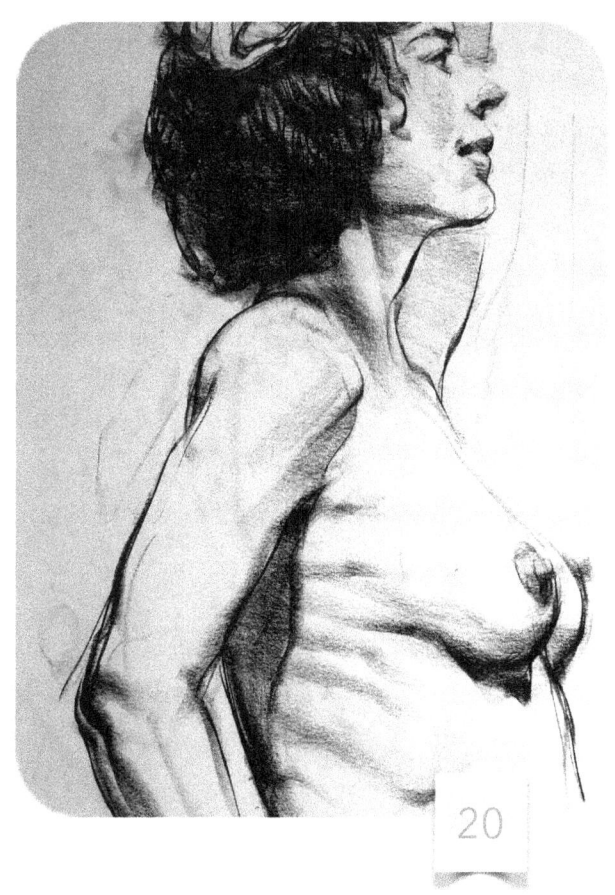

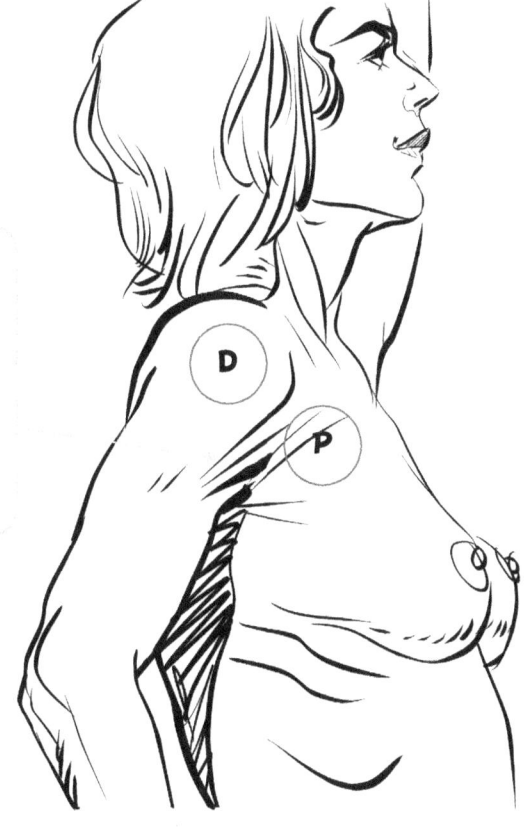

The chest muscle connects to upper arm bone humerus approximately here.

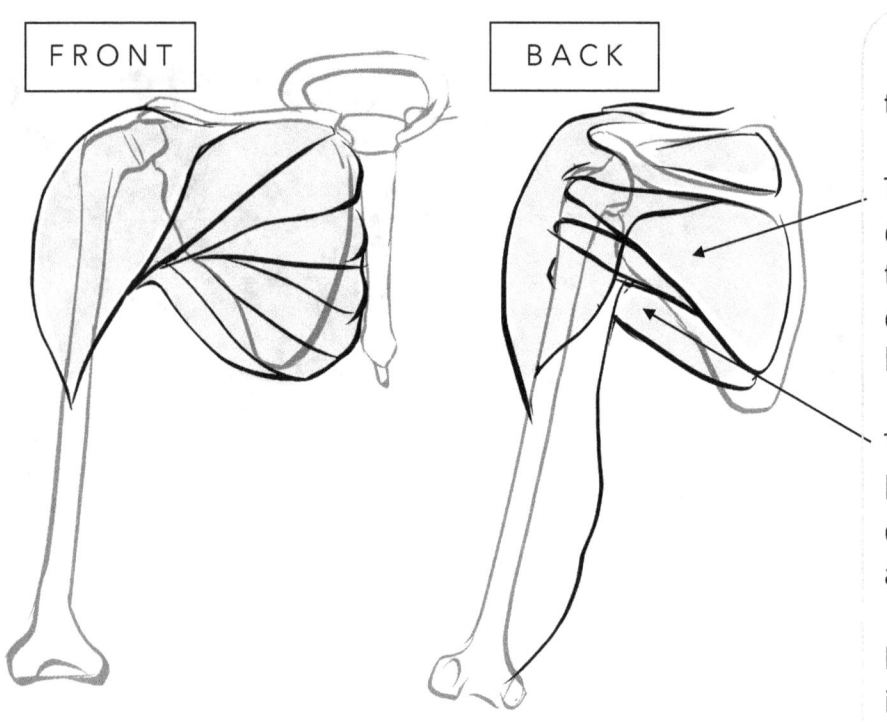

Identify the muscles and bones in the left two drawings. Note the connections.

The infraspinatus originates on the vertical edge of the shoulder blade and inserts at the top of the humerus bone. When it contracts, does it help lift the arm a little bit?

Teres major wraps around the humerus bone from back to front. When it contracts, does it rotate the humerus bone along its axis?

Do you really need to know this information to be able to draw well? Perhaps not. But curiosity never killed that many figure-drawing artists.

A few useful tips
- Length of breastbone (sternum) is
- equal to length of the collar bone (clavicle), which is
- equal to each of the vertical & horizontal sides of the shoulder blade (scapula), which is
- equal to the spine of the scapula, which is
- equal to the length from top of the head to bottom of the nose, which is
- equal to bottom of the nose to pit of the neck

You know how to use the head as a unit of measurements for the rest of the body. Of course, these are average measurements for an average adult.

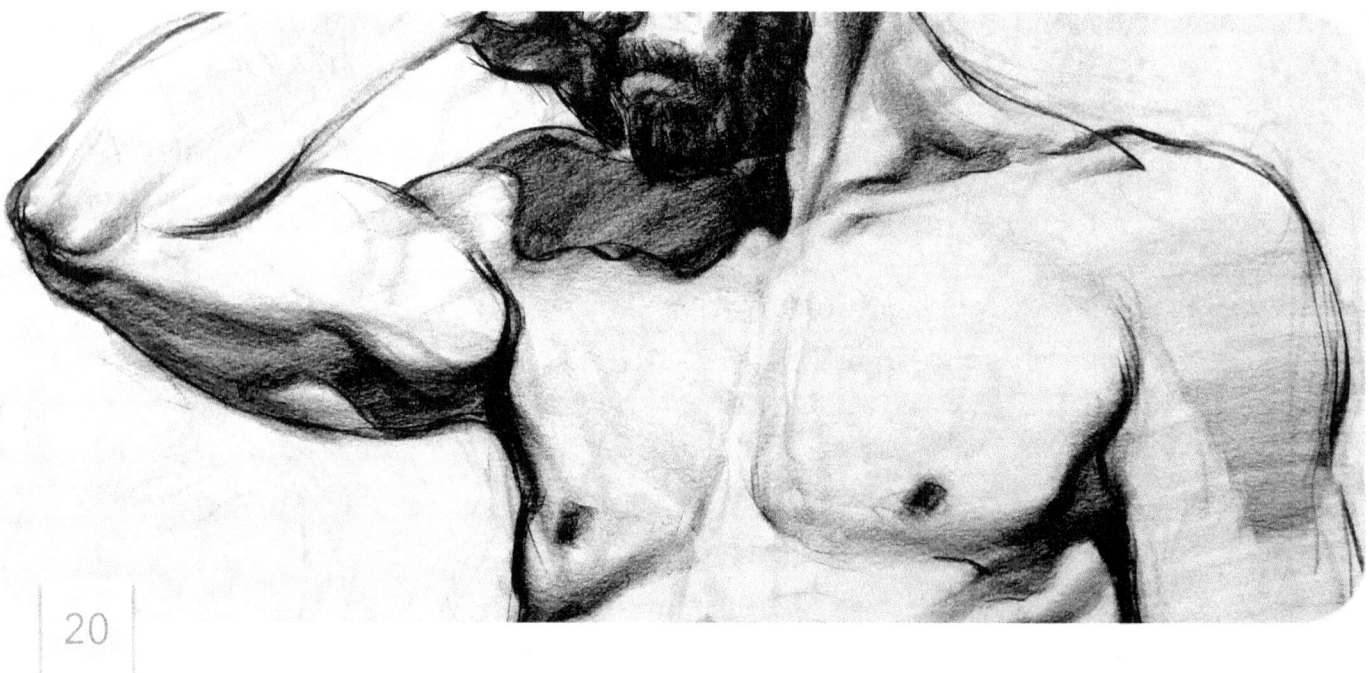

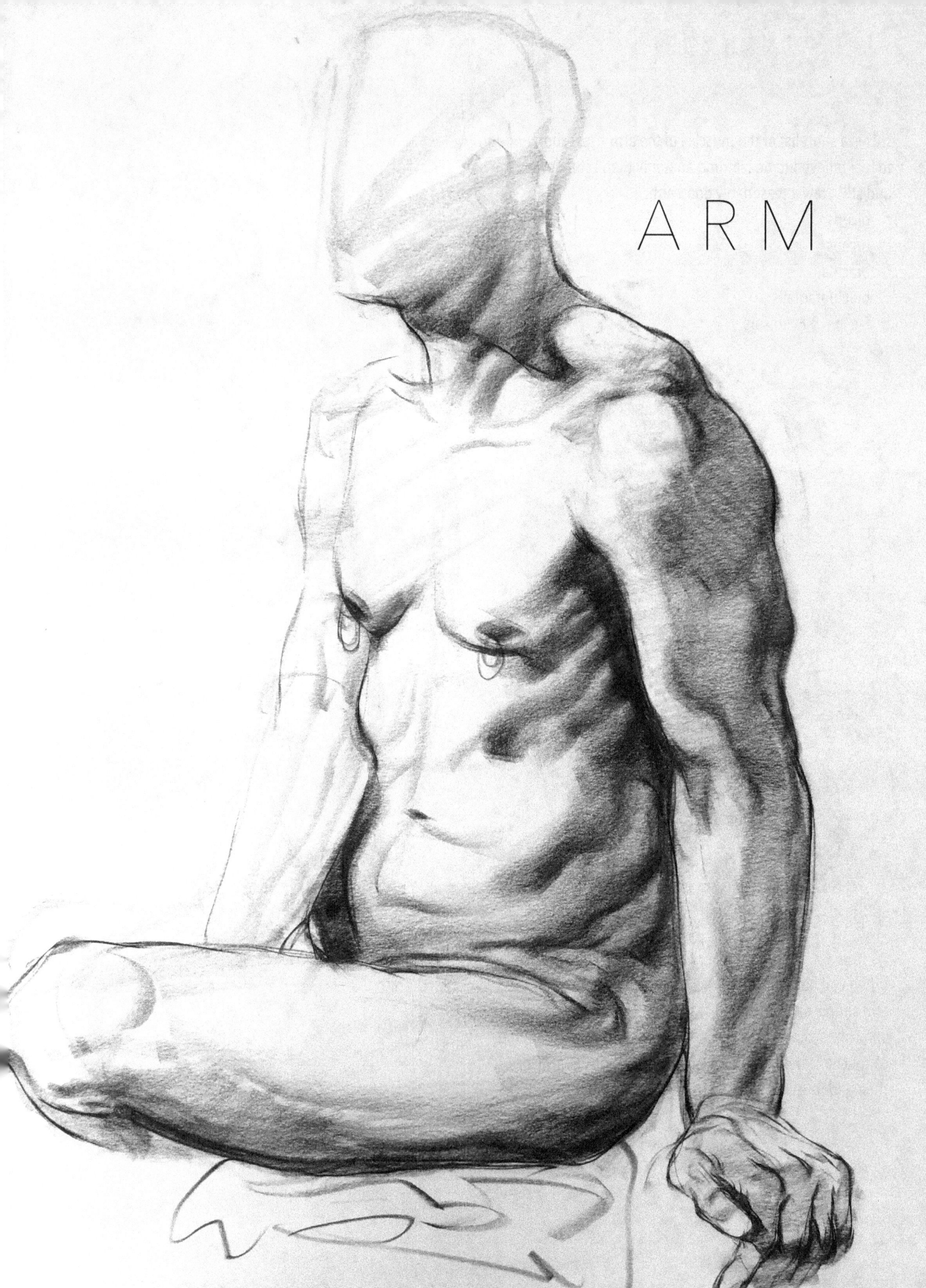

ARM

This is a short list of the muscles of the arm - just short enough to feel relieved to be learning anatomy than Latin declension and still draw a reasonably good arm.
- biceps
- triceps
- brachialis
- brachioradialis
- Flexors & Extensors

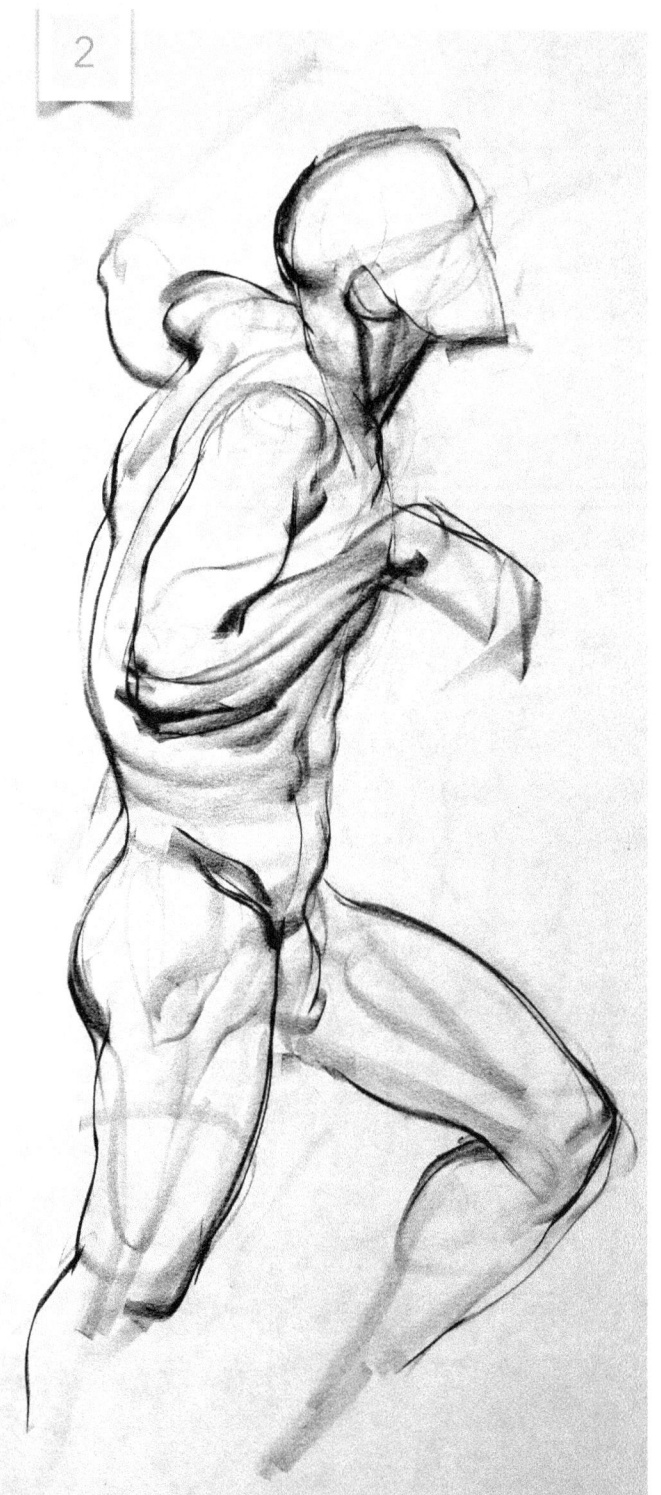

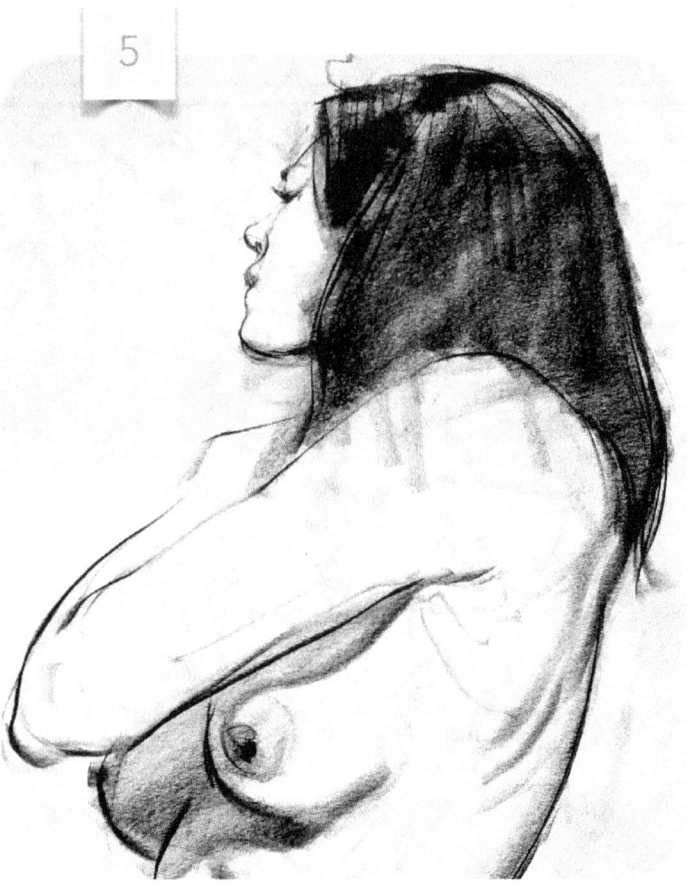

When you have a two-minute (or any short) pose, draw the arm simply as a tapered tube. Pay attention to proportions and connections. As mentioned earlier, making overlapping connections helps the forms feel three dimensional. Only then add muscle definition using line and tone.

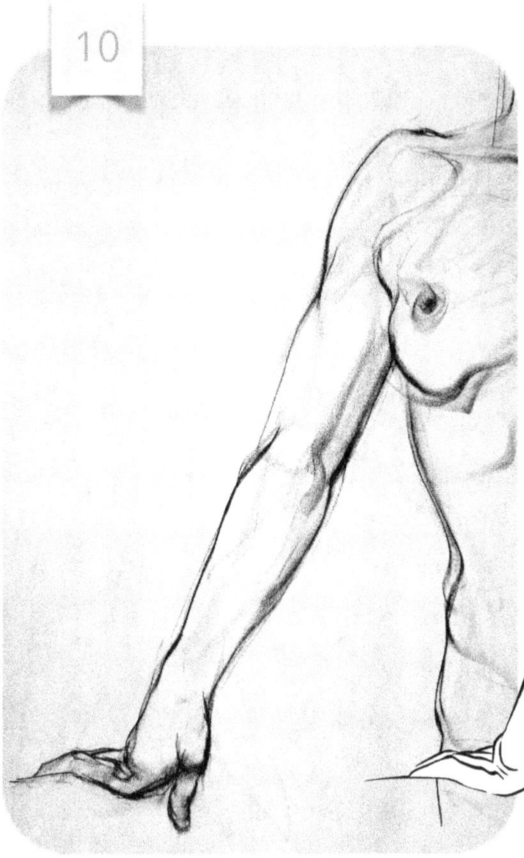

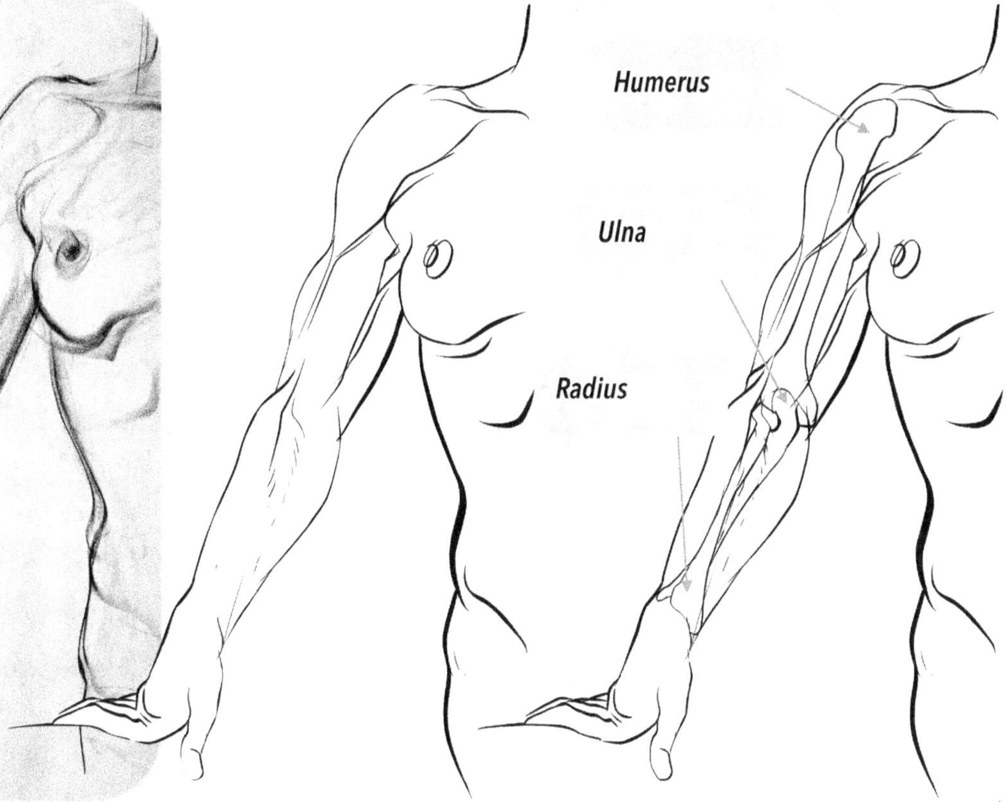

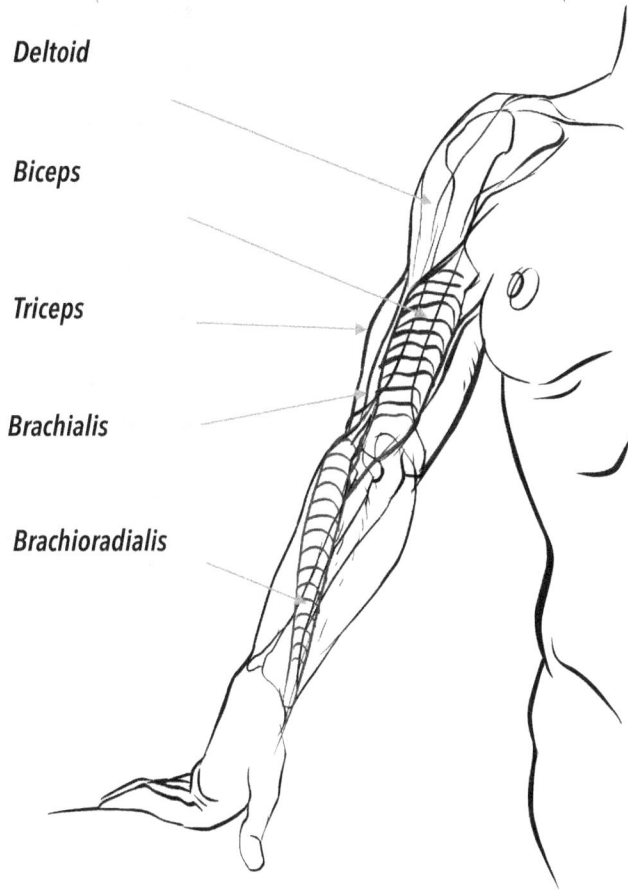

Let's analyze the arm above. If I were to draw the muscle definition separately, I'd see the biceps, a bit of the triceps, brachioradialis, and brachialis as shown in the bottom image..

Do you see the humerus and the lower arm bones ulna & radius? The radius ends on the thumb side of the hand. It also can rotate around the ulna. The ulna has a big head (elbow) and becomes narrow at the wrist on the pinky finger side.

The brachialis muscle is located between the biceps and triceps - usually you see a sliver of it on muscular arms.

Biceps & triceps perform opposite functions. The biceps bends the elbow and the triceps straightens the elbow.

Let's look at the functions of these muscles:
- Deltoid - connects scapula, clavicle and humerus - it pulls on the arm and can raise the arm so the hand is even with the shoulder.
- Biceps - connects the scapula to the radius and bypasses the upper arm bone. The biceps can bend (flex) the arm at the elbow.
- Triceps - connects the scapula to the ulna. The triceps straightens (extends) the arm.
- Brachioradialis - connects the outside, lower end of the humerus to the wrist on the thumb side. It rotates the lower arm.

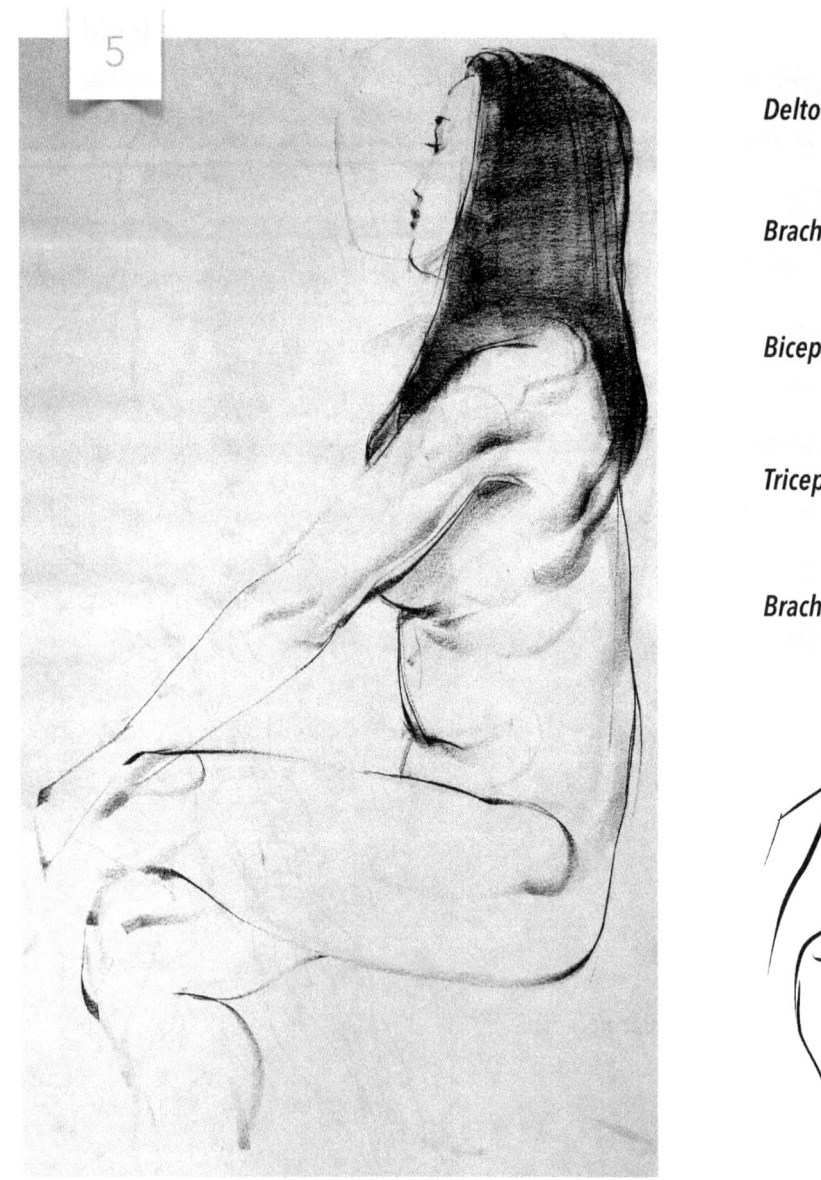
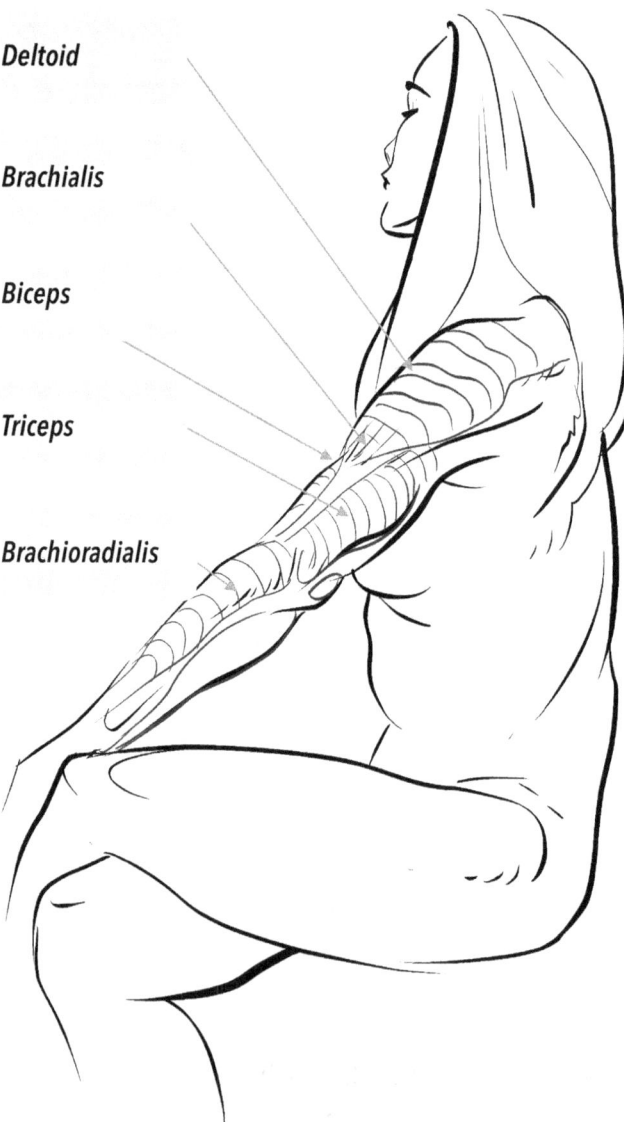

The above five-minute pose shows the arm with just a few indications of the muscles involved. Beginning artists go overboard delineating every bump and ripple. The arm in the life drawing overall still resembles a tapered tube.

When the arm bends, it is a result of the biceps flexing. Which is expressed as a bulge of the biceps. When the arm straights, it is a result of the triceps extending and will be seen as a bulge on the back of the upper arm . Every bump in your drawing has to have a reason to be there.

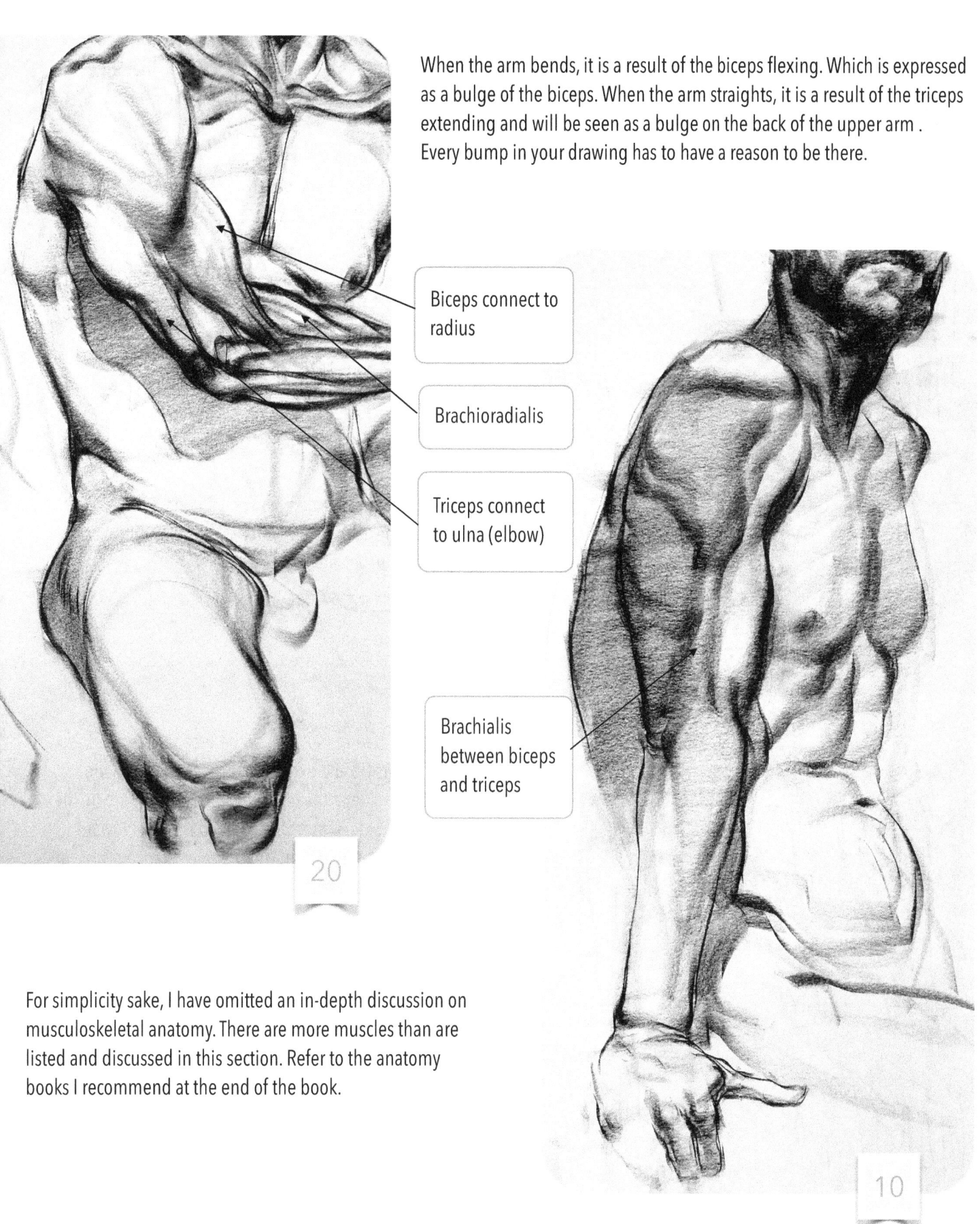

Biceps connect to radius

Brachioradialis

Triceps connect to ulna (elbow)

Brachialis between biceps and triceps

For simplicity sake, I have omitted an in-depth discussion on musculoskeletal anatomy. There are more muscles than are listed and discussed in this section. Refer to the anatomy books I recommend at the end of the book.

A few tips on drawing the arm

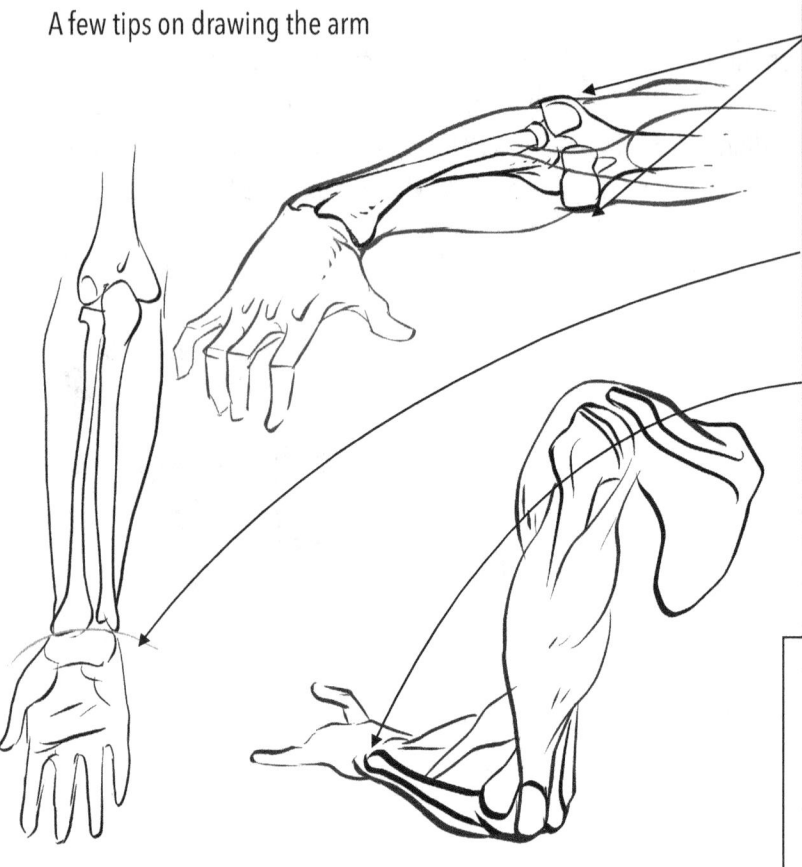

The humerus (upper arm bone) has two side protrusions at the elbow (condyles). They are visible as surface details. If you don't see them, don't draw them.

The ends of the radius & ulna form a curve into which the hand fits nicely.

The distal (furthest) end of the ulna (elbow bone) is a great landmark at the wrist. It's on the pinky finger side.

Note the gap between the hand and where the ulna & radius end. There are a few small bones (carpals) that occupy that space.

There is also a gap between fingers. Depending on the perspective, you may or many not see the gap; nevertheless, it's there.

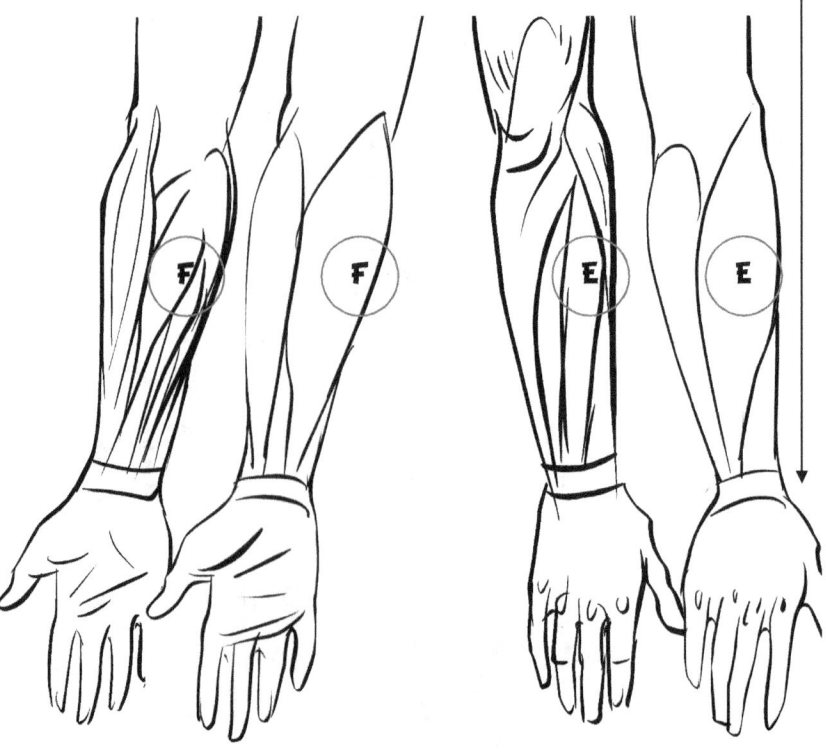

The forearm muscles can be broadly classified as flexors (F) and extensors (E). Flexors are on the palm side of the forearm, and extensors are on the other side. Flexors flex or bend the wrist inward (and also help form a fist), while extensors extend or open the wrist and fingers.

You may see a little dip on the inside surface along the length of the forearm, showing the flexor group. On muscular bodies, you may also see extensors on the back side of the forearm.

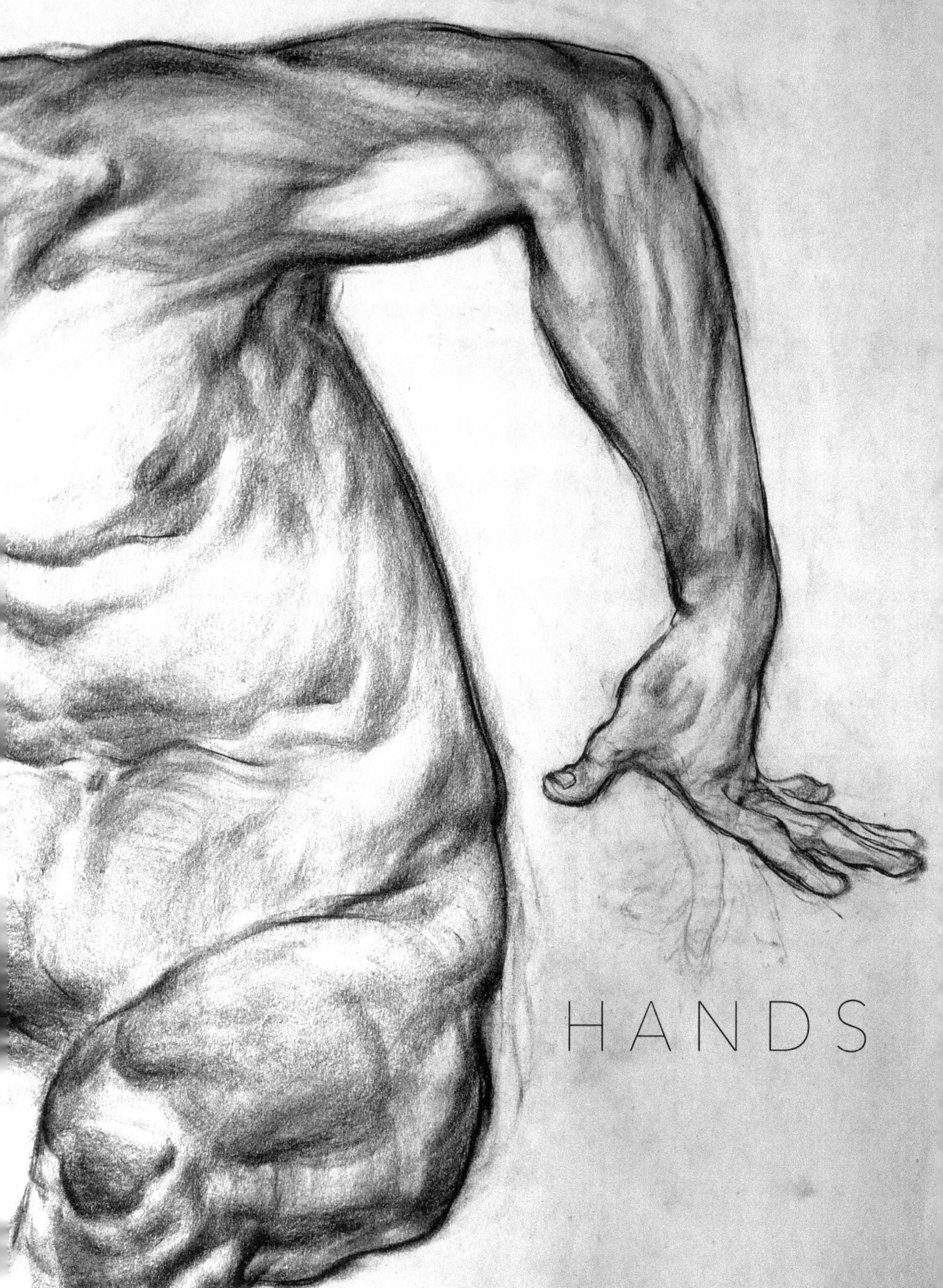

HANDS

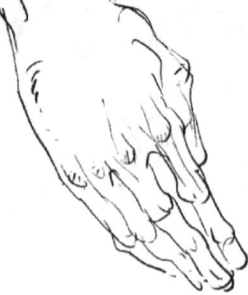

Drawing hands can be daunting, but it doesn't have to be. Simplify the forms: rectangular box for the palm, and tubes (*with gaps between them*) for the fingers. If you are intimidated by details, practice drawing gloved hands (surgical gloves).

The life drawings I've included in this section are all details of short poses - they are not as 'rendered' as I'd have liked; usually, I ran out of time. Getting proportions right is half the battle - the hand is slightly longer than three quarters of a head. The 'constructional' lines in the drawings below reveal the thought process. Note that palm is not always flat. It can also twist and arch.

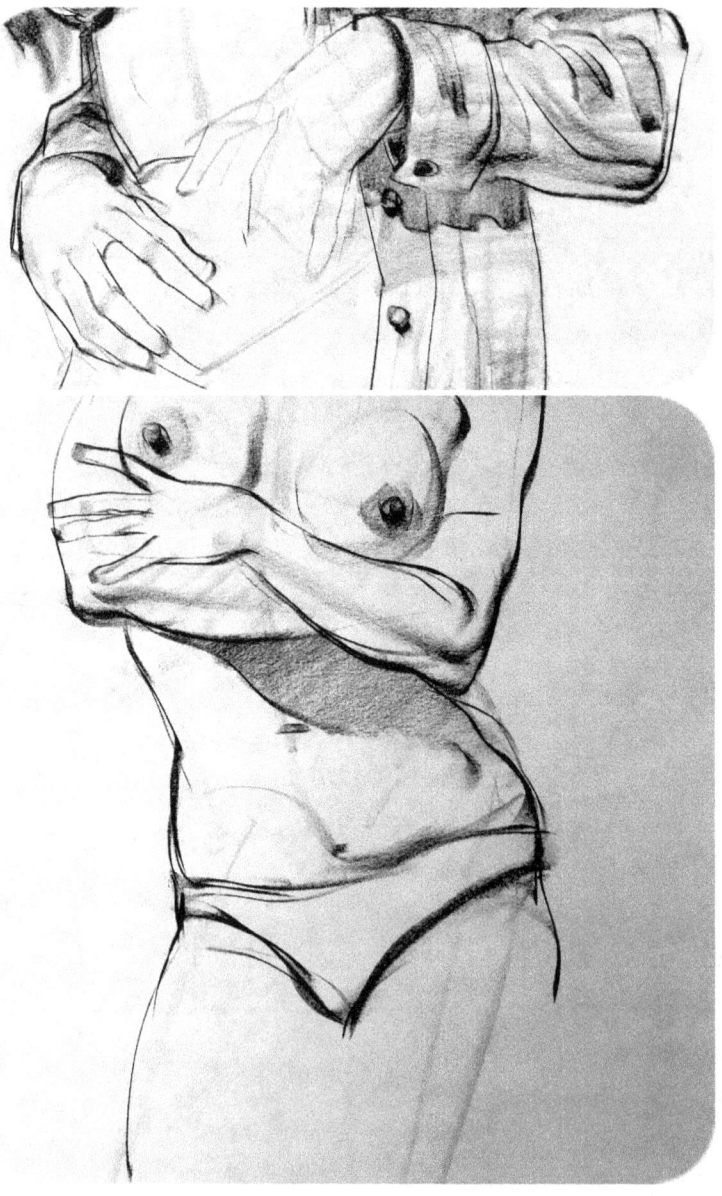
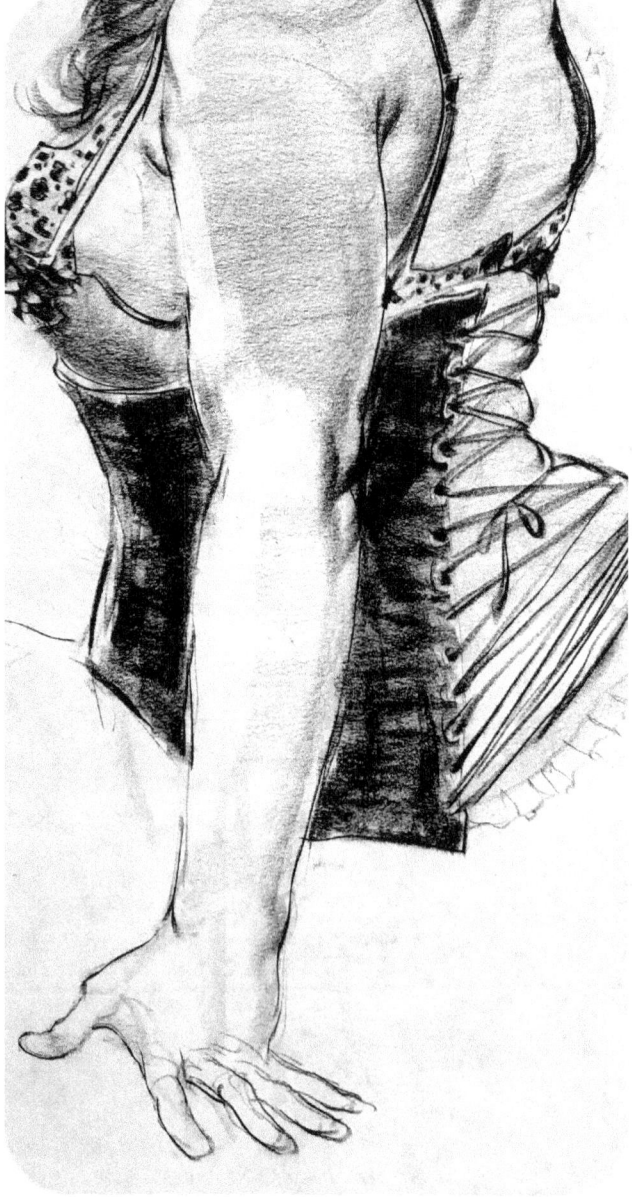

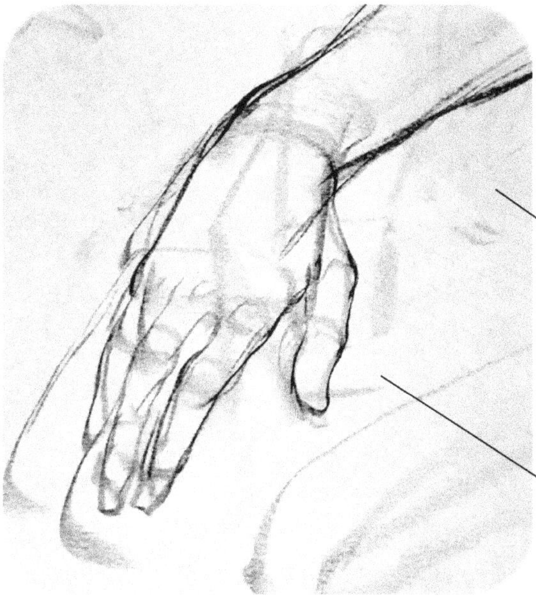

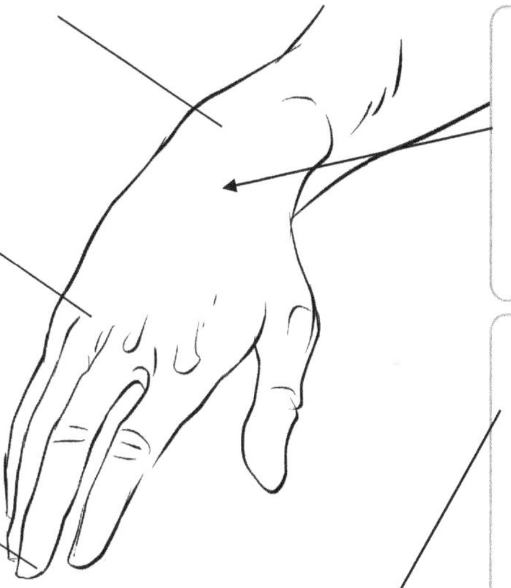

Seen from the back of the hand (dorsal side), the start of the fingers comes at the half way point in the length of the hand.

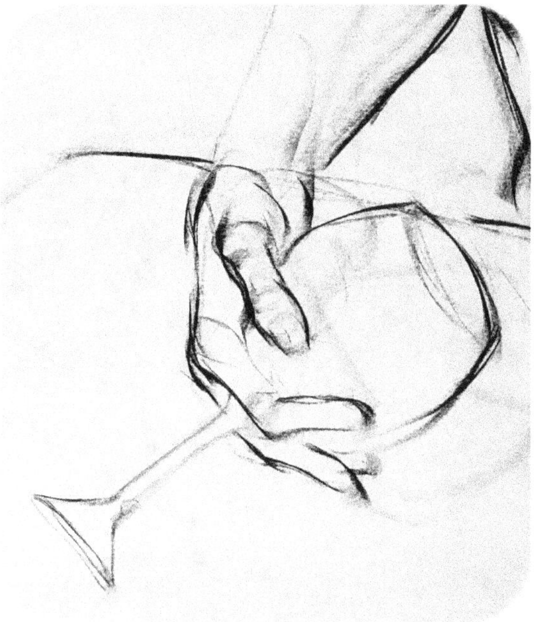

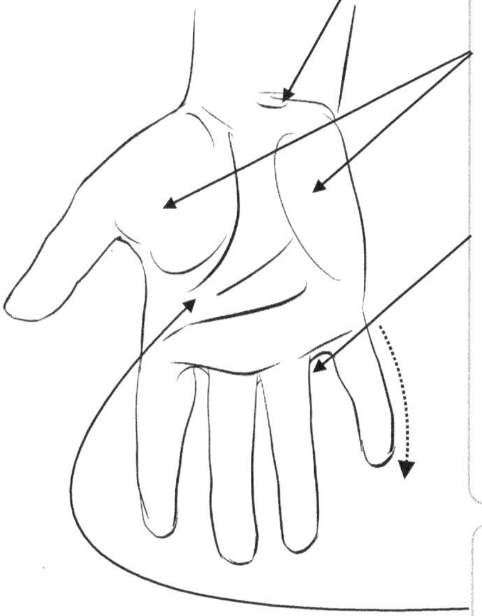

Width of the wrist is approximately three fingers wide (any three fingers).

On the palm side, fingers seem shorter than the palm.

Notice these lumps, one on the pinky finger side and the other on the thumb side.

The gap between the pinky finger and the third finger is the largest. Often that can make the fifth digit (pinky finger) bends inward toward the hand.

The palm shape is *almost a* square.

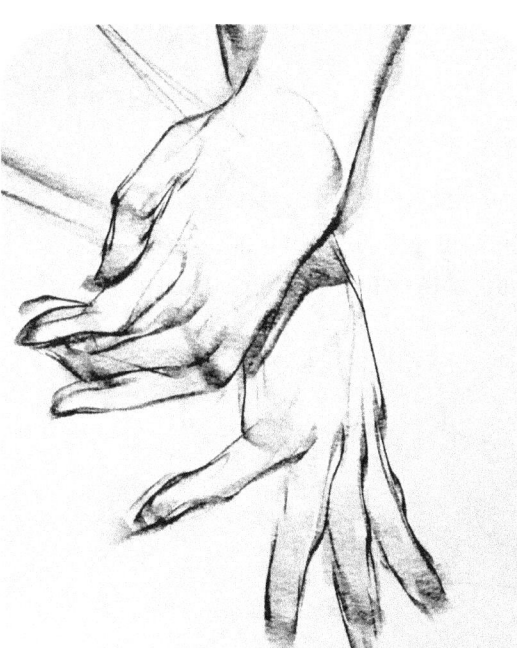

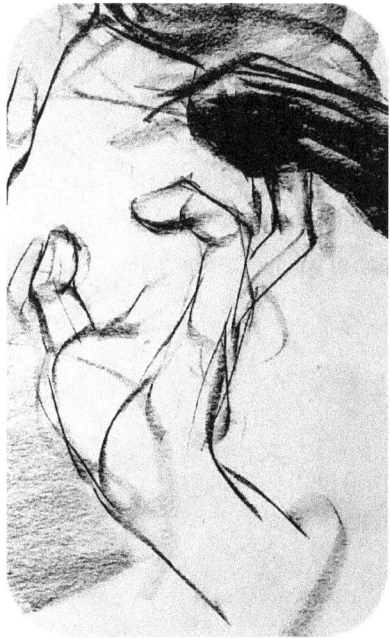

Fingers don't taper as much as we think they do. Start off with tubes of uniform diameter. After you get the length of the fingers right, add details where you see them. I approximate the length of the fingers with tonal lines first, then add tubes.

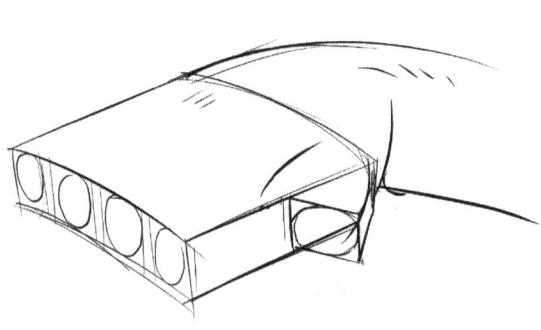 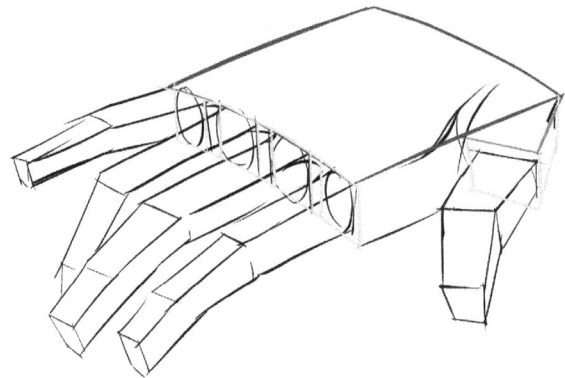

These two drawings demonstrate one way to draw the hands. A box for the palm, four evenly spaced 'squares' for the fingers. Add the thumb triangle and then the thumb. It's a bit difficult to follow this process literally during life drawing sessions, time being a big constraint. Perhaps we can simplify the process. Look at the following drawings:

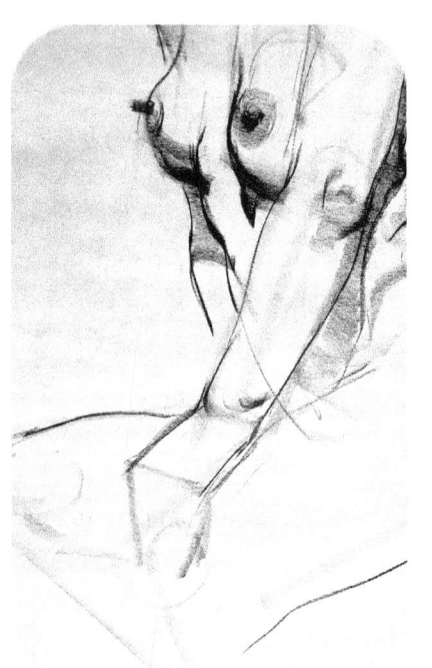 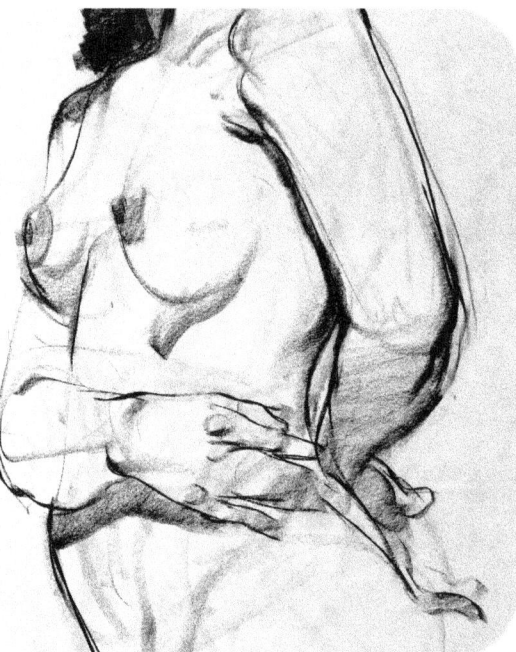 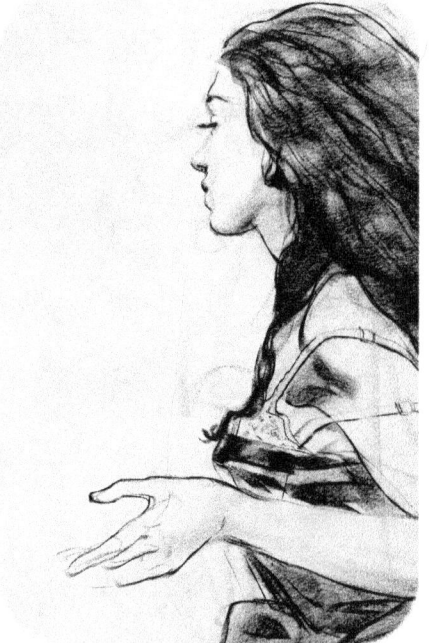

Get the proportions right (divide hand into two halves - fingers and palm), then add tubes to position the fingers. The middle fingers tend to stay closer together. The second and fifth digit (forefinger and the pinky finger) will usually have an expression of their own. The width of the first three fingers, or the last three, is the same as the width of the wrist. Add tonal detail for bends in the finger.

The more the fingers flex, the more the underside 'bunches up'.
Remember: three joints to each finger. The big joint (knuckle) is located 'in' the hand; the other two are in the finger.

Here are the dreaded drawings of the bones of the hand.
a. The palmer (palm) side.
b. The dorsal (back) side.
c. If you look at the slope of the webbing between the fingers, you will see why the fingers look longer on the dorsal side.

A closed fist is about two eyes wide at the knuckles. The length of the hand is about four fifths of the ulna - lower arm bone.

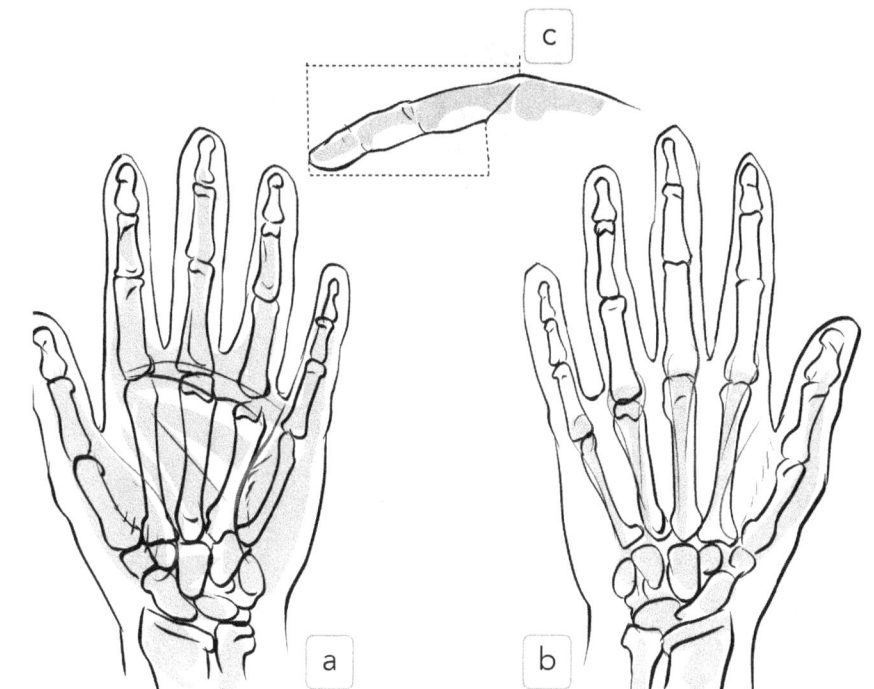

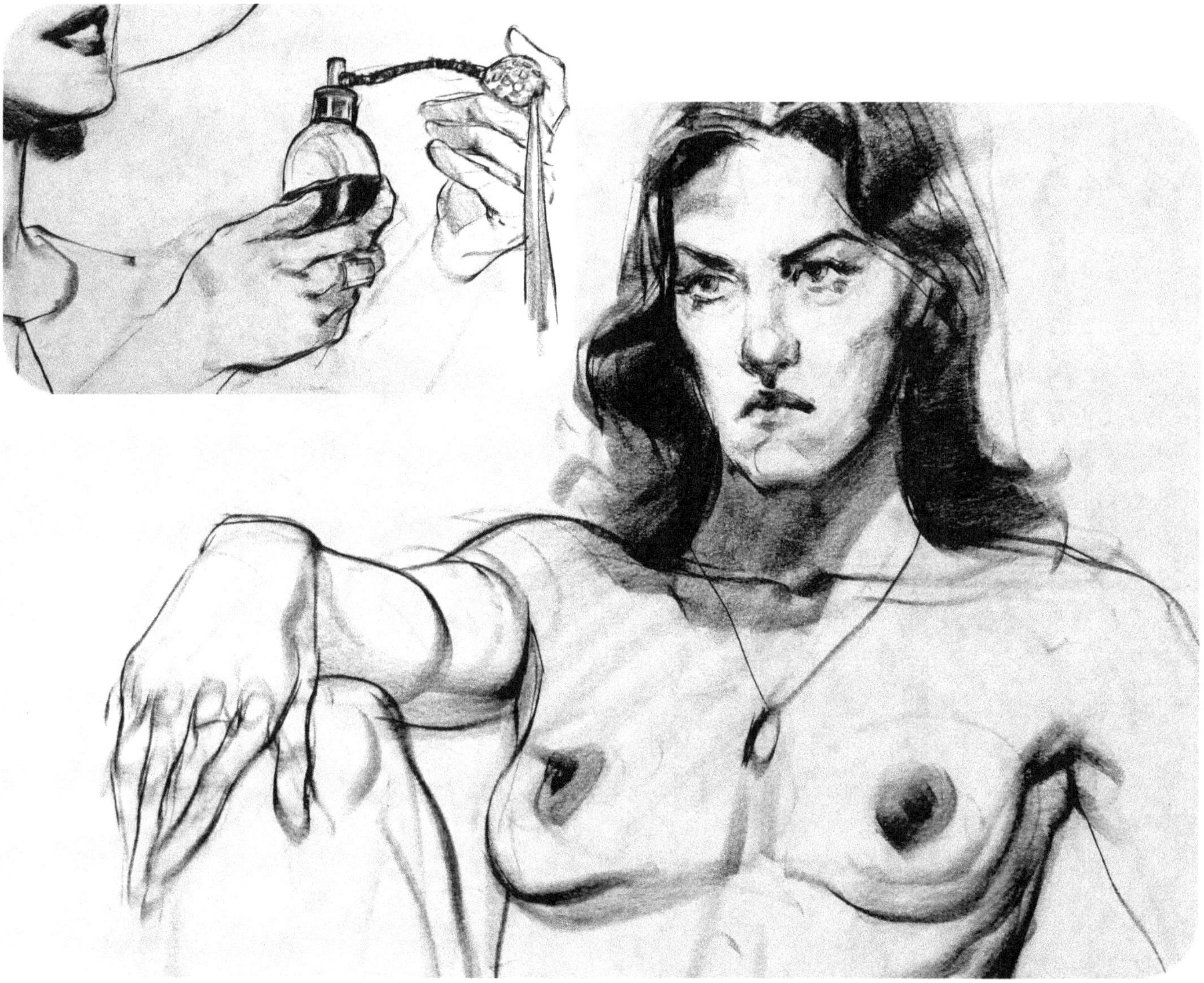

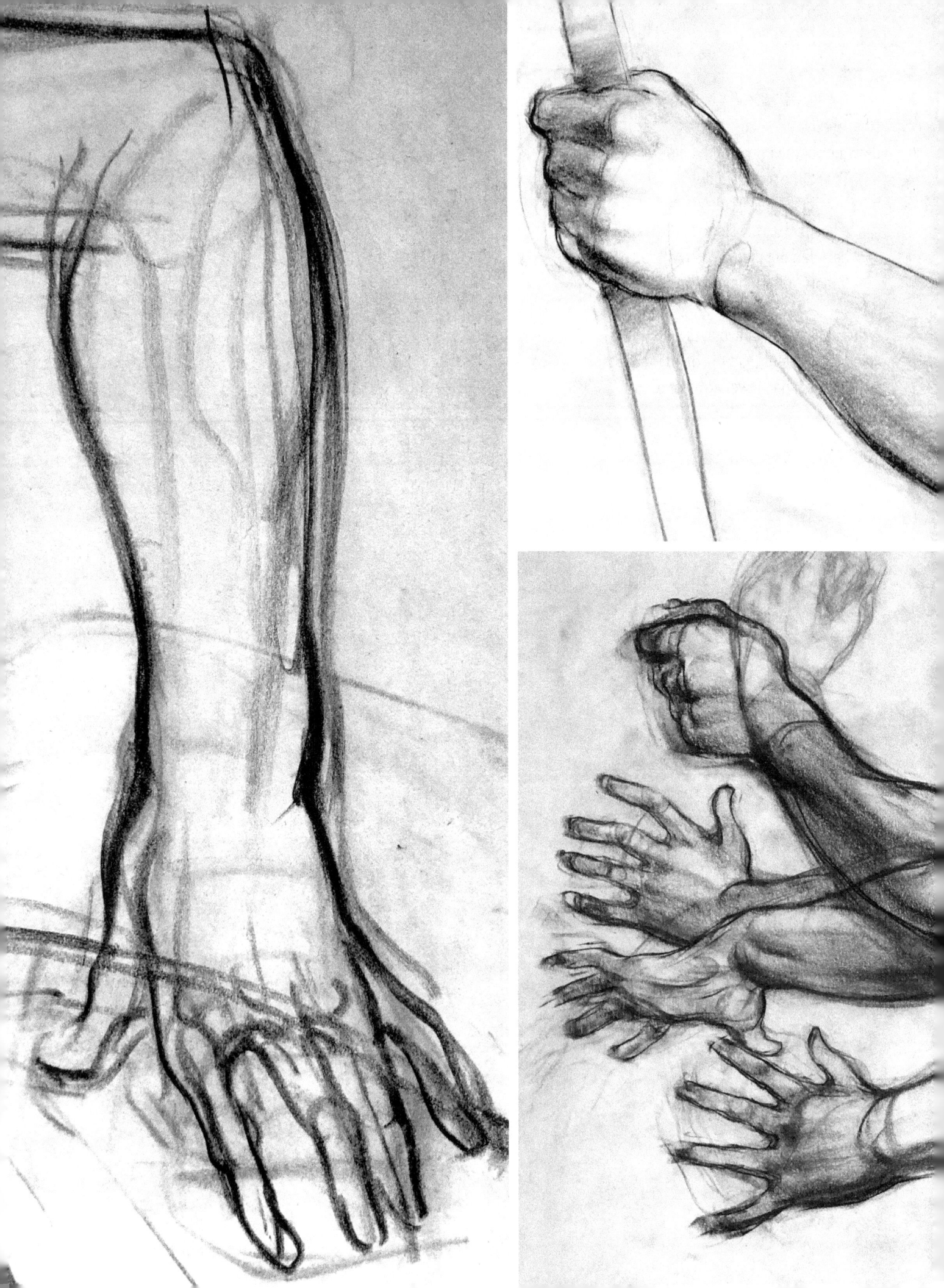

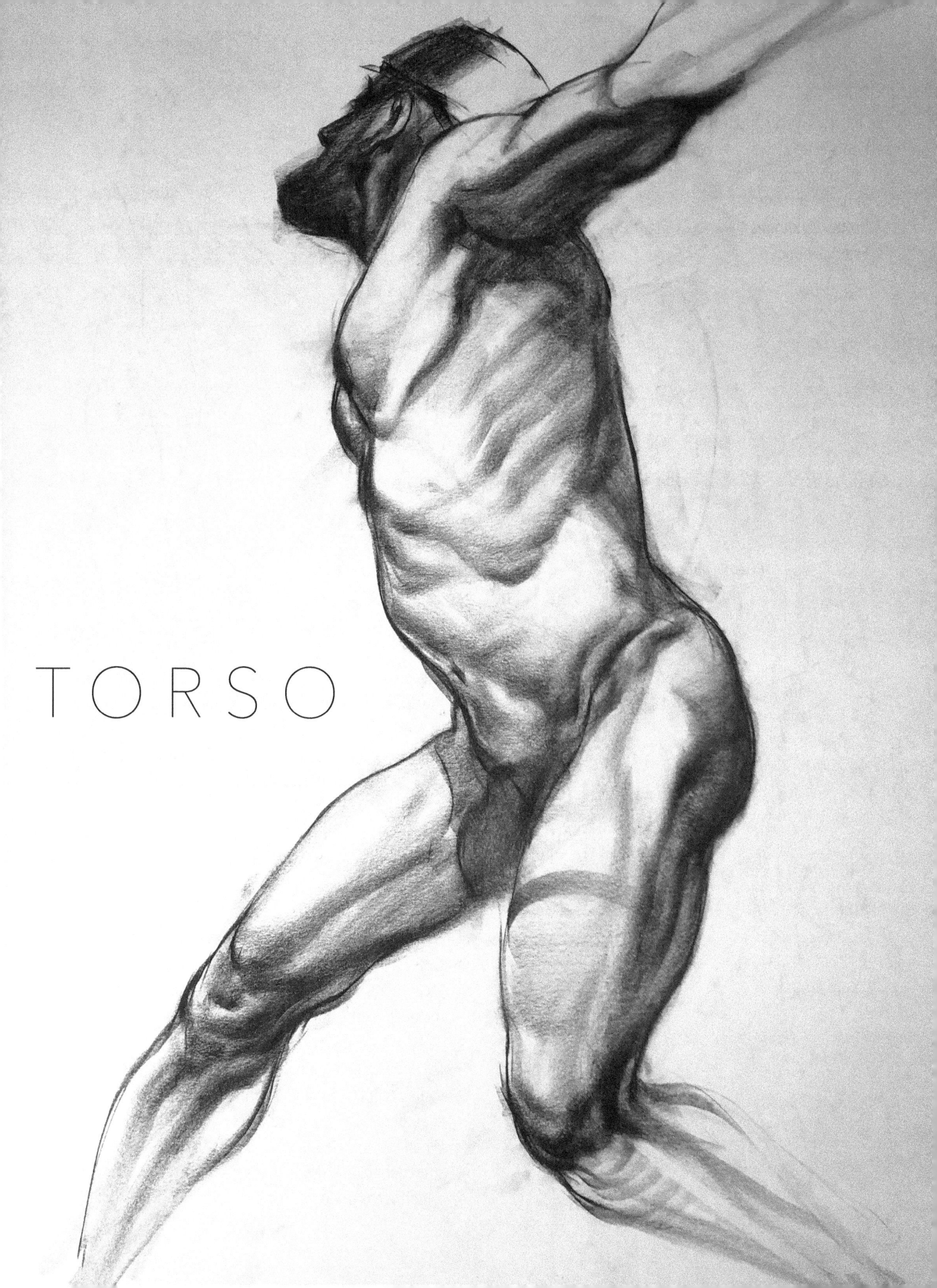

The muscles we are interested in for this section are:
- Latissmus dorsi
- Serratus anterior
- Rectus abdominis
- External oblique

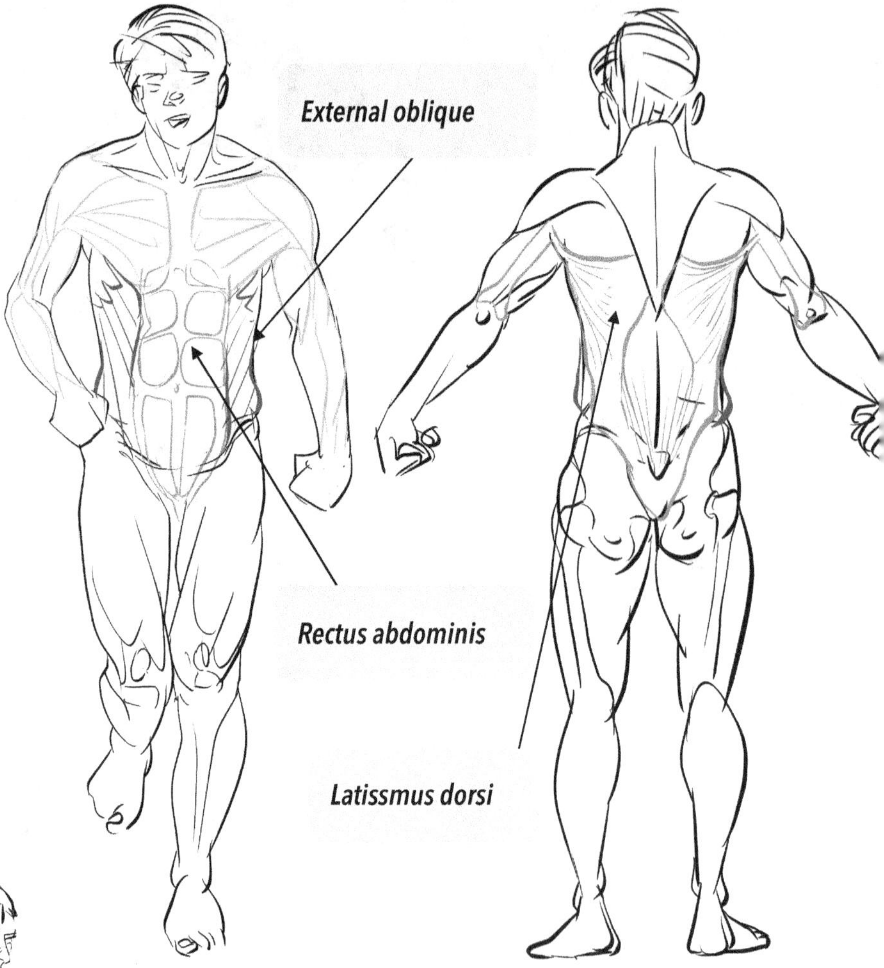

Latissmus dorsi

Serratus anterior

External oblique

External oblique

Rectus abdominis

Latissmus dorsi

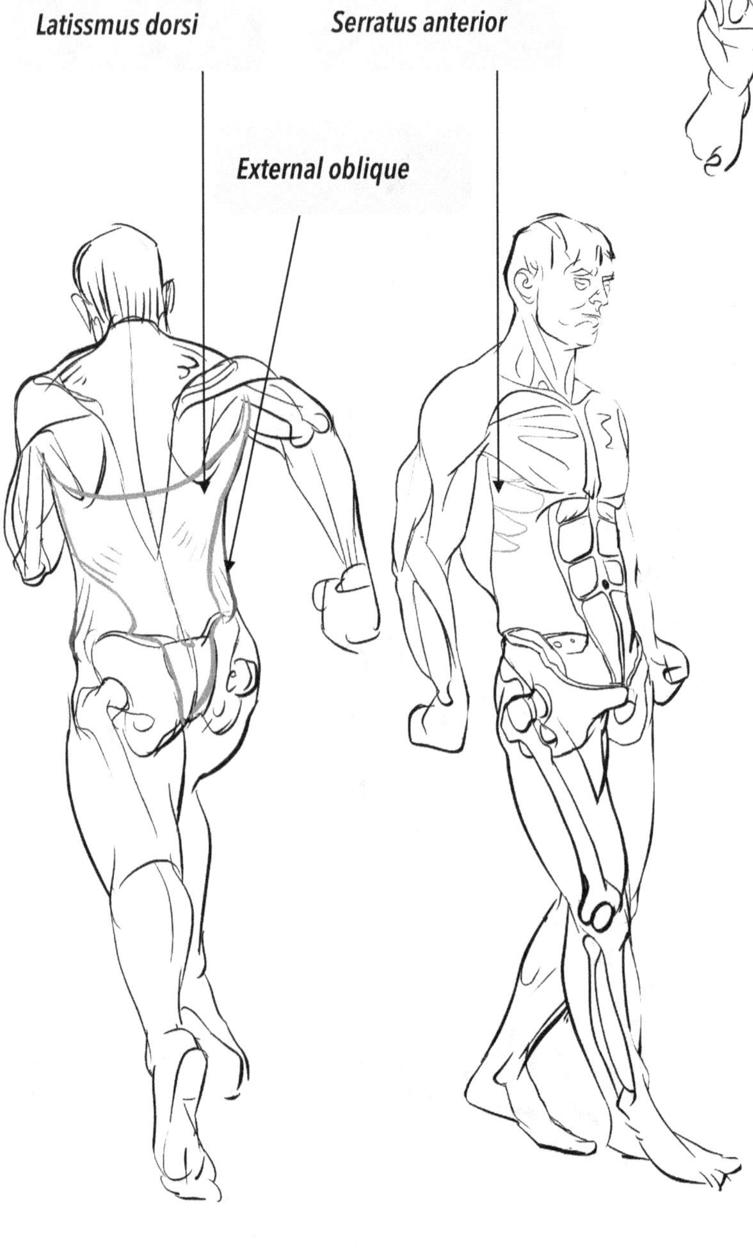

The latissmus dorsi is a back (dorsal) muscle that connects the upper arm bone (humerus) to the pelvis. The pelvic connection is fixed and a muscle can only pull - that means when the latissmus dorsi contracts, it pulls the arm down. Look for this muscle on olympic swimmers.

The rectus abdominis muscle (six pack muscle) is the front face of the lower torso. It connects the front of the ribs to the pubic crest.

The external oblique is located on each side of the lower torso. It's called the 'love handle' muscle (fat can accumulate here). It wraps around the iliac crest (top edge of the pelvis at the front).

The serratus anterior muscle (serratus means saw-toothed) connects to the ribs and the inside vertical edge of the shoulder blade. The rib connection of this muscle is fixed. When the muscle contracts, it will push the scapula/shoulder blade forward, thus extending the arm. Boxers and superheroes use this muscle.

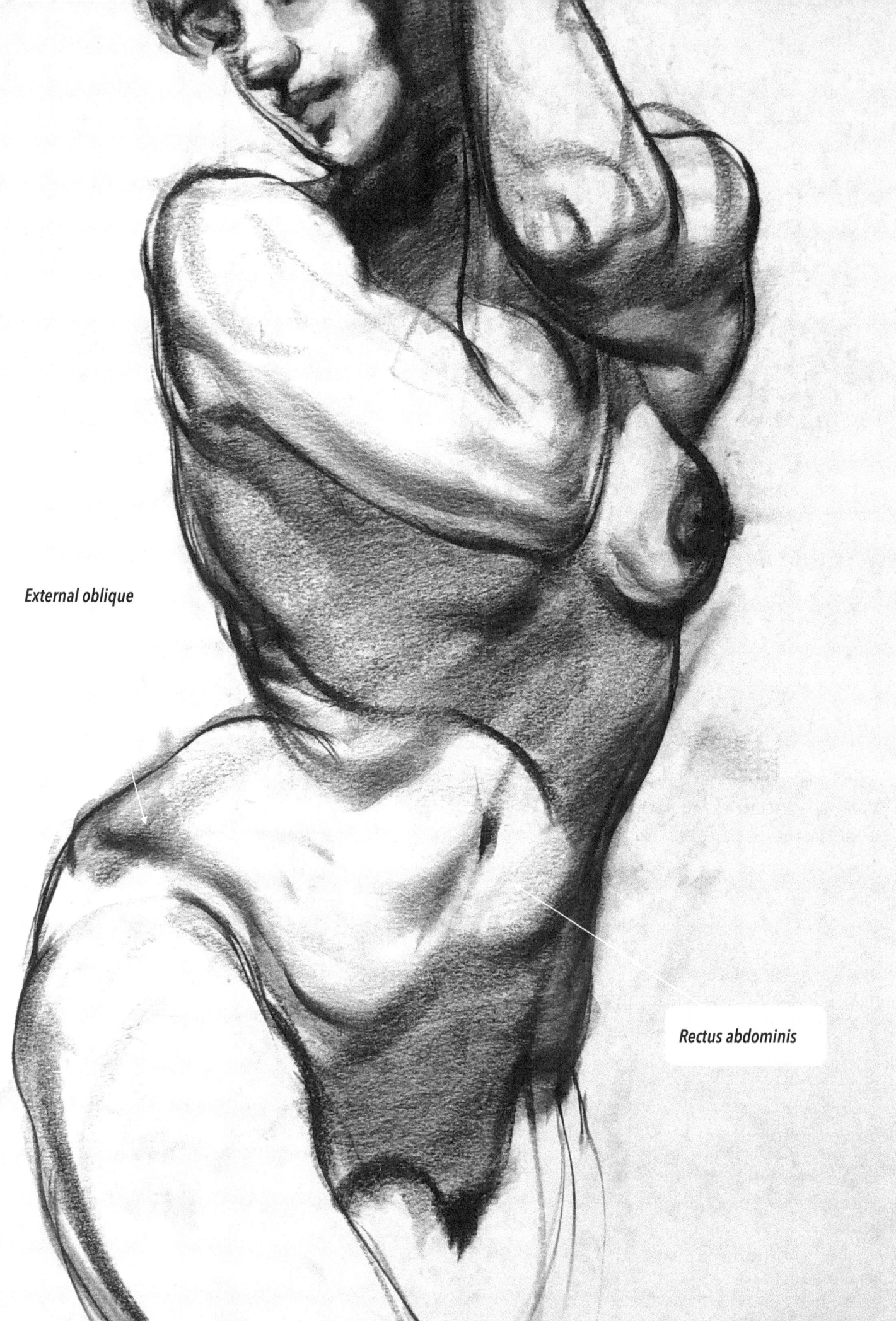

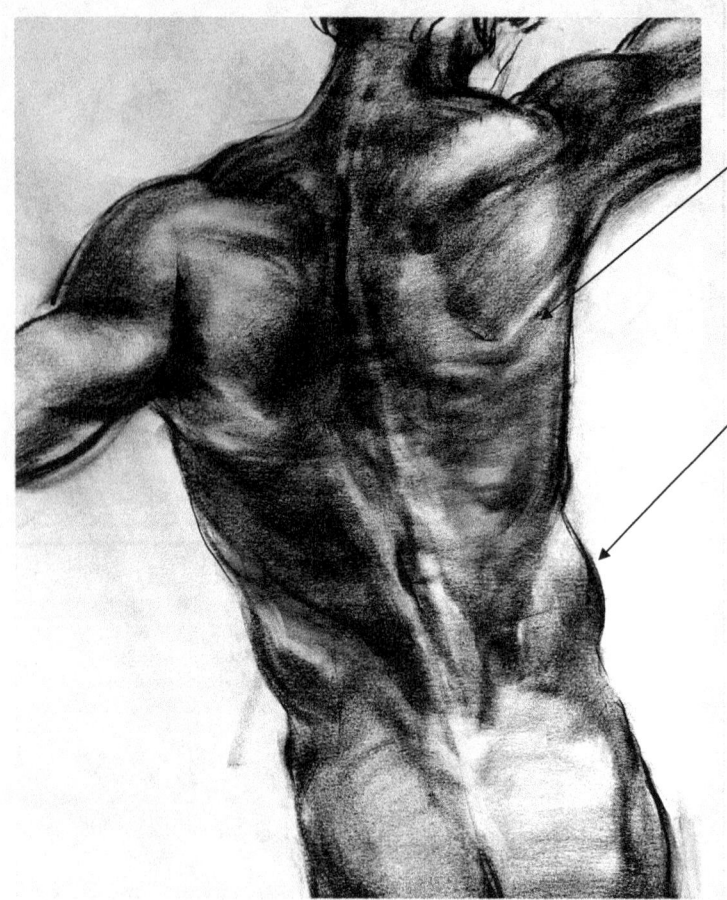

This is a subtle depiction of the latissmus dorsi muscle.

Here is a not-so-subtle external oblique, the love handle. This muscle helps us twist at the waist. The fibers run diagonally from outside to inside (same path as your arm if you place the hands inside the front trouser pockets). If there is an external oblique, is there an internal oblique? Yes, but it's internal & not a surface muscle, so we ignore it and don't need to draw it. See, this is easier than learning Latin declension - there you have to learn everything whether you use it or not.

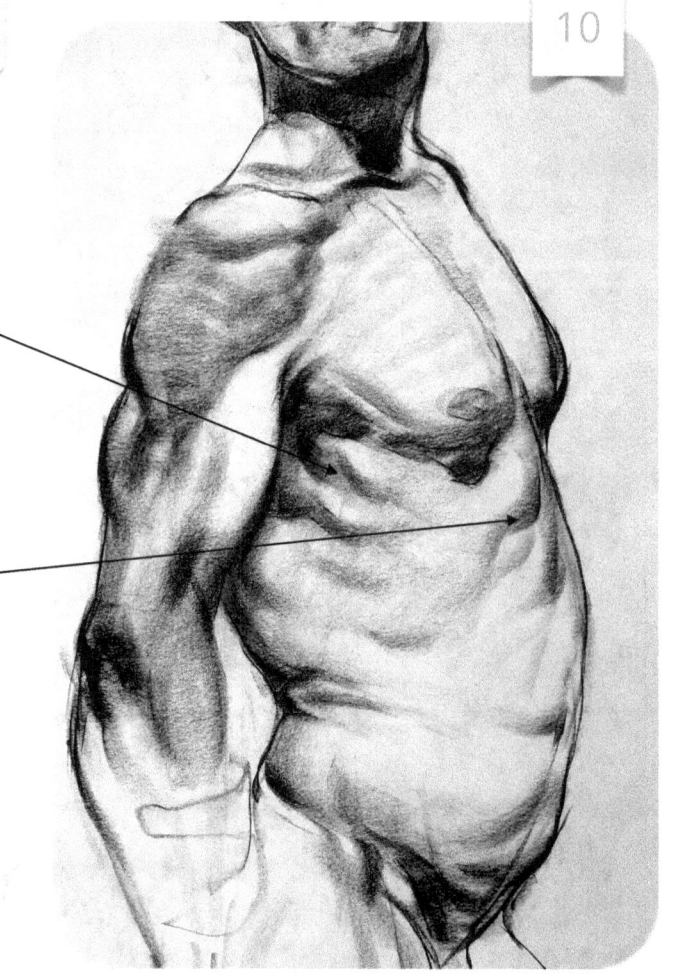

Serratus anterior - saw toothed muscle that helps boxers and superheroes. Imagine having muscles on the ribs.

Rectus abdominis, the stomach 'six-pack' muscle. The muscle has flat, tendinous material between each pack which gives the muscle its definition.

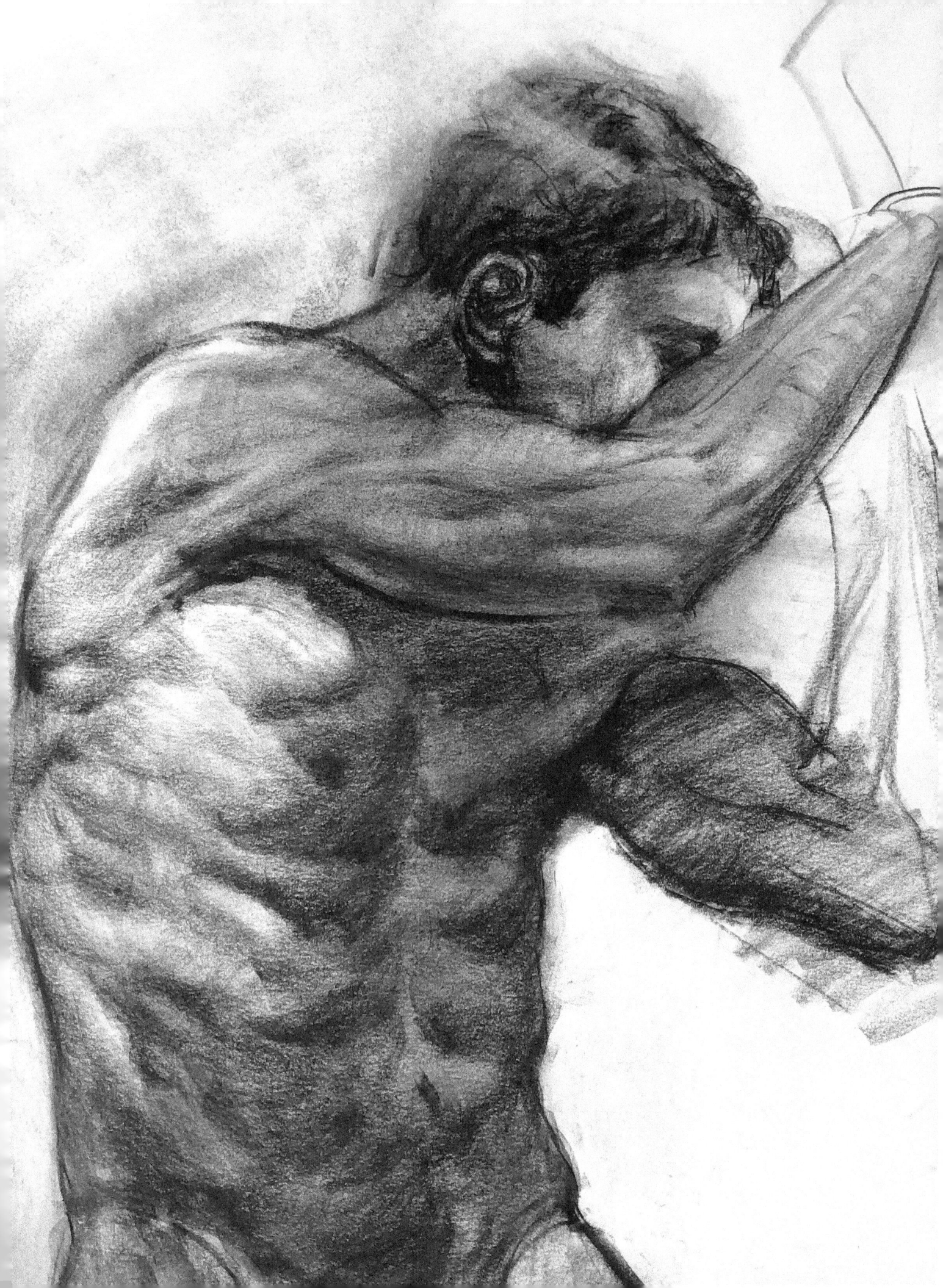

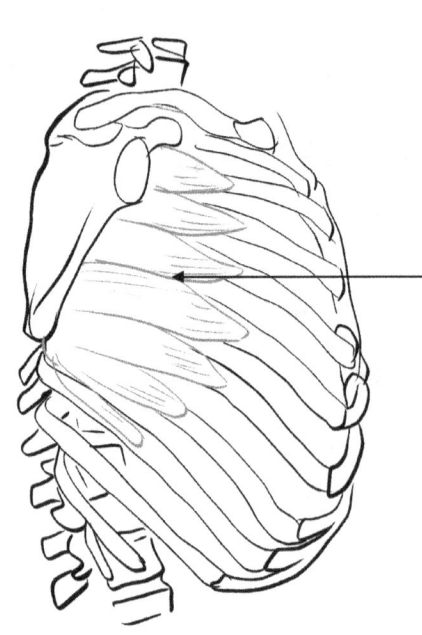

Latissmus dorsi

Serratus anterior

Rectus abdominis

External oblique

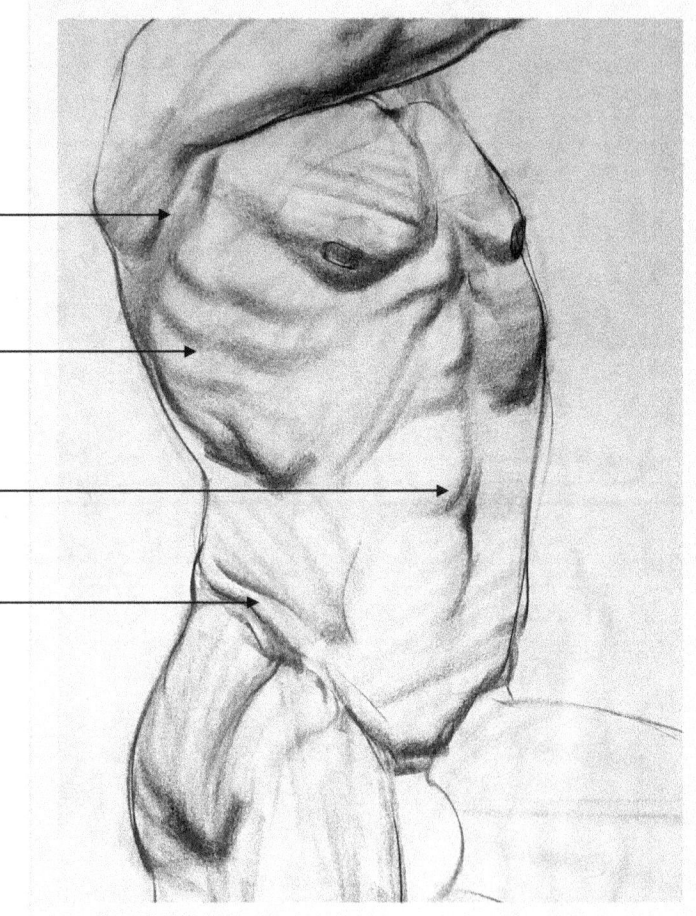

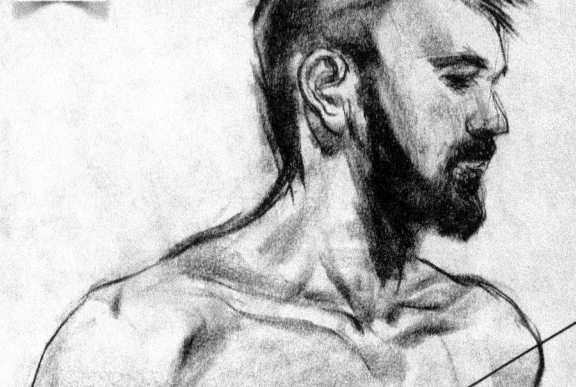

Pectoralis major is clearly defined here.

Rectus abdominis connective tissue forms bands and separates the muscle into four visible sections of alternating sizes. The pack closest to the sternum is shortest in height. The next one is slightly longer. The one below that is short again, and the horizontal connective tissue hovers near the navel. The last section of rectus abdomens is the longest and reaches pubic crest from the navel.

Here is the external oblique connected to the top edge of iliac crest.

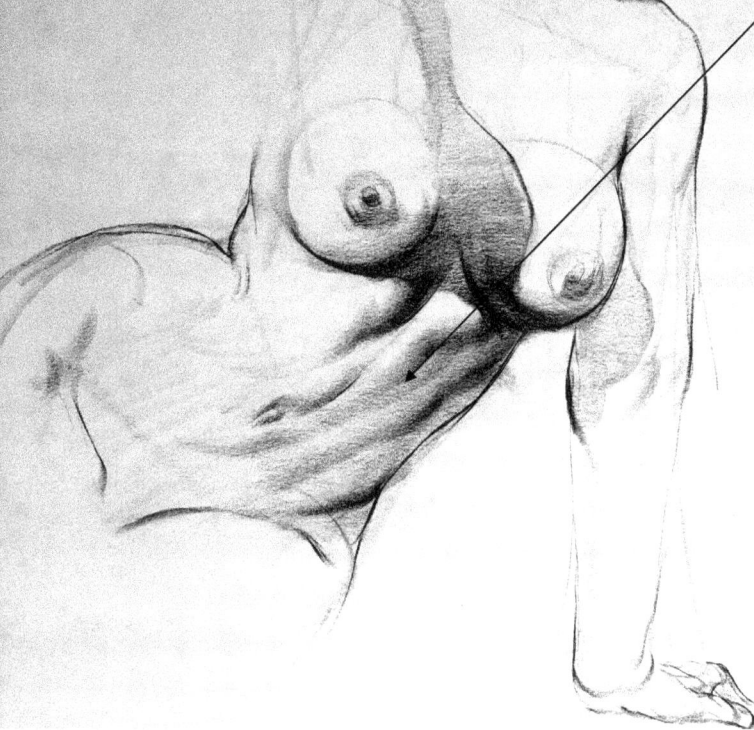

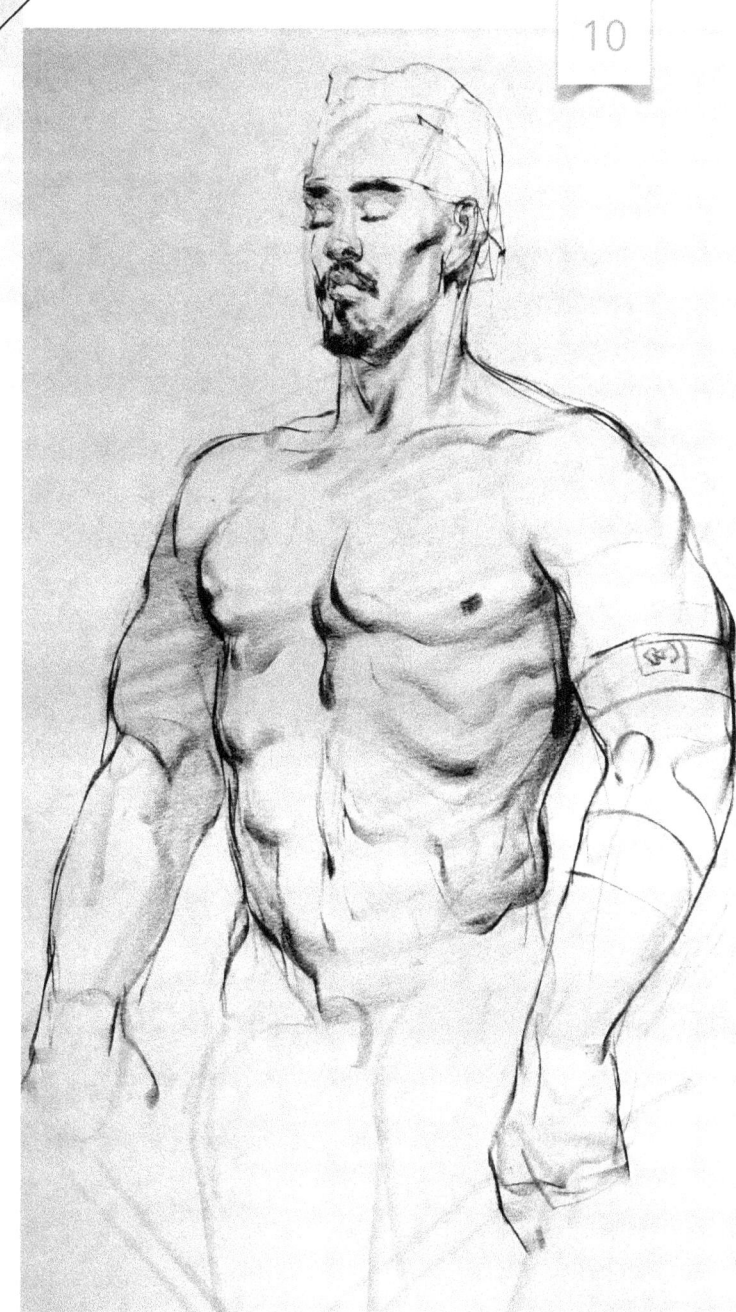

Rectus abdominis doesn't always look like a six or eight pack - the drawing on the left was a five minute pose with just a hint of rectus abdominis muscle.

When drawing short poses, you may not have time to render the entire figure. Choose what interests you and what you want to explore, and draw them. I hinted at musculature in the drawing on the right, but I was more interested in his face and his calm expression.

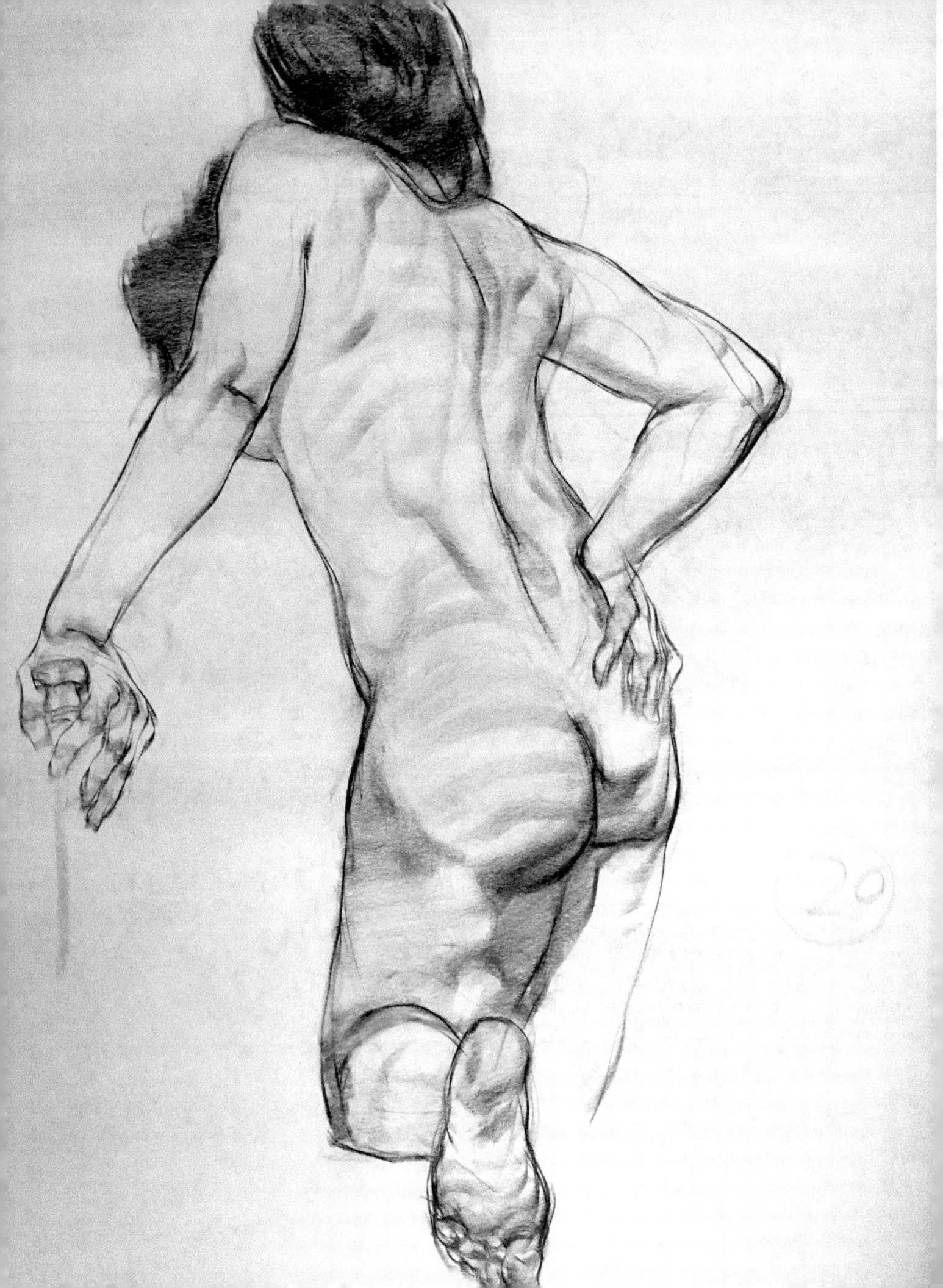

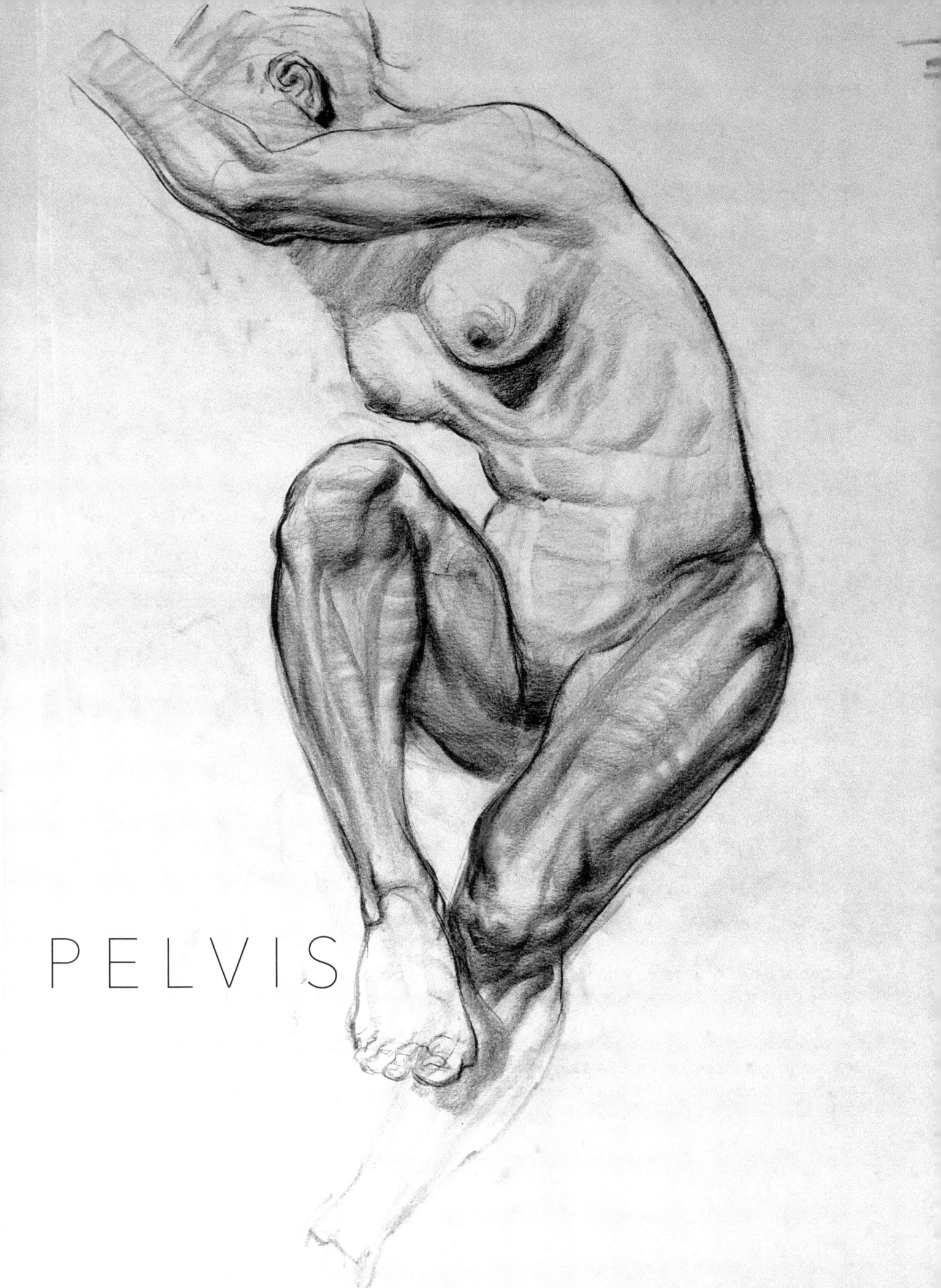

PELVIS

The four surface muscles on the pelvis that we are interested in are:
a. Gluteus maximus
b. Gluteus medius (on the side of pelvis)
c. Tensor Fasciae latae (front of pelvis)
d. Sartorius (thin long muscle connecting pelvis to Tibia)
e. Iliotibial band or tract

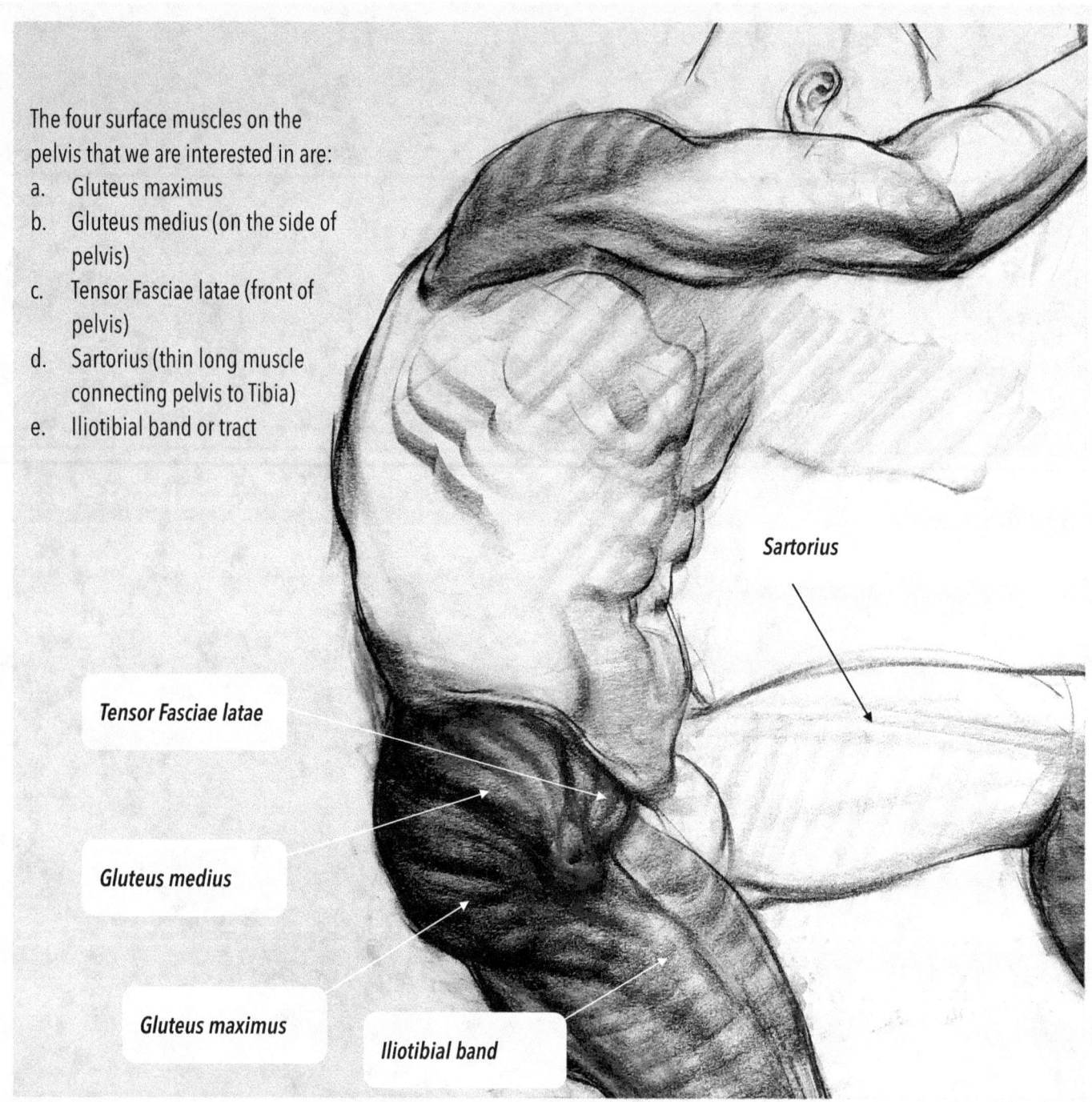

THE SARTORIUS MUSCLE DERIVES ITS NAME FROM THE LATIN WORD 'SARTOR' MEANING TAILOR. APPARENTLY TAILORS USED TO SIT CROSS-LEGGED IN THOSE DAYS AND THIS MUSCLE HELPS IN ADOPTING THAT POSTURE.

THE SARTORIUS LONG, THIN MUSCLE RUNS DIAGONALLY ACROSS THE FRONT OF EACH THIGH FROM THE HIPBONE TO THE INSIDE OF THE LEG BELOW THE KNEE - YOU CAN SEE HOW IT CAN HELP IN CROSSING THE LEGS WHEN IT CONTRACTS. IT'S A USEFUL MUSCLE TO KNOW, AS YOU WILL SEE IN THE NEXT PAGE.

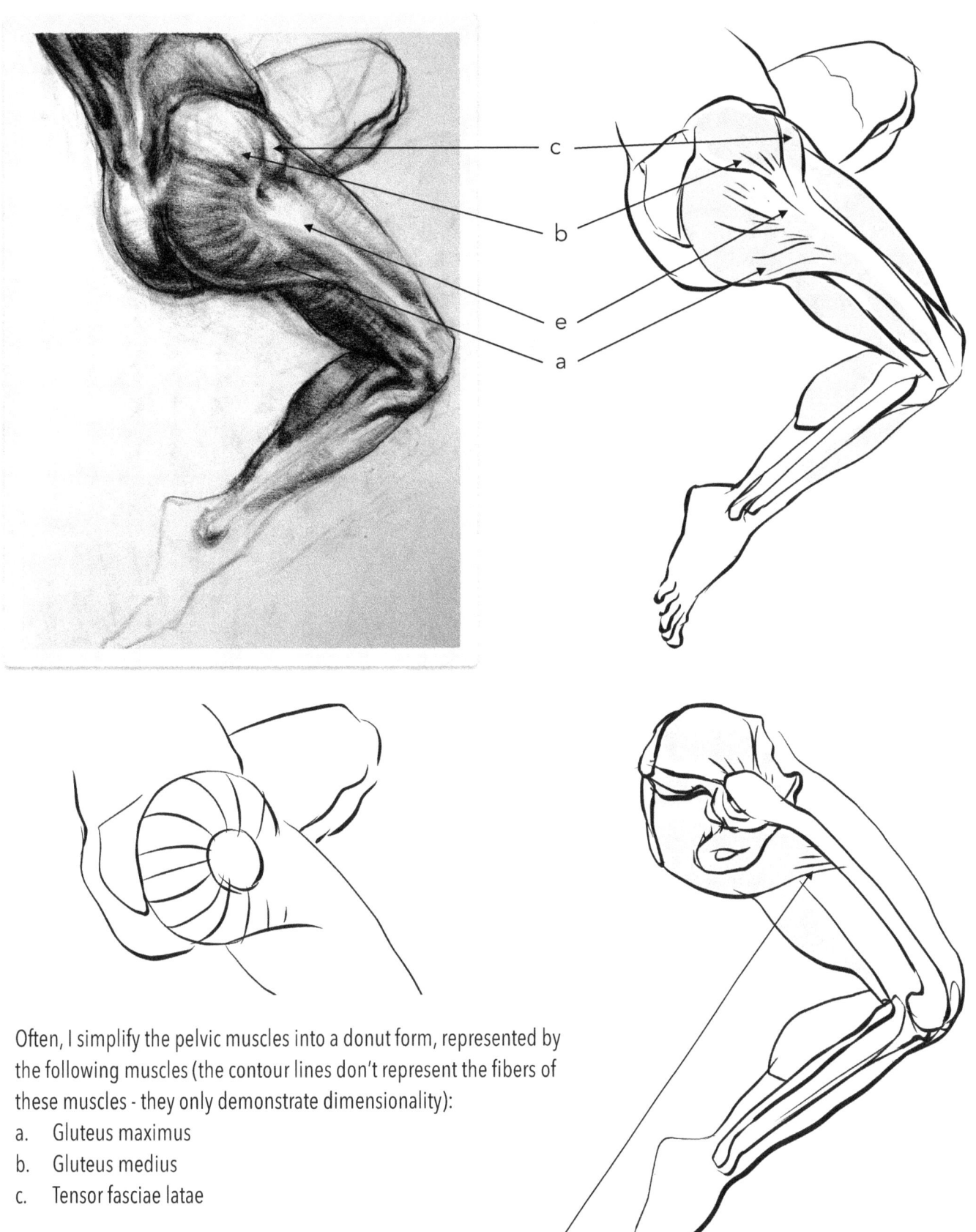

Often, I simplify the pelvic muscles into a donut form, represented by the following muscles (the contour lines don't represent the fibers of these muscles - they only demonstrate dimensionality):

a. Gluteus maximus
b. Gluteus medius
c. Tensor fasciae latae

The gluteus maximus muscle connects (inserts) to the femur, at about one third the length from the top.

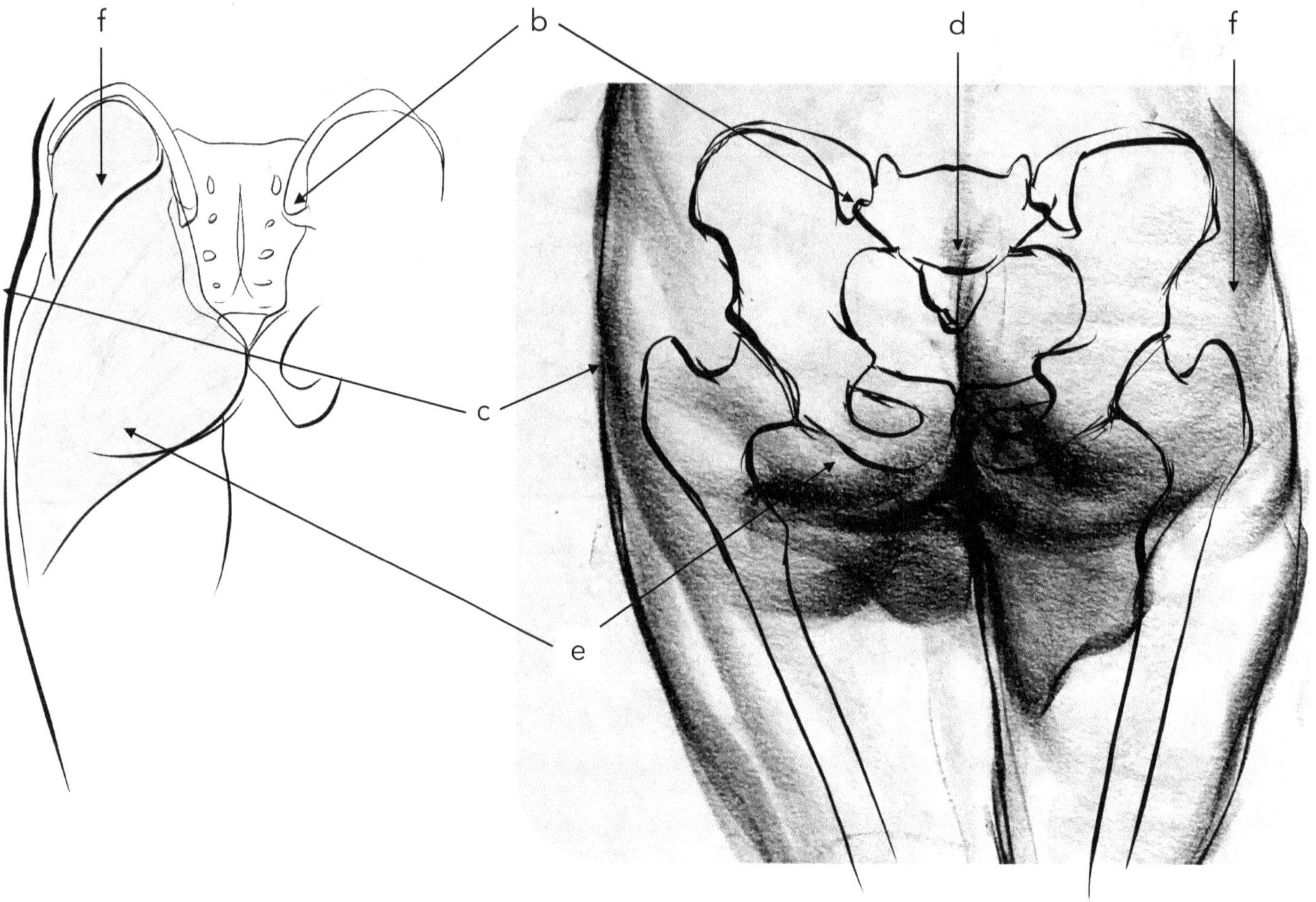

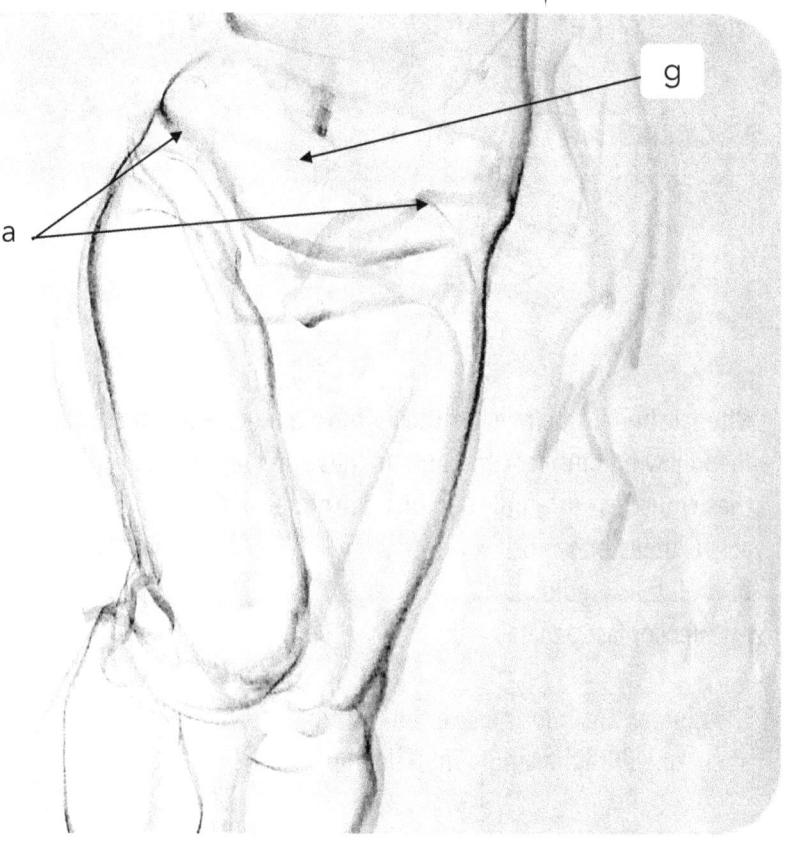

Surface landmarks of pelvic region:

a. Front edge of the pelvic bone (Anterior Superior Iliac Crest-ASIS)
b. Back edge of the pelvic bone (Posterior Superior Iliac Crest-PSIS)
c. Top of the upper leg bone (greater trochanter of the femur) on the side
d. Triangular sacrum (bone)
e. Bottom muscle of the pelvis (gluteus maximus)
f. Gluteus medius muscle

The one-minute drawing on the right shows light marks for ASIS of the pelvis. The imaginary line (g) connecting ASIS on both sides of the pelvis is a great aid for establishing the gesture of the pose.

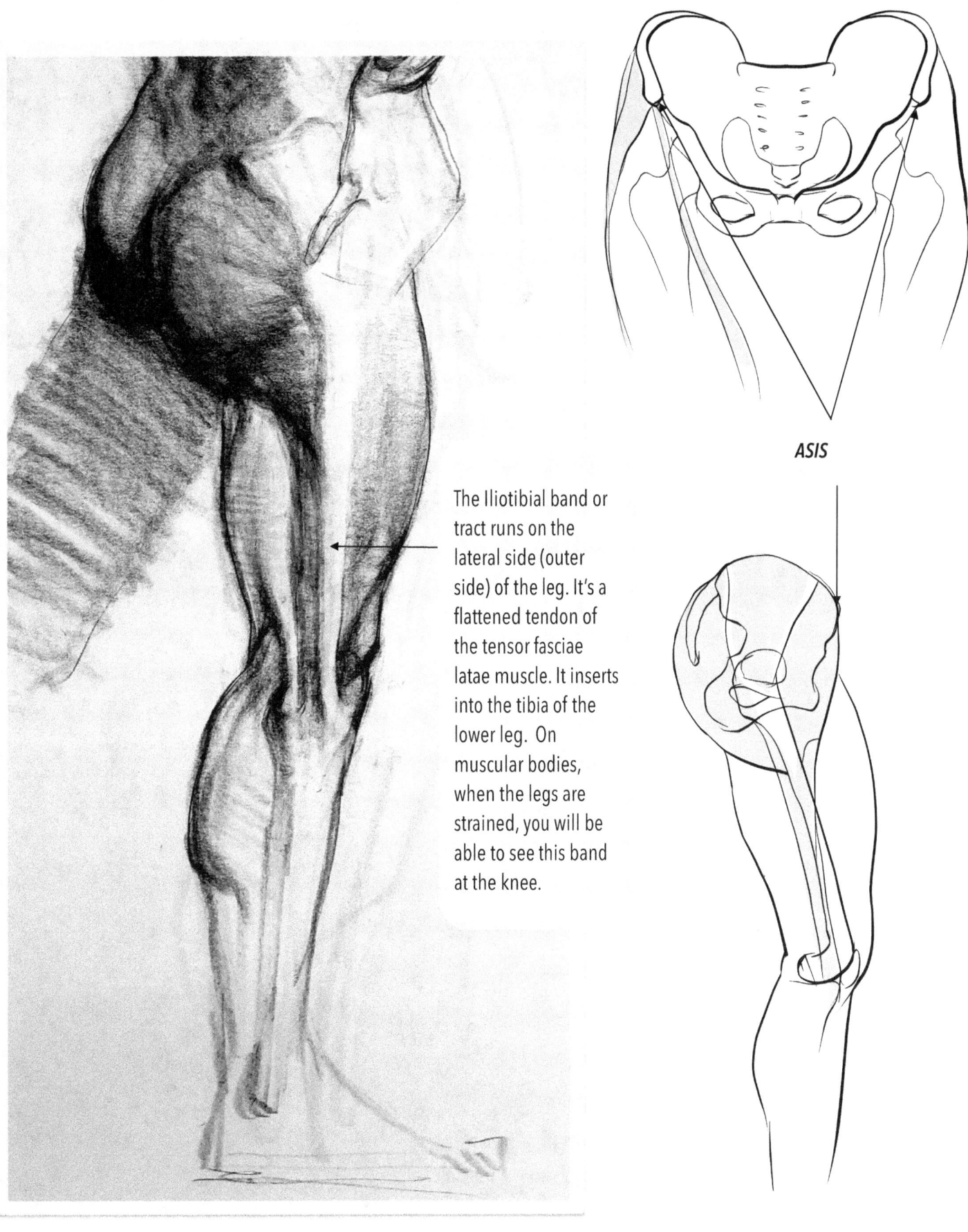

ASIS

The Iliotibial band or tract runs on the lateral side (outer side) of the leg. It's a flattened tendon of the tensor fasciae latae muscle. It inserts into the tibia of the lower leg. On muscular bodies, when the legs are strained, you will be able to see this band at the knee.

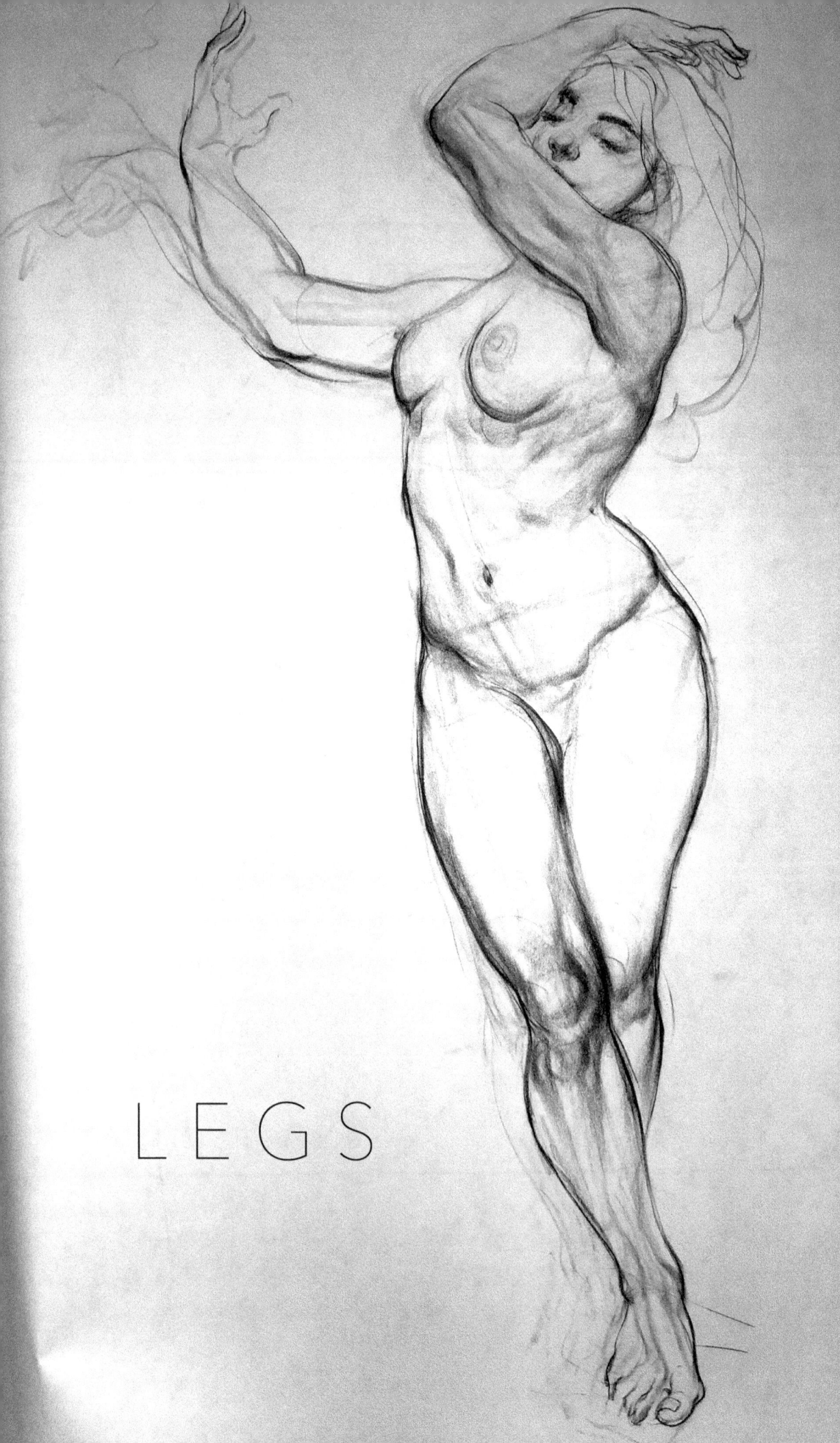

LEGS

Legs can be approximated as tapered tubes. We have already discussed proportions - the upper leg is two heads long and the lower leg is one and half heads long. If you include the foot, then the point where upper leg (femur) and lower leg (tibia) 'touch' (at the knee) is the mid point of the leg.

Important note: The leg starts at the Anterior Inferior Iliac Spine (AIIS), slightly (one and half eye lengths) below the Anterior Superior Iliac Spine (ASIS - the front surface bone of the pelvis). The leg muscle rectus femurs starts from AIIS.

The upper leg muscles we are interested in are listed below. The first three belong to the quadriceps group that straighten the leg at the knee. The hamstring muscles bend the leg at the knee.
- Rectus femoris
- Vastus lateralis
- Vastus medialis
- Hamstrings (three muscles: Biceps, semitendinosus, semimembranosus)
- Adductors of the upper leg

The sartorial muscle, the one that helps us cross our legs, is a great surface detail we can use in drawing the legs.

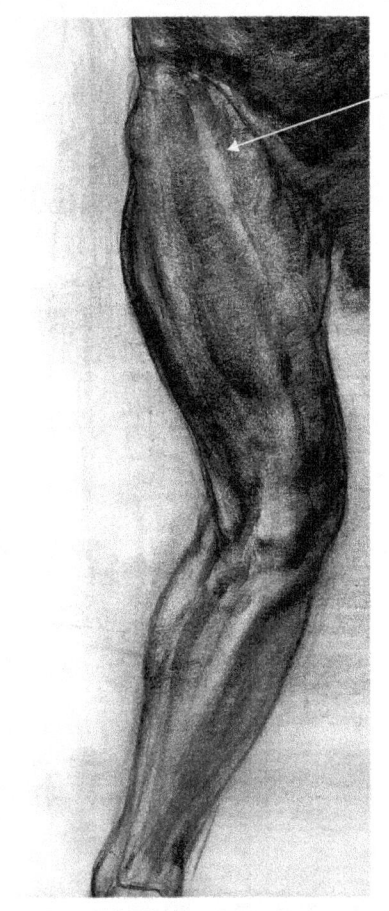

A hint of the sartorius (tailor's) muscle is in the image on the left.

The upper leg can be approximated as a tapered tube - wider at the top where it connects to the torso and narrow at the knee.

The sartorius muscle that runs diagonally across the thigh can be used to separate the thigh into two sections. The interior edge of the upper leg changes direction when it 'meets' the sartorius.

Drawing this muscle lightly can help in keeping the gesture of the leg.

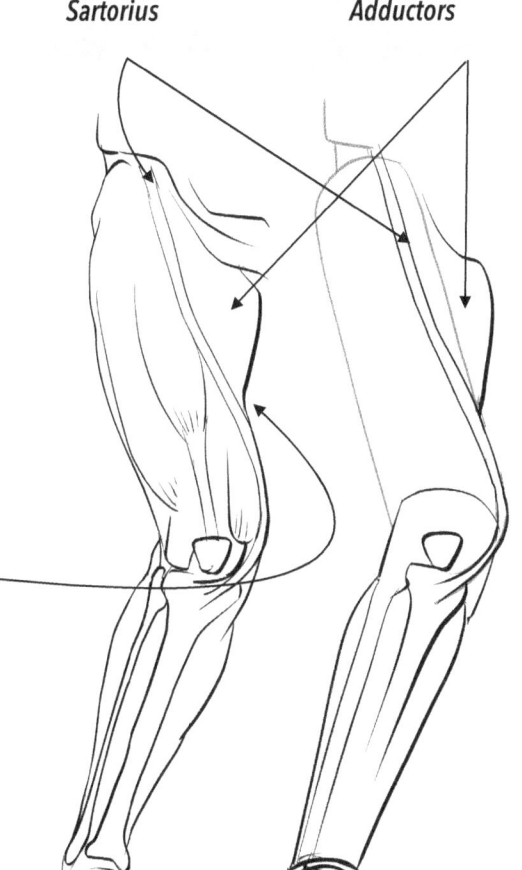

Sartorius *Adductors*

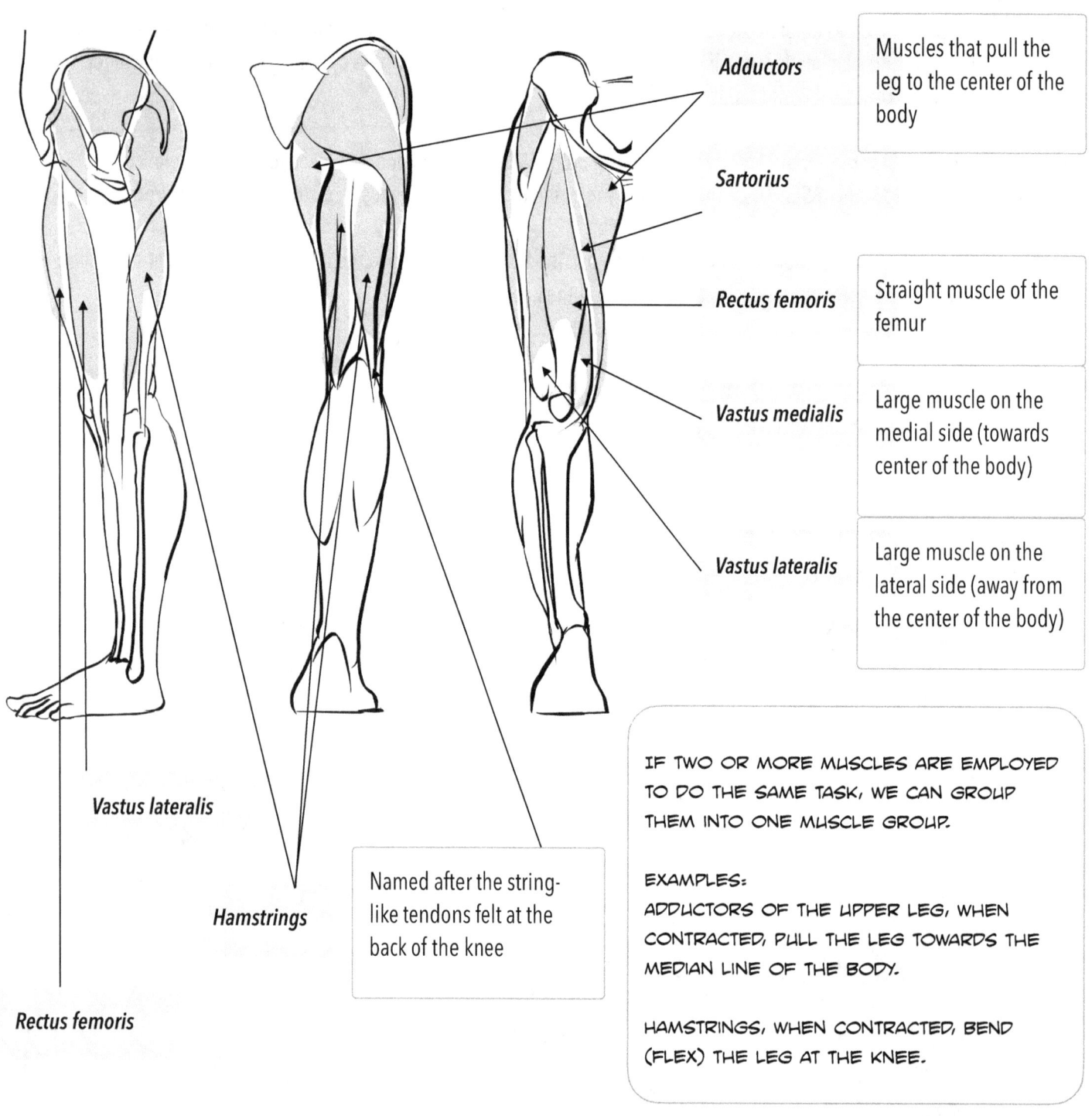

Learning terms like *adduction, abduction, flexion, extension, medial* and *lateral* side will help in your study of anatomy. We discussed *adduction*. *Abduction* is moving away from the center line of the body (the gluteus medius helps raise the leg away from the center line). *Flexion* is bending at a joint (hamstrings flex at the knee). *Extension* is the opposite of flexion (the rectus femoris helps straighten the leg at the knee).

In the drawing on the right, quadriceps, four muscles - the rectus femoris, vastus lateralis, vastus medialis, and vastus intermedius, (which we don't see on the surface) are combined into one large muscle shape.

You can also see the gluteus maximus and medius. The hamstrings connect (insert) at the lower leg bones. On the lateral side, the hamstring connects to the fibula, the thin bone in the lower leg.

Identify the upper leg muscles in the drawings below. Remember, the vertical center of the leg, including the foot, is roughly at the knee.

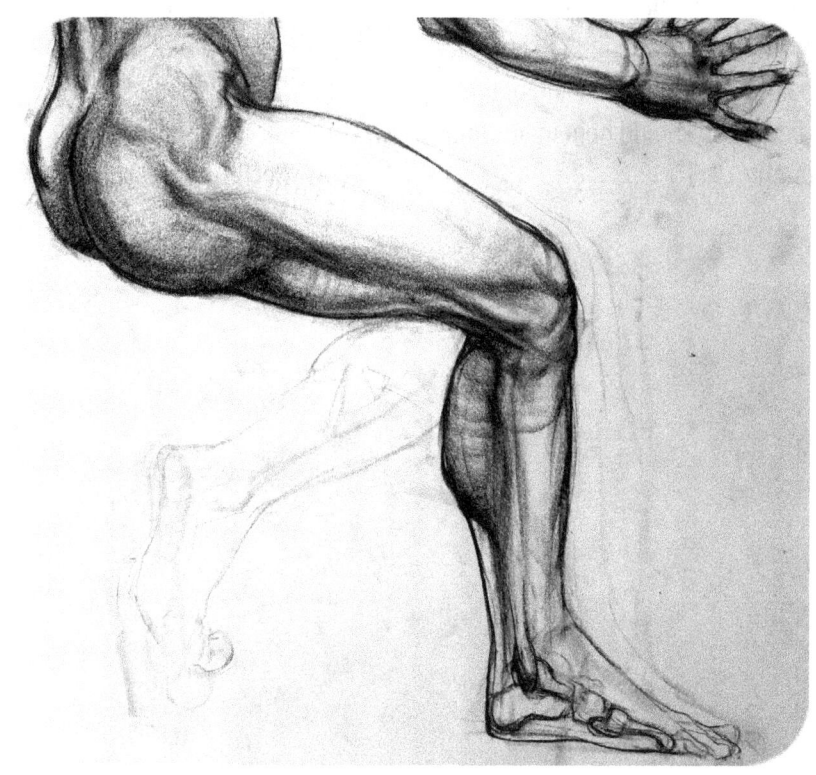

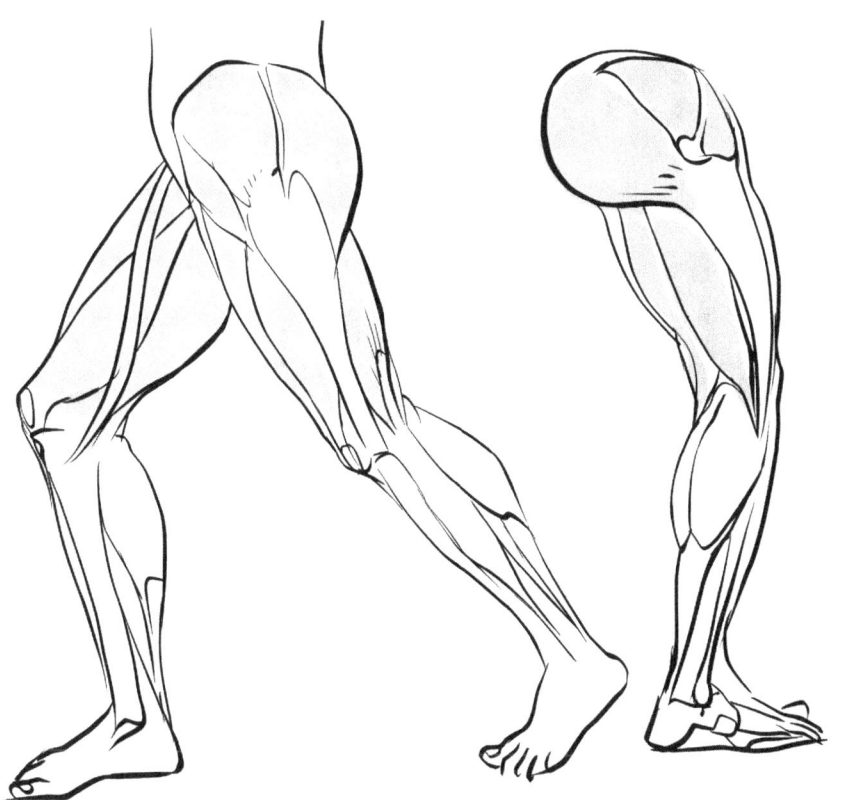

THE FIBULA, THE LOWER LEG BONE, IS A THIN BONE ON THE LATERAL SIDE. ITS NAME COMES FROM LATIN, MEANING A BROOCH. ITS SHAPE, IN COMBINATION WITH THE OTHER LOWER LEG BONE, THE TIBIA, RESEMBLES A CLASP OR SAFETY PIN.

THE TIBIA CARRIES THE WEIGHT OF THE BODY. ITS NAME DERIVES FROM A LATIN WORD FOR 'PIPE.' PERHAPS THESE BONES FROM ANIMALS WERE USED TO MAKE FLUTES? CHECK OUT CARAVAGGIO'S PAINTING 'THE LUTE PLAYER' - IS THAT A TIBIA IN THE FOREGROUND?

The surface muscles listed here are drawn or hinted at in the life drawing below. The digital drawing of the same pose should help in locating them.

a. Gluteus maximus
b. Gluteus medius
c. Iliotibial band
d. Biceps femoris
e. Rectus femoris
f. Vastus lateralis

Use simplified forms (cylinders, spheres, boxes etc) and get your proportions right. You can spend a lifetime refining those forms in making them look realistic.

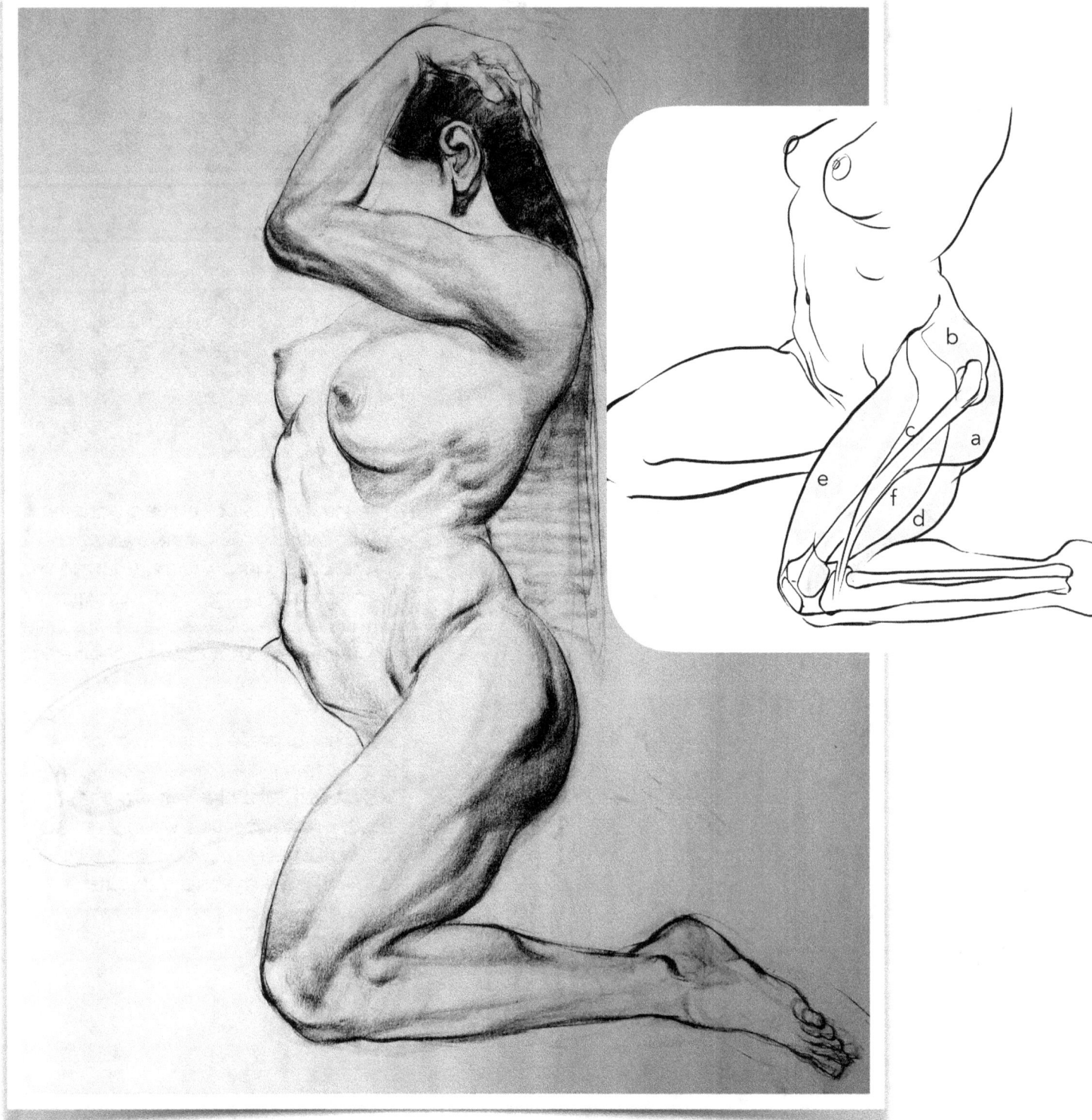

The lower leg muscles we are interested in are:
a. Calf muscle gastrocnemius
b. Calf muscle soleus
c. Tibialis anterior
d. Extensor digitorum longus
e. Fibularis longus

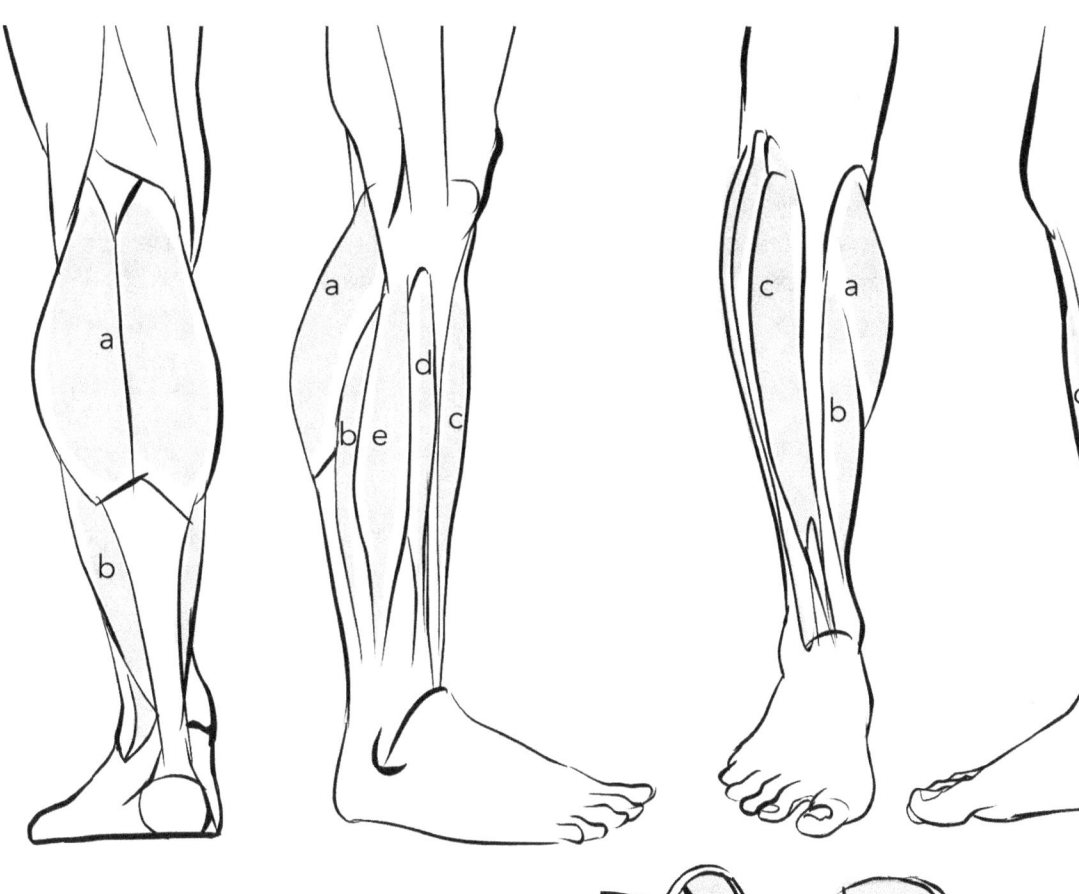

You can approximate the lower leg as a tapered cylinder and can capture its form by delineating, at the minimum, three muscles from the list above: the two calf muscles and the tibias anterior.

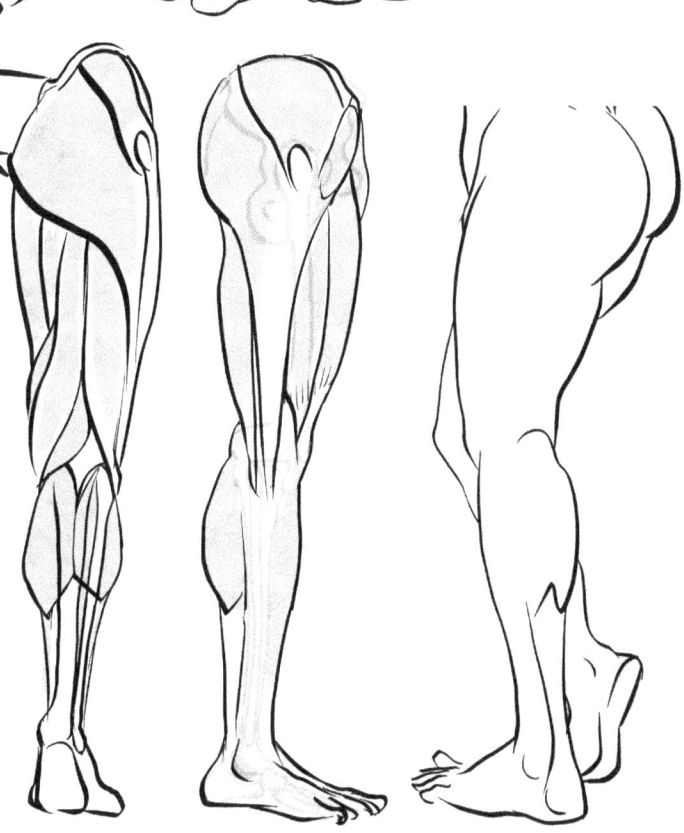

THE BULGE OF THE CALF MUSCLE DOESN'T EXTEND BEYOND THE HALFWAY POINT OF THE LOWER LEG. FOR MEN, THE MUSCLE ENDS EVEN HIGHER.

THE SHAPE OF THE BULGE IS NOT A SMOOTH CURVE. THE UPPER THREE QUARTERS OF THE LENGTH IS FLATTISH AND QUICKLY CURVES BACK INTO THE LONG TENDON THAT CONNECTS TO THE HEEL (ACHILLES TENDON).

THERE ARE MORE MUSCLES ON THE LATERAL SIDE OF THE LOWER LEG. THE MEDIAL SIDE (SHIN SIDE) OF LOWER LEG HAS FEWER MUSCLES. THE TIBIA BONE IS NEXT TO THE SKIN ON THE SHIN SIDE.

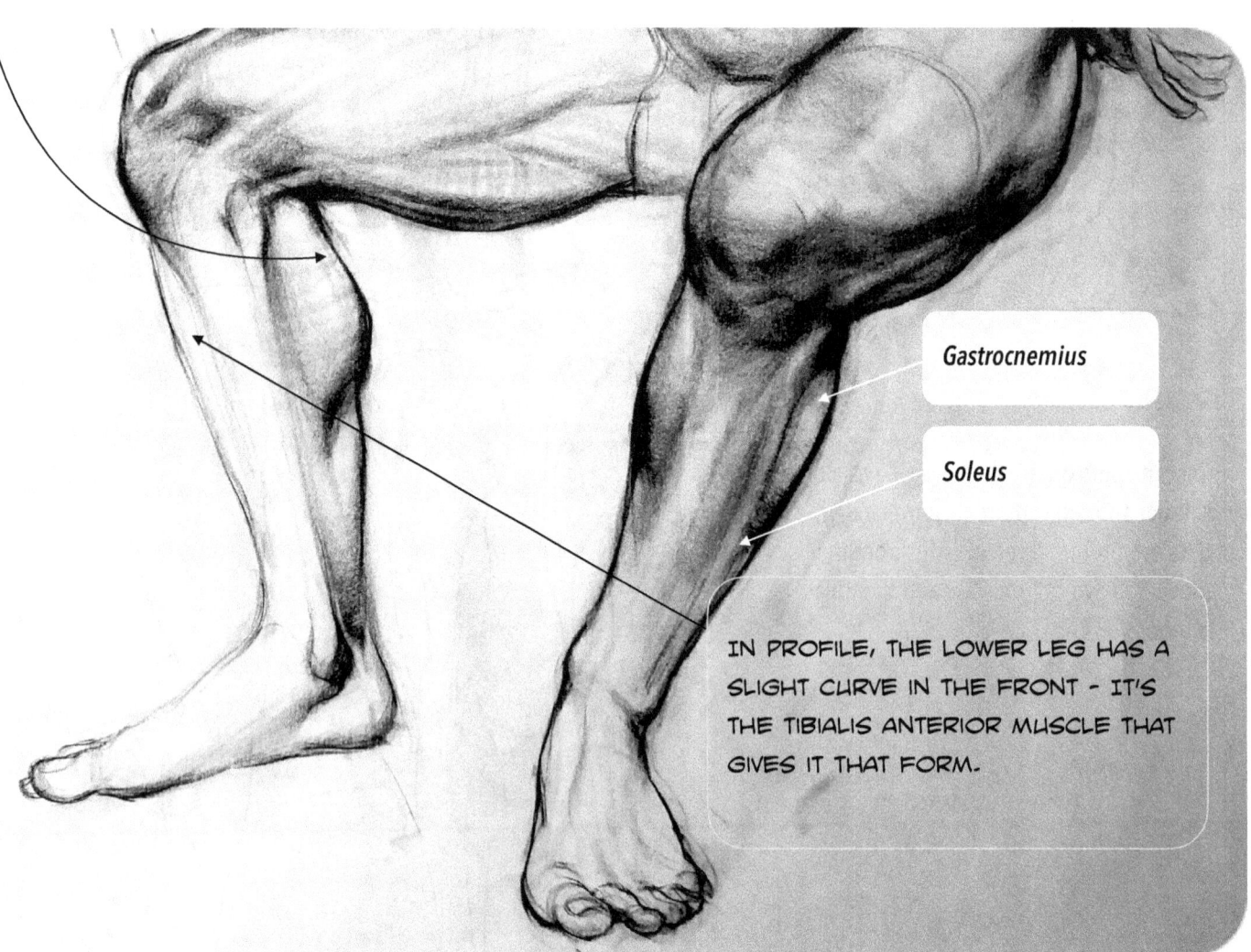

Gastrocnemius

Soleus

IN PROFILE, THE LOWER LEG HAS A SLIGHT CURVE IN THE FRONT - IT'S THE TIBIALIS ANTERIOR MUSCLE THAT GIVES IT THAT FORM.

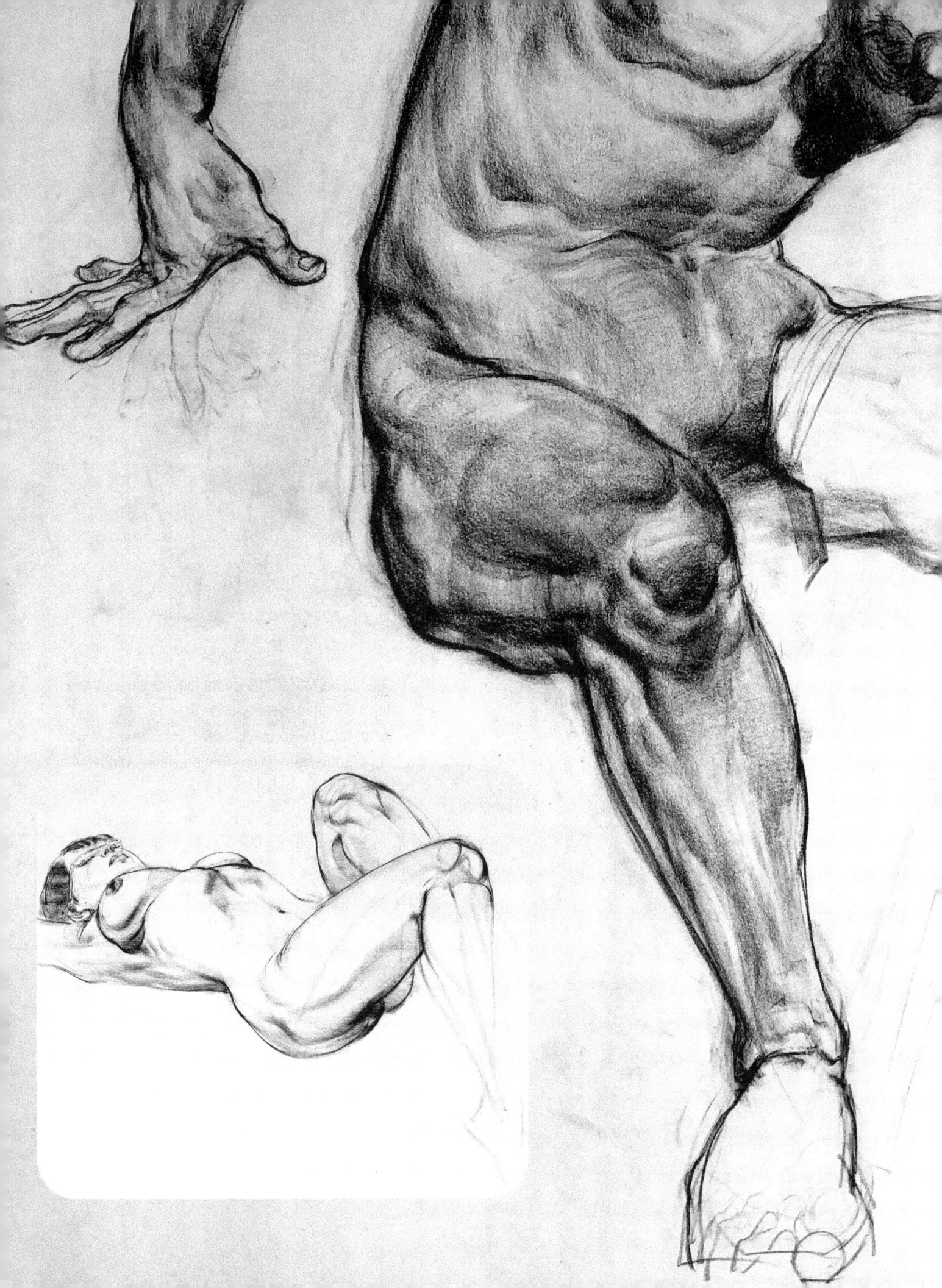

Legs aren't 'straight.' There is a change in the direction when the forms join (see the dotted line in the drawing to the right).

A few observations about the legs - the drawing on the right reveals these insights a bit more clearly:

a. Notice the simple forms.
b. a bowl for the pelvis.
c. Legs can be approximated as tapered cylinders.
d. 'Adductor' muscles connect to upper leg 'cylinder.'
e. The lateral side of the thigh is one single sloping curve. The same with the lower leg.

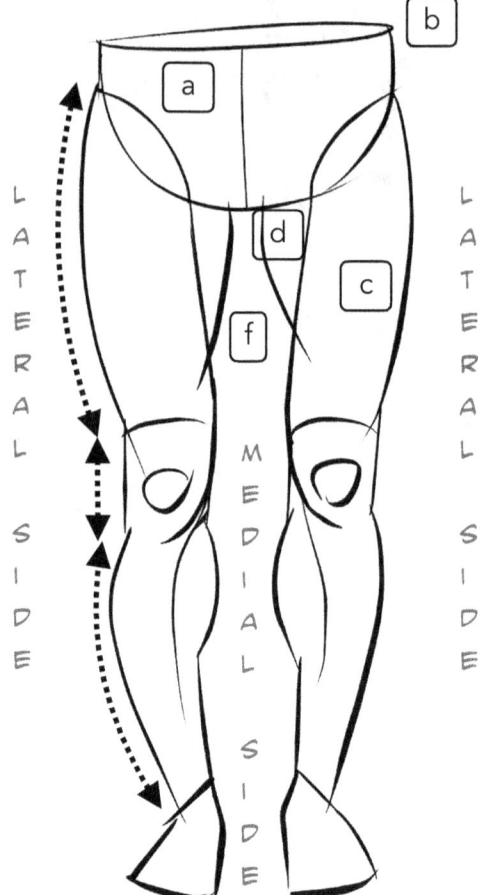

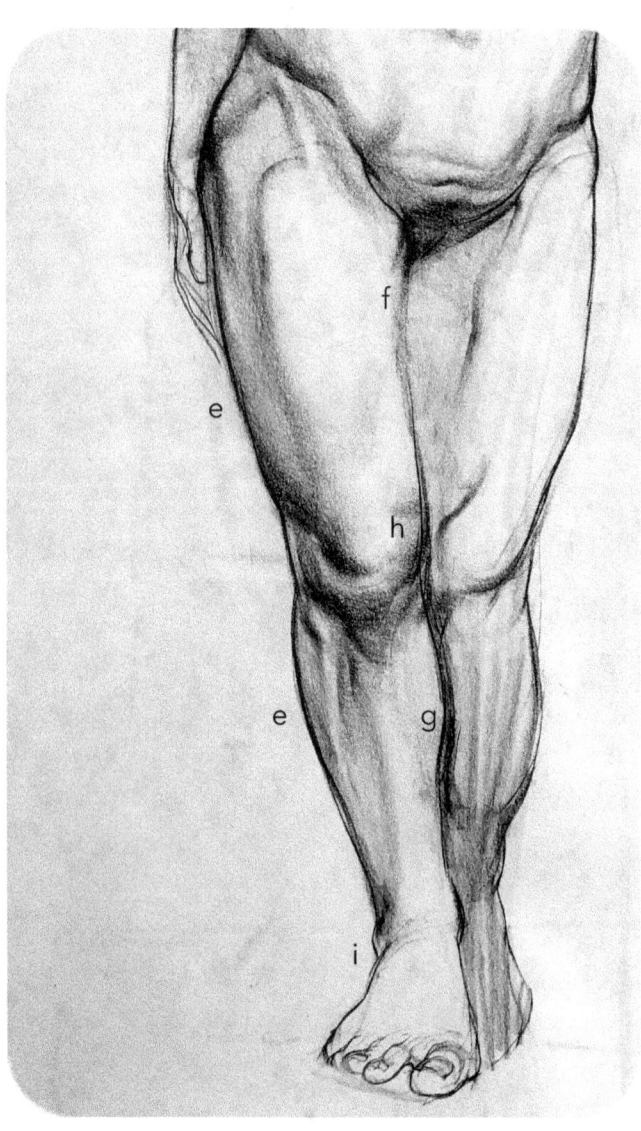

f. On the medial side of the upper leg, the contour line changes direction (clearer in the drawing above) as the adductor muscles connect to the thigh bone. See note on the sartorius muscle (section on pelvis) and its influence on the medial thigh line.
g. Similarly, on the medial side of the lower leg, the gastrocnemius muscle forms a bulge that breaks the medial edge line.
h. The medial side of the thigh ends lower than the lateral side. The vastus medialis (of quadriceps thigh muscle) protuberance is lower than the vastus lateralis (the other section of quadriceps thigh muscle).
i. At the ankle, the end of the fibula (the lateral side) is lower than the end of the tibia (medial side).

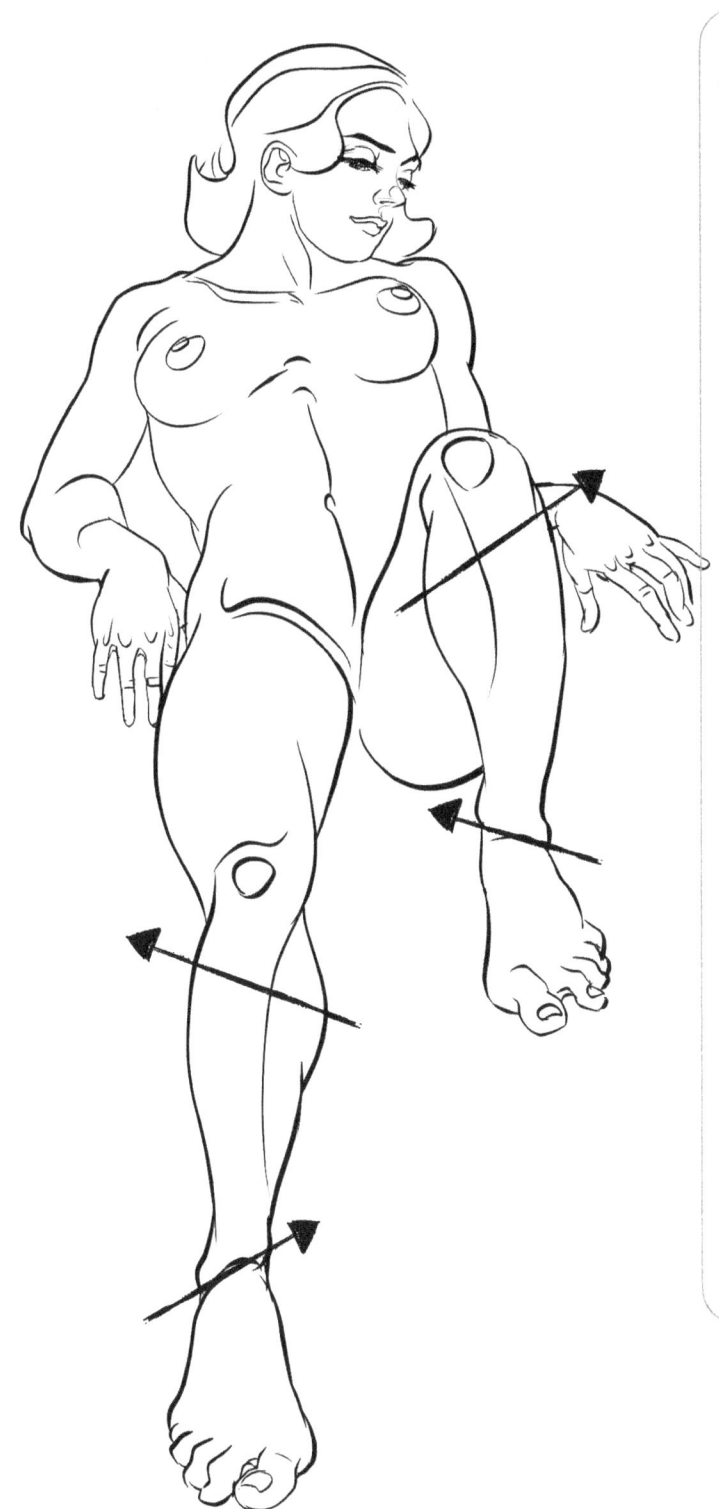

The surface ankle bone on the medial side is higher than the lateral side. The bulge of the calf muscle on the medial side is lower than on the lateral side.

To remember this, use either of the two hints - as arrows of opposing angles on each leg, or as the curves shown at right.

When connecting the foot to the lower leg, it helps to draw (very lightly) a 'connection line' as a construction line. Such lines appear to add 'stability' to the body. There is a good reason why: the tibia and fibula together form a vise-like structure that holds the foot in place.

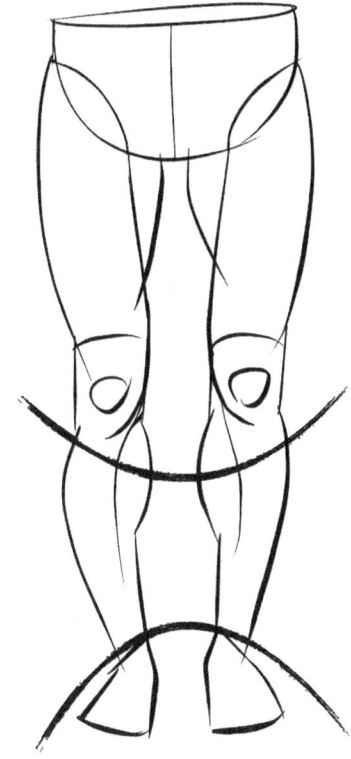

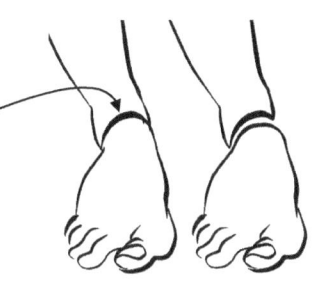

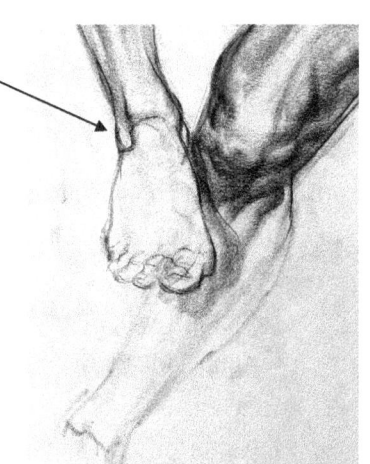

DRAWING FEET IS FUN! (not really)

Drawing feet can be difficult. Perhaps it's because they are harder to represent in simple forms, i.e., cylinders, cubes, or spheres. Or perhaps we don't have as much practice drawing feet–as children, we draw faces and landscapes; rarely do we see children's drawings of feet.

Learning the proportions and the bones of the feet will get you very far. There are a few muscles, but the foot's form is defined by its underlying bone structure.

Proportionally, a foot is slightly longer than one head.

Divide the foot into four sections: the **heel** is the large bone (calcaneus) at the back of the foot, the **tarsals** are seven small bones (just like the carpals in the hand, except there are eight carpal bones), the **metatarsals,** the long bones beyond the tarsals (meta means beyond), and then the **toes** (phalanges).

I learned that you can simplify the drawing process if you divide the foot into three cubes (see top diagram).

a. The heel occupies the first cube.
b. The tarsal bones end in the middle of the second cube.
c. The metatarsals start in the middle of the second cube and end about one-third into the third cube.
d. The center of the total length of the three cubes is where the metatarsals begin.
e. Notice the arch, which supports the weight of the body.
f. On the lateral side, the metatarsal of the little toe (fifth metatarsal) starts with a fairly large bump, which you can feel on the surface.

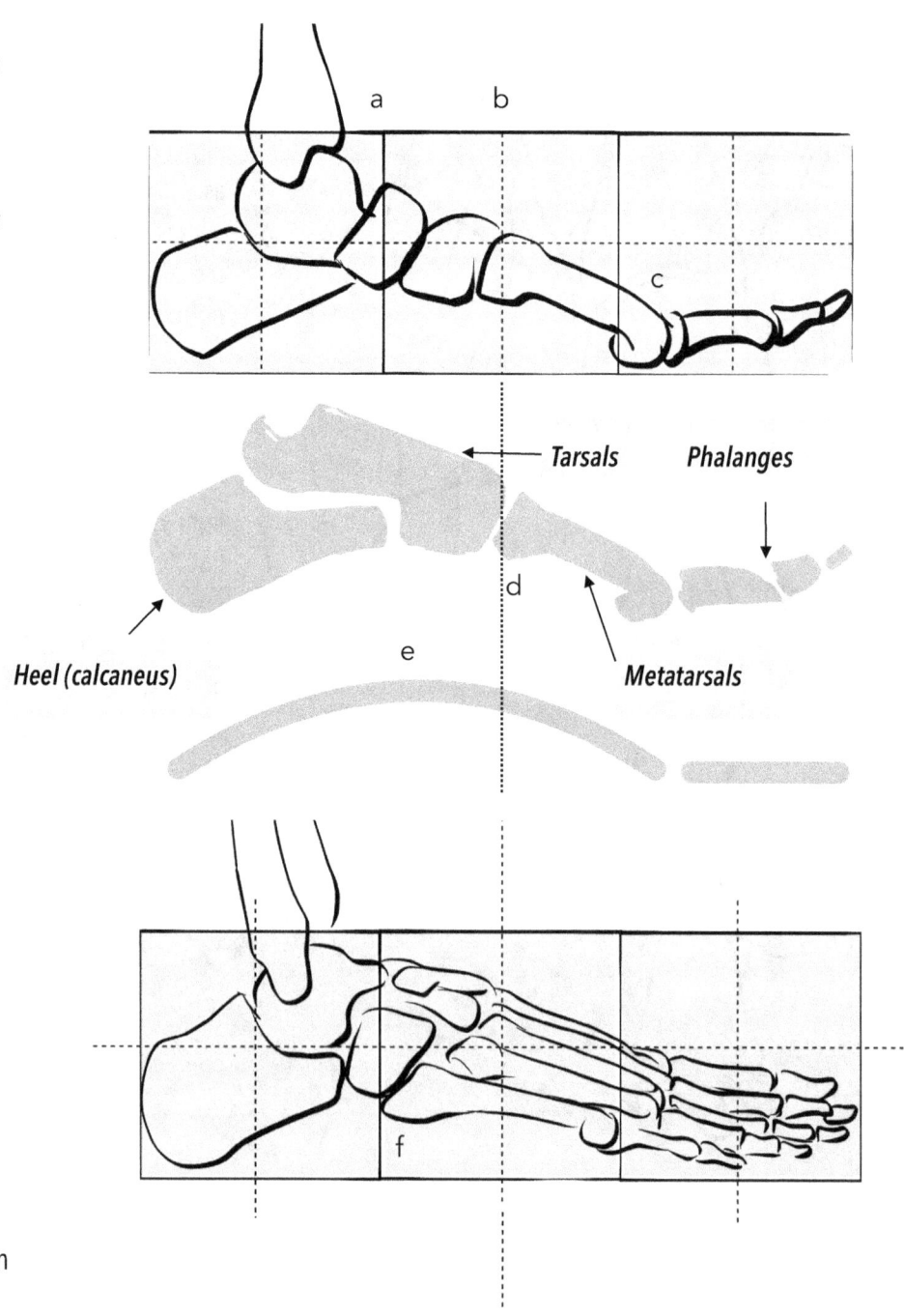

Umakanth Thumrugoti

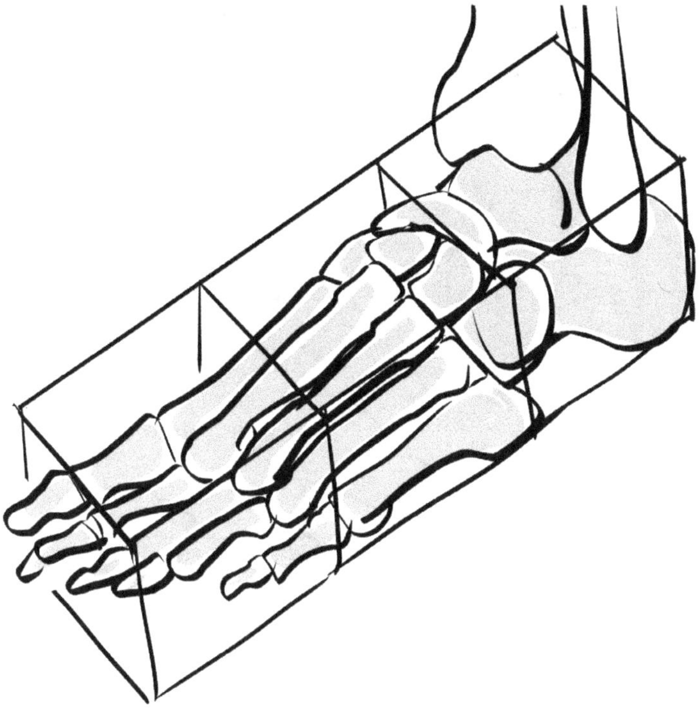

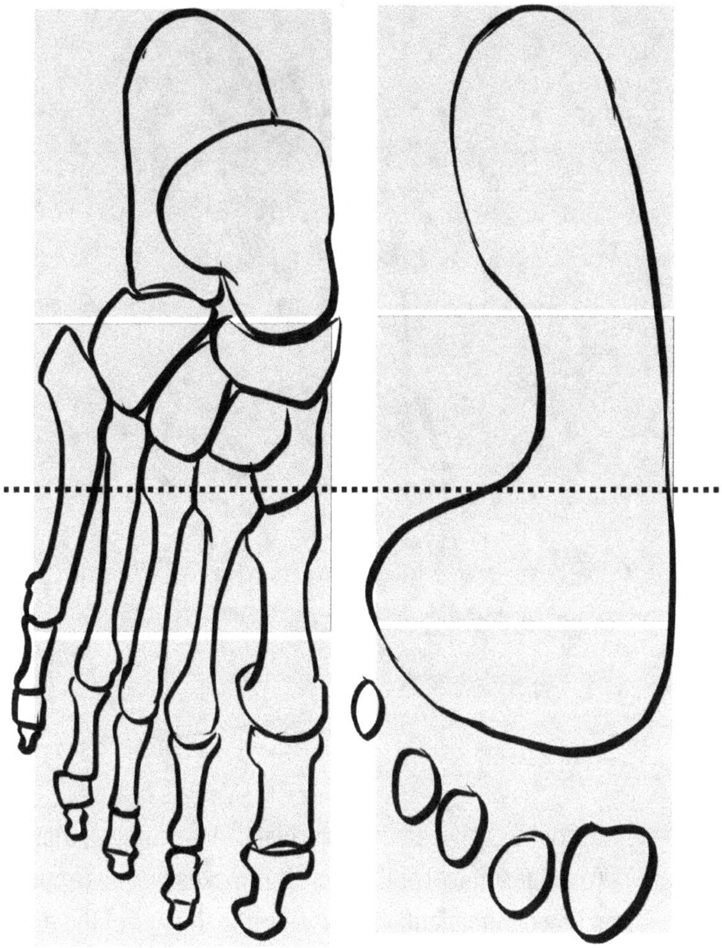

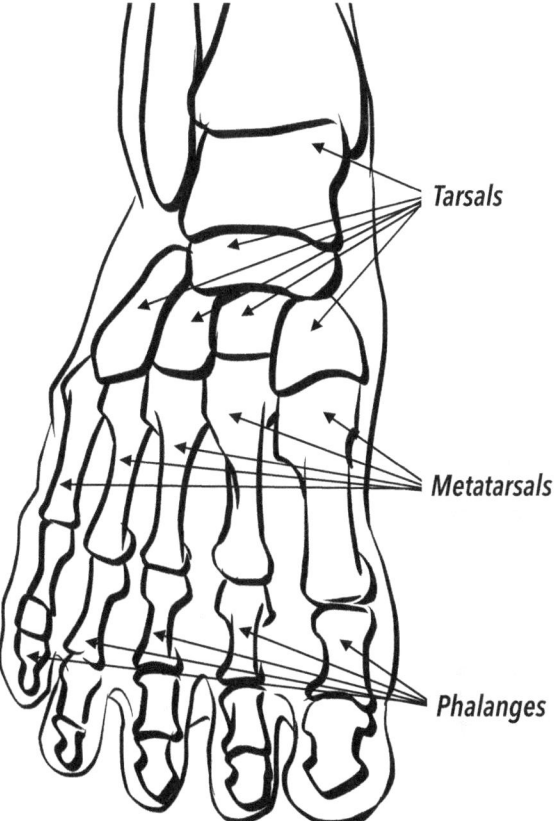

The three-cube (or squares for orthographic drawings) method should help with drawing the foot. These are rough guidelines:

a. The heel (calcaneus) bone occupies one cube.
b. Fifth metatarsal bone (for the little toe) ends at the third cube.
c. First metatarsal (for the big toe) extends into the third cube by as much as a third.
d. The center line of all three cubes will roughly fall where the big toe tarsal ends.
e. The heel bone is narrow - its width is half of the cube.
f. Fifth metatarsal (little toe) has a large bump at the head.

Drawing cubes as construction lines when drawing feet should help you if you can remember these tips.

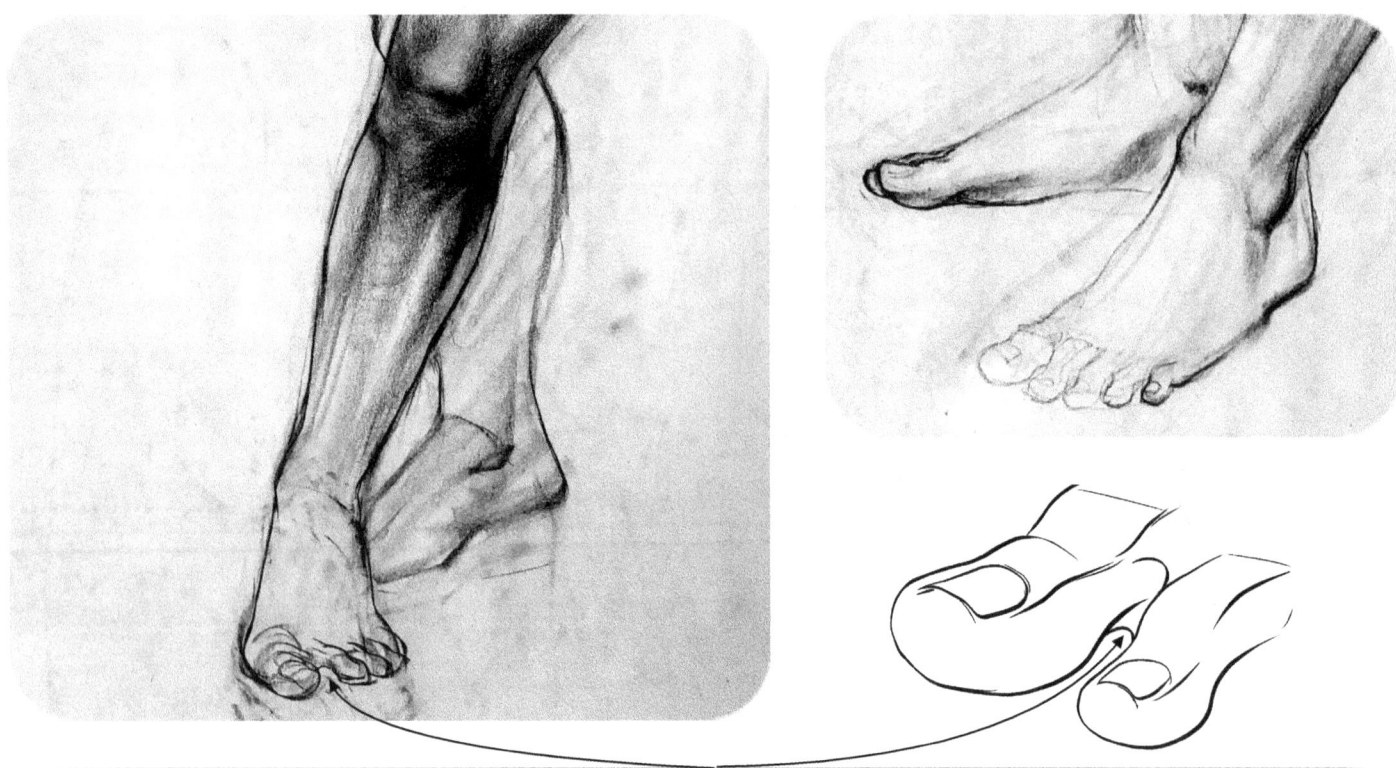

There is webbing between the toes (just like the fingers) that slopes from the top surface (dorsal surface) to the bottom surface (plantar surface) of the foot. This makes the toes appear longer on the dorsal side compared to the plantar side. The webbing line on the plantar side is closer to the tips of the toes because of that slope. Look for this line in other drawings in this book. *That line can help add dimensionality to the drawing of the foot.*

As you know, the lengths of the toes differ. Usually, the second toe is the longest.

a. A straight line from the beginning, at the base of the big toe roughly speaking, crosses the vertical center of the little toe.
b. Each toe has, again roughly speaking, four angles in its profile - up, flat, down and finally straightening out at the tip. See the image on the right.

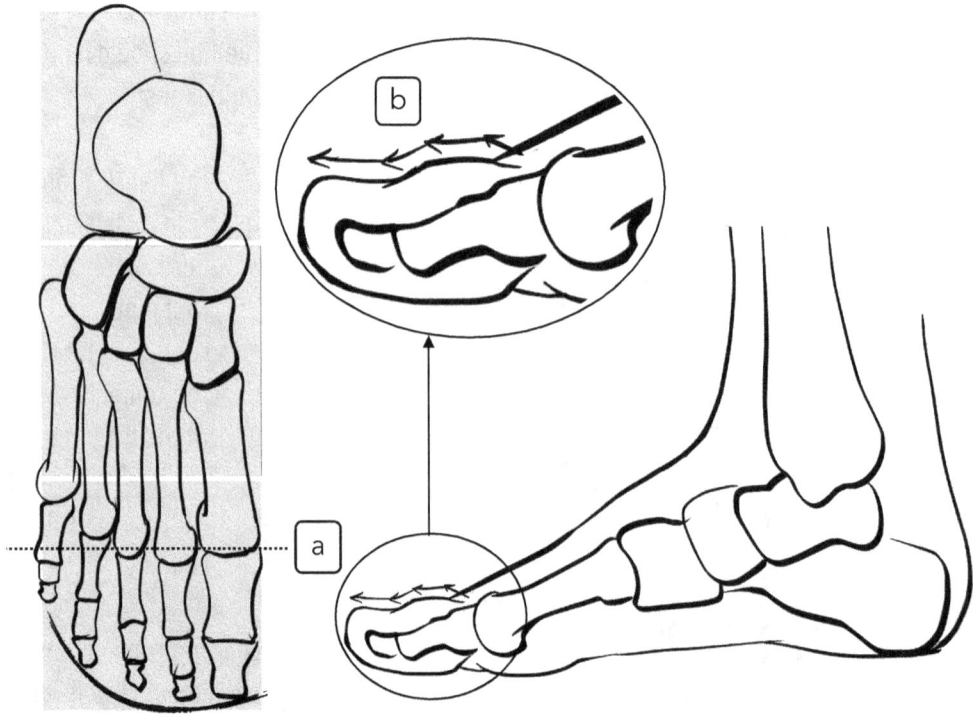

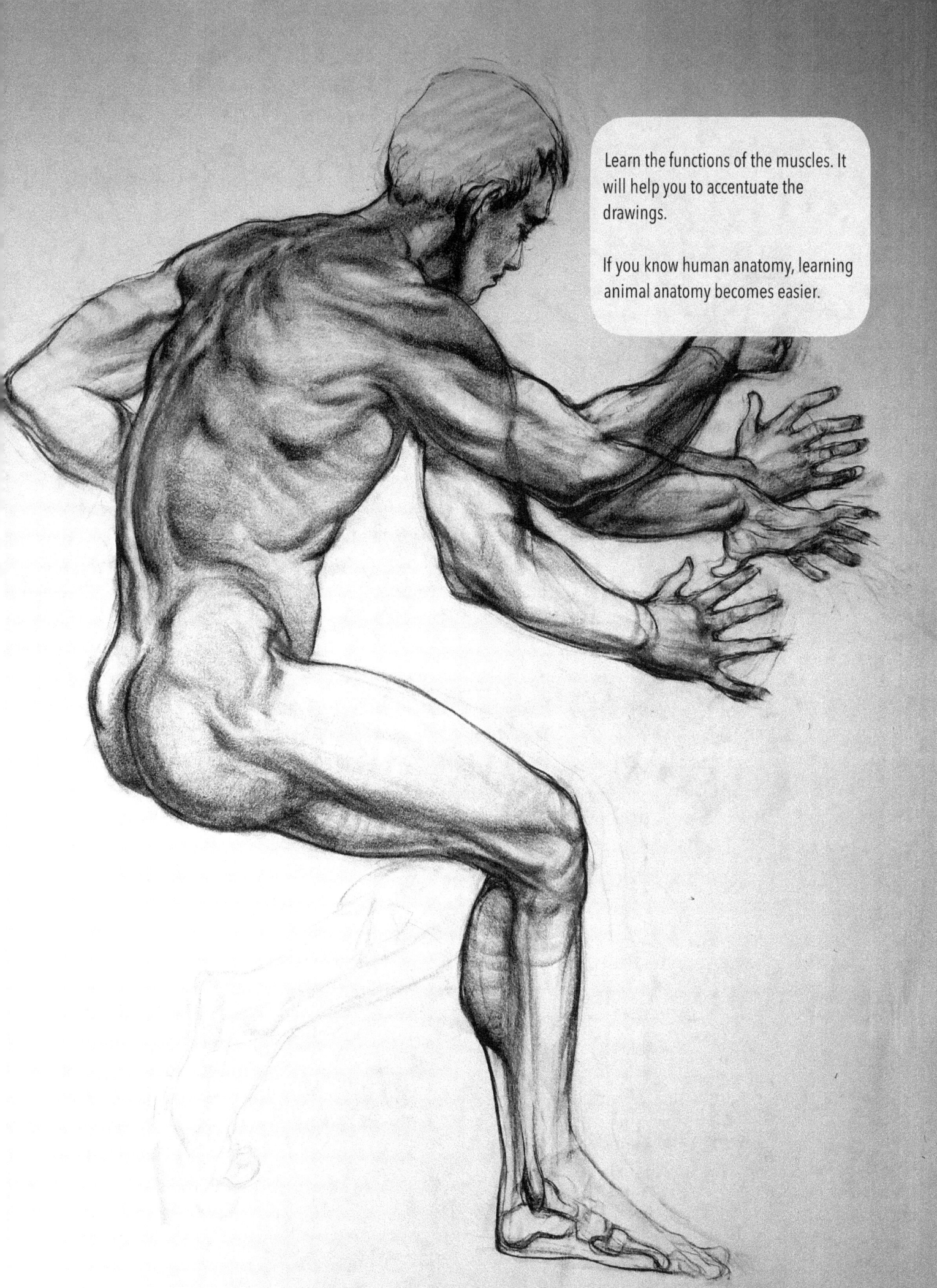

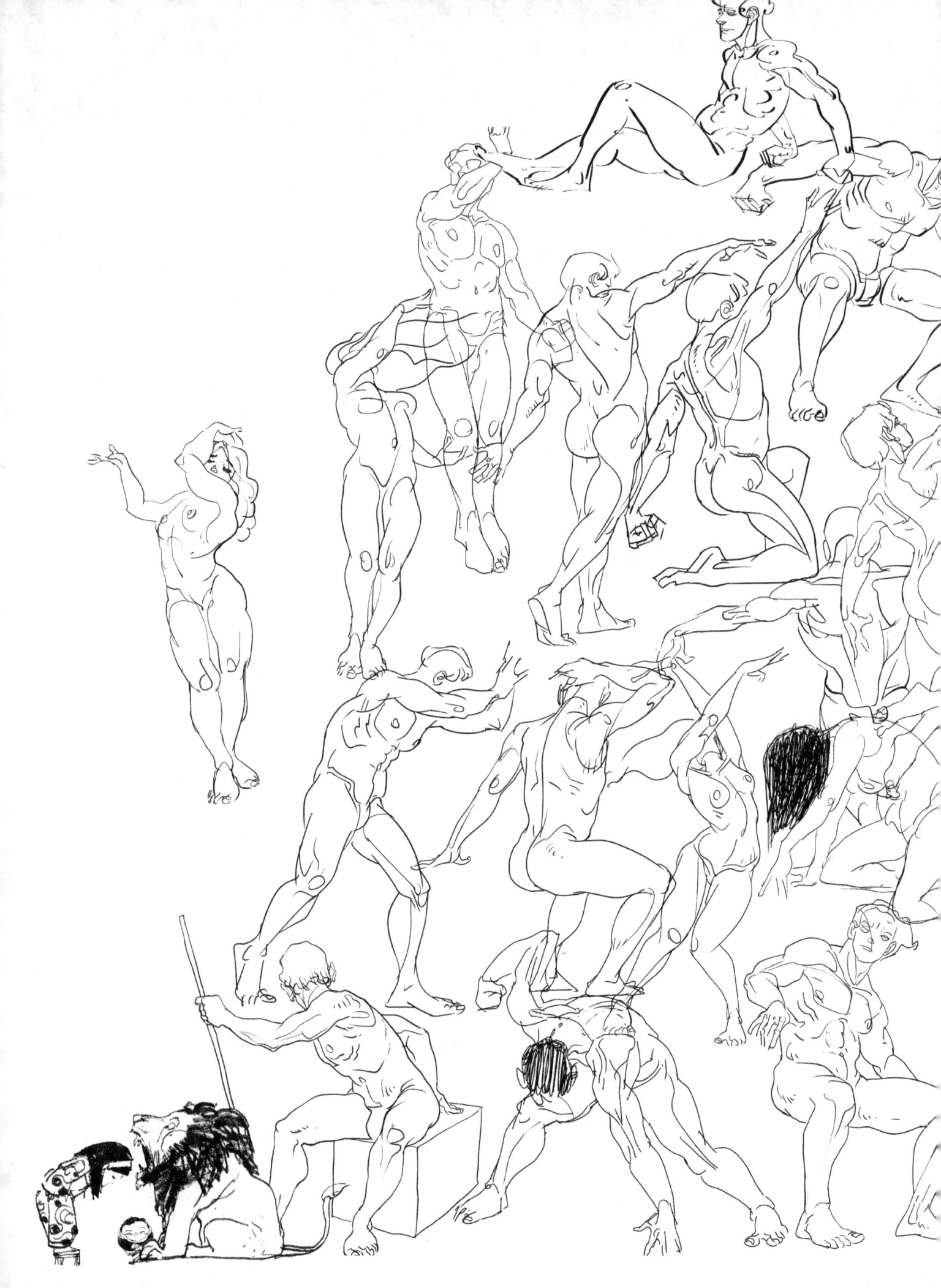

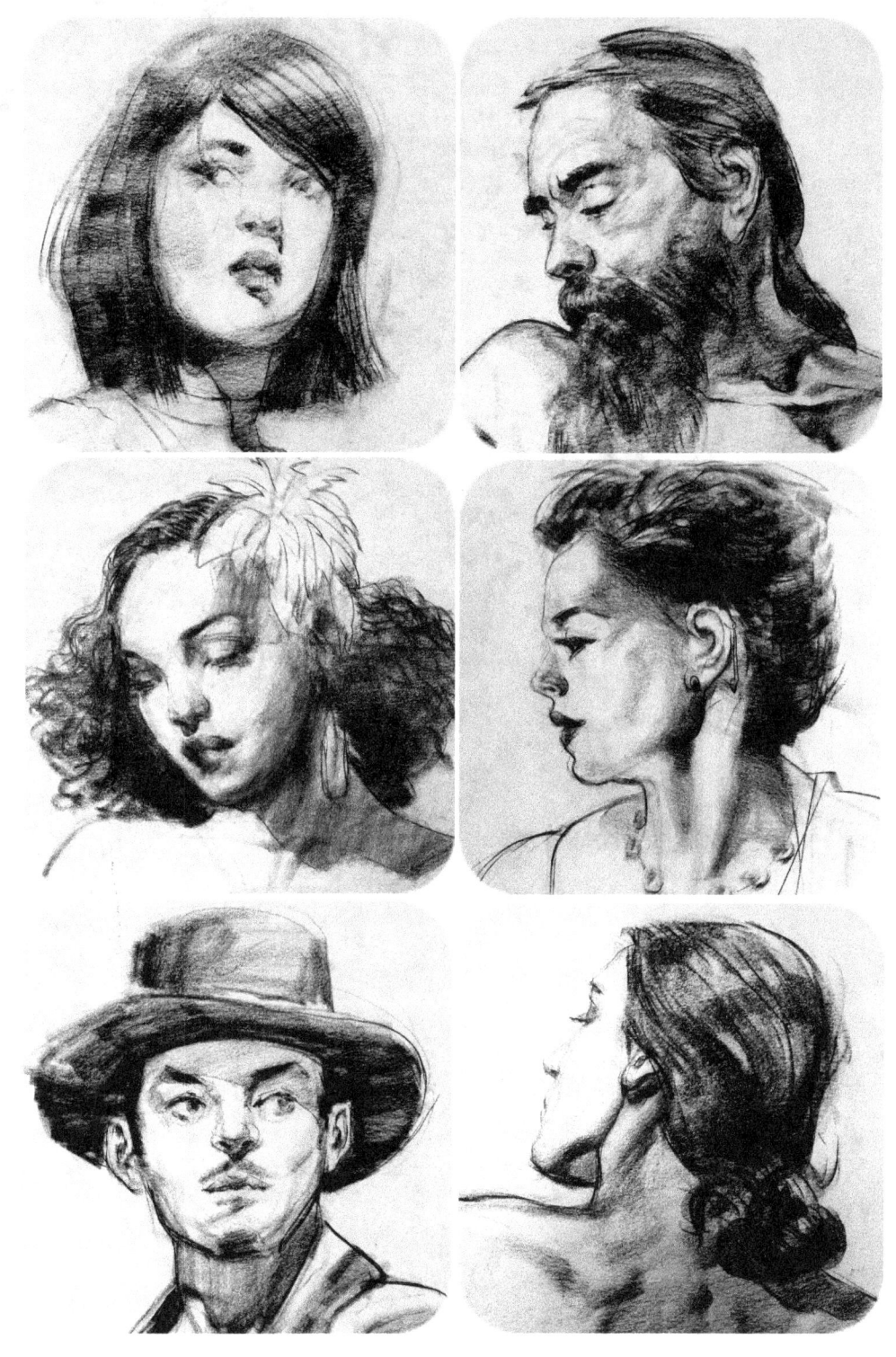

HEAD DRAWING

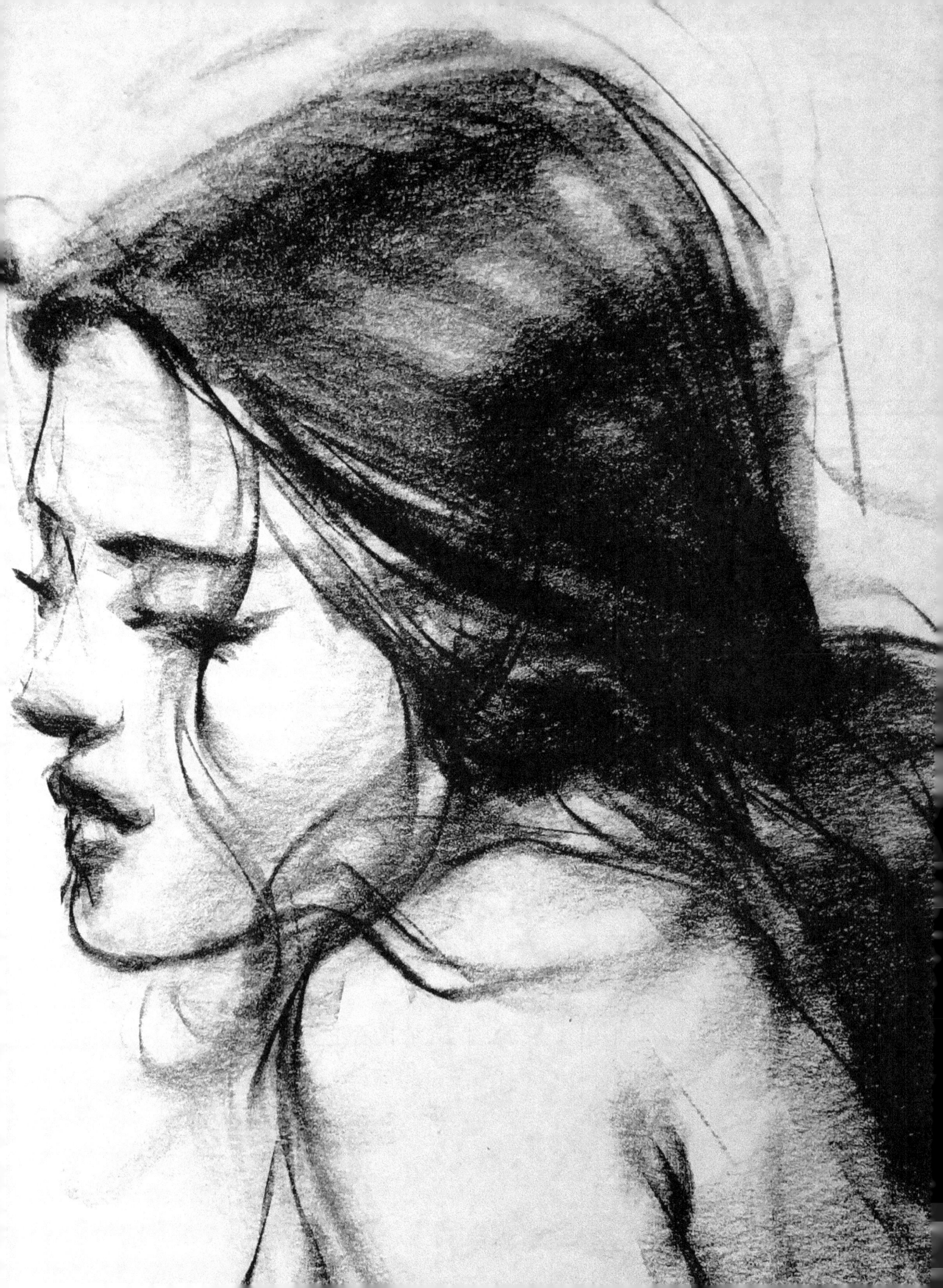

Here are two head drawings from life and their constructional breakdown below.

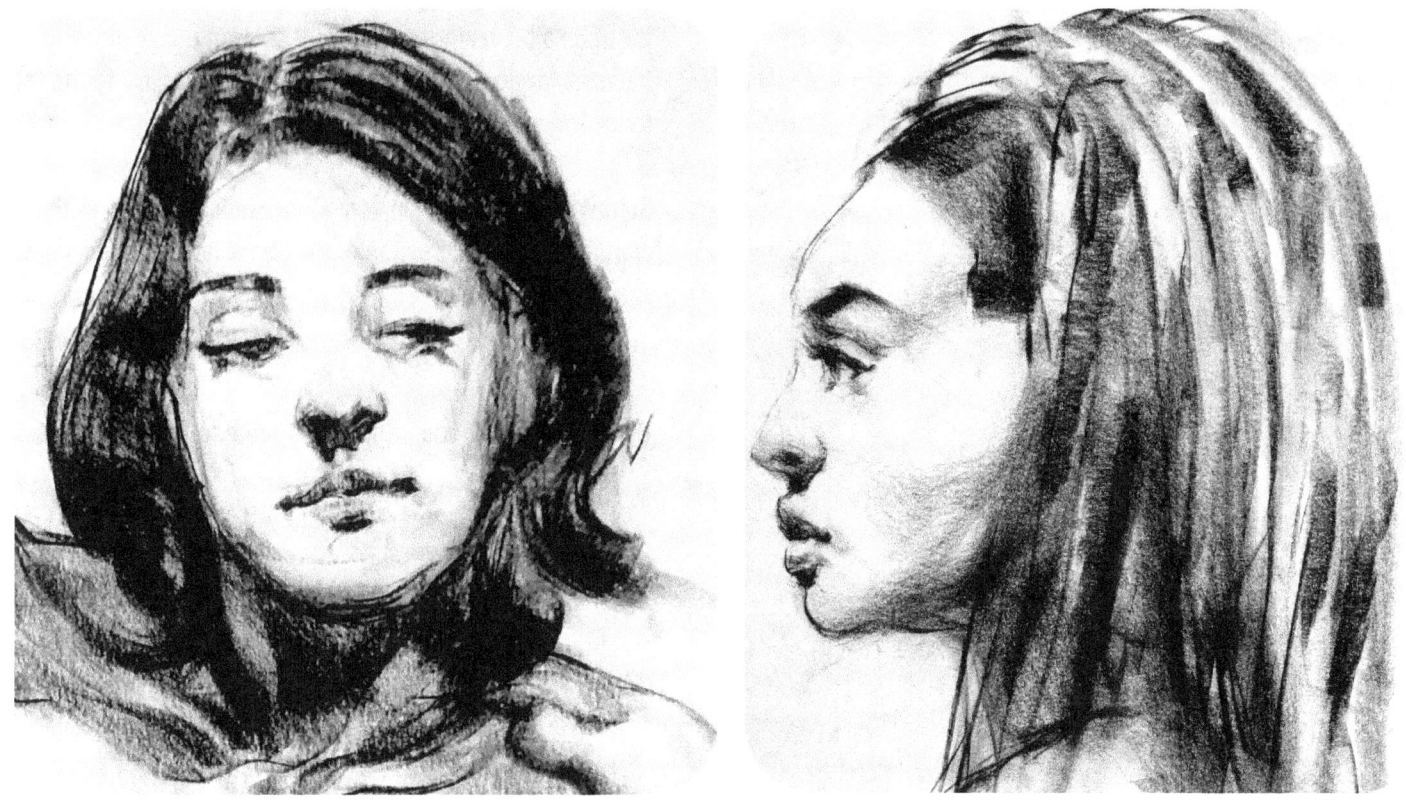

The eye line divides the head into two equal halves. From the hairline, the face can be divided into three equal sections. The head above the eyebrows can be divided into three equal thirds. In a profile view, the ear divides the head into two equal halves.

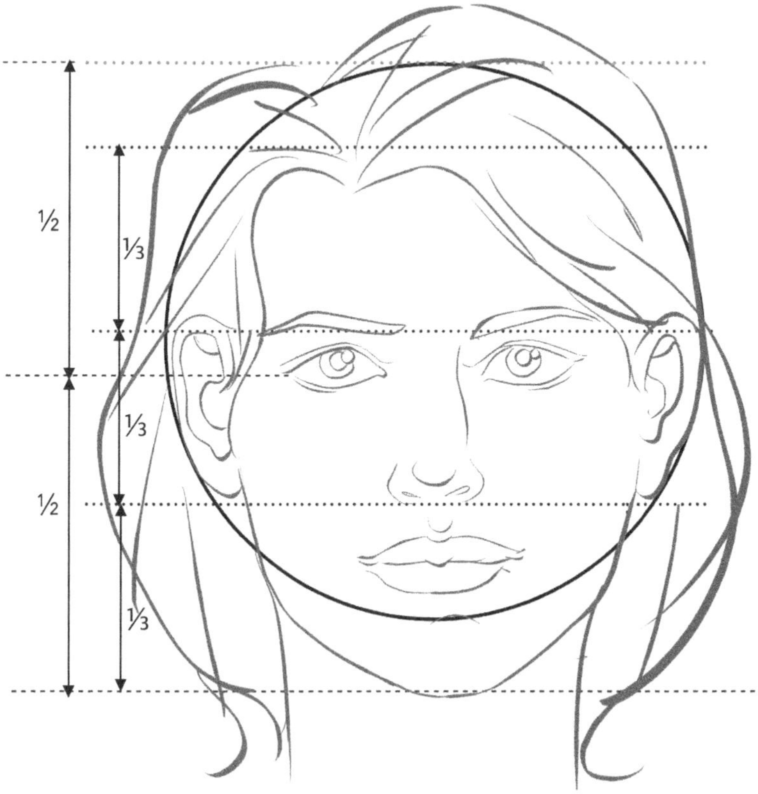

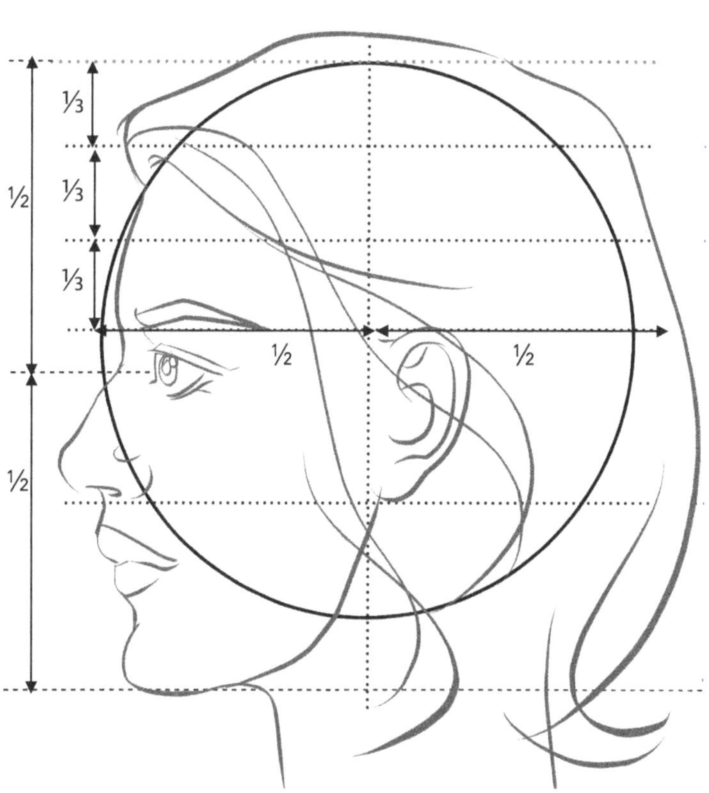

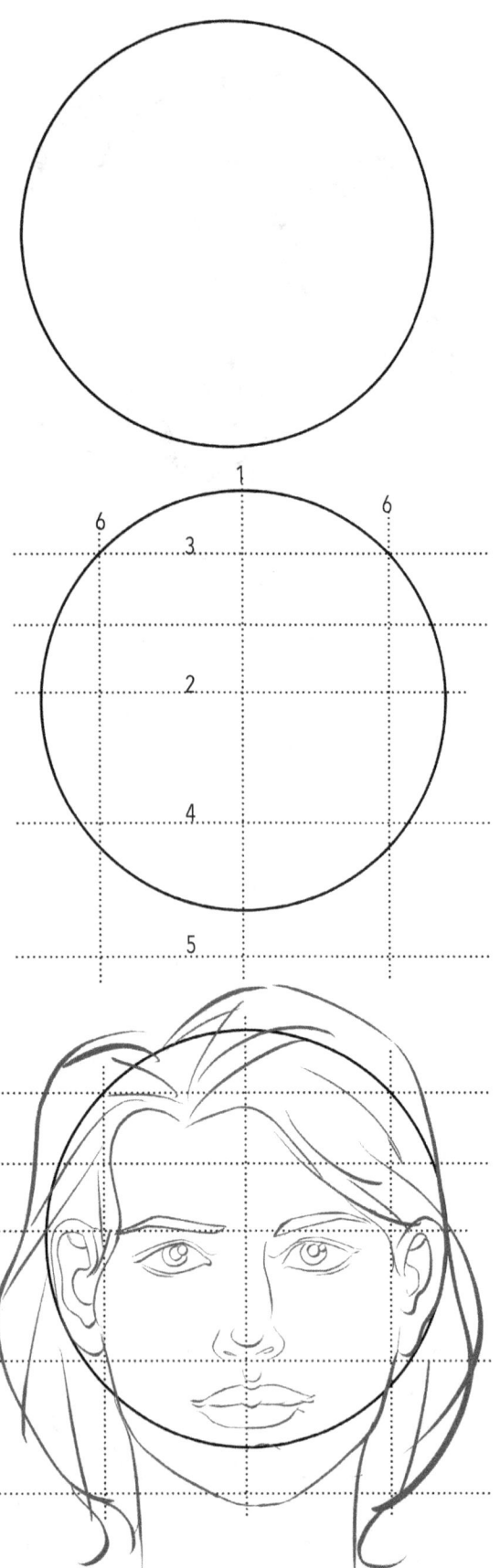

It can be a bit vexing when art instruction books present 'recipes' for good drawing as a list of steps. I have found the following steps to be very helpful - give them a try.

Start with a sphere, it's a very rough approximation of the cranium. The lower section of the head (jaw) extends below the sphere.

Draw the proportional guidelines in the following order:

- Line 1. The nose line establishes the center of the forehead. It runs through the nose, lips and chin.
- Line 2. The eyebrow line at the center of the sphere.
- Line 3. Divide top half of line 1 into three equal sections. This top line (line 3) is the hairline.
- Line 4 marks the bottom of the nose. Distance between line 2 and 3 is the same as the one between line 2 and 4.
- Line 5 is the chin line. It's at the same distance from 4 as line 2 is from 4.
- Line 6 is useful when drawing a front-facing head. It's a vertical line where the circle intersects line 3. This is where the ears are connected to the head.

You can use these guidelines in profile drawing, too.
- Line 2 gives you the eyebrow line.
- Line 3 gives you the hairline.
- Line 4 gives you the end of the nose - note it's where the wings of the nose connect to the upper lip. Line 4 isn't the location of the tip of the nose. The tip of the nose can be higher or lower than this line.
- Line 5 is where the chin is located.

Line 1 is more interesting. In *profile, the* ear connects to the face, roughly speaking, on line 1. Very useful in placing the ear, as we will discover in next few pages.

A few more observations:

- The length of the ear is roughly the length of the nose.
- The face can be described visually in thirds. The top third has eyebrows and hairline, second third contains eyes, nose, and ears, and the bottom third contains the mouth and chin.
- The location of the iris is roughly in line with the corners of the mouth. Draw a straight line from the corners of the mouth, parallel to the face. The line will go through the iris.
- The inner corner of the eye is in line with the outer edge of the nostril. If you draw a straight line parallel to the face from the edge of the nostril, it will connect to the inner corner of the eye.

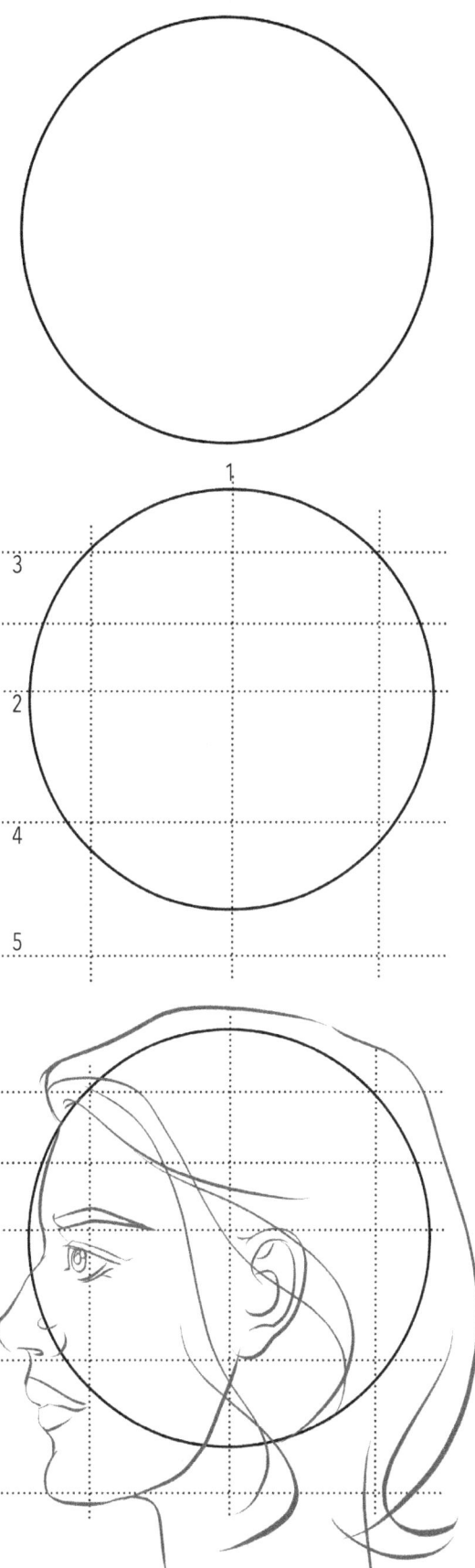

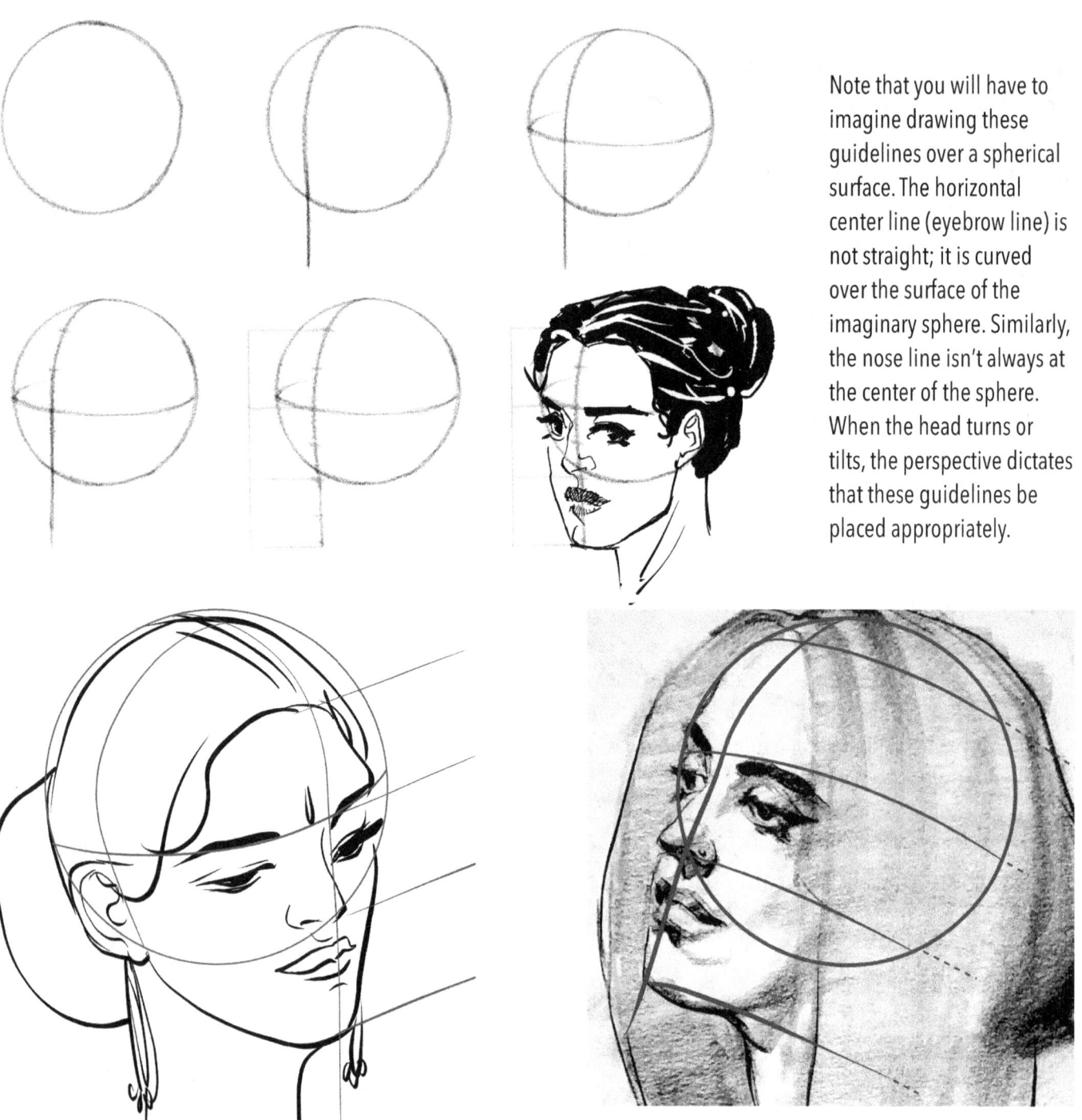

Note that you will have to imagine drawing these guidelines over a spherical surface. The horizontal center line (eyebrow line) is not straight; it is curved over the surface of the imaginary sphere. Similarly, the nose line isn't always at the center of the sphere. When the head turns or tilts, the perspective dictates that these guidelines be placed appropriately.

A DIFFERENT WAY OF MEASURING: THE HEAD IS SEVEN EYES TALL (FROM THE BOTTOM OF THE CHIN TO THE TOP OF THE HEAD), FIVE EYES WIDE (THE WIDEST PART OF THE HEAD ON THE EYEBROW LINE WHEN THE HEAD IS FACING THE FRONT) AND BETWEEN SIX AND SEVEN EYES DEEP (FROM THE FOREHEAD LINE TO THE BACK OF THE CRANIUM IN PROFILE).

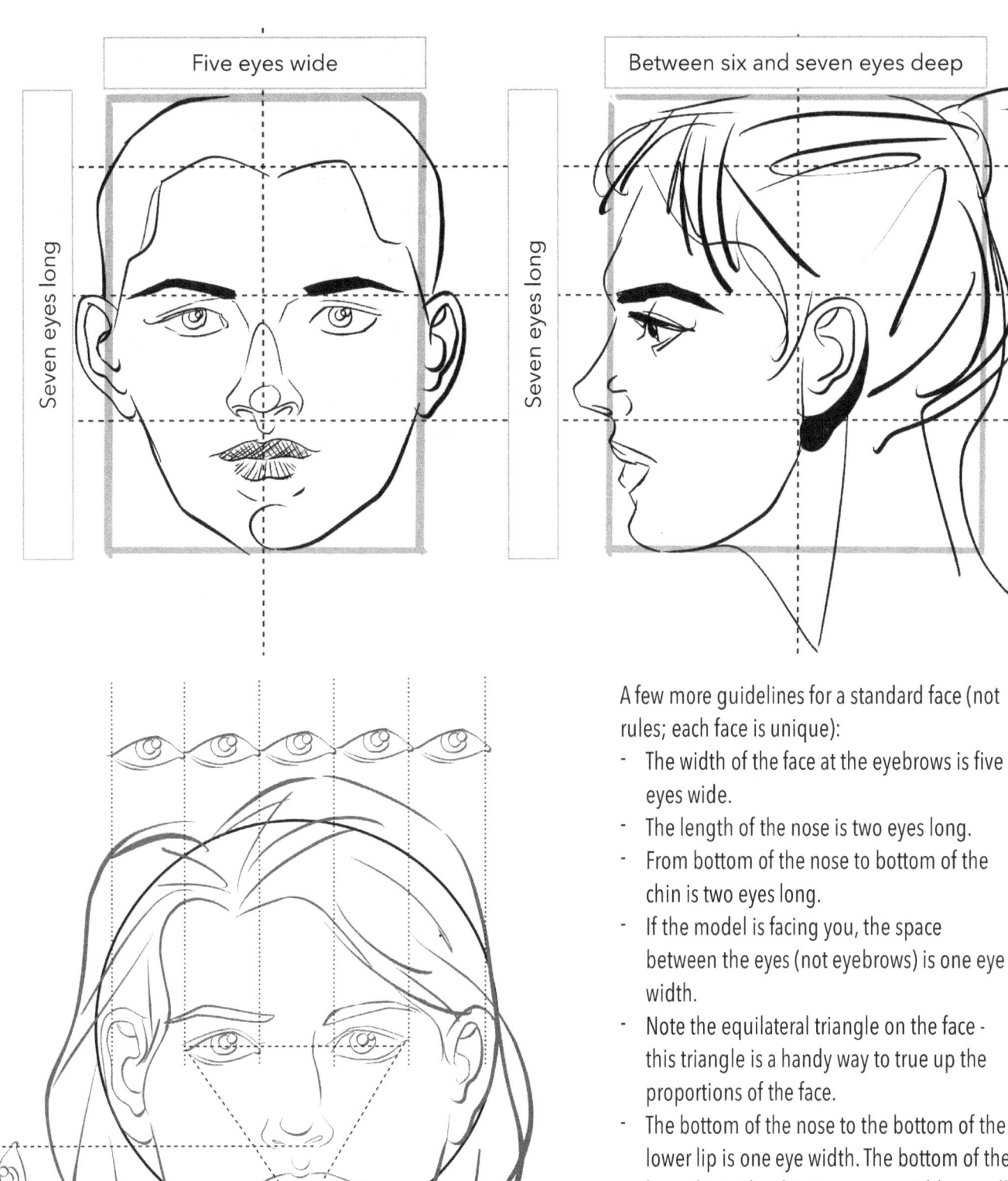

A few more guidelines for a standard face (not rules; each face is unique):
- The width of the face at the eyebrows is five eyes wide.
- The length of the nose is two eyes long.
- From bottom of the nose to bottom of the chin is two eyes long.
- If the model is facing you, the space between the eyes (not eyebrows) is one eye width.
- Note the equilateral triangle on the face - this triangle is a handy way to true up the proportions of the face.
- The bottom of the nose to the bottom of the lower lip is one eye width. The bottom of the lower lip to the chin is one eye width as well.
- It follows from the above guideline that the nose (eyebrows to bottom of the nose) is two eyes long. The forehead (eyebrows to hairline) is two eyes long.

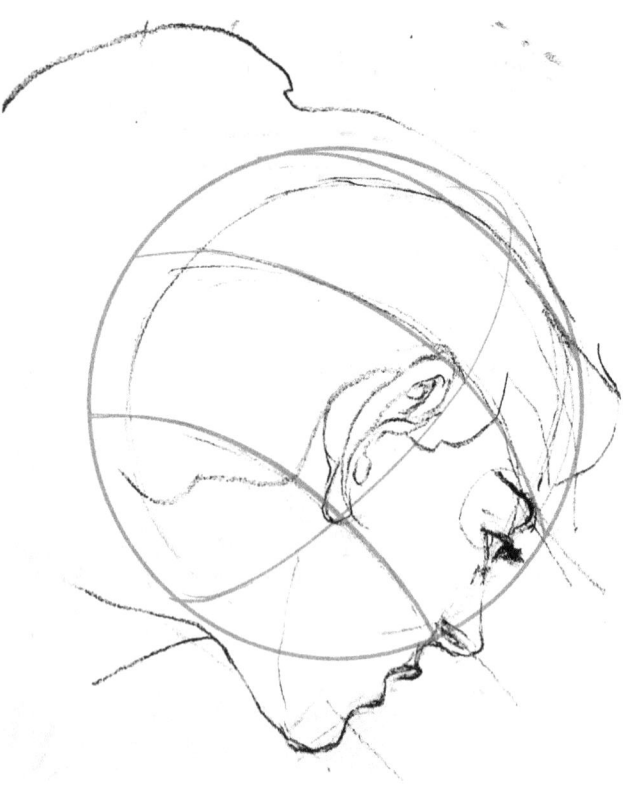
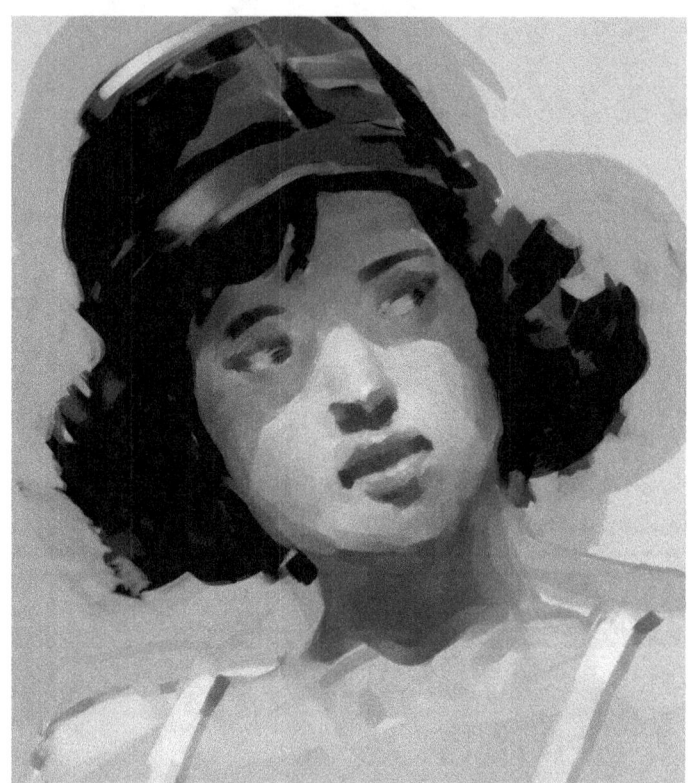

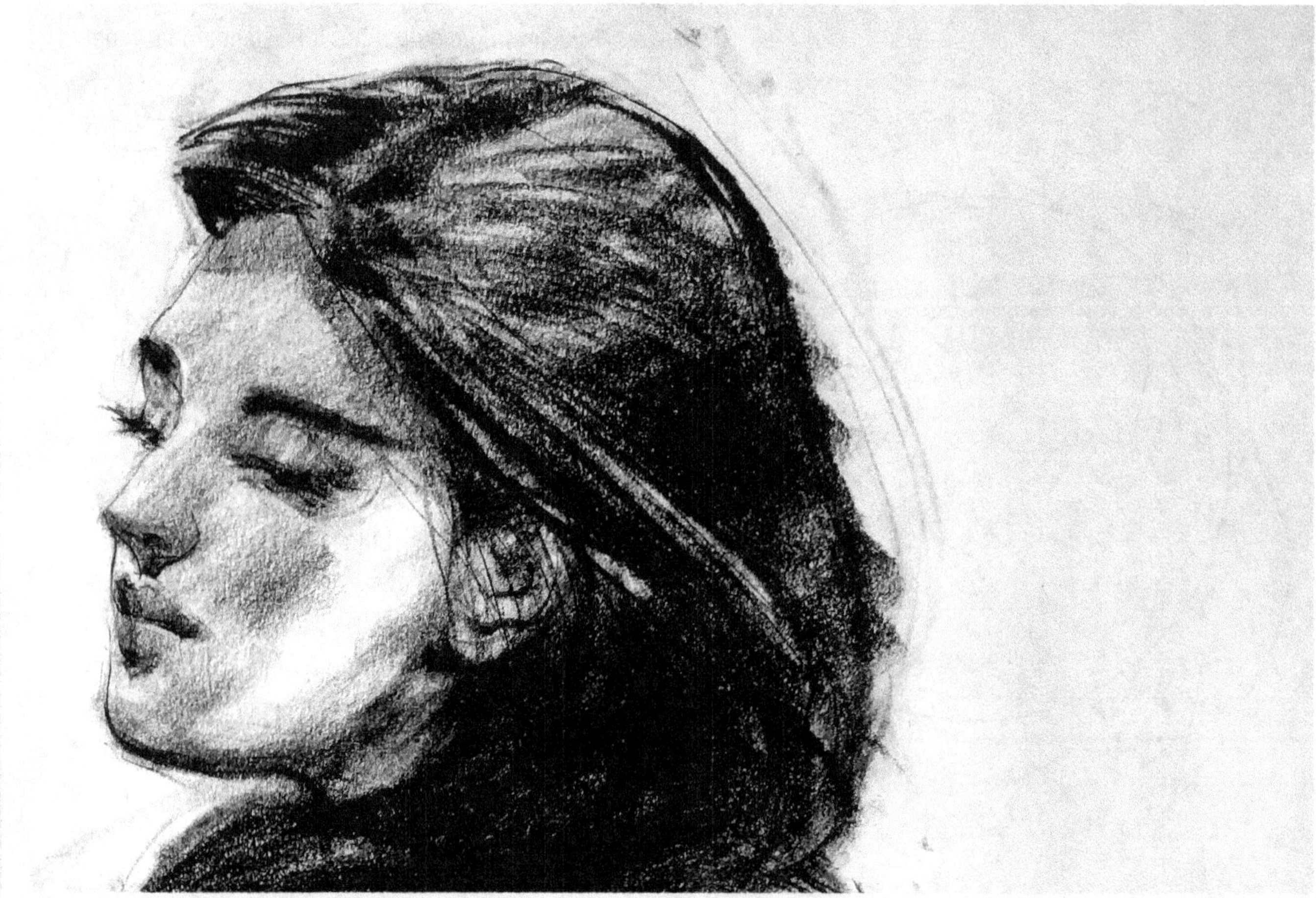

Umakanth Thumrugoti   Head Drawing

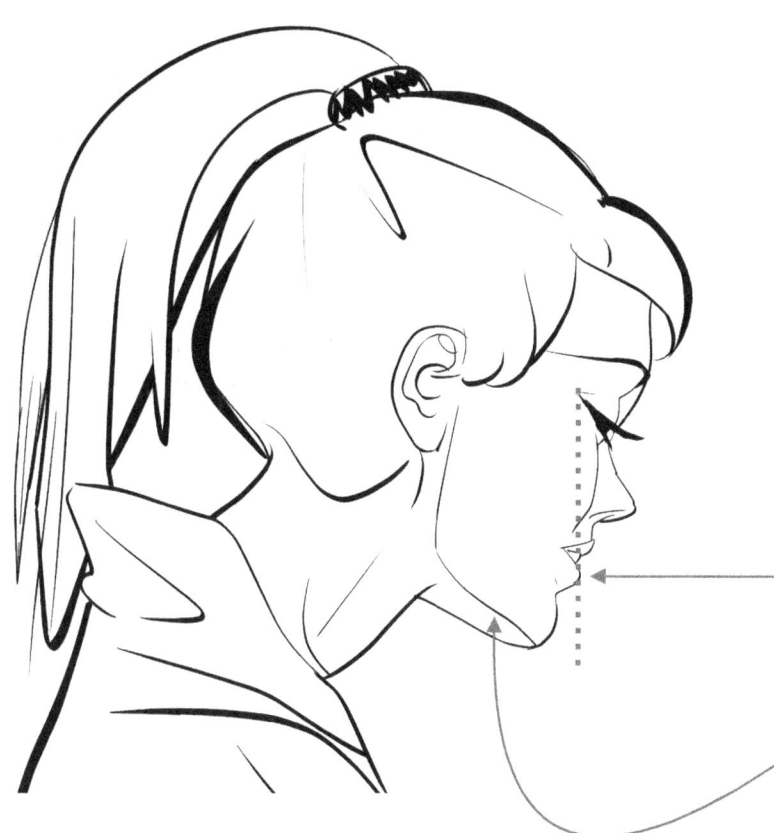

The guidelines mentioned so far are difficult to apply if the model's head position and angle is extreme. In the drawing on the left, the width of the eyes is difficult to get from the 'five eyes width' measurement. In such cases, use the tools from the discussion on human proportions. Observe alignment, both vertical and horizontal, on the model when the guidelines are not readily apparent.

In observing the model, a vertical guideline dropping down from the eye just touches the outer edge of the lower lip. Confirm that in your drawing.

Pay attention to this plane (this is a particularly problematic area for some artists). The plane of the jaw is important in establishing the perspective of the head in these kinds of poses.

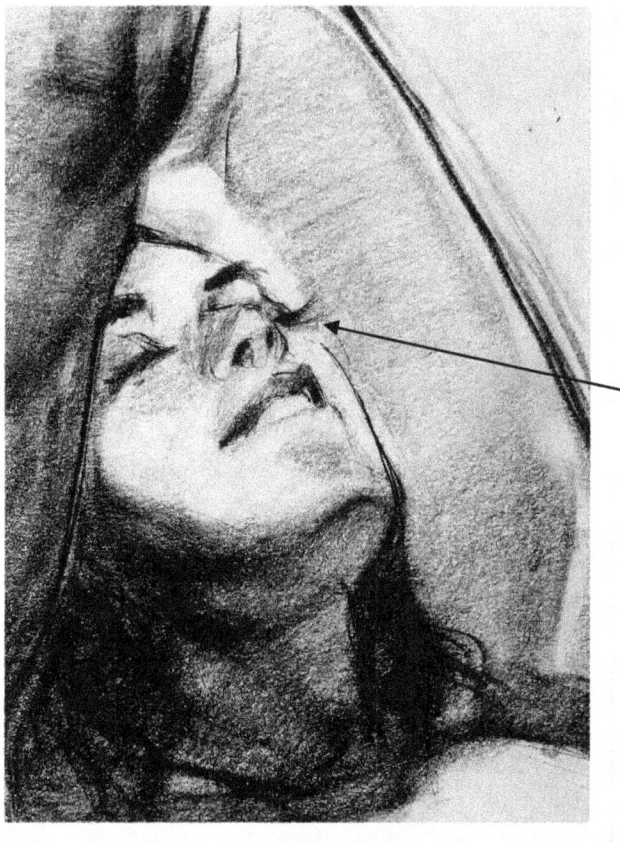

Notice how low the model's left eye is. It's almost in line with the tip of her nose. When the guidelines are not readily obvious, spend time studying the model. Make your marks and confirm on the model.

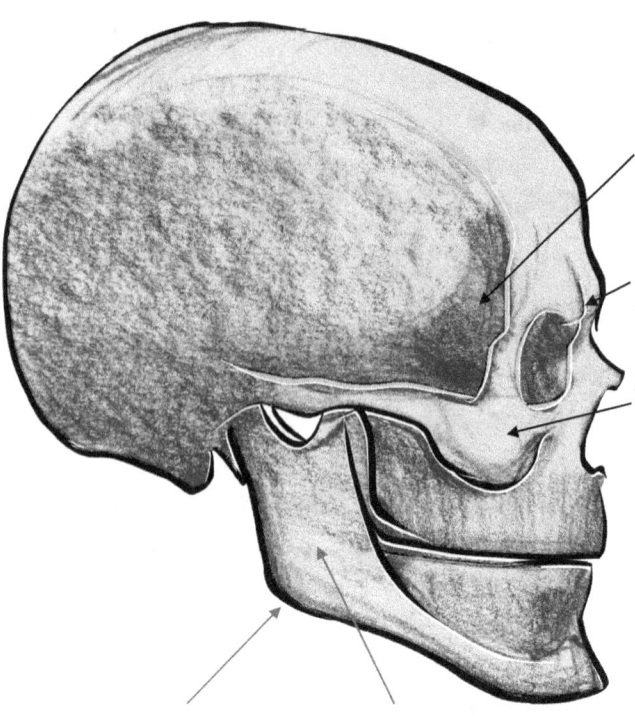

Sphenoid & Temporal

Superciliary arch

Zygomatic bone

Angle of the Mandible   **Ramus of Mandible**

We are interested in four surface landmarks on the skull outside of the obvious features like the eye sockets, nasal bone, etc.

- Forehead (superciliary arch of the forehead)
- Cheekbones (zygomatic bone)
- Jaw (angle of the mandible or lower border of the ramus of the mandible)
- Temple area (sphenoid & temporal bone)

Temple area is slightly shallow and hence there will be a tone.

The glabella is the space between the eyebrows covered by the procerus muscle; there is no need to delineate unless the model's face shows grief, anger, or any such emotion. However, the superciliary arch above the eyes shows.

The cheek bones are positioned slightly above (almost inline with) where the nose connects to the upper lip.

The angle of the mandible (the turn of the jaw) is usually in line with the bottom of the lower lip.

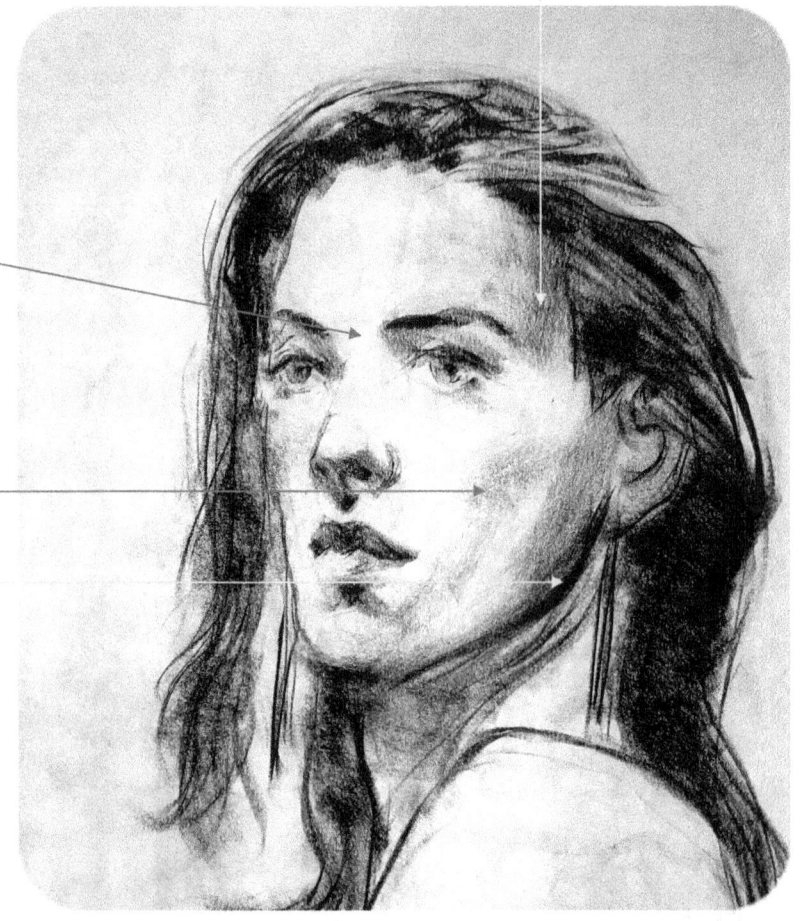

The basic facial muscles that we need to know are:

- Forehead muscle (frontal belly of occipito frontalis)
- Frowning muscle (corrugator supercilii)
- Line between eyebrows (procerus muscle)
- Cheek muscles (zygomaticus major and minimus)
- Elvis muscle (levator libii superioris alaeque nasi)
- Jaw muscle (masseter)

Let's not worry about other muscles that pull the lips up, down and sideways. If you are keen to learn those muscles, check out the anatomy books I recommend.

Corrugator Supercilii

Two tiny muscles, as shown here, in the enclosed spaces above the eyebrows. I guess they make you look supercilious?

Zygomaticus muscles, two of them, next to each other

Levator Libii Superioris Alaeque Nasi

Now you know why I call it the Elvis muscle - this muscle pulls the upper lip up as shown.

Masseter

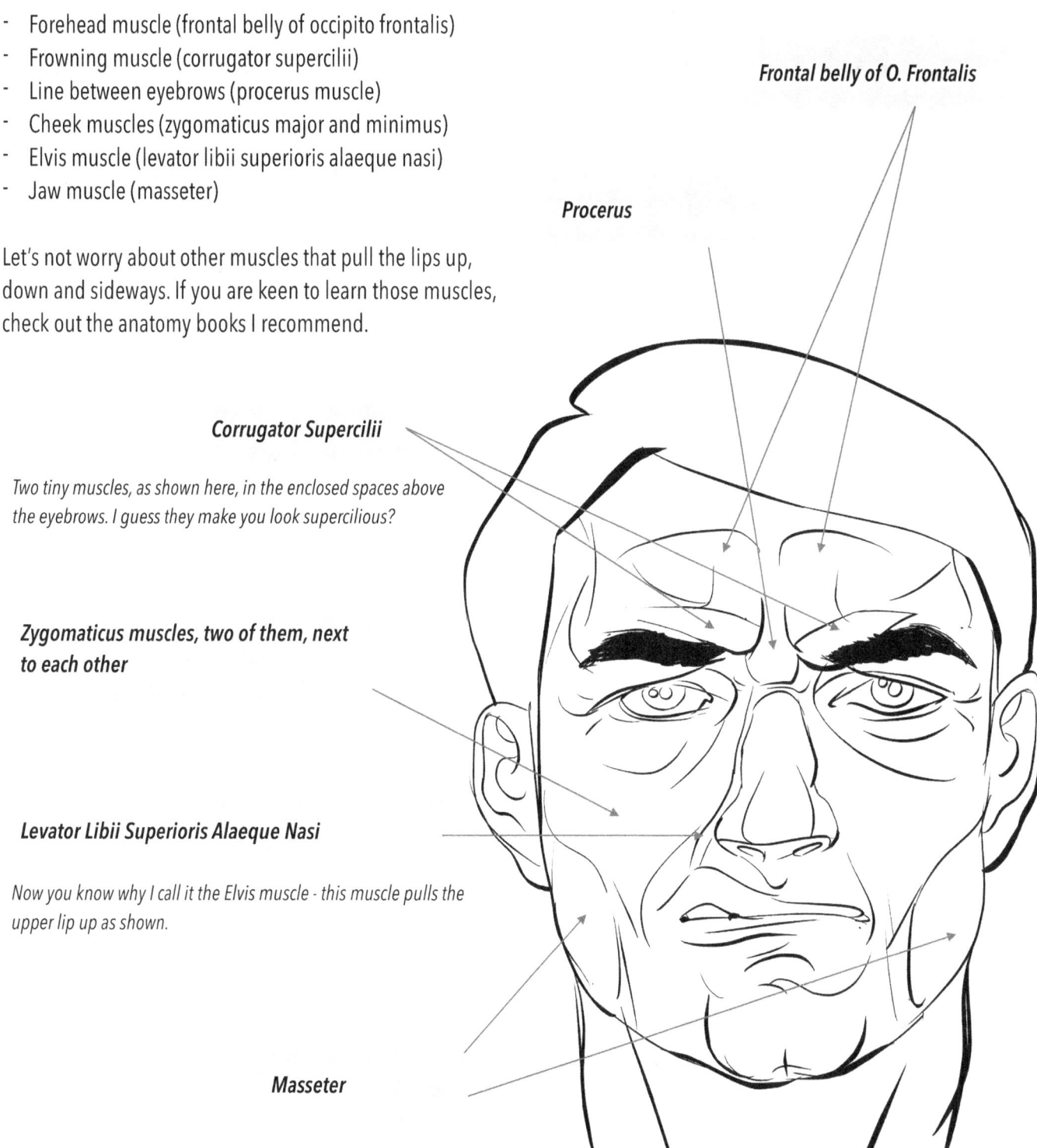

Frontal belly of O. Frontalis

Procerus

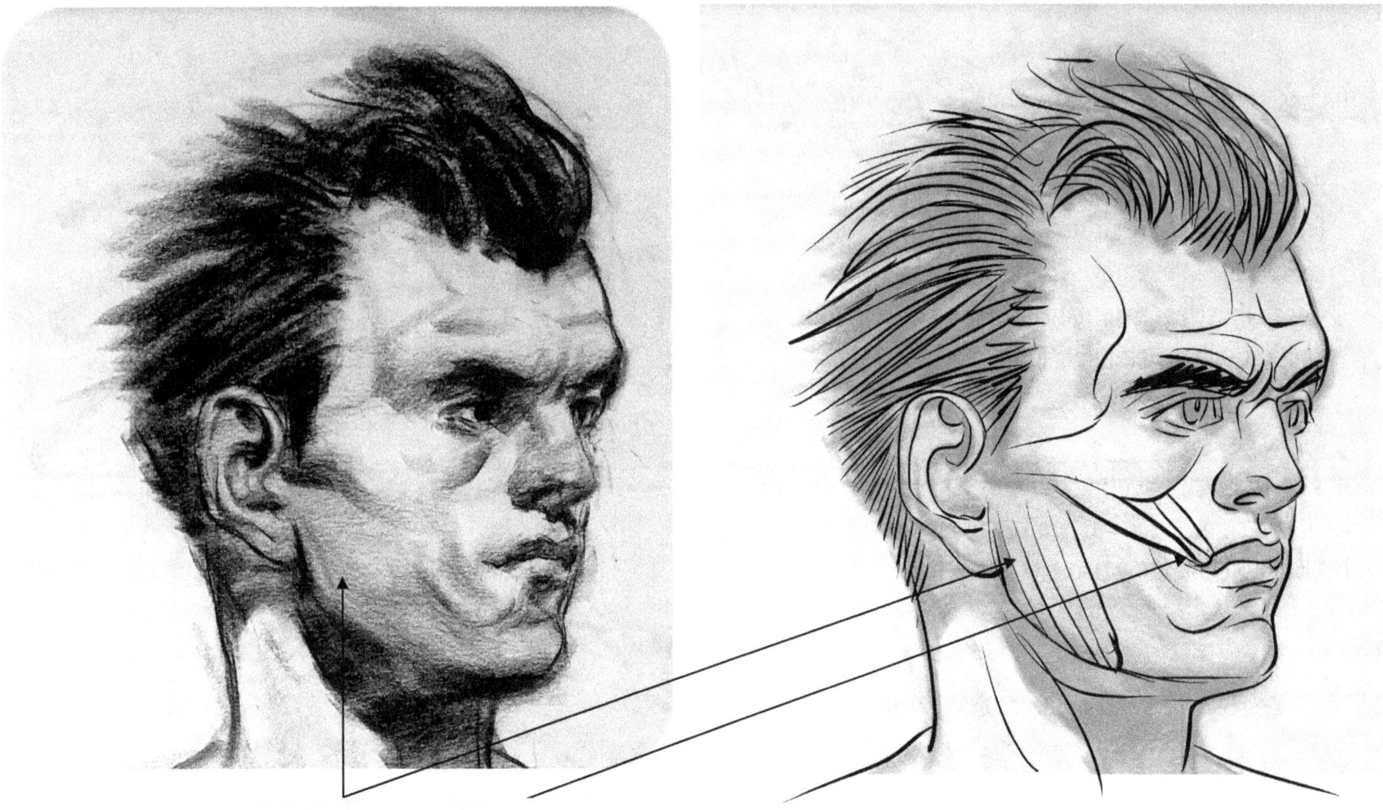

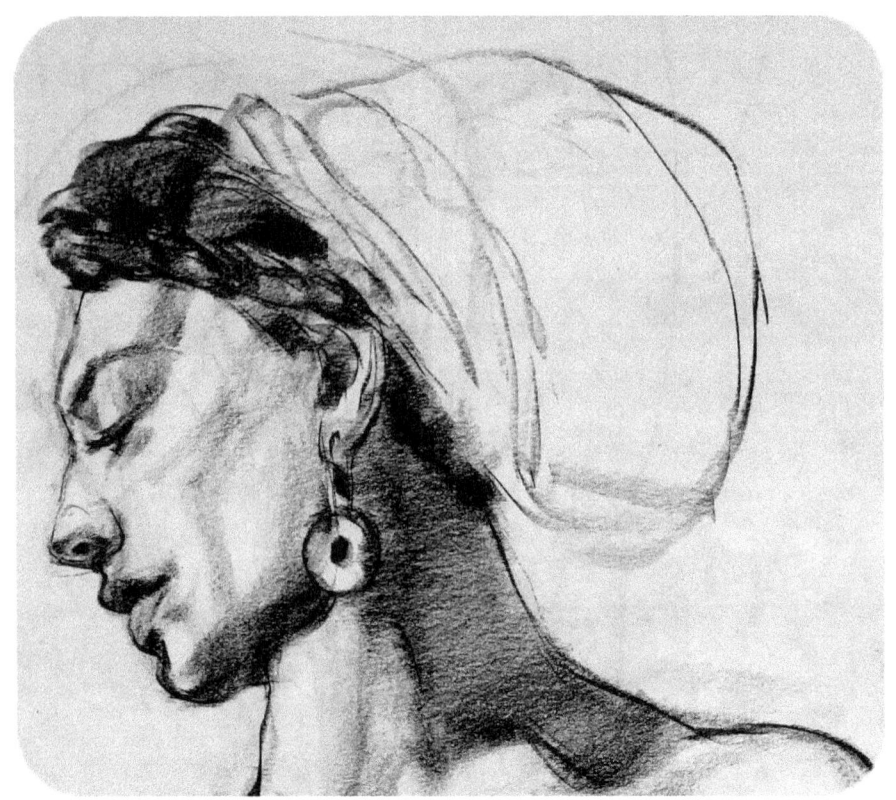

Masseter   **Zygomaticus muscles**

Keep delineation of the facial muscles in your life drawing simple. Use tone to suggest them. Your overall goal is to make your drawing read as one unified image. Over-rendering individual muscles can draw unwanted attention to the face.

In the drawing on the left, you can see the definition of masseter (jaw) muscle and a definition of zygomatic (cheek) bone. However, overall, the life drawing is cohesive.

A few more examples of head drawing - details from life-drawing sessions.

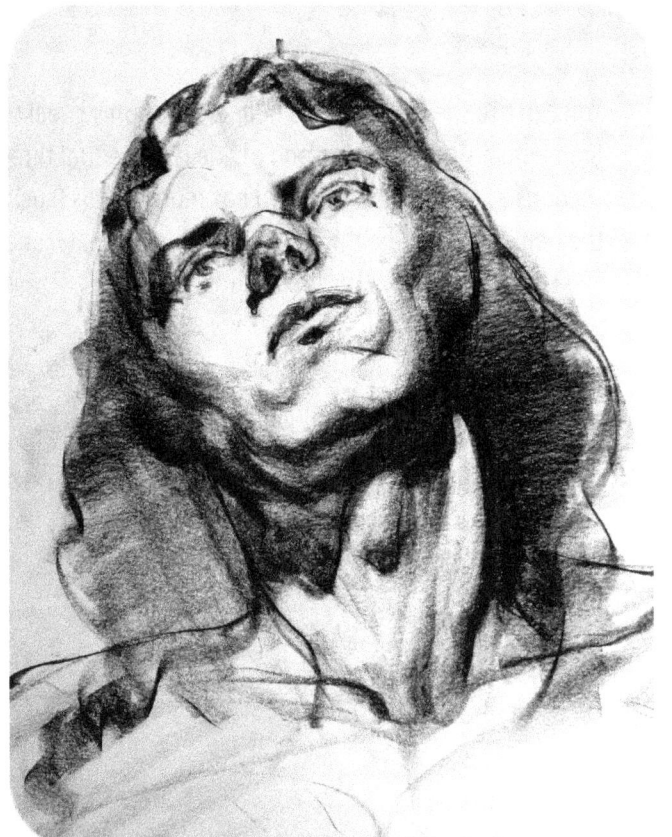
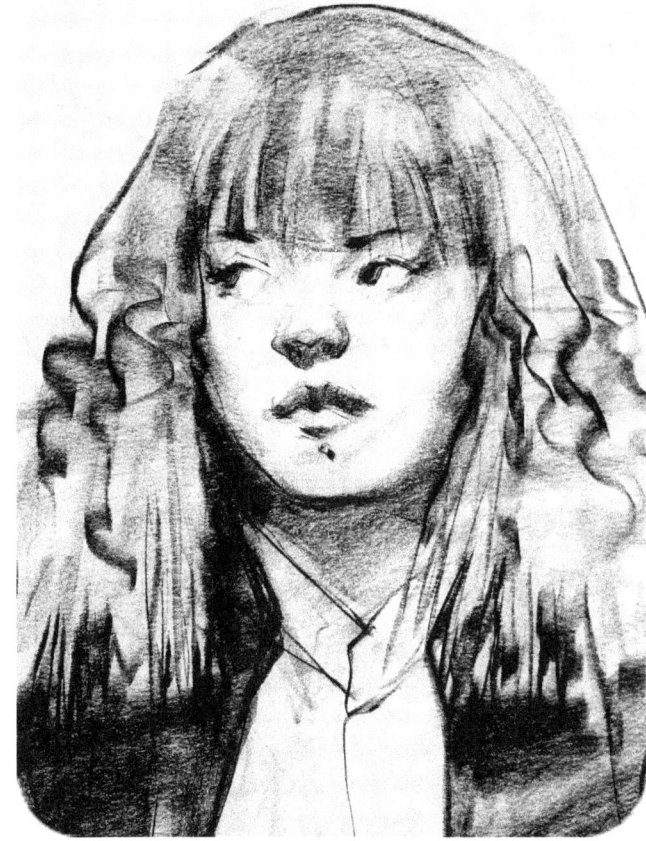
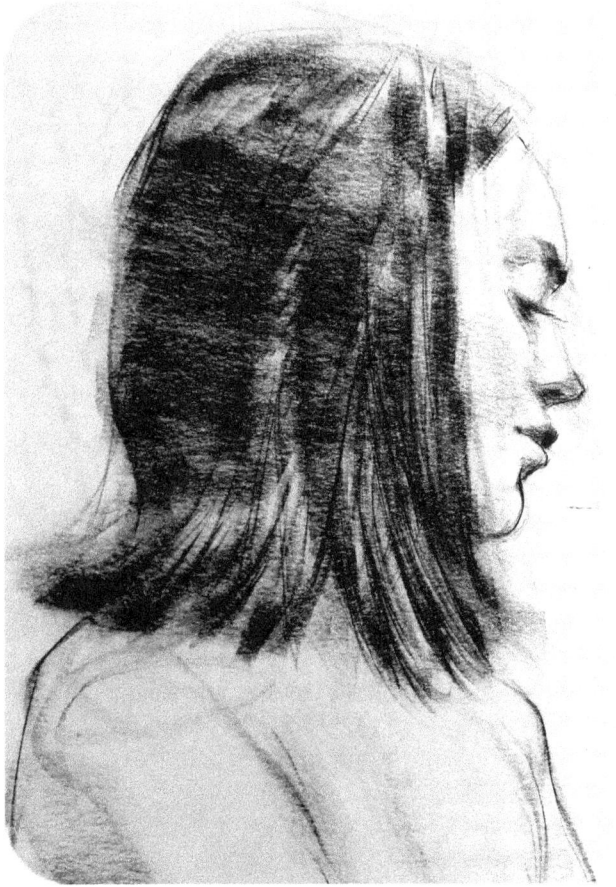
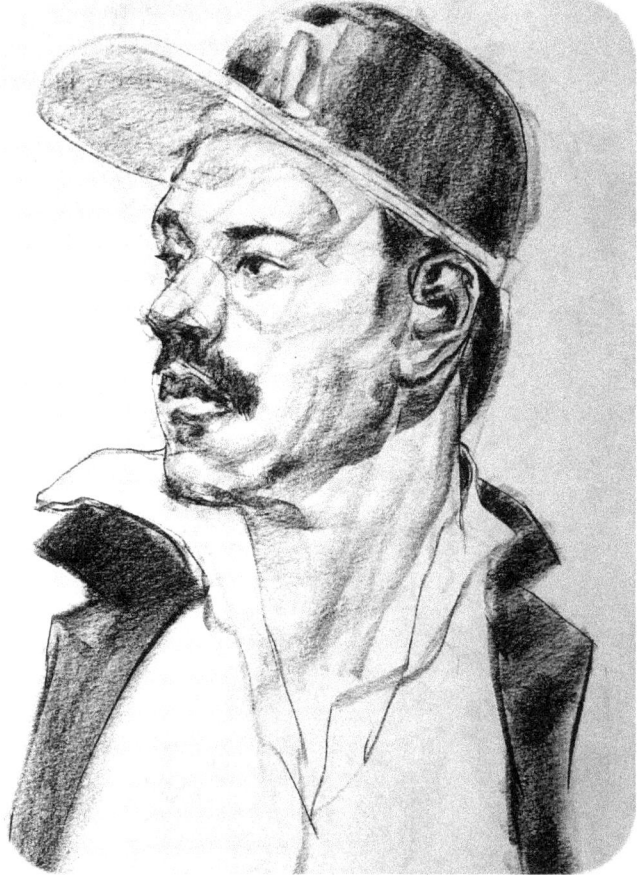

Ear, Nose, Mouth and Eyes

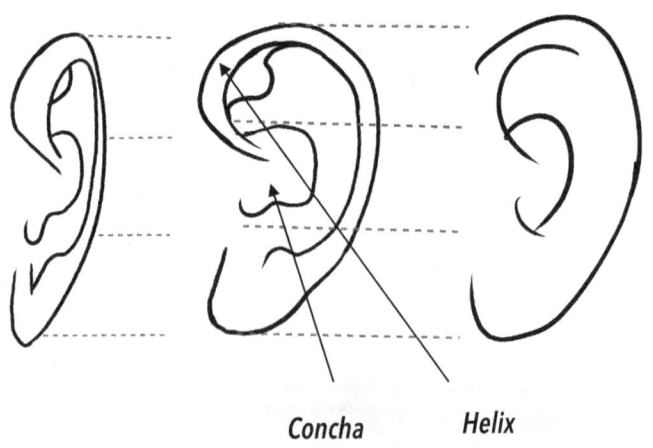

Concha *Helix*

You can use the rule of thirds here too - roughly speaking. Start with a simple C curve and divide it into equal three sections as shown. The top third has more details (such as the helix). The middle third includes the ear canal (concha). The bottom third features the fleshy earlobes.

If you are drawing small, don't cramp all the details into a small space. Simplify. Eliminate details.

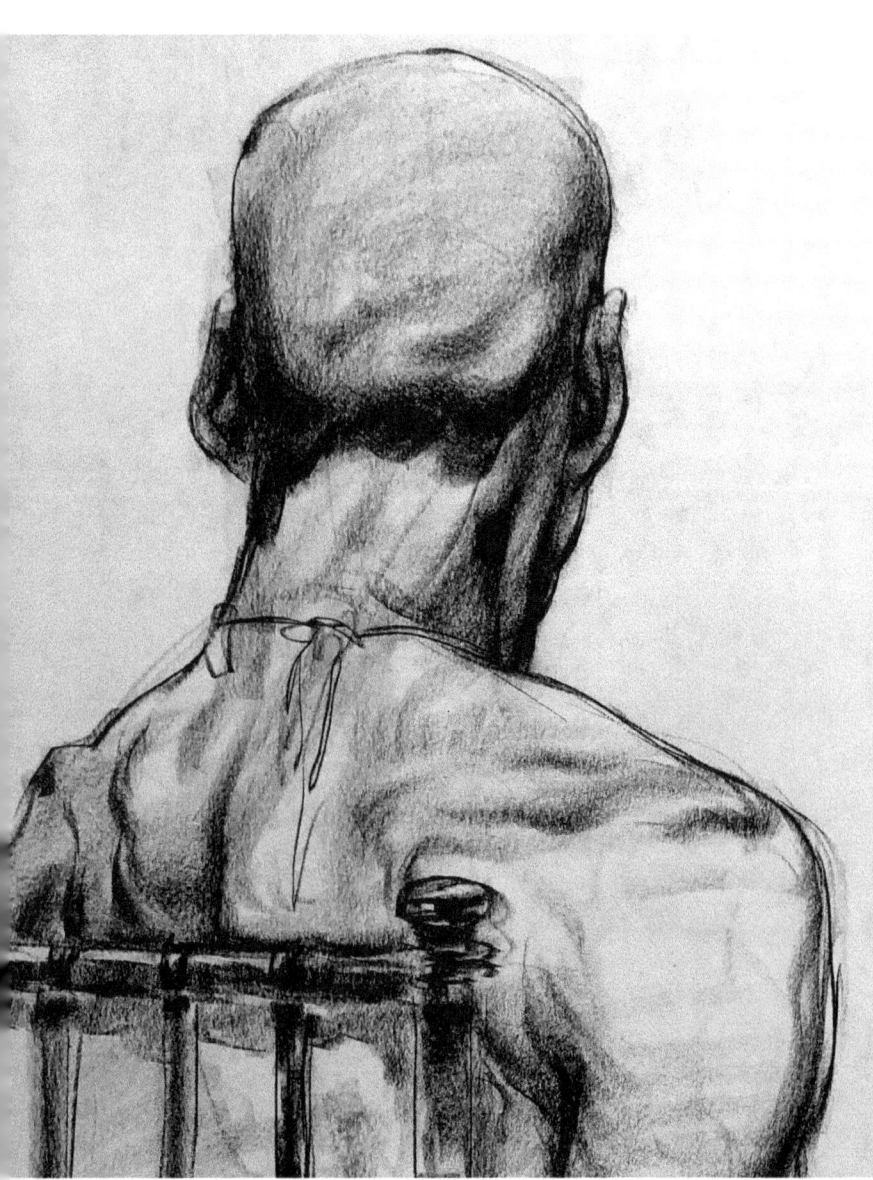

To the right shows a view of the ear from behind.

Sometimes the ears can take on more dramatic shapes, shown in the life drawing, left.

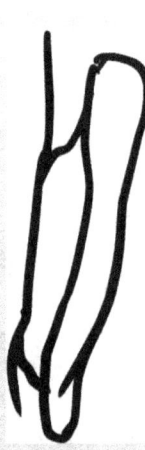

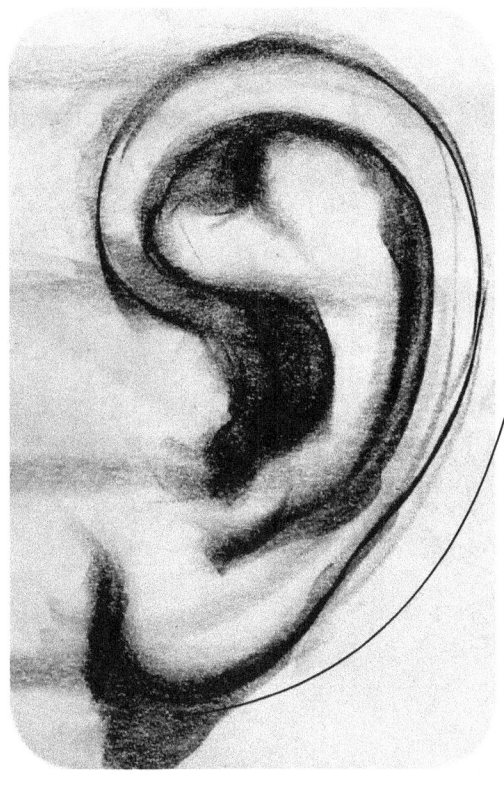

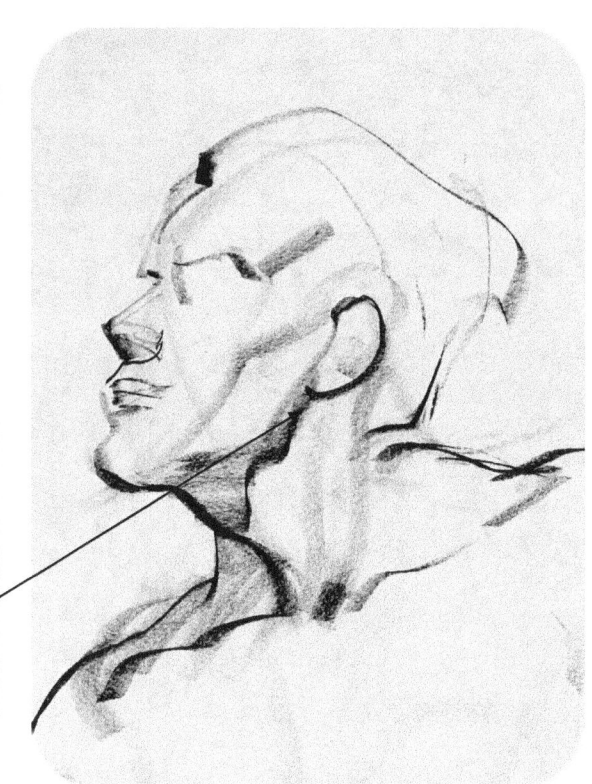

Always draw this contact shadow that connects the ear to the head. Floating ears can be distracting.

Detail from a two minute life drawing on the right. See how simple the ear form is. Anatomical details can be secondary if you get proportions right.

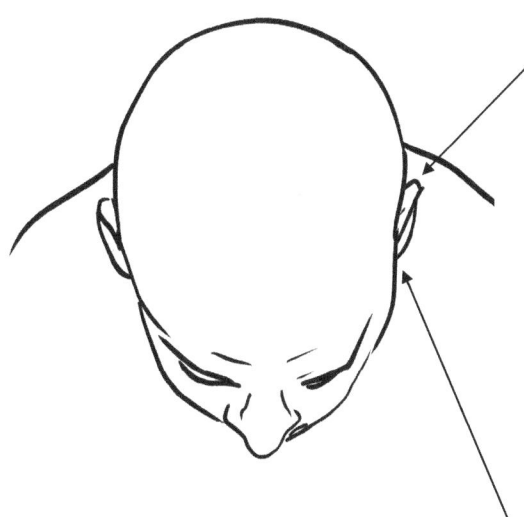

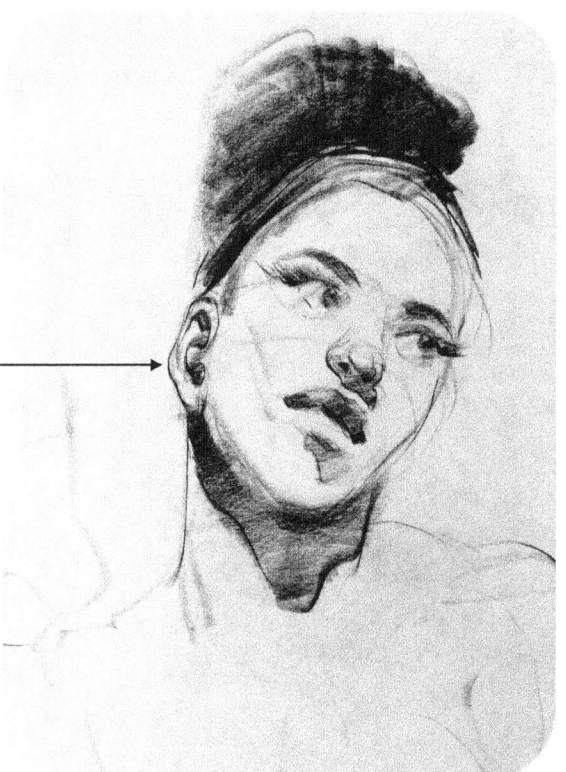

Top view of the ears is fairly simple. Often, we don't see them in this view, as most of the ear is blocked by the head or by hair.

When the head is tilted up, the ears appear to be lower than the eye-line. If the head is tilted down, the ears appear to be higher than the eye-line.

Umakanth Thumrugoti Head Drawing 163

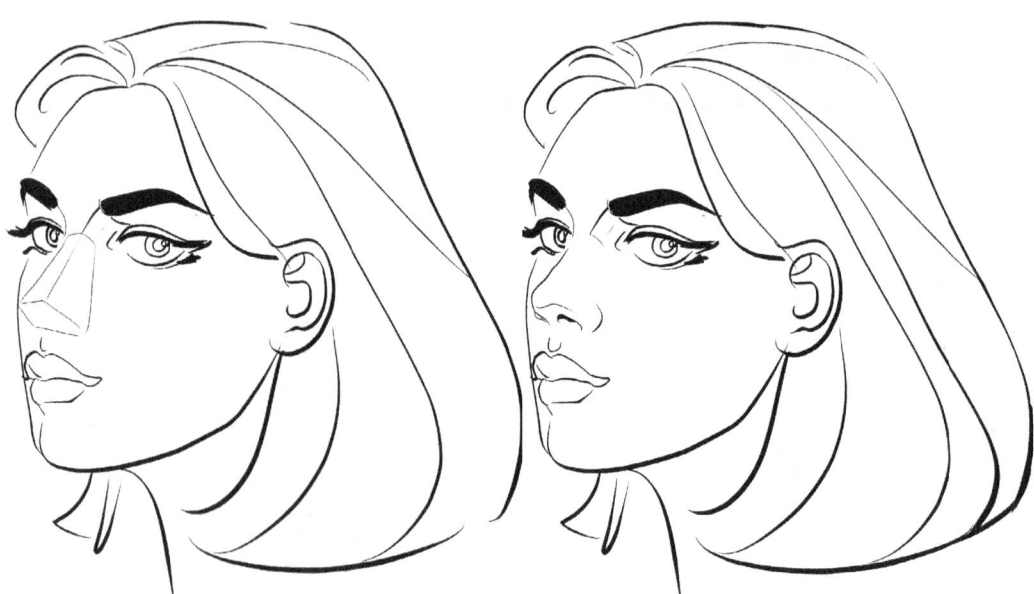

Noses come in many shapes and sizes - not all of them created equal (ask Cleopatra in the Asterix and Cleopatra graphic novel).

We can simplify them into a generic nose - a pyramid form enclosed by four planes: a top plane, two side planes, and a bottom plane, which contains the nostrils.

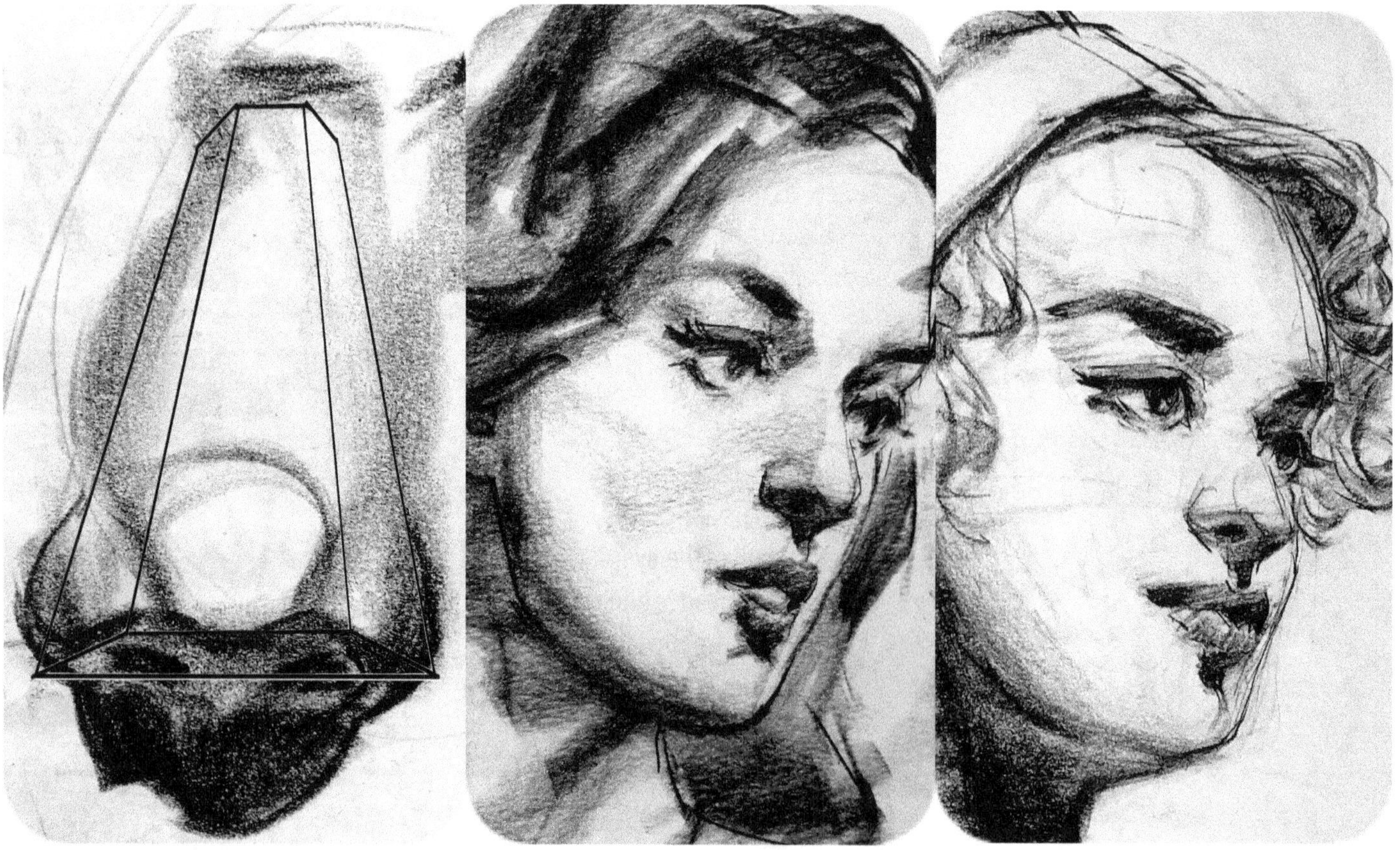

My initial rough lay-in includes a stretched sphere for the cranium, nose line, eye line, ear, rough eyebrow lines, two spheres for the eye sockets, a line for the nose and a ball for the tip of the nose, bottom plane, and a hint of the nostril and a hint for the mouth. After this, I finish the outline for the head by drawing the jaw, hair, and neck. Check out my two minute pose drawings in this book. For convenience, I'm including a quick iPad drawing next to this text.

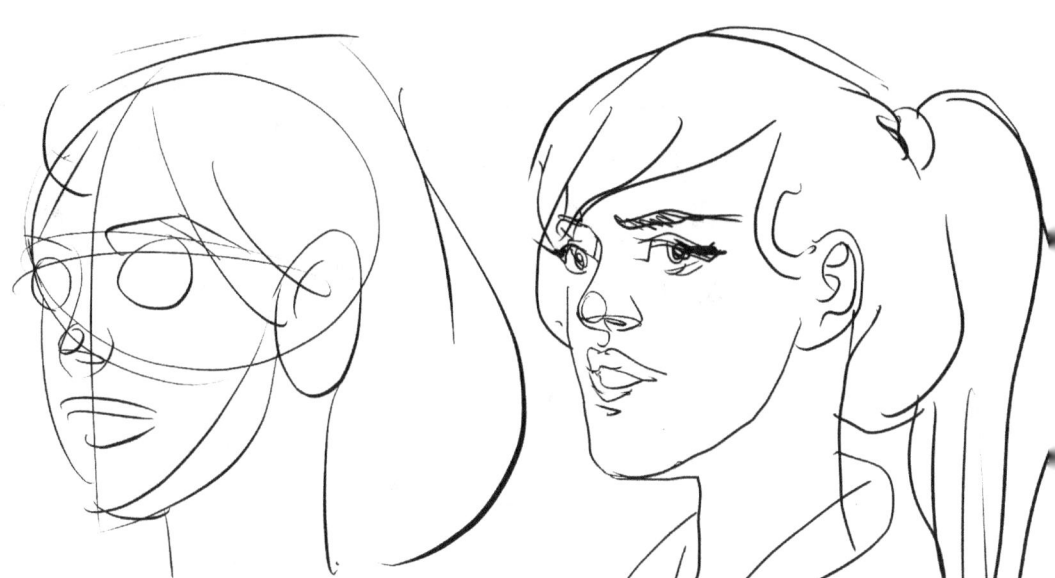

In the drawing above right, I removed all the 'construction lines' (above left) except for the ball at the tip of the nose. I find that drawing a ball for the tip of the nose helps me quite a bit. As you draw more, you will discover your own 'sign posts.'

The mouth, I think, is a bit simpler to draw. One important thing to remember is that mouth lies on top of a curved surface, our face. The corners of the mouth recede from the viewer compared to the center of the mouth.

Upper lip has three lobes and the lower lip has two. Compare the iPad drawing with the charcoal one - you will see those forms (lobes).

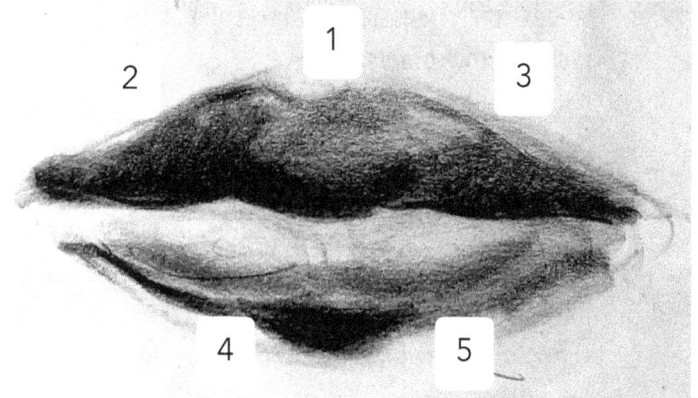

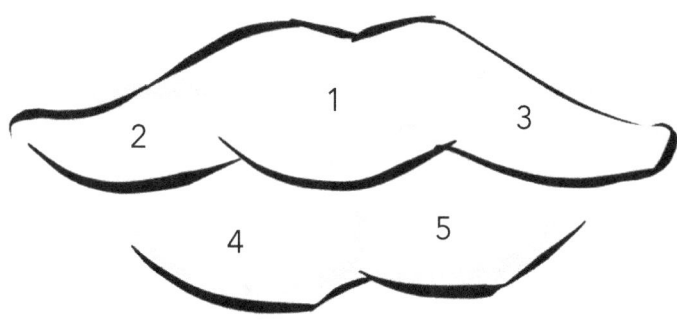

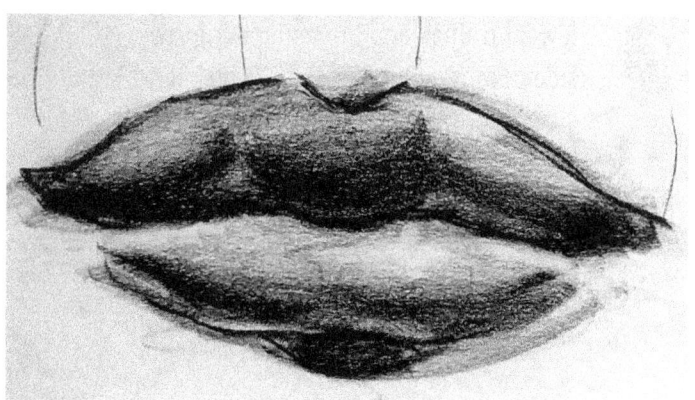

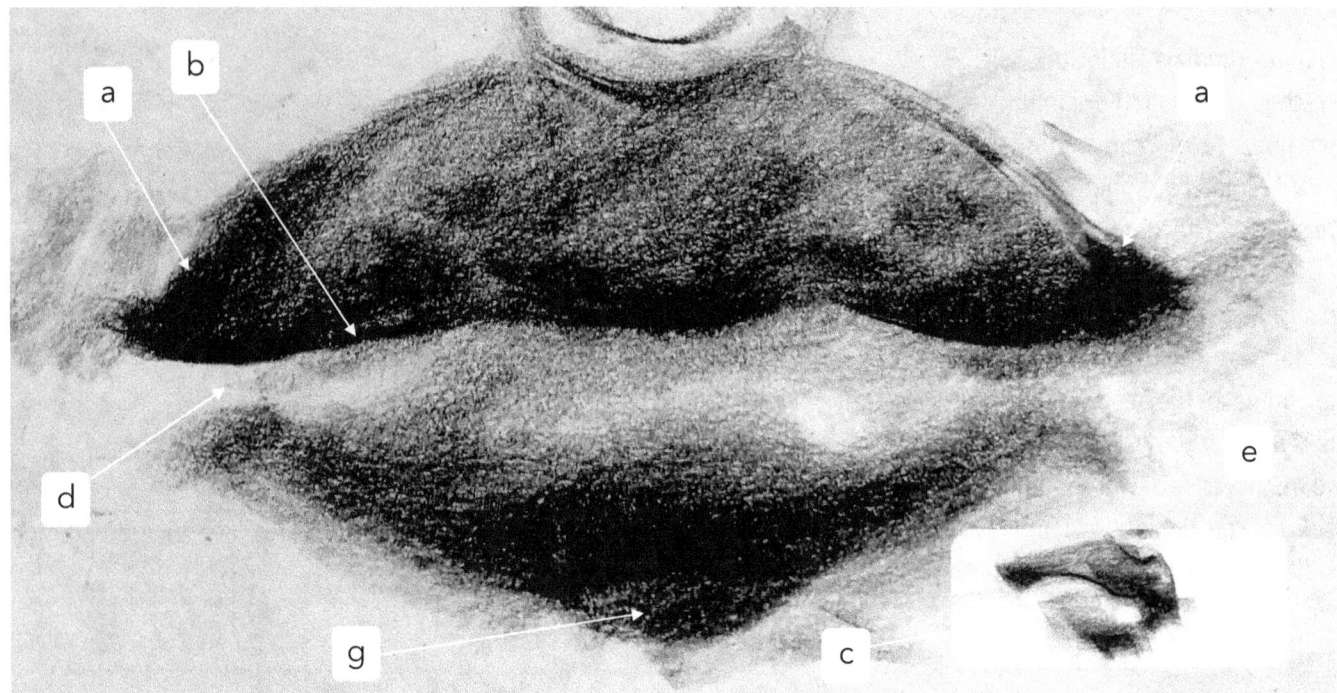

A few useful tips in drawing a mouth:
a. Value usually goes darker from center of the mouth to the corners.
b. If the mouth is closed, the contact line between the upper and lower lip would be the darkest line.
c. In most lighting scenarios, the upper lip is darker than the lower lip because it's turning under.
d. The lower lip gradually melds into the skin at the corners.
e. Keep the values to as few as possible. Start with two values - one each for upper lip and lower lip. Then add the center bump, two side bumps on the upper lip. Two almond shapes form the lower lip.
f. When drawing small (I'd consider a head drawing sized 2 by 3 inches for example), eliminate detail. No definition of the bumps needed on the lips.
g. The lower lip usually casts a shadow.

Study the life drawings in this book to see how different head positions influence the rendering of the mouth.

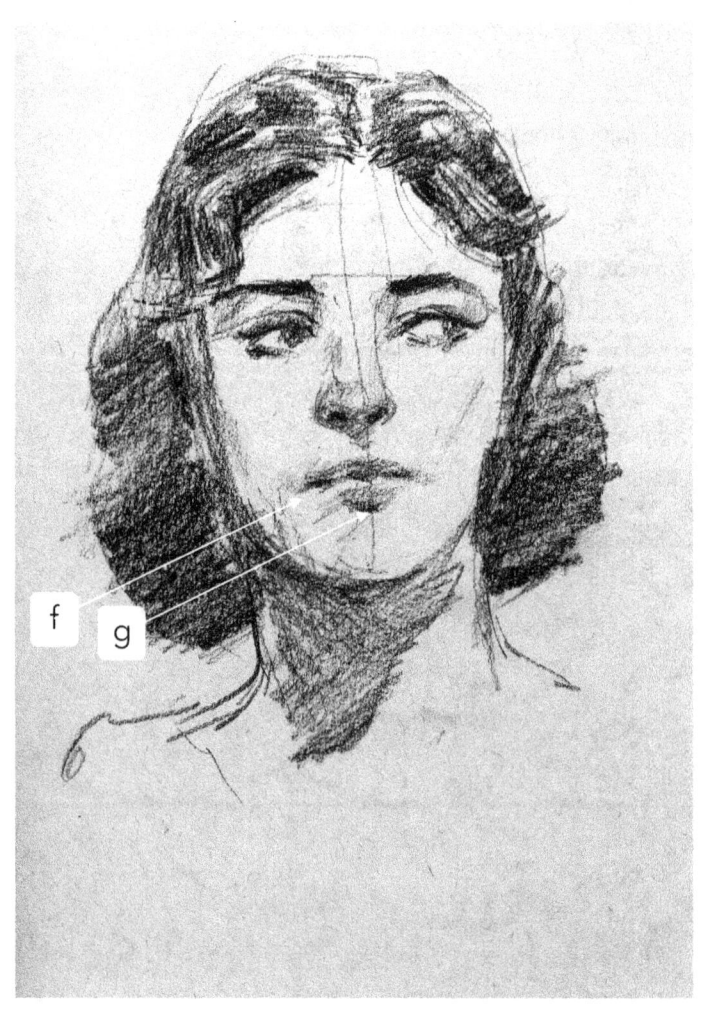

Eyes are the hardest for me to draw (or paint) - for a good reason. Its structure is complicated. We tend to look at eyes when interacting with our fellow human beings and so are very familiar with them. Minor errors in drawing them become very obvious to us.

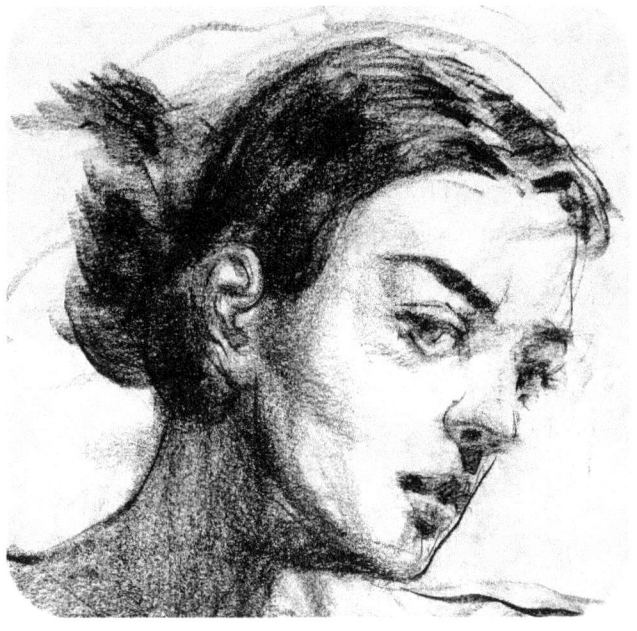

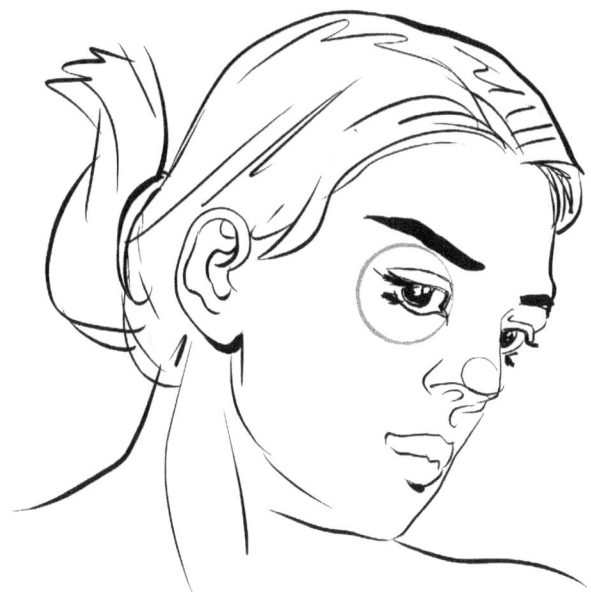

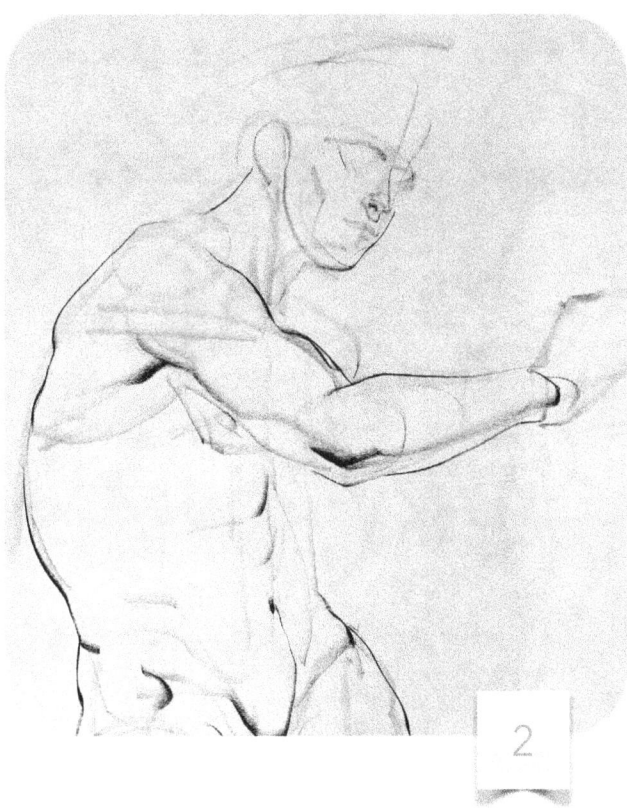

Visualize the eyeball below the eyebrows. In the iPad drawing above right, the structure underlying the drawing of the eye is indicated by a perfect sphere. The two minute life drawings to the left and right show how I suggest the approximate position of the eye.

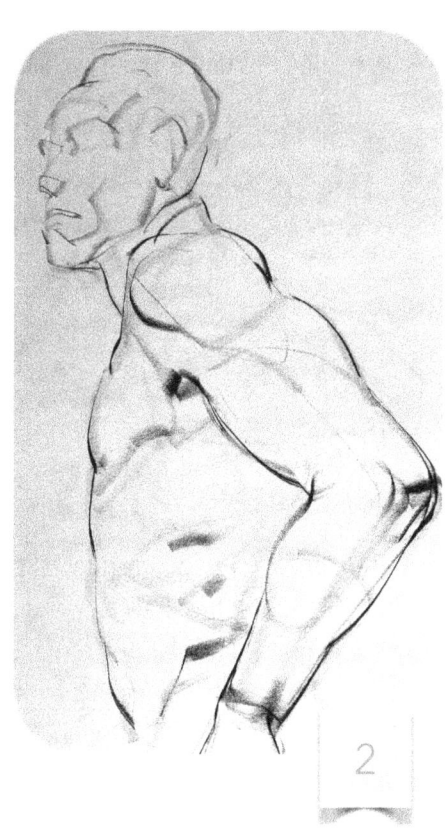

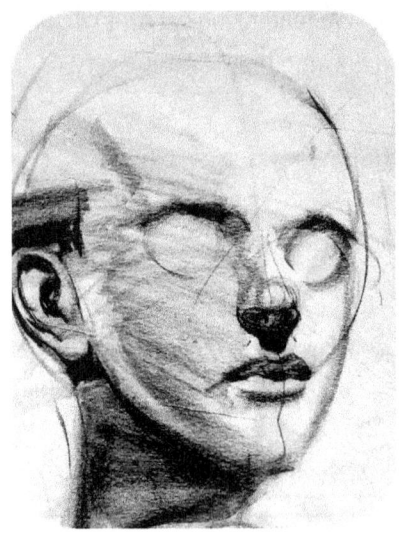
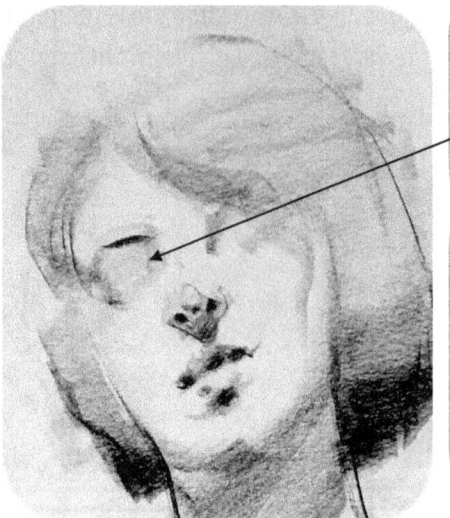

You can use tonal-line to create a rough approximation of eyeball. The goal is to draw a sphere very lightly.

Next, draw the eyelid line, keeping in mind the eyes' proportions. Perhaps drawing the nose first might help, as width of the nose (at the nostrils) is one eye width.

a. The upper lid usually covers almost half of the iris (the colored part of the eye)
b. The shape of the eye has an axis - it's not a perfect almond. The widest part of the eye is at the dotted line.
c. Eyelids have thickness. Upper eyelid/leashes cast shadows.
d. The specular hi-light (the brightest spot) is usually placed in the top half of the iris if the light source is at or above the eye level. It floats above the pupil. Light travels and scatters behind this bulge of the eyeball (acqueous humor) and can create a softer hi-light on iris.

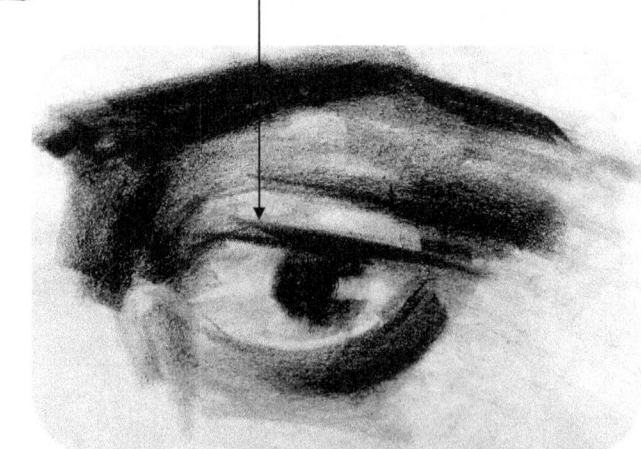

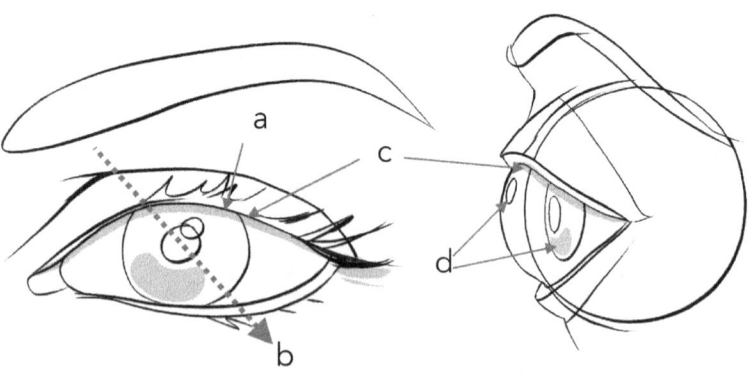

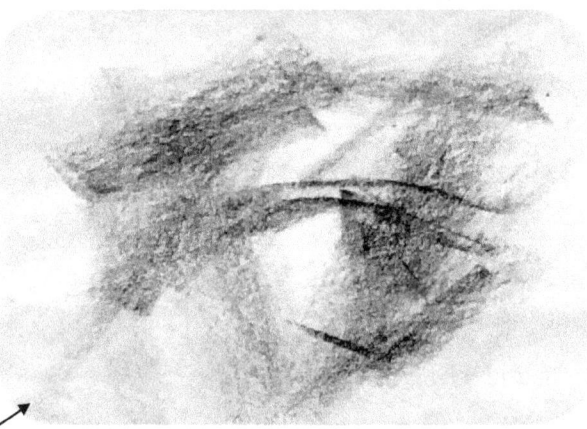

The enlarged sketch on the right reflects all the points discussed above. Note that this drawing was done with just two values - medium gray for tonal-lines and dark gray for axial-lines and pupil. <u>Eliminate details when drawing small.</u> Learn to distinguish between realistic drawing and an accurate drawing.

Actual size of the drawing.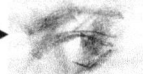

Umakanth Thumrugoti — Head Drawing

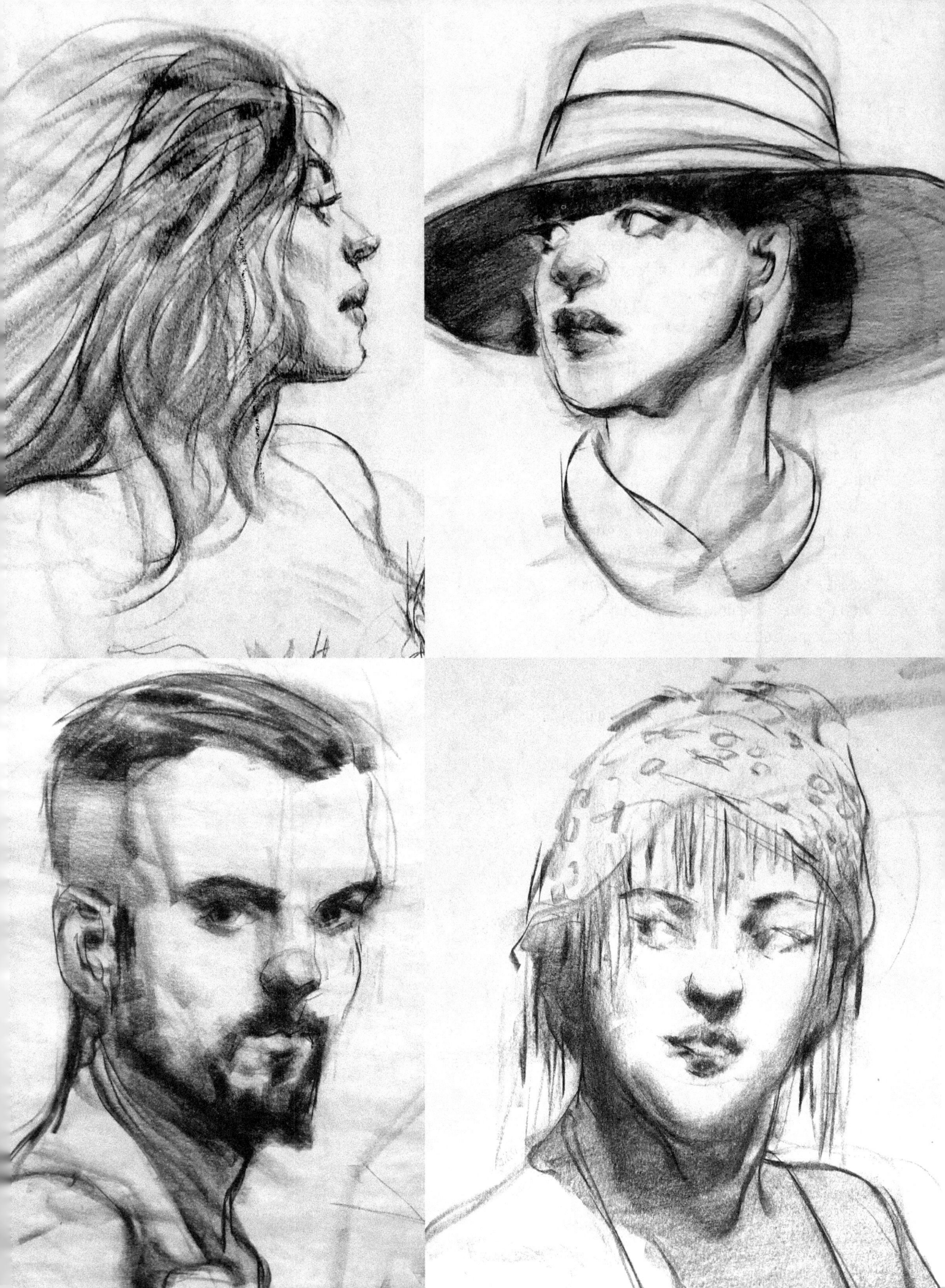

Hair

Follow the form when drawing hair. Hair has volume, and there are darker and lighter sections of the hair. Concepts like 'anisotropic' reflection, light scattering etc., are a bit harder than Latin declension to model with mathematical precision but terribly easy to draw from a model. Just draw what you see. A few suggestions:

a. Broadly speaking, treat hair as a single volume with a top surface and side surfaces. Usually, I interpret that volume with two tones - a lighter tone for the surface facing the light, and a darker tone for the rest of the surfaces.
b. If I were to squint, these two values will seem one, i.e., there isn't much difference in value between them. This is very important. Most hair details are from highlights (specular reflection).
c. After the tone is laid down, identify clumps of hair that make up secondary volumes within the mass.
d. Sections of the clump either face or turn away from the light. Show that in your drawing using your lights and darks.
e. Each clump has volume and 'planes' enclosing that volume. These planes can twist and turn, reflecting light.
f. Overall, hair has a flow - support it in your drawing.
g. Make use of tone and tonal-lines. Makes your life easy. Add clump details using axial-lines.
h. If the hair is in layers, let me make the obvious point that interior hair is usually darker.
i. Get into the habit of drawing the head (cranium) lightly (tonal lines first), then draw the hair on top.

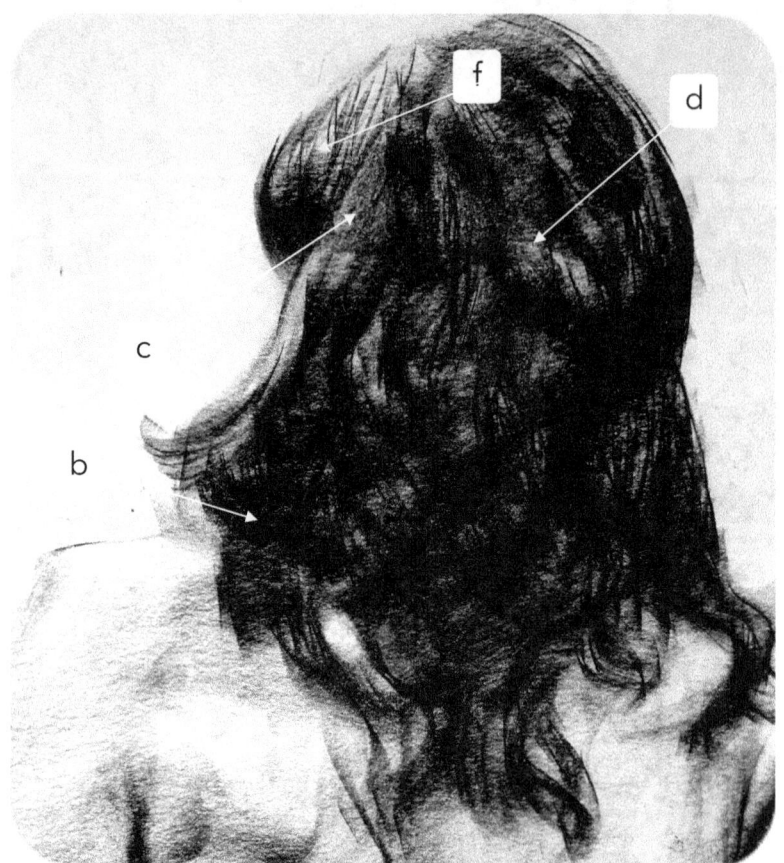

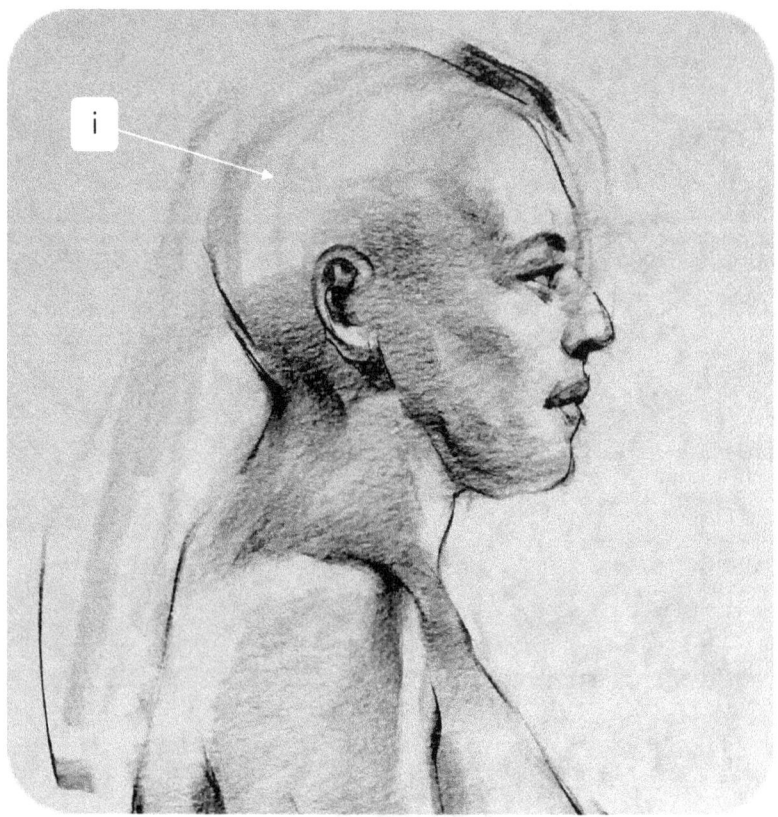

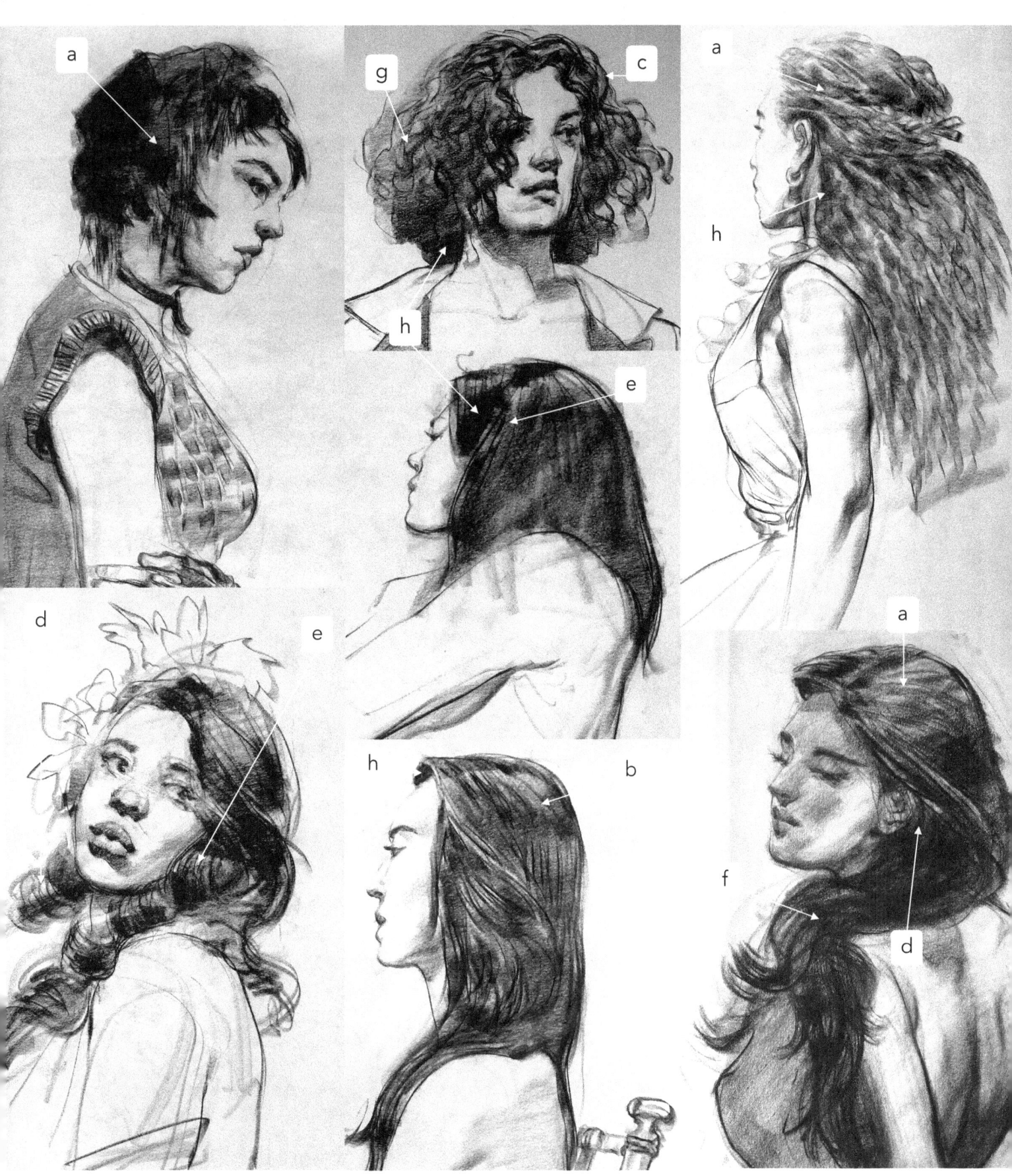

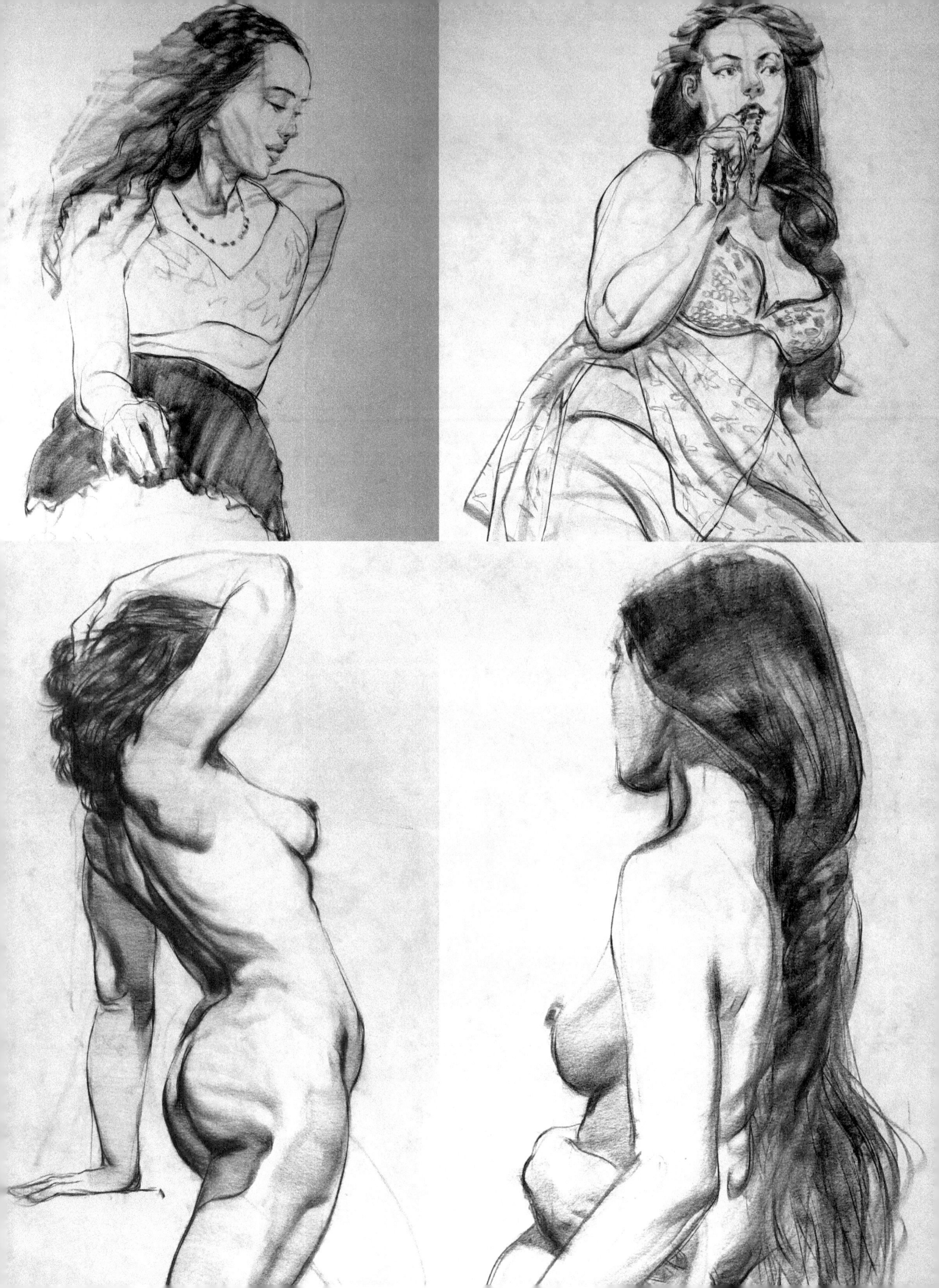

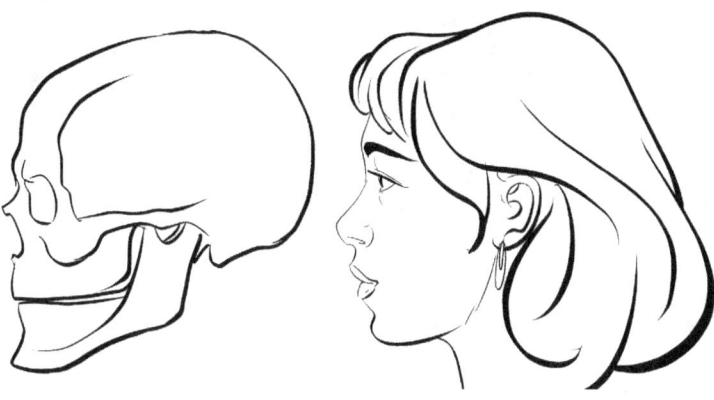

Heads come in all shapes and sizes. Divergence from the standard head can make for an interesting model and drawing. In the iPad drawing above, is the eye placed higher than it normally is in a head?

The model who posed for the drawing on the right had a prominent forehead, an unusual jawline, and a strong underbite. It was a fun sketch session - the theme of the session was Burlesque Sketch Night. As mentioned earlier, always draw what you see.

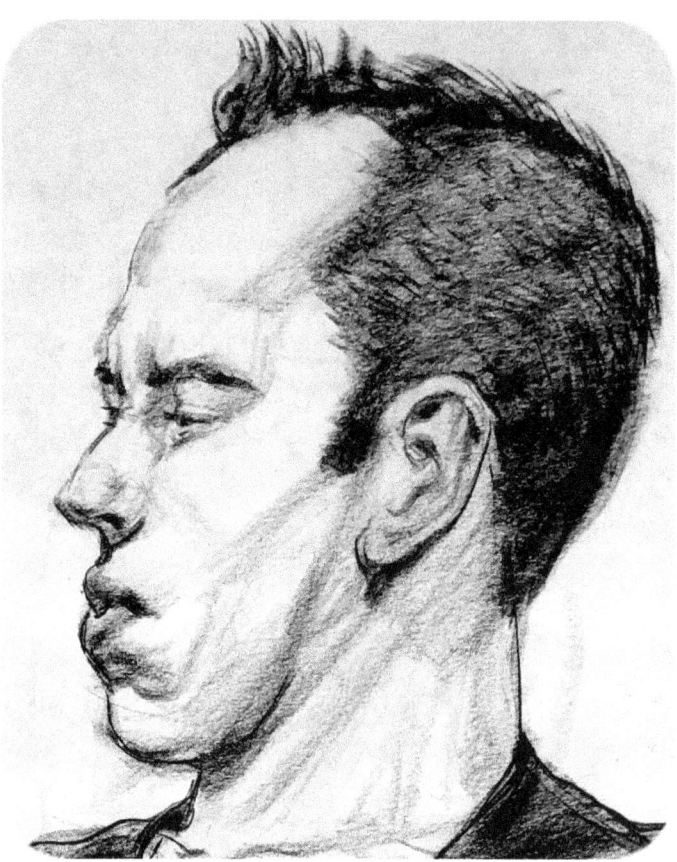

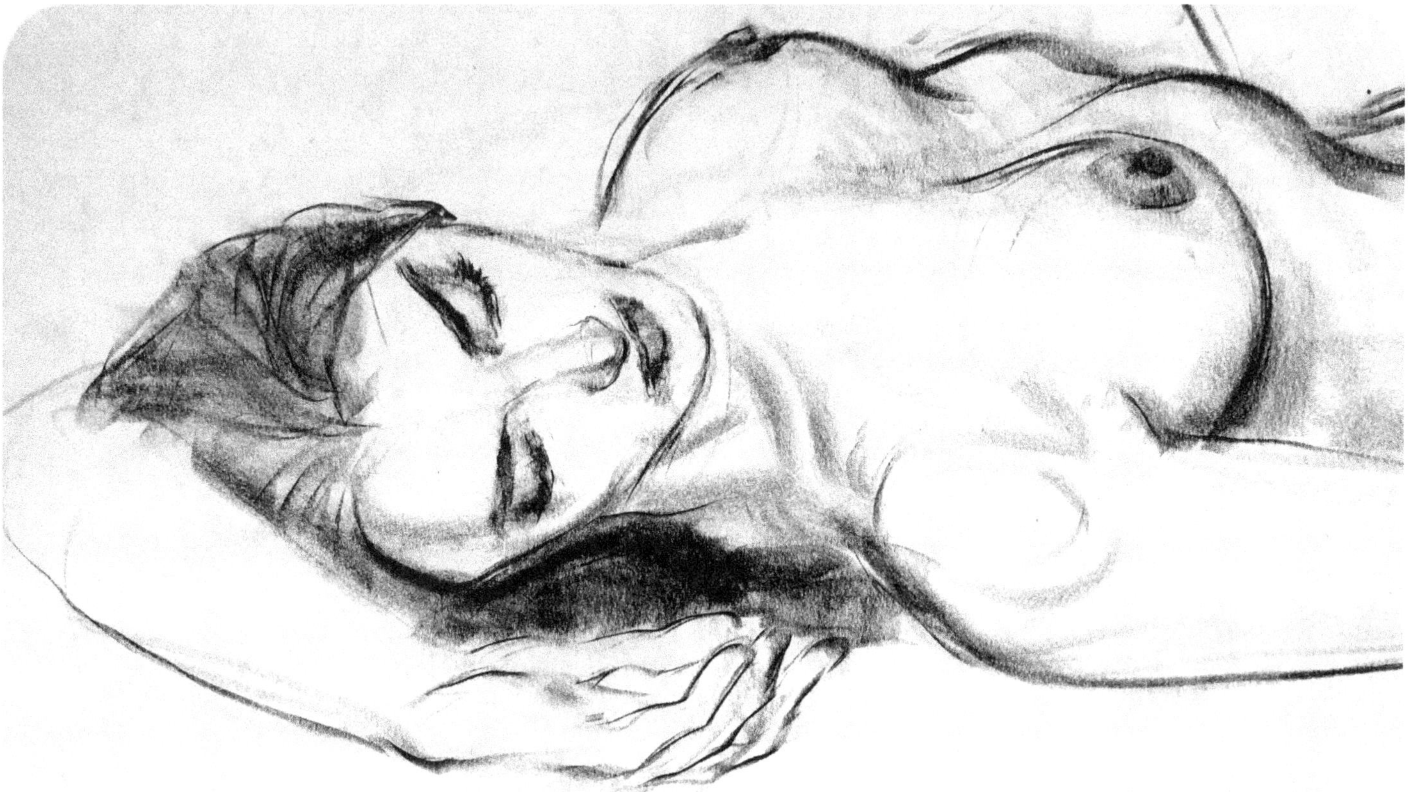

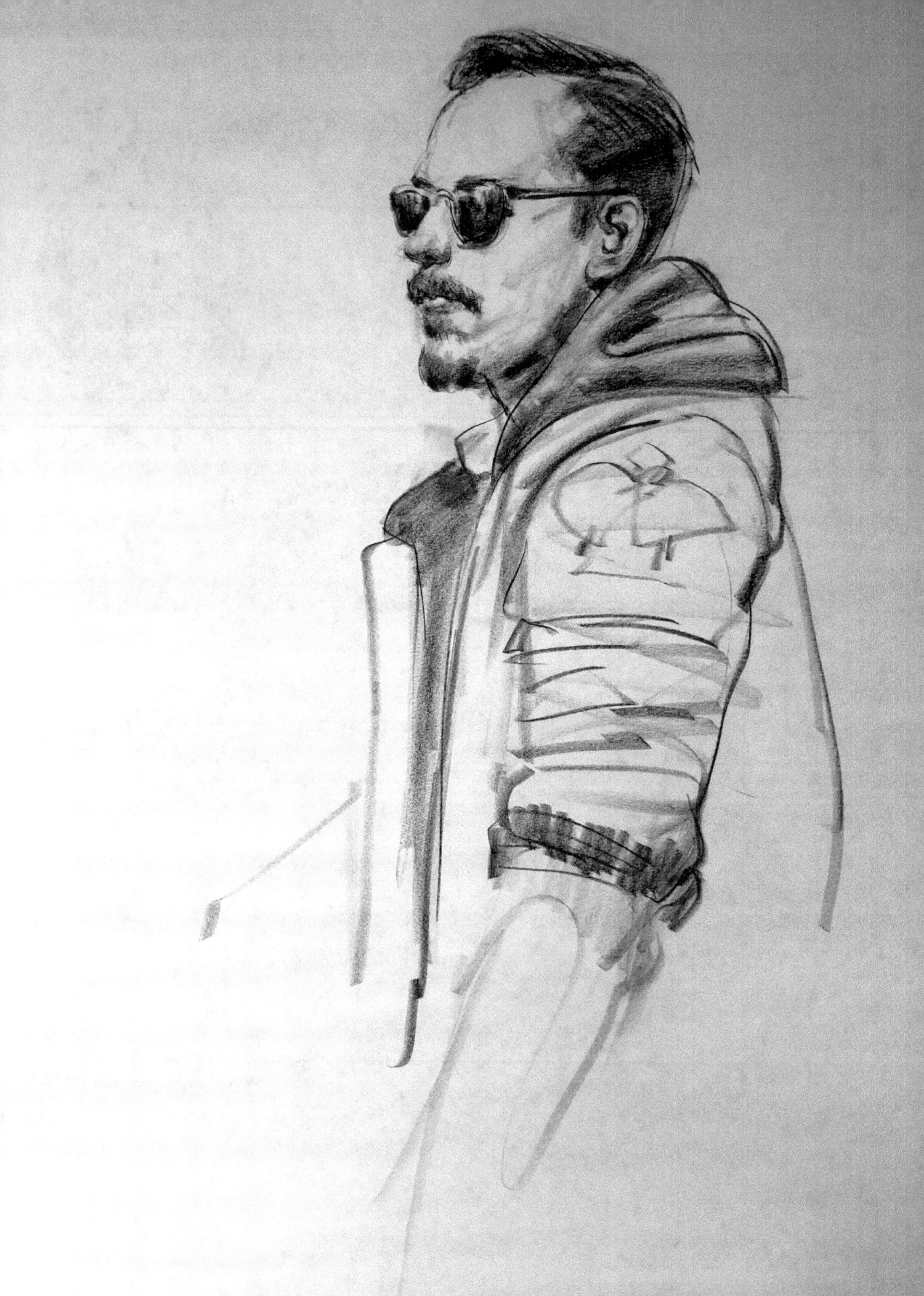

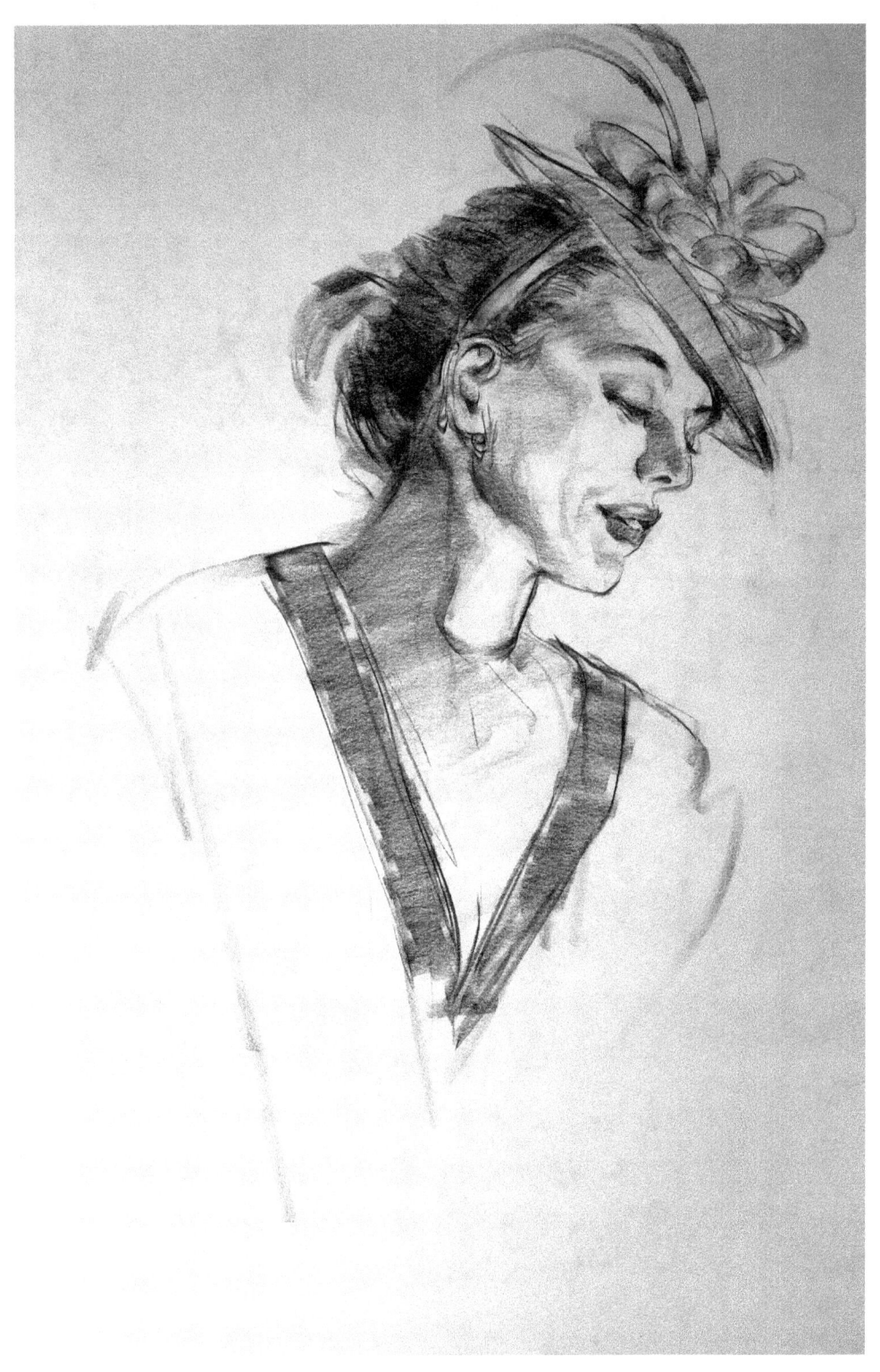

LIGHTING & PERSPECTIVE

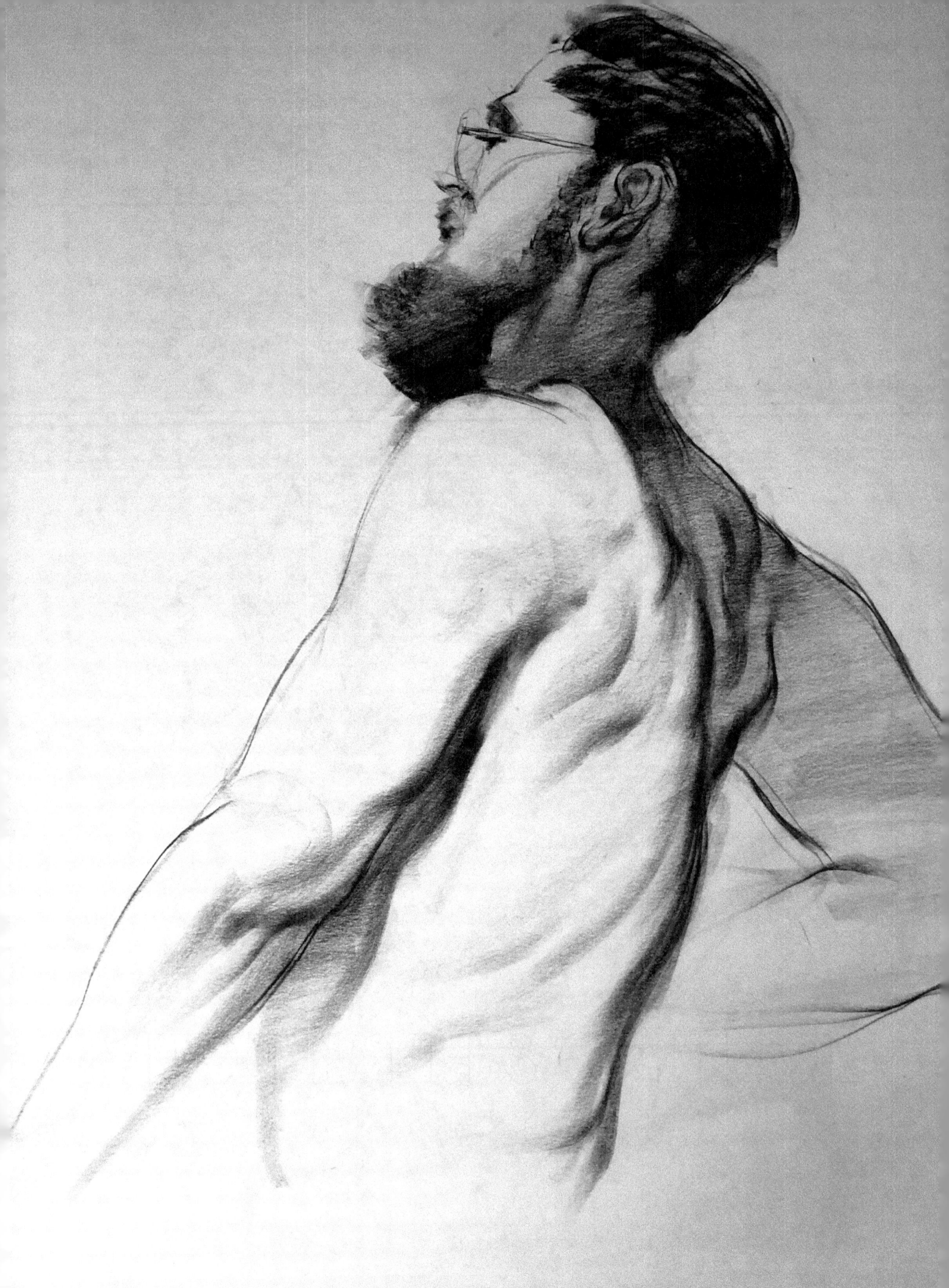

Lighting model

Rendering a drawing with lighting information adds both life and dimensionality to the drawing. Most lighting scenarios in life drawing include at least a main light (key-light), and a complementary fill (or ambient) light. The contrast between the key and fill light intensities will result in a dramatic lighting of the models. Florescent lighting is an example of omni-directional lighting. It emits light in all directions, thus eliminating well defined shadows. Avoid this type of lighting unless there is a reason for it.

We can use a simple form (a sphere) and analyze our lighting model.

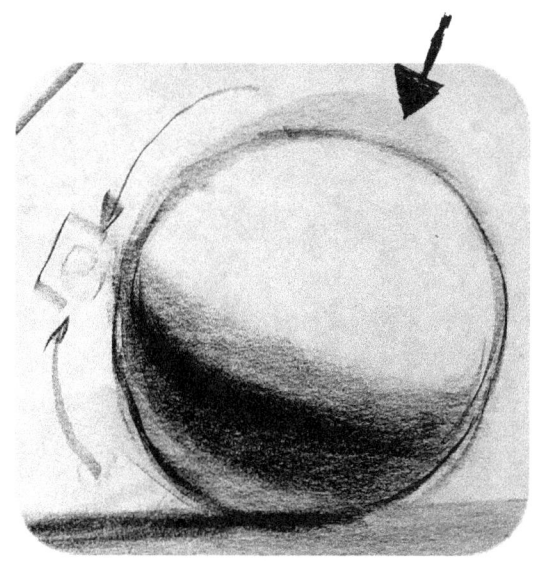

Assume a key light and a fill light are lighting the sphere at right (often in life-drawing sessions, ambient light may serve as a fill light).

Lit area on the object receives direct light from a key light. It's usually the brightest area.
Local tone is the entire shaded area on the sphere. It receives reflected and fill (ambient) light but not the key light.
Core shadow is the area that receives neither direct light nor the reflected light. It's the darkest tone on the form.
Reflected light is the light that is reflected from an adjacent surface back into the tonal side of the form.
Cast shadow is the shadow cast by the lit object. An example is a head casting a shadow on the neck and shoulder. Cast shadows are sharpest and darkest at the point of origin (contact points).

Compare the lighting on the sphere in the sketch below.

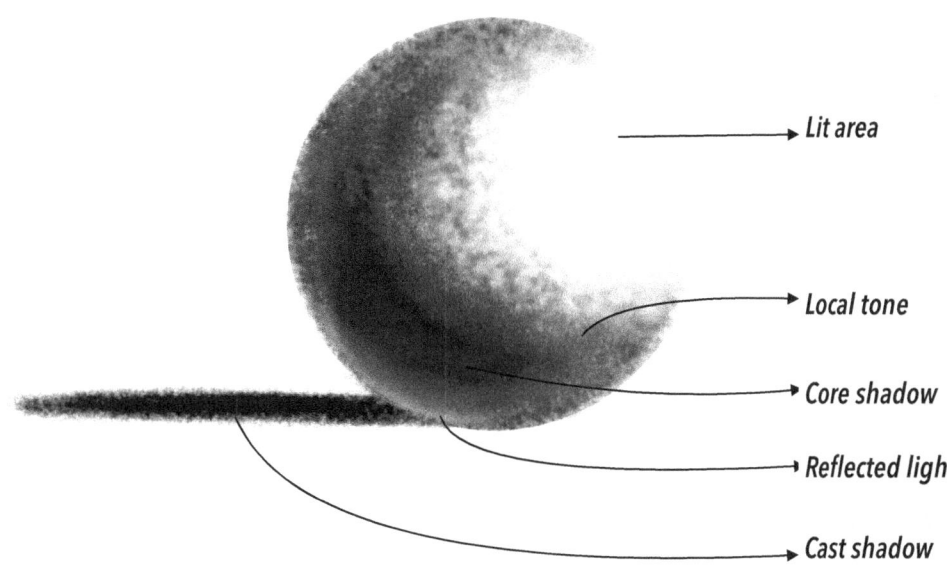

A few suggestions

- Keep values to three when doing short poses - lit area, local tone, core shadows, and cast shadows.
- Save the darkest lines/tone for the end; avoid drawing dark early in the pose.
- Keep interior lines a shade lighter than the outline.
- If you are running out of drawing time, keep the shadow details to the minimum.
- If it is a long pose, make sure the value structure in the shadow area doesn't compete with the value structure in the lit area. The lightest area in the shadow should be darker than darkest area in the light.
- Cast shadows can help define the form. Cast shadows follow the form(s) they fall on.

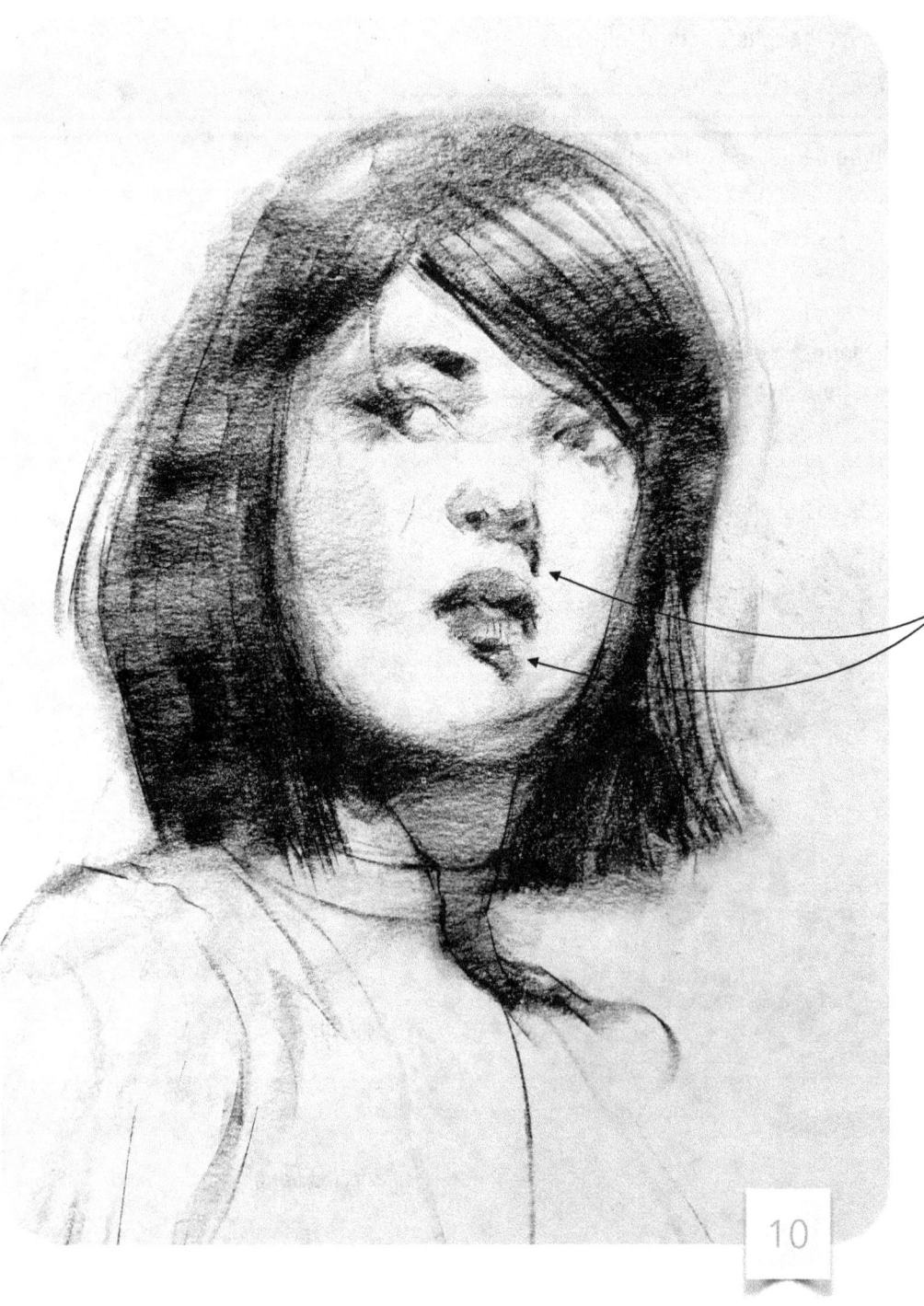

The nose casts a shadow on the upper lip. The form of the upper lip is solely defined by the shape of the cast shadow. The same is true for the lower lip. Make shadows work for you.

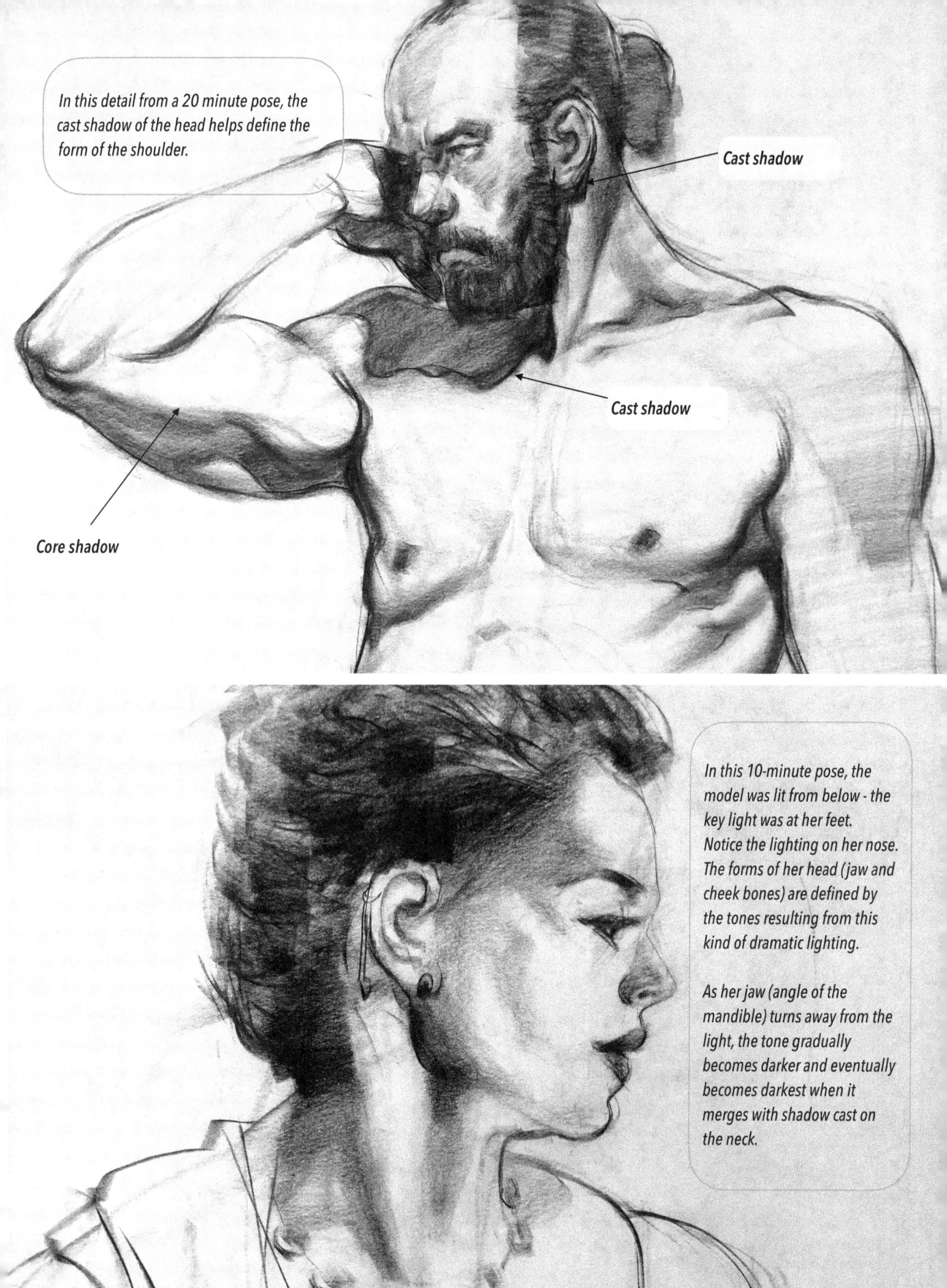

In this detail from a 20 minute pose, the cast shadow of the head helps define the form of the shoulder.

Cast shadow

Cast shadow

Core shadow

In this 10-minute pose, the model was lit from below - the key light was at her feet. Notice the lighting on her nose. The forms of her head (jaw and cheek bones) are defined by the tones resulting from this kind of dramatic lighting.

As her jaw (angle of the mandible) turns away from the light, the tone gradually becomes darker and eventually becomes darkest when it merges with shadow cast on the neck.

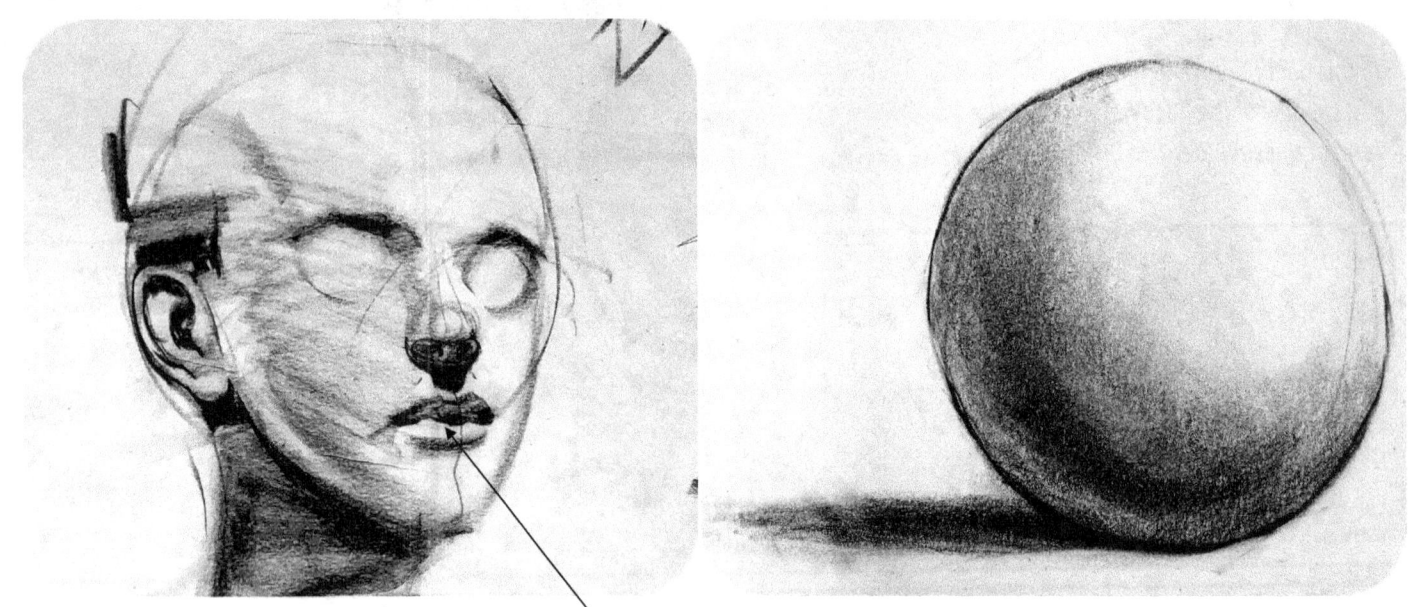

Contact shadow

The quick sketch above demonstrates the similarities between lighting a sphere and a face. The lit area, local tone, core shadow, cast shadow, and reflected light are shown both in the sphere drawing and the head drawing. Notice the cast shadows under the nose and the ear, as well as the reflected light on the bottom surface of the nose.

Contact shadow is the cast shadow at the point of origin - it is the sharpest and darkest area of the cast shadow (for example, the darkest line between the lips). No light reaches that contact point. Cast shadows lose density the farther away they get from their point of origin.

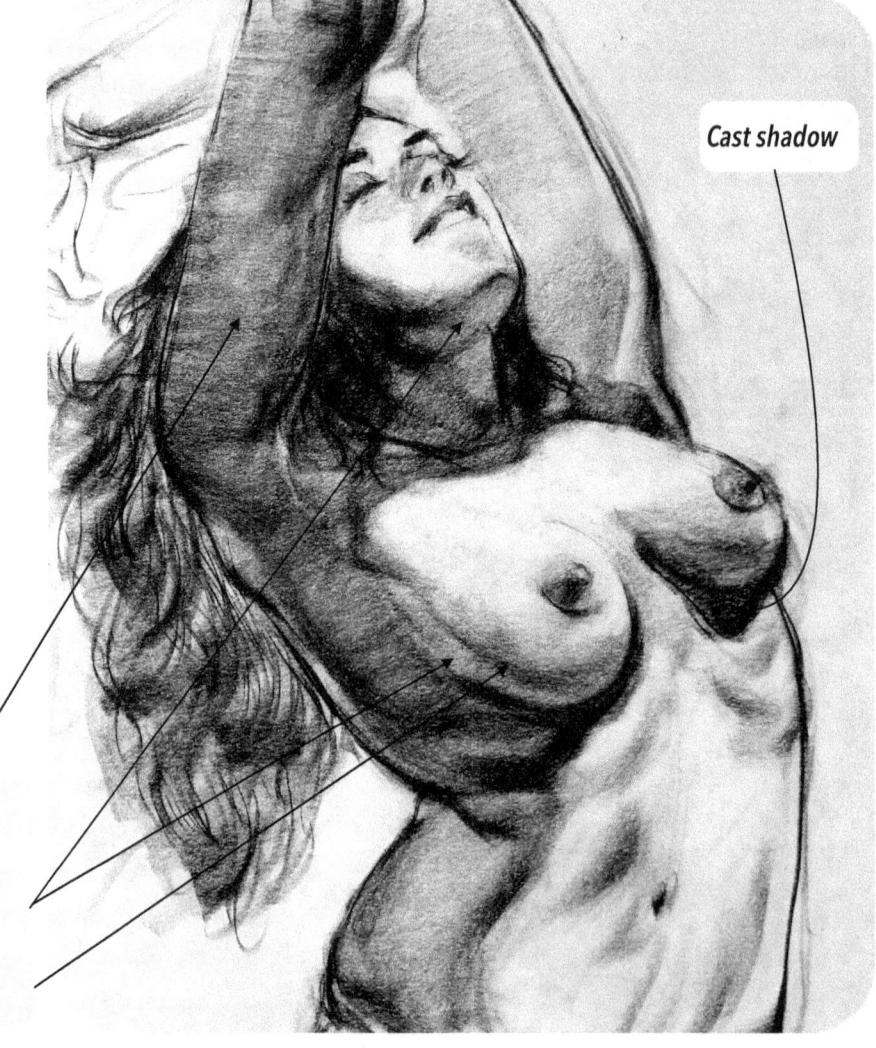

Cast shadow

Local tone

Reflected light

Core shadow

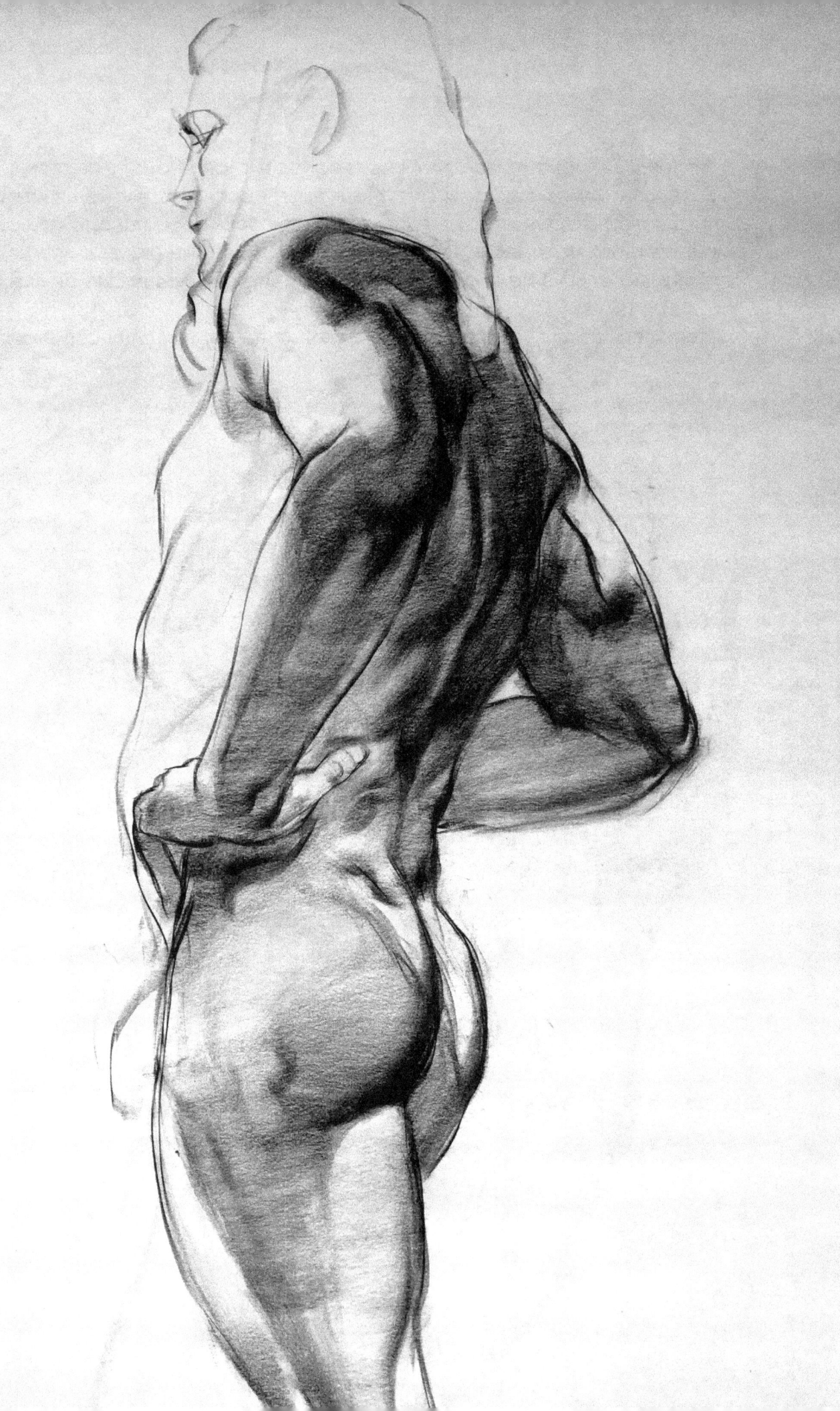

IF THE LIGHTING AT A LIFE-DRAWING SESSION IS BAD OR IS OMNI-DIRECTIONAL WITH FLORESCENT LAMPS, FOLLOW A SIMPLE GUIDELINE - SURFACES FACING UP ARE LIT AND SURFACES FACING DOWN ARE IN THE SHADOW. I HAVE HAD GOOD RESULTS FOLLOWING THIS SIMPLE IDEA. AN ARTIST ONCE SAID PERHAPS IT'S BECAUSE THE HEAVENS ARE UP THERE IN THE SKY SHINING LIGHT ON US DOWN HERE THAT SURFACES FACING UP ARE LIT.

ALTERNATELY, IF YOU DON'T BELIEVE IN HEAVEN UP THERE, YOU CAN DO THE OPPOSITE.

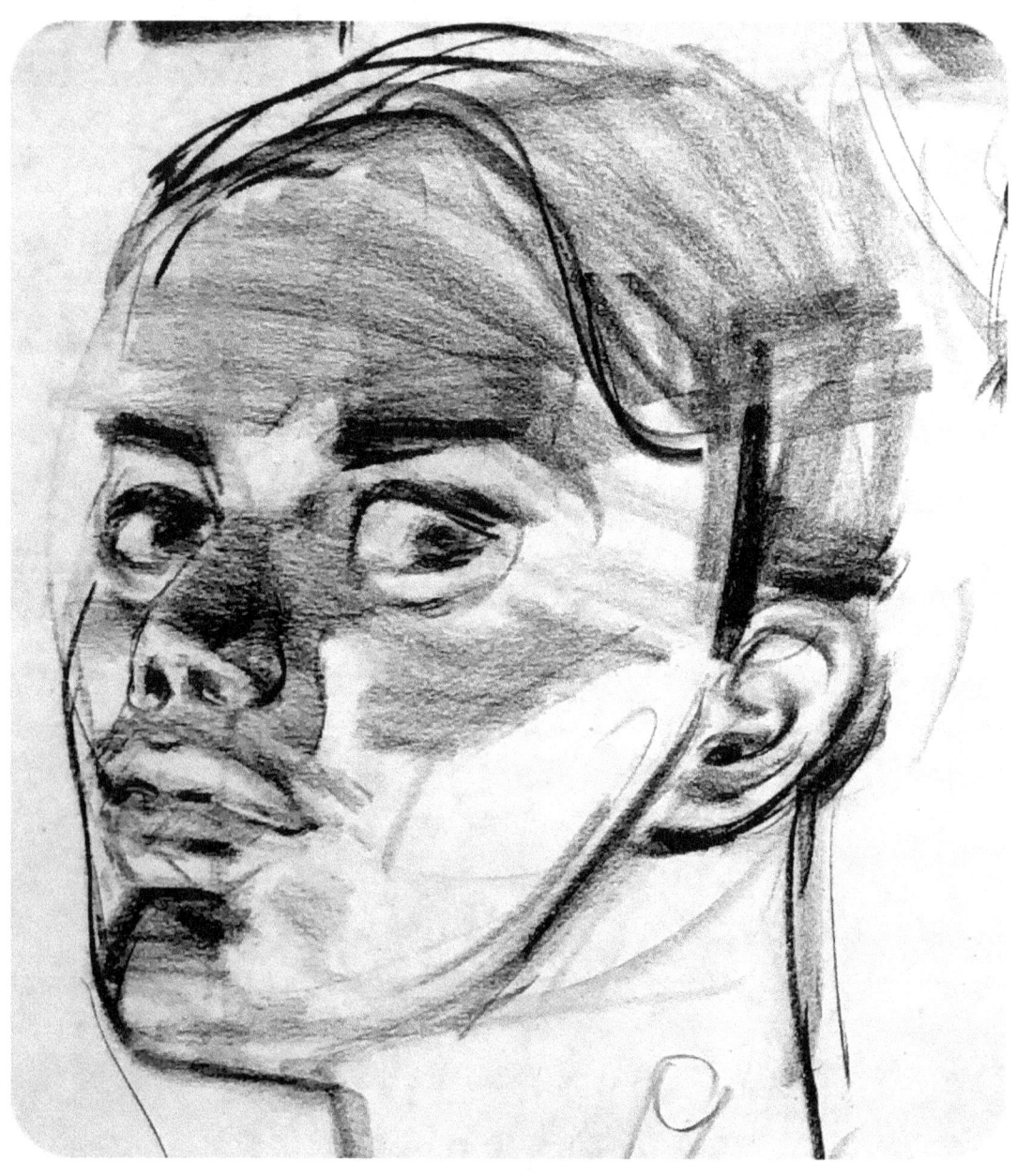

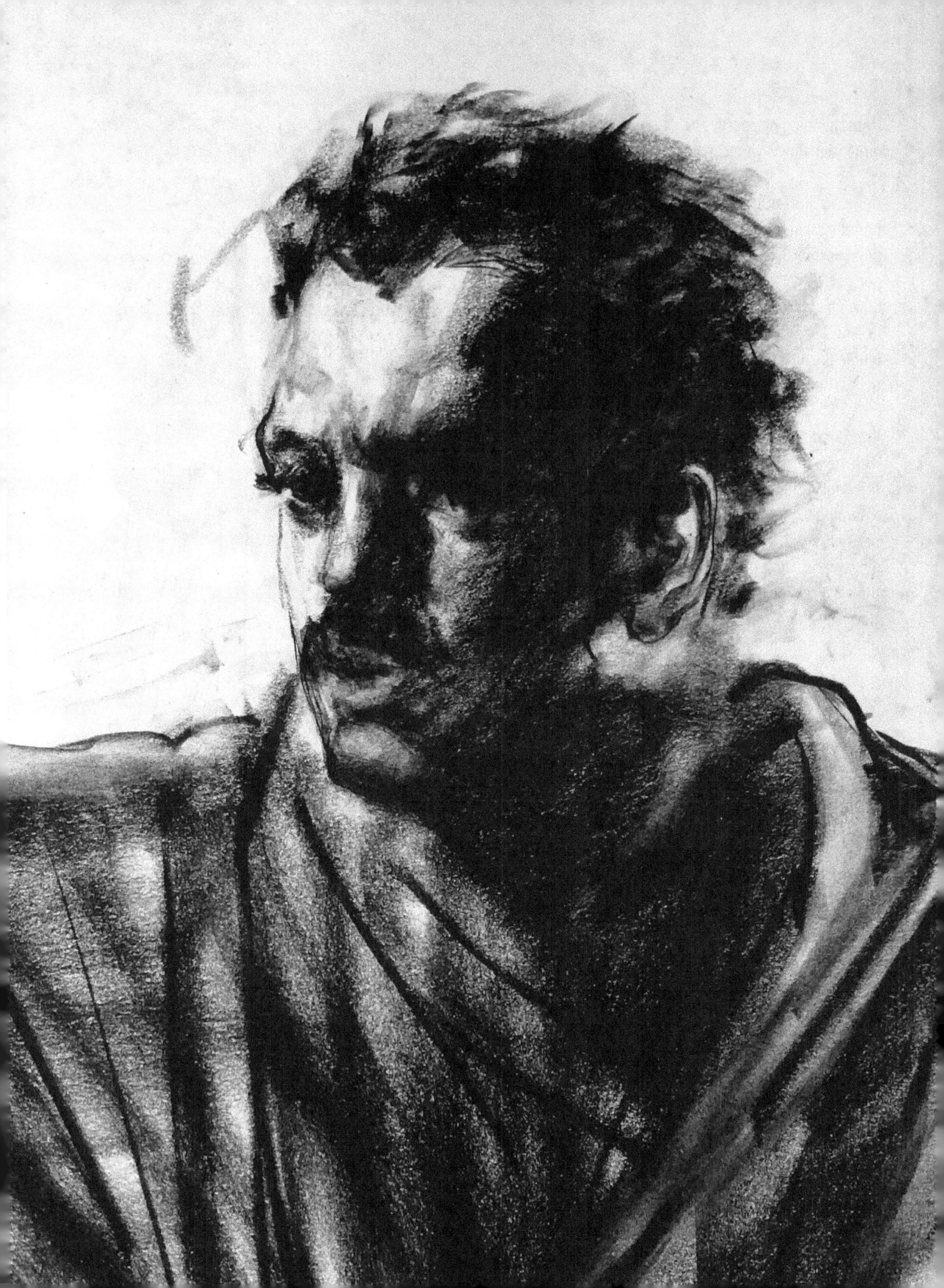

Understanding perspective helps add dimensionality to your drawing.

There is value (as in merit, not a measure of brightness) in learning one, two, and three-point perspective. Any good book on perspective will discuss these in detail. In life-drawing sessions, though, the models usually pose in close physical proximity, so we can ignore the nitty gritty math of using vanishing points, horizon lines, etc.

If you were to approximate the human body with boxes instead of spheres or tubes, your drawings would be in perspective by default - assuming the boxes are placed accurately in perspective. This is a quick way to establish top surfaces, front/side surfaces, angles of turn, and the relationship of masses. However, approximating human body as boxes can be difficult.

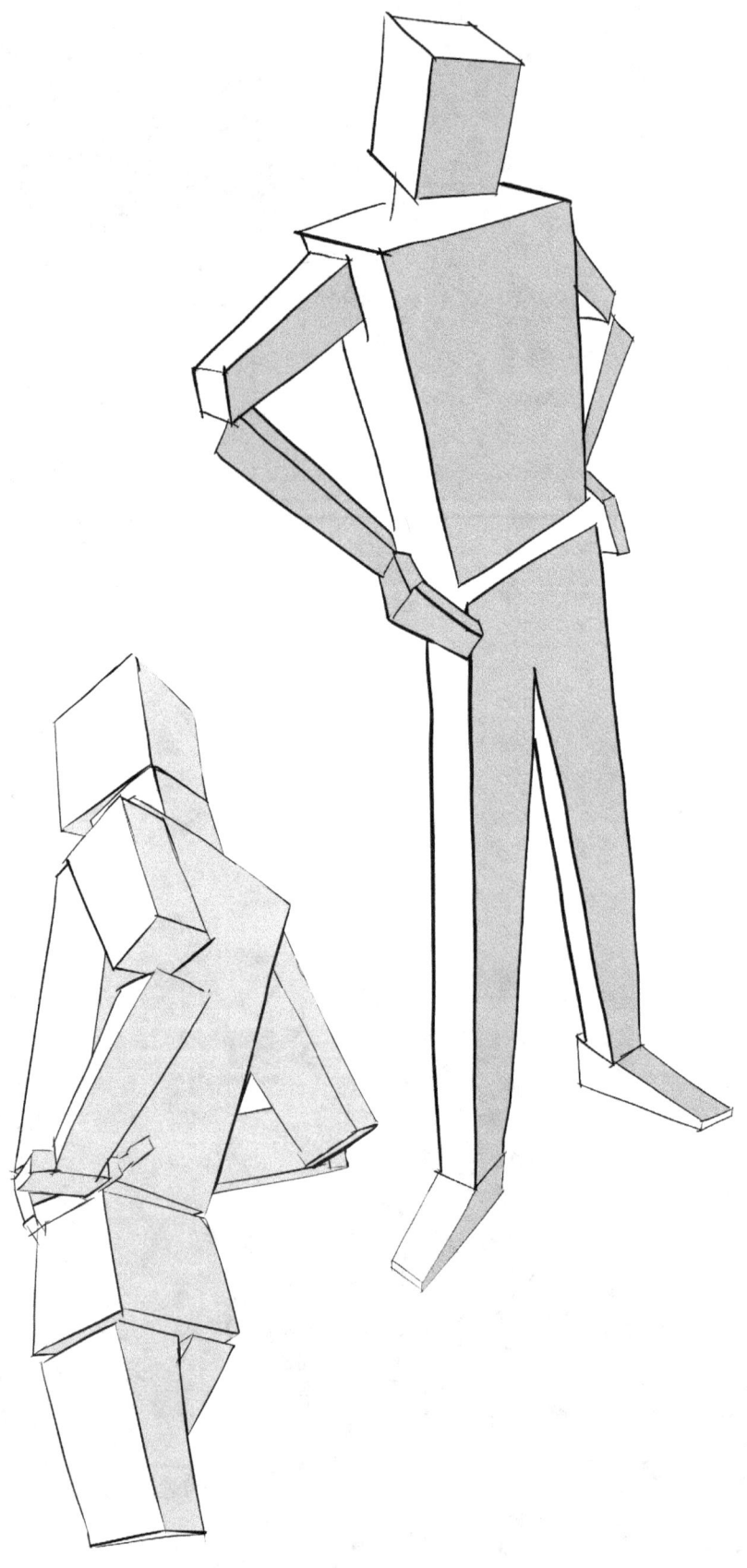

WHEN YOU ARE DOODLING, IT IS USEFUL TO DOODLE BOXES IN PERSPECTIVE. IN THE BEGINNING, YOU WILL STRUGGLE DRAWING THEM ACCURATELY, ESPECIALLY IF DOODLING IS SECONDARY ACTIVITY TO SOMETHING ELSE (BEING ON THE PHONE ETC), BUT IT WILL BE WORTH IT.

WHENEVER YOU ARE KILLING TIME, DRAW PEOPLE USING SIMPLE FORMS LIKE SPHERES, TUBES OR BOXES, AND DRAW CONSTRUCTION LINES AND PLAY WITH LIGHTING.

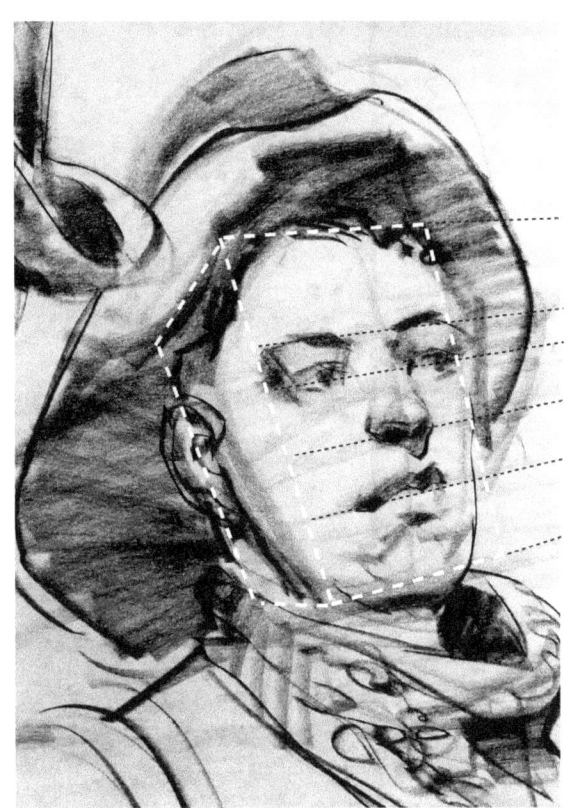

Check out the perspective guidelines (dotted lines in black) in the two head drawings to the left.

Notice how the perspective guidelines are almost parallel. Usually, the model is so close (physically) that we can simply draw them as parallel lines. The eyes lie on one of the guidelines. The edges of the mouth also lie on one of these lines. If we can to see both the nostrils of the nose, they would both lie on their perspective guideline.

You can apply the same idea to full figures. In a standing, neutral pose, the perspective guidelines (which would converge at a vanishing point in a true perspective drawing) pass through the left and right side of the body at the same point. For example, the left and right shoulder are on the same guideline, as are the elbows, wrist, knees and heels.

Use these guidelines to make marks that help you draw in perspective.

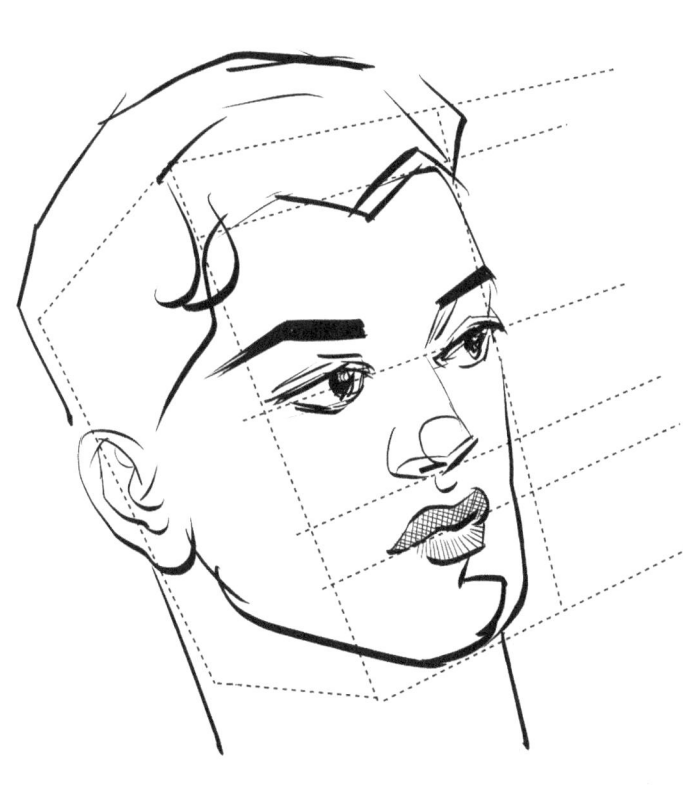

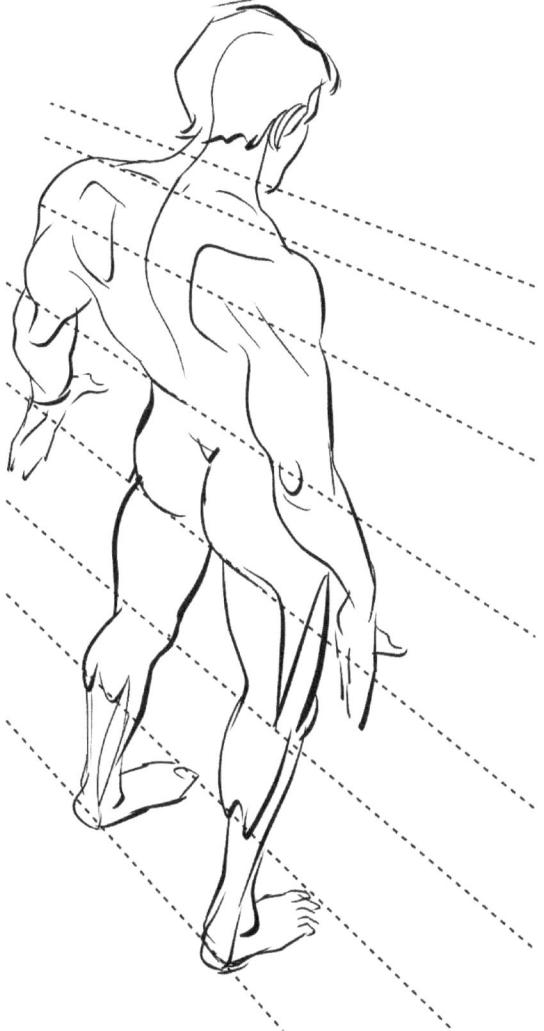

In the *Proportions* section, we discussed how to make your drawings three dimensional. Here is one more idea : add details that support the perspective you want to draw.

Imagine a column with rubber bands stretched horizontally around it. The rubber band at the eye level is a straight line. The bands above eye level will appear convex giving the effect of looking up. The bands below eye level will look concave, giving the effect of looking down. Adding these curved lines to a cylinder supports the illusion of a three dimensional column.

We can use this idea in life drawing when the model is posing above our eye level or below. These "rubber bands" function as construction lines.

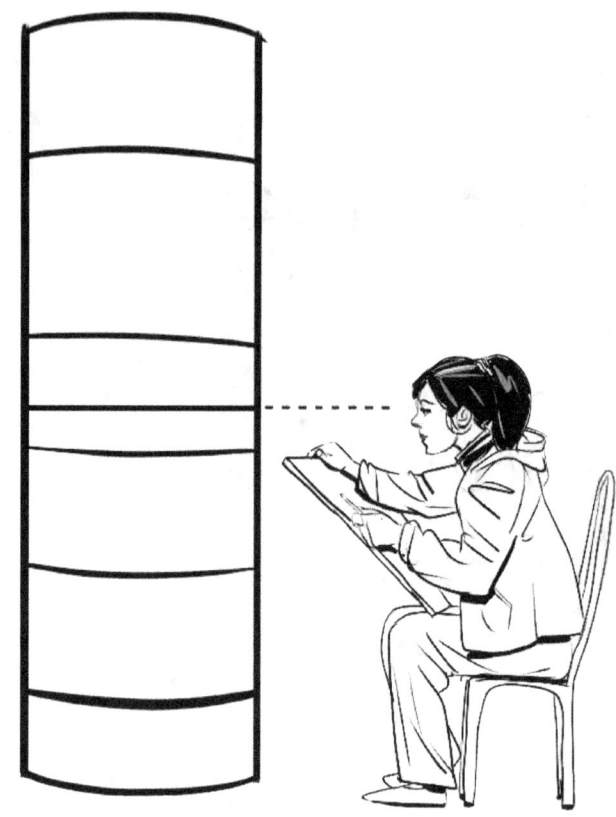

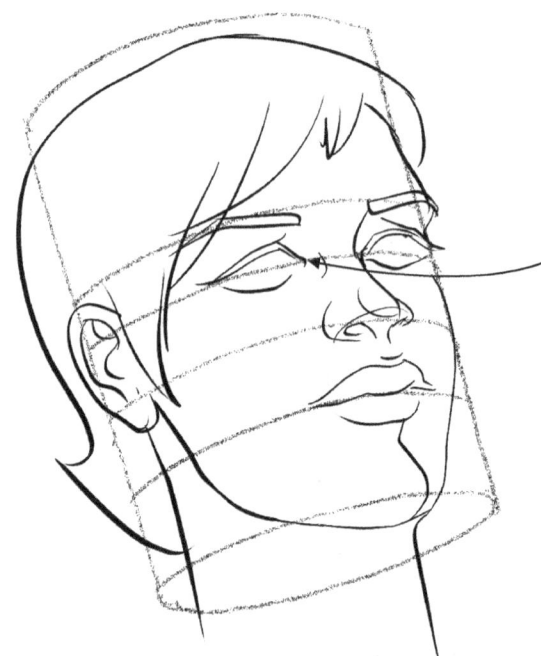

The rubber bands are lightly indicated on the cylinder at the left. We are looking 'up' at her. The details at the center of the cylinder are higher than the details at the edges of the cylinder. For example, the inner corner of her right eye, which is closer to the center of the cylinder, is placed higher than the outer corner.

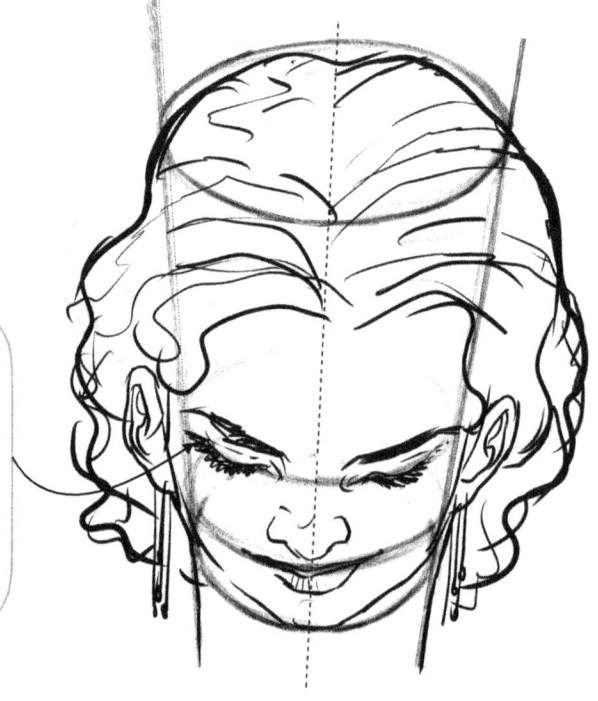

When looking down at the head, the construction lines appear as concave lines. The edge details are at a higher point compared to the center details. The outer corners of the eyes are placed higher relative to the inner corners of the eyes in this case. It's the same with the wings of the nose compared to the tip of the nose. The more the head is tilted down, the more you will see this difference.

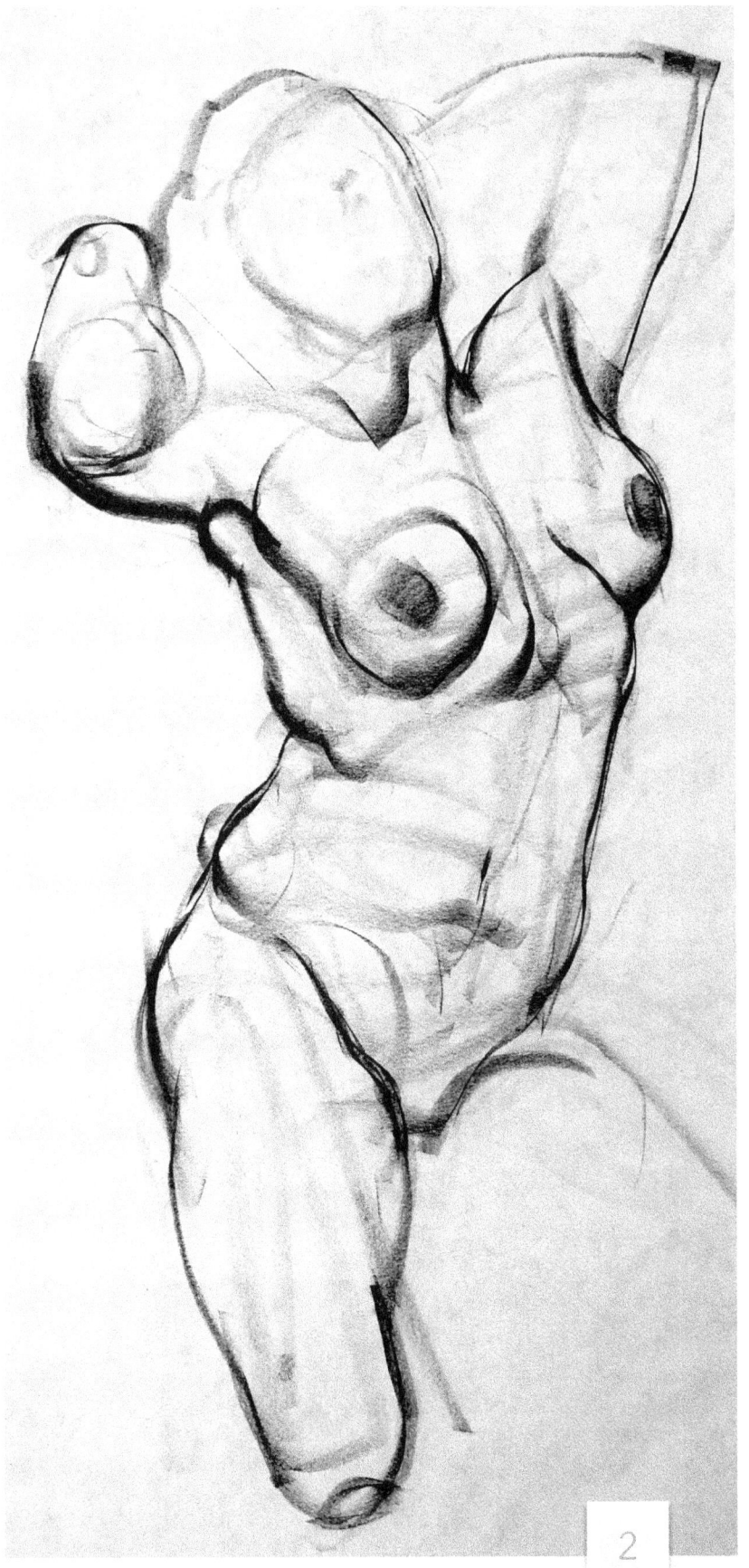

Use construction lines to accentuate the form or volume of the figure.

The two-minute pose on the left contains many construction lines drawn to follow the form.

Construction lines should work toward expressing one single 'idea' at a time. If the form (the upper torso in the drawing on the left) is tilted up, the construction lines should all be convex on the form. The shadow lines below her left breast do not support that idea.

The dark outline helps enclose the form. With the help of insertion lines, construction lines, and the relationship between the edge and center details (remember the rubber bands), you will achieve greater three dimensionality of the figure.

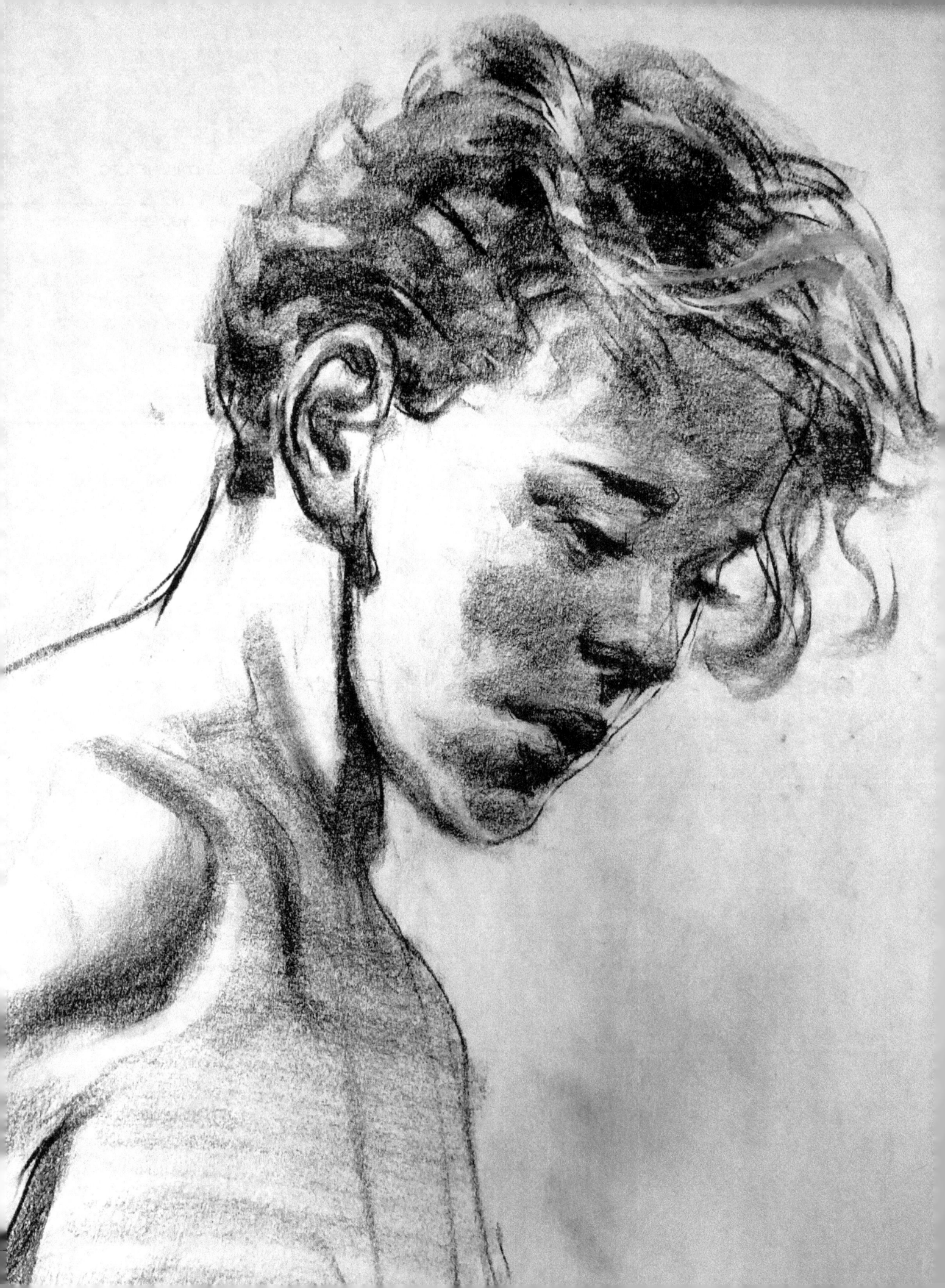

"...But all I have done before the the age of 70 is not worth bothering with. At 75 I'll have learned something of the pattern of nature, of animals, of plants, of trees, birds, fish and insects. When I am 80 you will see real progress. At 90 I shall have cut my way deeply into the mystery of life itself. At 100, I shall be a marvelous artist. At 110, everything I create; a dot, a line, will jump to life as never before...."

"...the Old Man Mad About Drawing"

CLOSING STATEMENT

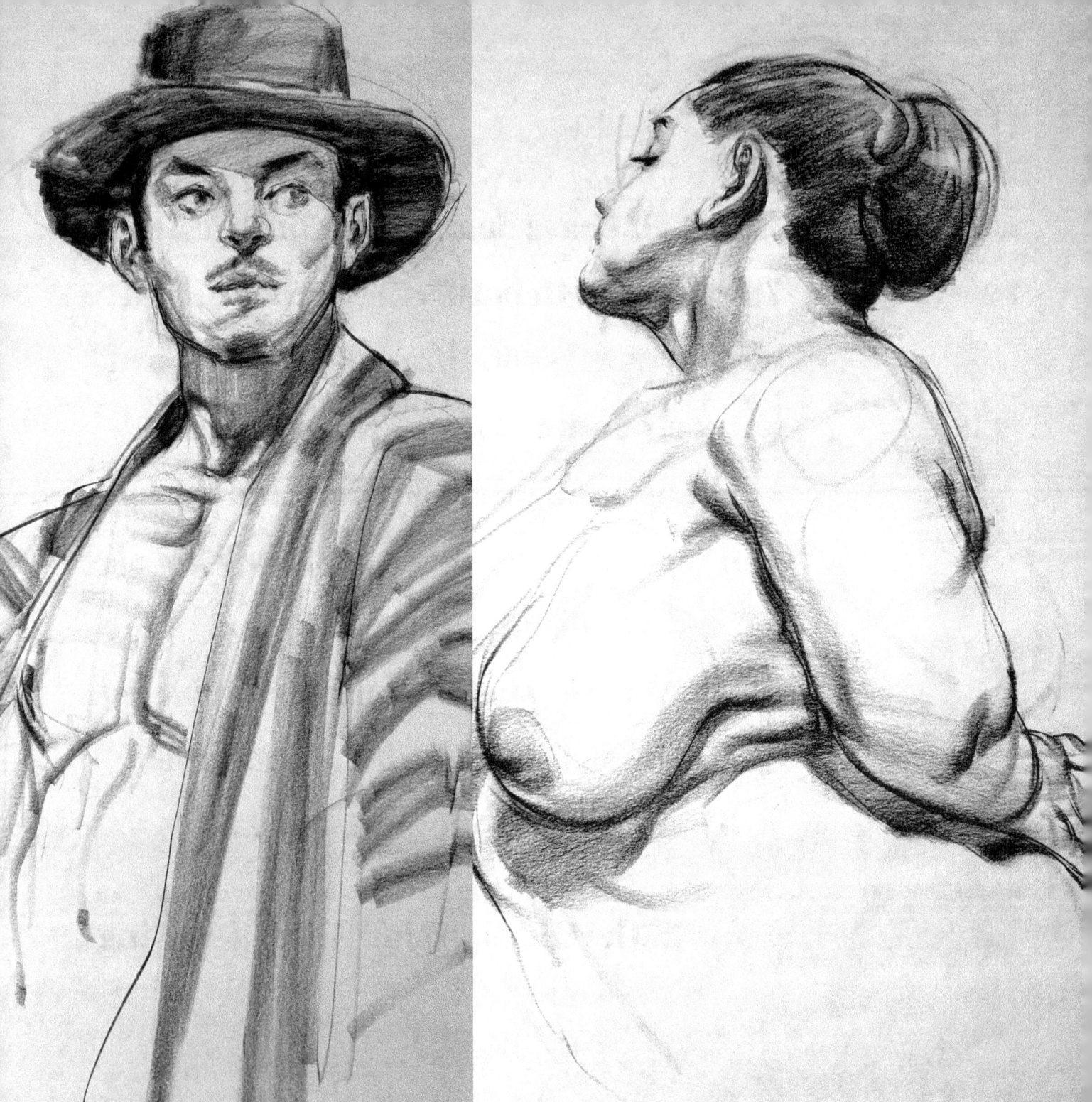

There are many good books on anatomy. I found the following two particularly useful and the artwork compelling.
- The Complete Guide to Anatomy for Artists & Illustrators by Gottfried Bammes.   Published by Search Press.
- Human Anatomy for Artists - The Elements of Form by Eliot Goldfinger. Published by Oxford University Press.

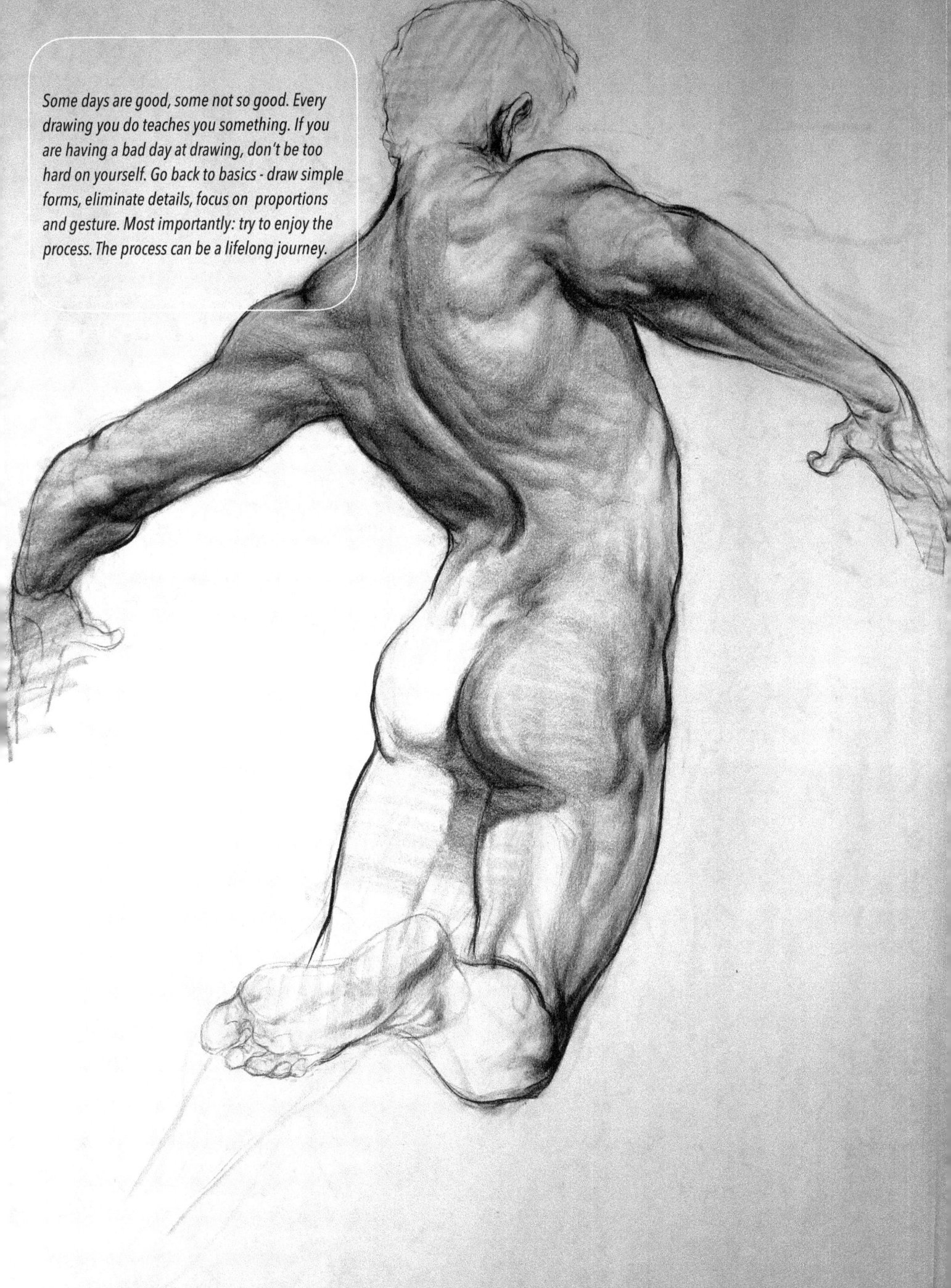

Some days are good, some not so good. Every drawing you do teaches you something. If you are having a bad day at drawing, don't be too hard on yourself. Go back to basics - draw simple forms, eliminate details, focus on proportions and gesture. Most importantly: try to enjoy the process. The process can be a lifelong journey.

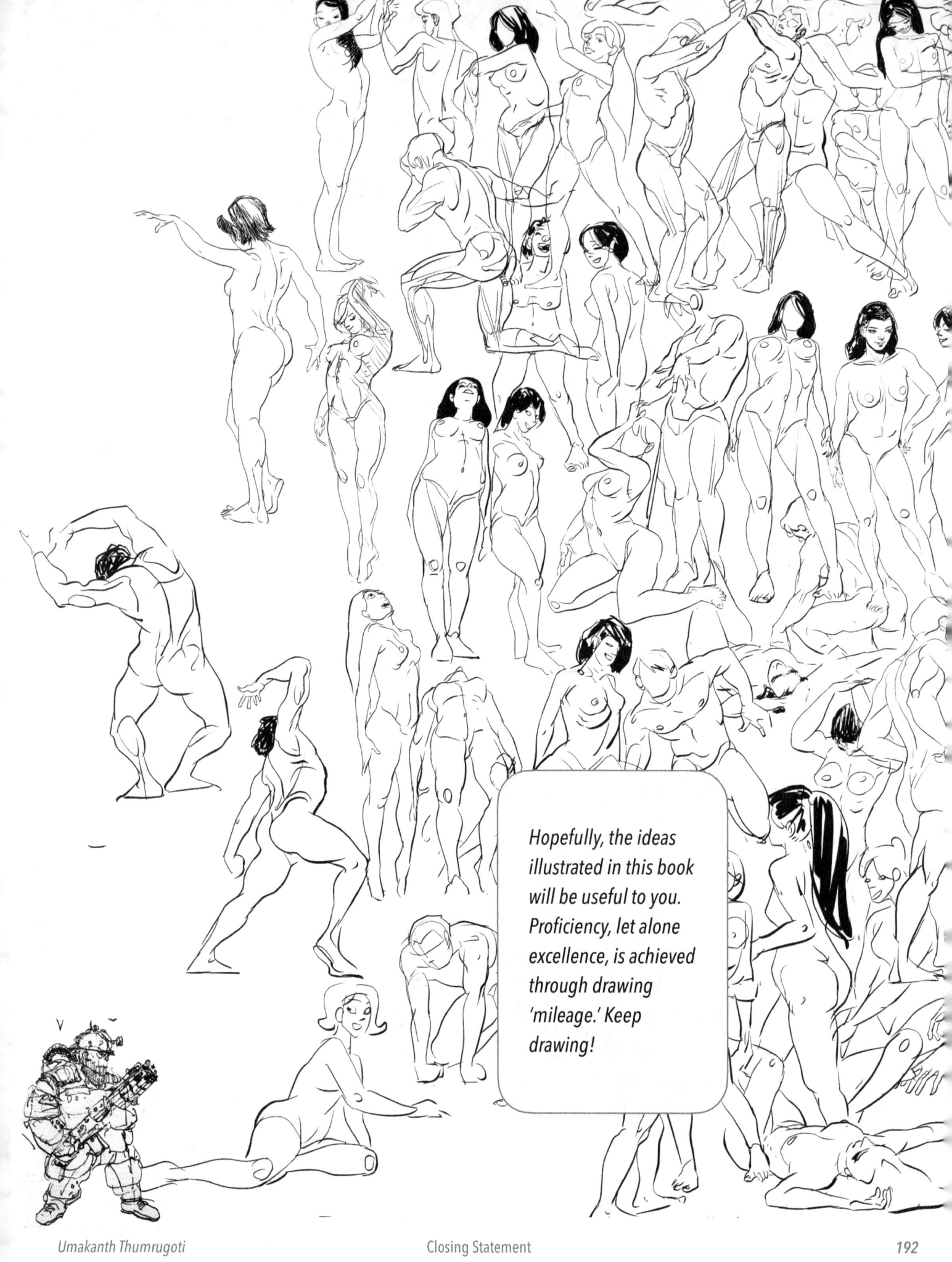

www.ingramcontent.com/pod-product-compliance
Lightning Source LLC
Chambersburg PA
CBHW082246220526
45469CB00009B/2898